INVANTAGE, INC.

One Kendall Square, Building 200
Cambridge, MA 02139

W9-BDP-415

THE
SOFTWARE DEVELOPER'S
AND MARKETER'S
LEGAL
COMPANION

APPRECIATION OF

The Software Developer's and Marketer's Legal Companion

"Read the **Legal Companion** and protect your software property rights. . . . This step-by-step guide is an essential book for any software company."

> *J. Richard Iverson, President and CEO, American Electronics Association*

"A guide that every software developer and entrepreneur should read. . . . Loaded with practical business tips on how to turn the law into an ally and how to avoid obvious traps."

> *James Geisman, President, Marketshare, Inc. and Consulting Editor,* **Software Success Newsletter**

"Astonishingly readable. . . . An excellent summary of the complex legal issues central to the computer software industry. . . . This guide ought to be on the bookshelf of every manager of a software business and every venture capitalist investor."

> *David Boucher, Founder and Chairman of the Board of Interleaf, Inc. and Venture Capitalist*

"Extremely valuable. . . . Timely. . . . For individuals from software entrepreneurs to CIOs of user corporations. . . . Makes software law easier to understand."

> *John Cullinane, Founder of Cullinet, Inc., and author of* **The Entrepreneur's Survival Guide**

THE
SOFTWARE DEVELOPER'S
AND MARKETER'S
LEGAL
COMPANION

Protect Your Software and Your Software Business

GENE K. LANDY

Addison-Wesley Publishing Company
Reading, Massachusetts   Menlo Park, California   New York
Don Mills, Ontario   Wokingham, England   Amsterdam   Bonn
Sydney   Singapore   Tokyo   Madrid   San Juan
Paris   Seoul   Milan   Mexico City   Taipei

Library of Congress Cataloging-in-Publication Data
Landy, Gene K.
    The software developer's and marketer's legal companion : protect
your software and your software business / Gene K. Landy.
      p.   cm.
    Includes index.
    ISBN 0-201-62276-9
    1. Software protection--Law and legislation--United States.
    2. Computer software--Law and legislation--United States.
    I. Title.
KF3024.C6L37   1993
346.7304'82--dc20
[347.306482]   93-19050
                                                 CIP

Set in 11-point Palatino by Benchmark Productions, Inc.

1 2 3 4 5 6 7 8 9-MA-97 96 95 94 93

First Printing, August 1993

Addison-Wesley books are available for bulk purchases by corporations, institutions, and other organizations. For more information please contact the Corporate, Government, and Special Sales Department at (617) 944-3700 x2915.

ABOUT THE AUTHOR

Gene K. Landy, Attorney at Law, holds degrees from the Massachusetts Institute of Technology, Harvard Graduate School, and Harvard Law School. His love of computers began when he wrote Fortran programs for mainframes at M.I.T. Now a partner at the law firm of Shapiro, Israel & Weiner, P.C. in Boston, Massachusetts, he has had more than a decade of experience in computer law; including advice to companies, contract negotiation, and hardware and software litigation. He is a member of the Computer Law Association and a member of the American Bar Association's Section of Patent, Trademark and Copyright Law and its Committee on Computer Litigation.

To My Parents

CONTENTS

CHAPTER 2

**Software Trade Secrets and
Confidentiality Agreements**   **45**

CHAPTER 15

Software Patents   **247**

APPENDIX D

Software Business and
Intellectual Property Resources   **525**

INDEX   **531**

ACKNOWLEDGMENTS

This work is founded on the insights and experience of many computer professionals, computer lawyers, and friends who gave guidance and reviewed the text. Although words cannot repay my debt of gratitude, my heartfelt thanks go to all those who helped, including:

I. Cary Armistead, Counsel, Digital Equipment Corporation, Maynard, Massachusetts.

Cynthia Canady, Counsel, Apple Computer Corporation, Cupertino, California.

Peter Chapman, President, Windowcraft Corporation, Acton, Massachusetts (who conceived the idea for this book).

Michael Dornbrook, President, Sound Information, Inc., Arlington, Massachusetts.

Douglas Ferguson, Vice-President, Lotus Development Corporation, Cambridge, Massachusetts.

William Franzblau, Counsel, Hemagen, Inc., Waltham, Massachusetts.

Lynn Fructer, Of Counsel, Cowan, Liebowitz & Lattman, P.C., New York City.

Professor Bernard A. Galler, University of Michigan, Ann Arbor, Michigan.

Neal D. Goldman, Counsel, Lotus Development Corporation, Cambridge, Massachusetts.

Leon Glazerman, Partner, Palmer & Dodge, Boston, Massachusetts

David Hays, Partner, Fenwick & West, Palo Alto, California.

Lou Katz, Partner, and Paul Bijkersma and Russell Stein, Associates, Shapiro, Israel & Weiner, Boston, Massachusetts.

Lindsay Kiang, Counsel, Digital Equipment Corporation, Maynard, Massachusetts.

Seth Muriph, Vice-President, Windowcraft Corporation, Acton, Massachusetts.

Richard Stein, Partner, Hutchins, Wheeler & Dittmar, Boston, Massachusetts.

Bruce Sunstein, Partner, Bromberg and Sunstein, Boston Massachusetts.

Dorothy Swithenbank, President, AudioFile, Inc., Lexington, Massachusetts.

Penelope Wilson, Patent Counsel, Digital Equipment Corporation, Maynard, Massachusetts.

William A. Wise, Jr. General Counsel, Analog Devices, Norwood, Massachusetts.

In addition, the United States Copyright Office, in particular, Mary Beth Peters, Esq. and Nancy Lawrence, gave invaluable assistance on the copyright sections.

These people were incredibly generous with their time. I am now convinced that anyone who wants to reaffirm their belief in the essential goodness of human nature should write a book. Of course, any inadequacy in this work is solely my responsibility.

I am also indebted to my editors, Chris Williams, Deb Kaufmann, and especially to Amy Pedersen, who has the patience of Job and the tact of a diplomat, as well as all the people at Addison-Wesley who helped with this book. And my thanks go to Michael Mark and Paul DiLascia, who helped me find the right publisher.

Finally, I owe the greatest debt of all to my wife Sylvia and my daughter Beth.

Gene K. Landy

A NOTE FROM THE AUTHOR

I would like to hear from you about the ways in which this book has helped you and about ways that it could be improved. And I am always interested in new technologies, innovative legal techniques, new legal issues, and new problems to solve.

Feel free to write me at my firm at the following address:

Gene K. Landy, Attorney at Law
Shapiro, Israel & Weiner, P.C.
100 North Washington Street
Boston, Massachusetts 02114

You can also send me a fax at (617) 742-2355 or contact me at my Compuserve e-mail address: 72366,2456. Through Internet, you can send me e-mail at 72366.2456 @compuserve.com.

FOREWORD

Gene Landy has written an exceptionally valuable book on software and the law. This book is also extremely timely because the body of law affecting issues of copyright, trade secrets, contracts, patents, look and feel, etc., has grown dramatically in recent years. Software now pervades all aspects of our lives and will only become more prevalent in the future. It used to be that a good company could be put out of business by bad software. Now, bad software *contracts* can put a good company out of business.

As more power is concentrated in a few mega-software companies, individuals, from software entrepreneurs to CIO's of user corporations, need to have access to the latest legal perspectives in terms they can understand easily. *The Software Developer's and Marketer's Legal Companion* is more than a book of law, it is a guidebook for the non-lawyer, making it much easier to understand software legal issues and to cope with them successfully.

As someone who has been in the computer software and service business for more than thirty years, and as someone who often wrote my company's legal agreements out of necessity, I could have used this book on numerous occasions in the past.

—*John Cullinane*
President, The Cullinane Group

*John Cullinane is the founder of Cullinet, Inc., the first software company to be listed on the New York Stock Exchange and the first to reach a billion dollar valuation. He is also the author of a recently published book, **The Entrepreneur's Survival Guide**.*

Using this Legal Companion

Your Need to Know the Law

To compete in the software industry, you need to have basic information about software law. Imagine playing in a complex variant of chess with scores of players—where there are rules and moves that your opponents know and you do not. That is what it's like to deal in the software business without understanding the legal rules that apply or the tools that the law provides.

Computers have had a role in business since the late 1950s, and began an explosive expansion in the late 1970s that continues today. Computers are now a huge part of the global economy. Computer hardware is seen as a mere commodity; the value that customers pay for is in the software.

As the software industry has grown, the legal system has been working out the rights and duties of software owners and users. Many of the legal rights that are discussed in this book hardly existed 10 or 15 years ago. Now there is a considerable body of law on software that vitally affects every software business.

I am a lawyer who handles computer-related litigation and I have been an advisor in many negotiations concerning software. I have seen many companies make smart moves to protect their rights, and I have seen the damage caused by costly legal mistakes. Everyone that deals in software has the ability to structure their legal relationships in ways that maximize legal protection, reduce ambiguity, and minimize conflict and risk. This book is designed to help software businesses accomplish just that.

This book will give you the basic knowledge you need to see opportunities, to make better deals, to protect yourself, and watch for common traps. It will not free you from the need for lawyers. But it will help you know when you need a lawyer and when you do not, how to use legal counsel in the most cost-effective way, and what to expect from the legal system.

Who Is This Book for?

This book is written for anyone who needs to understand how the law affects a software business, including:

- Individuals and businesses that write, buy, sell, or license software.

- Dealers, distributors, value-added resellers (VARs), and original equipment manufacturers (OEMs) who license software to customers.

- Software publishers.

- Contract programmers and custom software developers.

- Executive, sales, and technical staff in software development, distribution, and publishing companies.

- Management information system (MIS) managers and chief information officers (CIOs) who make important software purchases.

- Investors and venture capitalists who need to evaluate software businesses and to understand software-related intellectual property rights.

Topics Covered

This book covers the major aspects of law that people in software-related businesses need to know.

- **Copyright law** is the most important body of law protecting software. This book explains how to protect and exploit your software copyright and how to avoid copyright infringement liability.

- **Trade secret law** protects confidential techniques and business information. This book explains how to protect your trade secrets and how to avoid taking trade secrets from someone else. Confidentiality agreements and non-competition agreements are covered as well.

- **The law of contracts** governs relations between and among programmers, software owners, publishers, distributors, dealers, and customers. This book covers, in nine chapters, **contract negotiations** and **common software con-**

tracts including beta test agreements, confidential disclosure agreements, software assignments, development agreements, publishing agreements, distribution and dealership agreements, shrink-wrap licenses, and end-user license agreements. Annotated samples of these contracts and checklists for negotiations are provided both in the text and on diskette (in both WordPerfect and ASCII formats).

- **Trademark law** protects the unique name of your software product. You will find an explanation of how trademark protection works and practical guidance for protecting your trademark.

- **Patent law** grants monopoly protection to many software inventions. The costs, scope, and means of software patent protection are explained, and there is a discussion of what to do if you are threatened by a patent infringement suit.

- There is an introduction to the practical and legal issues in **software distribution in foreign markets** and to **international intellectual property protection** for software.

- This book discusses an **overall strategy for intellectual property and contract management**—a method to monitor the legal health of your software business.

In addition, at the end of the book are appendices where you will find:

- **Copyright registration instructions:** A step-by-step guide to obtaining copyright registration including a United States copyright application form (bound in the center of the book), detailed instructions for using it, and instructions for recording software copyright assignments and licenses.

- **Software trade and intellectual property resources:** A collection of the names, addresses, and phone numbers useful for software trade and business, including government agencies, trademark search firms, software escrow companies, and resources for international software sales.

- **Glossary:** A compendium of the legal terms that are found in computer contracts and computer law in general.

How to Use This Book

This book is written to be used in two ways. First, it is a plain-language primer on software law, designed to give you a basic understanding of law that affects your business. Second, the book is designed as a reference book for practical guidance—a resource to pick up when you face legal problems or important negotiations and need direction or specific facts.

Intellectual Property

The legal meat and potatoes of the software industry is bargaining about intellectual property—in the form of copyrights, trade secrets, patents, and trademarks. The players in the software industry create, transfer, license, sublicense, and sometimes steal intellectual property. All the various forms of intellectual property are the creation of the legal system. Intuitive notions of property, which are based on things that you can touch and see, are a poor guide to the workings of intangible legal rights. You should therefore read the portions of this book that discuss intellectual property law pertinent to your business.

Commercial Negotiations

You not only need to understand your intellectual property rights, but you need to put them to use in commercial negotiations and agreements. Much of this book—particularly Chapters 4 through Chapter 12—is devoted to this subject. I suggest that you scan the table of contents and read those chapters that relate to subjects important in your business.

I have also included a number of form agreements and negotiation checklists for use with various chapters, all of which are found in Appendix C and on the diskette included with the book. I had a professor at Harvard Law School who loved reading contracts; he delighted in finding clever wording, new issues, and new solutions to old contract problems. But my guess is that few of you will experience the same delight in reading these form agreements. Nonetheless, the "fine print" in agreements has extremely important consequences for your business. I recommend that you read and use these forms and checklists when you are actually in the midst of a negotiation. That is the time to delve into the nitty-gritty of the these form documents.

More Reference Materials

As I noted earlier, there are two appendices for reference use. One is Appendix B, a glossary of legal terms, which you can use whenever you have a question about the meaning of a legal term. You may also wish to browse through Appendix D, a list of computer trade organizations, relevant government agencies, and the like.

CHAPTER 1

Software Copyright Law

Federal copyright law is the most important form of software intellectual property protection. Whenever you say that you "own" a program, it is primarily the program copyright that you are talking about. Whenever you make a contract to license software, it is primarily the copyright that is being bargained for.

In this chapter, you will learn the fundamentals of copyright law, including:

- How to get a software copyright and the legal rights it gives you.

- How to put your software copyright to work.

- How to register your software copyright with the United States government.

- How to respond if your copyright is infringed: What you can do and what it will cost to do it.

These topics are critically important to anyone who creates, owns, or deals in software. In addition, in Chapter 16, there is a discussion of international copyright protection, including software copyright law in Europe and Japan, the largest foreign software markets.

The Nature of a Software Copyright

Fundamentally, a software copyright is just what it sounds like: the legal right to control who copies your software. It also governs who can distribute and sell copies or prepare works based on your software.

Copyright protection in the United States is governed by the Copyright Act, a statute passed by Congress. The purpose of copyright law is to encourage creation and expression by granting a legal monopoly for a new book, song, or computer program, known under copyright law as a "work." Copyright law gives the copyright owner a remedy in court when someone else sells copies of a "work" without permission of the copyright holder. For many years, copyright protection included books, articles, graphic works, dance, and music. A 1980 amendment extended coverage to computer programs.

What is meant by a "program" in copyright law? It means just what you think it means: code that can be run in a computer and tells the computer to do something. In the copyright statute, Congress gives the following formal definition:

> A "computer program" is a set of statements or instructions to be used directly or indirectly in a computer in order to bring about a certain result.

Under copyright law, a program can be written in any computer language— COBOL, C, XBase, BASIC, Hypertalk, or anything else. It could be an operating system, a game program, a word processor, a subroutine meant to be incorporated in other programs, or anything else that runs on a computer. It could be a few lines of code or millions of lines. A "program" under the Copyright Act may also be a combination of programs that work together and are sold together.

A fundamental concept of copyright law is that it grants exclusive rights to the particular *expression* that constitutes the work. The Copyright Act expressly provides that copyright protection does *not* extend to "any idea, procedure, system, method of operation, concept, principle, or discovery" underlying the program.

The (Very Modest) Requirement of Originality

Under copyright law you can only get a copyright on a work, including a computer program, that is "original." However, the level of originality required is very, very low, and meeting this requirement is easy. The legal test contains two elements: (1) a level of originality described by judges as "very slight" or "minimal," and (2) independent creation. This means that if you wrote a software program, even if quite pedestrian and ordinary, it will usually be original enough.

Registration of Your Copyright: Strongly Recommended

A frequently asked question is: Do you have to register your software in order to get a U.S. copyright? The answer, surprisingly, is "No." To get a copyright on your software, all you have to do is to get your program into some tangible form, such as a printout, diskette, or ROM chip. The rule is that a copyright is secured *automatically* when the program is recorded in some solid form for the first time. Registration with the United States Copyright Office is, however, required in order to bring a lawsuit to enforce your copyright.

Even though you won't lose your copyright if you don't register, I strongly advise that you do register—and that you do it promptly. As I will discuss later in this chapter, registration is very easy and there are very important advantages from registering your software in a timely manner.

The Copyright Notice

You've seen a copyright notice (also called a "copyright legend") on books and on software many times. A typical notice looks like this:

Copyright © 1993 Jack Smith, Inc.
All rights reserved

Is a notice legally required to secure copyright protection? Under the Copyright Act, the answer is "No," *if* the software was published *on or after March 1, 1989.* If the publication took place after that key date, there is no legal requirement that you mark your software in any special way in order to preserve your copyright. Copyright protection is *automatic*. Software is "published" when it is first put into general distribution or public sale. Private showings to friends, investors, or publishers is not publication.

Nevertheless, *you should always use a copyright notice on software and computer documentation*—even before publication. The notice serves to deter illegal copying and helps you in litigation against infringers. Later in this chapter there is a discussion of the correct forms for a copyright notice for use with software.

For software published *before* March 1, 1989, putting that copyright notice on the work was and remains absolutely *essential*. Generally speaking, if your computer program was published before that date and if you have published more than a relatively small number of copies without a copyright notice, your copyright may be lost—and the program may then be in the public domain, that is, it may belong to everyone. There is a provision that may save your copyright if you have registered the copyright within *five years* of publication and you take reasonable efforts to put copyright notices on all copies not yet in the hands of the public (such as those in stores and warehouses)—which may be an expensive and difficult proposition. Another provision applies if a publisher was obligated by contract to put on the copyright notice but failed to do so. If neither of these escape provisions apply, the copyright is gone forever. If you fear that you might have inadvertently lost a copyright for software published before March 1, 1989, *you should seek legal counsel without delay.* (For works created before March 1, 1989, certain errors in copyright notices can also eliminate copyright protection—and other errors are harmless. For example, misspelling a name is normally a harmless error, but omission of the publication date can be a serious problem. This is another situation where potentially serious errors may be curable with prompt action. If you have distributed works of this vintage with an inaccurate or defective copyright notice, you should seek legal counsel immediately.)

The Duration of Copyright Protection

Copyrights last a *very long* time:

- If the copyright program is a "work-for-hire," the copyright lasts *75 years* from the date of publication. The concept of "work-for-hire," which usually means programs written on the job by the employees of the copyright owner, is discussed later in this chapter.

- If the program is the work of a single individual, the copyright lasts for *the life of the author plus 50 years*.

- If the program is the joint work of several authors, the copyright lasts for *the life of the last surviving author plus 50 years*.

In other words, the copyright will outlast by decades the commercially useful life of any computer program yet known to humankind. As a practical matter, the expiration date is irrelevant.

There is another long-term rule under the Copyright Act, a special rule that applies if an author has licensed or transferred any rights to a copyright. The author (or his or her heirs) has the right to revoke the transfer or license 35 years after publication or 40 years after the license grant, whichever comes first. This rule is to protect the creators of works of literature and art that show their true value only many years after creation. Because this rule requires the passage of such a long period, it appears to have no practical relevance to software.

Putting Software Copyrights to Work

How do parties turn copyrights into profits? On occasion, companies develop software only for their own internal use. In that case, the function of the copyright is simply to stop others from using the program. Most often however, software is licensed or transferred. The software industry has evolved a series of commercial transactions and arrangements to exploit copyrighted software. Some common types are listed below.

- **Software Assignments**. In a software assignment, the copyright owner transfers all ownership rights in a software copyright to a new owner. These transactions are discussed in Chapter 7.

- **Software Development Agreements**. In a software development agreement, a developer agrees to create software to specifications and then to transfer or license the copyright to another party—typically for a negotiated schedule of cash payments. These agreements are discussed in Chapter 8.

- **Software Publishing Agreements**. In a software publishing agreement, a developer grants to a publisher a license to duplicate and market the copyrighted software. The publisher then sells the software. The publisher makes royalty payments to the developer based on a percentage of the sales revenue from the software product. The licensed software may already exist, or the developer may create it under the agreement. The negotiation of these rather complex agreements is discussed in Chapter 9.

- **Software Distribution Arrangements**. Under software distribution arrangements, the publisher of the copyrighted software (who may also be the developer) makes an arrangement with a software distributor to sell the software product to others. Sales might be retail, by telemarketing, by mail order, by direct mail, or through other channels. The distributor gets the right under the copyright to grant licenses to users. These arrangements are discussed in Chapter 10.

- **End-User Agreements**. In these agreements, a developer, publisher, distributor, or dealer grants an end-user a license under the copyright to use (but not to copy or sell) the software, in exchange for a fee. The negotiation of these agreements is discussed in Chapter 12. Software licenses used in mass-market software sales, known as "shrink-wrap" licenses, are discussed in Chapter 11.

"Licensing" Versus "Selling" Software Products

It is common for people in the software business to talk about "buying" and "selling" software products—as, for example, in the discussion of putting software copyrights to work that you just read. But, as you may have noticed, virtually every written agreement concerning software products talks about "licensing" the software.

"Licensing" means that one person or company is granting someone else *permission* or *license* to use the software under specified conditions. In reality, most transactions involving software products are *licensing* transactions, not sale transactions. (In some cases, a sale of a software product might be a *sale* of the diskette and the *license* of the program on the diskette.) This is an important distinction that can have major legal consequences.

There is, for example, a rule in copyright law known as *the principle of first sale*. The basic concept is that once you *sell* a copy of a copyrighted work, you cannot forbid or control the resale of the copy. For example, if I sell you a copy of a copyrighted novel by Steven King, you can resell *that copy* of the novel whenever you want, to whomever you please, for any price that you can get. (Of course, it would be illegal to copy or reproduce the novel without the permission of the holder of the copyright.)

However, this principle of first sale does not apply in licensing. If I license software to you, you and I can validly agree that the license cannot be transferred to a third party without my permission. And we can agree on how you may and may not use the software. The licensor's control of the transfer and usage of the software product by a licensee is essential for a great variety of common business transactions in the software industry.

As a legal matter, in most situations where two parties sign an agreement that says that a software product will be licensed, the result will be a licensing transaction under copyright law—and if there is patented technology in the software, under patent law as well. To avoid possible problems under the "first sale" principle, it is important that in your agreements and other formal documents, and in your business correspondence, you use the terminology of "licensing" and avoid the words "sell" and "sale" when referring to software product transactions.

Nonetheless, in common language, we speak every day of "selling" software. It is very cumbersome to speak of everyone who sells software products for a living as a "licensor" rather than a salesperson. It is odd to refer to a company's sales for the month as its "revenue from licensing activities." In this book, I will often use ordinary language and refer to "sales" of software products. However, you should note that it is *licensing* that we are discussing—and you should remember that the use of licensing terminology in documentation is important.

There is one complication in this matter of terminology. In many cases, a transaction can be a *licensing* transaction under the copyright law, and still be considered a *sale* under the law relating to sale of goods and warranties. (Discussion of matters relating to sales and warranties can be found, in various contexts, in Chapters 9, 10, 11 and 12, which cover various commercial software transactions.) It is a measure of the complexity of our legal system that inconsistent concepts of the nature of a bargain can coexist in a single software transaction.

The Scope of Protection Under Copyright Law

As I noted at the beginning of this chapter, the Copyright Act prevents unauthorized copying of computer programs. But the question is: What kind of copying is forbidden? Answering that question is more difficult than it sounds, because there are so many aspects of software that might be copied.

Software programs are fundamentally different from all other copyrighted media. The elements in a novel or a play are all there in black and white: the words, the phrases, the plot, the characters—everything is on the printed page. With software, the images and words that the user sees on the screen are only one small element of the program. Indeed some programs have no visible aspect and operate only in the background.

Quite distinct from each of the visible (or audible) elements of a program is the object code of the program, which consists of millions of on-off signals that the machine perceives and executes. The object code in turn is quite different from the source code that the author wrote and used to generate the object code—source code that in most cases is never sold to the user. All these elements are conceptually different from the internal organization and structure of the program. And different still is the overall appearance of the program.

What is it then that the Copyright Act protects from copying: pictures and words on the screen, object code, source code, internal structure, or overall appearance? The text of the Copyright Act doesn't say. In the course of decisions rendered since 1981, the federal courts have had to sort out which of the many elements and aspects of software are protected by the Copyright Act. We now have many answers, but some of the rules are still hazy.

In this and the next several sections, you will learn the scope of software protection. First, we will look at the areas where it is reasonably clear that copyright protection applies. Then we will look at what is excluded from that protection. Finally, we will review the "gray areas" where the answers are still unclear.

Unauthorized Copying of Copyrighted Computer Code

One aspect of the law is crystal clear. It is illegal to copy object code or source code without permission and use it or sell it. Similar protection against copying applies to the text of the user documentation that comes with the program, in printed form or on diskette. There is one narrow exception. Under the Copyright Act, every buyer of software has the right to make *one copy* of the program for *archival purposes only*.

It is often said that half of personal computer software in use in the United States consists of illegal copies. This is a guess; no one really knows how many billions of dollars worth of illegal copying takes place each year. Every year major software companies catch corporations committing wholesale violations of the Copyright Act. The copyright holders must threaten suit or actually sue to terminate these violations and to collect the money that should have been paid for the software.

Of course, an individual user of mass-market software can make an illegal copy without fear of repercussions, because it is not cost effective for a publisher to pursue an individual in court. For this reason, personal computer software publishers must rely on the customer's desire for the benefits that come only from purchasing the program, such as the user manual, technical support, access to upgrades, and bug fixes.

During the mid-1980s, personal computer software was commonly sold with a software-based copy protection "lock" designed to abort attempts to create copies.

This method of deterring illegal copying proved unsatisfactory. Customers didn't like it, and there were programs generally available—both in the retail marketplace and through bulletin boards—to defeat the software locks and permit copying. Business application software for personal computers has now generally abandoned copy protection, although some vendors use hardware lock system featuring a "key" that attaches to the serial port of a computer. Game programs have abandoned software locks, but now typically begin with a query that can only be answered by reference to the user documentation. This makes it cumbersome to copy game software, because the would-be copyright violator needs both a computer and a photocopy machine to make a usable copy.

Criminal Violations of Copyright Law

There are criminal provisions in the Copyright Act, but criminal prosecutions are brought only when violators engage in substantial criminal enterprises, such as large-scale pirating. In 1992 and 1993, for example, the government prosecuted large-scale importers of counterfeit copies of Microsoft's MS-DOS 5.0.

Notwithstanding the "FBI warning" on rented videotapes, the government does not have the resources to stop small-scale violations of the Copyright Act by private citizens.

Pieces of Software Programs

Under copyright law, it is also illegal for someone without authorization to copy *part* of the code of a copyrighted program. Programmers sometimes leave a job with pieces of software that they or others have developed, and use the code in their next job. Sometimes programs are decompiled and pieces of code are then copied into other programs. If someone else's software code gets into your software, even without your knowledge, it is still copyright infringement.

"Salting" a Computer Program to Detect Copying

To aid in detection of illegal copying by competitors, many developers include nonfunctional code in their programs—a practice known as "salting" the code. If this "salt" shows up in a competitors' program, it helps prove that the developer's program was copied, because the competitor cannot claim to have independently developed identical nonfunctional code for its product.

Salting works best if the "salt" consists of short segments of code in essential portions of the program. It is harder to detect the code as "salt" if it is encrypted.

External Characteristics of Computer Programs

A computer program is *active*. It may display a list of commands for you to choose from, retrieve data, solve equations, draw graphs, present pictures and sound, etc., all in response to instructions delivered by keystrokes and mouse clicks. The term in vogue for these visible and audible aspects of a software program is "external characteristics." Sometimes the external characteristics of the program, together with its internal structure, sequence, and organization are called the "non-literal elements" of a program, because the "literal" program is the source and object code.

For some of the external characteristics of computer programs, copyright protection is obviously available. For example, copyright law will protect the pictures and designs that appear on the computer screen, including animation, as well as music and sound. A copyrighted picture from a screen cannot be copied without permission any more than a picture from a copyrighted magazine or a scene from a movie can be. If your computer program displays an original poem, that text would be protected by the Copyright Act just as much as any poem that appears in *The New Yorker*.

The external characteristics of a program are of course quite independent of the source code. One could duplicate the menus, graphic displays, and other aspects of a program, say, Excel, without copying any of its code. Excel is written in C, but you could "clone" it in a completely different language, like Pascal. If you did so, not one line of code in your program would be the same as Excel's code. Nonetheless, if you made your clone without permission from Microsoft, and if you appropriated its external characteristics lock, stock, and barrel, you would be in violation of the Copyright Act.

Recent Cases Involving the Lotus 1-2-3 User Interface

The exact degree to which external characteristics are protected by the Copyright Act is still a bit unsettled, and different federal courts have arrived at different conclusions. As of this writing, however, it appears fairly clear that the trend is to a substantial degree of protection for external characteristics. Recent case law in cases involving Lotus 1-2-3, for example, has underlined the protection accorded to the spreadsheet user interface.

Several years ago, Lotus sued two companies that (each independently of the other) "cloned" Lotus 1-2-3 by duplicating its menu structure. Both are now out of business, at least in part because of decisions against them in litigation.

In 1992 Lotus won an important ruling in a suit against Borland International, Inc., whose Quattro spreadsheet offered the user the choice of using a interface copied from Lotus 1-2-3 or Quattro's own menus. The judge decided that Quattro's wholesale incorporation of the Lotus menu structure was an infringement of the Lotus 1-2-3 copyright.

The Analysis of Similarity of External Characteristics

You may have heard that one can copyright the "look and feel" of a computer program, but that is not accurate. Although the terms "look and feel" are used as a shorthand expression in some judicial opinions, the fact is that no court has been willing to grant rights to abstractions as vague and undefined as "look" or "feel." Rather, the analysis of external characteristics is done by comparing the visual and audible elements of the two programs in question. It is reasonable to expect that this mode of analysis will continue in the future.

> **Example:** You get an inspiration for a new type of computer game based on the legend of a macho super-hero, and then you program a highly original game called Hercules. You register the game copyright with the United States Copyright Office and publish it. Then your competitor brings out a strikingly similar game—so similar in every feature, element, and design that it clearly is a copy—called Thor. What are your rights? Can you and your lawyer get Thor off the market?

To begin with, you cannot copyright the *concept* of a game based on a mythological hero. You can't even protect the idea of a game based on the life of Hercules. Remember that the Copyright Act forbids extending copyright protection to any "idea" or "concept." On the other hand, your competitor cannot evade copyright law just by giving his game a different name and making a few minor changes.

A lawsuit would usually turn on an analysis of the functional, thematic, and graphic elements of the two games. The more the author of Thor borrows the external characteristics of your game Hercules, the more likely it is that he will be found liable for infringing your copyright. The test is one of "substantial similarity." In the case of the external characteristics of a game, that would basically translate into whether, based on the similar elements, an average user would perceive Thor as a copy of your game.

To prove an infringement case, you would also have to show that the author of Thor had *access* to your game and, in considering substantial similarity, the court would have to *disregard* that any elements copied were in the *public domain*. I will return to the case of Hercules and Thor and discuss these additional elements in the context of infringement litigation later in this chapter. Suffice it to say for present purposes that if the copying is clear, there is an excellent chance that you *can* get Thor off the market.

Derivative Works: One Work Based on Another

Suppose that you write a brilliant software game program based on the latest Steven King novel and begin selling it. What will happen? Unless you have a license from the holder of the rights to create computer games from the novel, you will surely be sued.

In copyright law, a "derivative work" means a work based on another work. The legal rule on derivative works is quite clear and is just what you would expect: If you want to sell your work, you need the permission of the holder of the rights that your program is based on. Your copyright in a derivative work covers only your contribution and creation.

A derivative computer program could be:

- An update, new release, or new version of any existing computer program.
- A translation of a program into a foreign language version, or into another computer language, or for a different hardware or software platform.
- A program substantially based on an another computer program.
- A program based on another medium such as a novel, a movie, or a game that is itself copyrighted.

- A novel, television show, or Broadway musical based on a computer program.

Sometimes there is litigation over the question of whether a work is derivative or not. The analysis is just like the inquiry we discussed in the preceding section, based on the functional, thematic, and graphic elements of the two works in question. Indeed, the concept of what is derivative is logically and legally linked with the concept of copyright infringement. For this reason "derivative work" is commonly defined in contracts as: "A work sufficiently based on a copyrighted work such that copying it without permission would infringe the copyright of the prior work."

"Thin" Copyright Protection for Computer Databases

You *can* copyright computer databases, that is, data compilations on computer readable media. However, there is an important limit to that protection. If the data itself is not copyrighted then your copyright extends only to the arrangement of the database, and if there is little or no originality to the arrangement, you may have no copyright protection at all. Lawyers say that the protection afforded to databases is "thin."

> **Example:** You distribute a computer database consisting of the names and addresses of all restaurants in southern Florida. Your database supplies the data in alphabetical order. Do you have a valid copyright?

In this example, you certainly have no ownership interest in the names and addresses, which are public information. The alphabetical arrangement is not even slightly original. There would therefore be no valid copyright. Even if you arranged the names and data in some original way, your copyright would only extend to the arrangement itself. Others would be able to copy the names for their own database without violating the law.

Note that it is possible to have a database in which each entry in the database, and therefore the contents of the database as a whole, is protected by copyright law. For example, the entries in a database might be brief custom-written reviews of the southern Florida restaurants.

Limits of Software Copyright Protection

There are pragmatic limitations on the reach of software protection under copyright law. In general, copyright protection does not cover functional or commonplace elements of copyrighted works. File formats are not covered. There are important areas of intellectual property that are quite beyond the reach of copyright law altogether.

No Protection for Functional Elements Inherent in the Idea of the Application

Software copyright protection does not cover *functional elements* that are inherent in the *idea* of a particular application.

> **Example:** You write and market a copyrighted medical office program that manages a doctor's appointments, bills, and patient records. Your program allows the physician to input the time of her appointments and to display each patient's medical history, and it allows the staff to print out an invoice before the patient leaves. Your competitor brings out a program that also provides for patient names, appointments, medical records, and invoices. Is your copyright infringed?

It is clear that the features of the competitive program—managing appointments, bills, and medical records and the like—are intrinsic to the *concept* of a medical office system, and the competitor may use them all.

The same principle would apply if you wrote a word processing program. You could include insert, backspace, word wrap, footnotes, spell checking, paragraph numbering, and other common features without fear that you would be infringing the copyright of WordPerfect for Windows. All these features, and many more, are intrinsic to word processors.

Even though all competitors can offer the same collection of features, that doesn't mean that they are immune from infringement claims. For example, the hypothetical medical office system might well include organizational, presentation, and design elements that are protected from copying, because they were *not* determined by functional considerations.

The cases involving Lotus 1-2-3 discussed earlier illustrates this point. Every option in the Lotus interface was functional. But a spreadsheet is complicated enough that a virtually endless variety of spreadsheet interface designs were possible. The judge reasoned that copying the interface was not required to duplicate the functions of 1-2-3, and therefore found exact copying to be infringement.

No Protection for Commonly Used Software Elements

Copyright protection does not extend to software elements that are in common use. Suppose that you write a program that uses the following message when a user exits without saving a file: "Do you want to save your work before exiting? Y/N". A competitor can use the exact same message without raising any infringement concerns, because hundreds of programs use essentially the same message. Similarly, there are only a few ways to implement a "print" function in a program, and therefore none of them are likely to get protection.

No Protection for Use of Interfaces and File Formats Needed for Compatibility

It is generally accepted that copyright protection does not prevent use of interfaces or file formats needed to achieve compatibility or allow interaction with another program. Therefore you can create an application that writes files in Paradox or Oracle or any other format, or you can write a word processor that includes a utility to convert WordPerfect macros to your own macro language—all without fear of a copyright infringement claim based on your use of the format. You can also sell macros that work with Excel or WordPerfect or any other program without running afoul of the copyright laws. Of course if you copy someone else's Paradox or Oracle code, you may well have a serious copyright infringement problem.

"Clean Rooms": Duplicating Without Copying

Perhaps it is an obvious point: There can be no copyright infringement unless there is *copying*, and a key element of proving infringement is proving that the alleged infringers had access to the allegedly copied material. If one person *independently* creates a program, it doesn't matter if it coincidentally is very much like another program. This principle has been used in so-called "clean room" software operations to duplicate the functions of a competitor's program without copying.

A "clean room" operation works as follows: Say that you wish to duplicate the functions of a competitor's program that has no "external characteristics" and operates invisibly as far as the user is concerned. Examples are the programs that manage computer or network resources. Or say that the external characteristics consist entirely of elements that you may use without infringing the program, because singly *and* in the aggregate they are commonly in use or are in the public domain.

You might decompile the competitor's program and then copy it by means of reverse engineering, but that would clearly be copyright infringement. (See the discussion of reverse engineering later in this chapter). So instead (1) you hire engineers who know nothing about the workings of the competitor's program (because of their lack of knowledge of the competitor's code, these engineers are sometimes known as "virgins"), (2) you have your engineers in an isolated and secure "clean room" environment where they are told the *functions* of the competitor's program but can learn nothing about the competitor's code, and (3) you have them write a new program that duplicates these functions. All of these procedures to isolate the engineers from the other product are scrupulously documented.

The end result of this "clean room" operation should be a program that acts the same as the competitor's program—but nothing was copied. The most famous example of this "clean room" technique is the Phoenix BIOS (used in many IBM clones), which was designed to perform all the same functions as the IBM-PC BIOS. It is generally believed that this "clean room" process avoids copyright infringement claims, but only where there are no copyrightable external characteristics in the competitor's program. This sort of operation requires careful planning and documentation, and must be carried out with the assistance of counsel.

Intellectual Property that Copyright Law Does Not Cover

There are important aspects of intellectual property protection for software products that copyright law simply does not provide for, including the following.

Inventions   Inventions are covered by United States patent law. Over the last decade, thousands of software patents have been issued. Typically, a software patent will grant a monopoly on certain functions and a means to accomplish them using software on a computer. Software patents, a cause of growing concern in the software industry, are discussed in Chapter 15. A copyright on a program that had patentable elements would only cover the particular *expression* of the invention that constitutes the program itself.

Product Names   The names of your software products (used on packaging, diskettes, screen displays, and in computer manuals) are covered by trademark law. Your software copyright does not protect them from use by others. The use and protection of trademarks is discussed in Chapter 14.

Secret Technology and Techniques   Software may use unique and secret methods of data storage, graphics display techniques, character recognition methods, encryption and compression techniques, speed optimization methods, etc. The law that prohibits employees from disclosing these secrets—and prevents competitors from stealing them—is state trade secret law. Trade secrets law is discussed in Chapter 2.

The Gray Areas of Software Copyright Law

There are a number of areas of software copyright law where the rules of the game are still quite unclear. These are obviously areas in which you will want to tread with caution, and with the benefit of legal advice.

Uncertain Protection for the Internal Structure of a Program

An open question (at least as of the writing of this book) is whether copyright protection extends to the internal structure, sequence, and organization of a program. Even if one does not copy the code of a program or its appearance, one might copy its overall internal structure. For example, one might copy the way that the program modules are organized, internal data structures are arranged, errors are monitored, or techniques are used for managing memory, etc. (One might learn these things, say, from a former employee of the other company. This circumstance might raise serious issues under trade secrets law, discussed in Chapter 2.)

In the mid-1980s, it looked like structure, sequence, and organization were going to be broadly protected, and that to copy these program "internals" was therefore copyright infringement. Now the decisions are going the other way. The courts are beginning to conclude (correctly in my view) that many of these "internals" are in fact "ideas" and "methods of operation" that cannot be covered by copyright protection. It seems that the trend is toward less protection for these "internals," but there is still no clear rule. In fact, federal courts in different areas of the country may give different results.

All that can be said with certainty is that the line between what is allowed and what is forbidden is unclear. Any imitation of significant aspects of the internal structure of another company's software program is a dangerous business that should only be undertaken after seeking legal advice.

The Unresolved Question of Reverse Engineering

A topic much discussed in software copyright law is whether it is copyright infringement to reverse engineer (without actually reproducing the code or selling copies). Reverse engineering means decompiling or disassembling the object code of a program to figure out how it works. The law on whether this is permitted is not yet fully clear.

It seems quite clear that reverse engineering—for whatever purposes—is unauthorized *copying*. In reverse engineering of software, the first step is to decompile the program in question and then printout the source code for detailed study. The printout itself is a copy. The question is whether it is an illegal copy.

The answer to the question of when reverse engineering is permitted involves a rather hazy doctrine of copyright law known as "fair use." Generally the "fair use" doctrine permits any copying that is socially beneficial. For example, parodies are clearly derivative works, but the courts have ruled in most cases that because they are social commentary parodies are "fair use" and therefore not a copyright infringement. The critic's right to use quotations from a play or novel in a review is also "fair use." There are, however, no hard and fast rules about what is "fair use." This is law that the judges must create as they decide new issues.

Based on recent decisions, it looks like reverse engineering will *probably* be "fair use" if discovery of information, rather than reproduction and sale of the program, is the goal, and as long as other means of discovering information about the program are unfeasible.

In a recent case, Accolade, a California software game company, reverse engineered the operating software used by Sega Enterprises of Japan in its Genesis game console. Accolade did not seek to use Sega's code or to market copies of the Sega Genesis software. Rather, Accolade used reverse engineering to learn the interface between the Sega game console and the game cartridge. Accolade used this information to make its own game cartridges work with the Genesis unit. The reverse engineering was *necessary*—that is, no other means of access to the interface information was available. The court found that under these circumstances the "fair use" doctrine protected Accolade from a copyright infringement claim.

On the other hand, if you reverse engineer another company's program *and then copy much of it*, you will probably be found liable for copyright infringement. What if you reverse engineer another company's program to discover its "methods of operation" (which are not protected by copyright law), and then use these methods with entirely new code? What if there is no other practical way to discover these methods? Is this reverse engineering permitted? The answer is unclear. As of now, the line between what is permitted and forbidden is very indistinct.

If you are thinking of reverse engineering another company's software product, be wary. This is a dangerous area where there are many risks and the law is in flux. You definitely need get the advice of counsel before travelling down this road.

The Dangerous Game of Creating "Near Clones"

Let's go back to our example of Lotus 1-2-3 (although we could use any program as an example). An obvious question is: How close can your program get to Lotus 1-2-3 and still be legal? If you create your spreadsheet by copying all or most of the menus of Lotus 1-2-3, or make your program appear to the user to be a copy or close to a copy of Lotus 1-2-3, then you are probably in the soup. But what if you make your program similar in some functions and different in others? What if only 70 percent of the functions are the same, or only 30 percent?

How close can one program get to another program and not infringe it? There is unfortunately no clear line that separates legal from illegal programs. The closer you get to the other program, the greater the risk. If you have any doubt as to how far you can go, or as to whether your program is infringed by a "near clone," you should talk to legal counsel.

Problems When Parties Fail to Specify Who Is to Own the Copyright

When a contractor or consultant provides software under a contract, the parties all too often forget to specify who will *own* the software copyright. The result can be uncertainty that leads to conflict. The following illustrates the problem.

Example: A large poultry producer, United Chicken, wants a program to calculate its need for grain over time and to budget for grain expenditures at the lowest overall cost. They also need several other business programs updated and debugged. United contracts with Smith, a programmer, to do the required jobs, and the contract says nothing about who will own what.

Smith writes computer code at home and at United. He works closely with United's headquarters staff who assign him additional work. After six months, Smith has done everything required, including the creation of a brilliant grain-buying program called Econo-Grain that runs on a Macintosh. Econo-Grain gathers information on worldwide grain prices, makes recommendations, and saves United millions of dollars each year.

After the program is written, Smith sees that he has a winning program that United's competitors will all want and pay big money for. He puts his copyright notice on Econo-Grain, and advertises it for sale in *Chicken World* magazine. Meanwhile, believing it has all rights to the program, United has registered the copyright in its own name. Seeing Smith's advertisement, United sues Smith to stop him from selling the Econo-Grain program. Who really owns the copyright, and who will win the struggle for ownership?

The legal question in this case is whether Smith's program created for Econo-Grain was "work-for-hire." The answer to this legal question is unclear, and therefore it is also unclear who owns the copyright.

The Legal Question of "Work-for-Hire"

Generally speaking, if an *employee* of a company (or a person subject to the degree of control and supervision that a company normally has over its employees) writes a program while on the job, the program is "work-for-hire." This means that legally the company is the author of the program and owns the copyright.

Generally, if an *independent contractor* writes a program then it is *not* "work-for-hire." The independent contractor owns the copyright for the program unless the contractor has agreed to transfer it.

The problem is to determine whether a particular relationship is more like an employment relationship or more like the relationship with an independent contractor. The decision in Smith's case involves consideration of matters like these:

- Did United have the right to tell Smith *what* work to do and *how* the work should be done, as it would with an employee? The more control that United had over detail, the more likely that it will prevail. The more Smith worked on his own, the better his case will be.

- Where was his work done? If it was predominantly done on site at United, that would help United's case. If most of the work was done at Smith's home that would help him.

- How was Smith paid? Was he paid on a weekly or monthly basis? Were taxes withheld? Did Smith get any employee benefits? The more Smith's compensation looks like employee compensation, the better United's case is.

- Was Smith to be paid on delivery of the software? Was Smith to be paid on the basis of cost savings produced? If so, then Smith looks less like an employee and much more like a contractor.

The bottom line in this high-stakes dispute between Smith and United is that the lawyers could fight about it for years—assuming that Smith and United can afford that fight. Until the case is settled or tried, ownership of the copyright will be unclear, and the persons with the most to gain will be the lawyers.

(There is another specialized and rather technical circumstance in which a program is "work-for-hire" under the Copyright Act. Specifically, the provision makes a work into work-for-hire if (1) there is a written contract, (2) the contract *states* that the work will be work-for-hire, *and* (3) the work is part of a larger work, is a translation, is supplemental to another work, is part of a fact compilation, or is an instructional text.)

Avoiding This Problem

This type of dispute is common. The copyright issues in these "work-for-hire" cases in fact can get even more complicated in many cases, because the lawyers could also argue that the contractual relationship between the parties determines who owns what. Ambiguous contracts are also grist for the litigation mill.

The important point to remember is that *this kind of issue should never arise in the first place*. Every software development contract should make it *explicitly clear* who will own the rights to the software product. Software development agreements that deal with this issue are discussed in Chapter 8.

Copyright Notices for Your Software

You Should Always Use a Copyright Notice

As I noted earlier, you should *always* put a copyright notice on your software programs. This is true even when a notice is not necessary to prevent loss of a copyright under the Copyright Act (because the software was first published after March 1, 1989). The copyright notice provides three major advantages:

- The notice proclaims to the world that your work is copyrighted. Therefore it helps to deter would-be software infringers, pirates, and cloners.

- The notice makes a lawsuit against an infringer stronger, because it makes it clear that the infringer acted in willful disregard of your rights. No one can claim that they "innocently" infringed a copyright if a notice of the copyright is on the face of the software.

- A copyright notice is required for copyright protection in some foreign countries.

The copyright notice has to be tailored to fit matters of ownership and publication. But it is really very easy to get the copyright notice right. If you read through the following examples, you will get the idea.

Basic Form of Notice

The basic form of a copyright notice is this:

Copyright © 1993 Jack Smith, Inc.
All rights reserved

Legally, this formulation is redundant. The © symbol means the same thing as the word "copyright," and either alone would be sufficient under the law. The words "All rights reserved" are not strictly required, except in some Latin American countries. However, the form above is customary, and has the benefit of making it perfectly clear that you claim the full protection of the copyright laws.

In using this format there are two very important points that you should pay attention to:

- **The Right Name:** The name to use in the notice is the *owner* of the software, which may be different from the author, as is discussed later.

- **The Right Date:** The date to use in the notice is the date of *publication*, not the date when the software was written.

Form of Notice for Work-for-Hire

In the case of work-for-hire, the corporate employer is both author and owner. For example, if Janet Jones, in her capacity as an employee of XYZ Corporation wrote software, then the author and owner of the software is XYZ Corporation. The copyright notice should therefore be as follows:

Copyright © 1993 XYZ Corporation
All rights reserved

Form of Notice for Software that Has Been Transferred

If *all* rights in software have been transferred to a new owner, it is the *new* owner's name that should appear in the notice. For example, if Jack Smith, Inc. wrote a program but then sold "all rights, title, and interest" in it to ABC Corporation, the copyright notice should say:

Copyright © 1993 ABC Corporation
All rights reserved

In Chapter 7 I will discuss how to accomplish this type of transfer.

Form of Notice for Software that Has Been Licensed

If Jack Smith, Inc. has licensed its program, the question of whether the licensee may put its name on the copyright notice depends on whether the license is exclusive or non-exclusive.

Assume that Jack Smith, Inc. has licensed to ABC Corp. the *exclusive* right to reproduce its program for sale in California. Jack Smith, Inc. retains all other rights. In this case, ABC Corp. can show itself as the owner on the copyright notice on copies of the software that it sells, because it has an exclusive license. It would also be proper to show Jack Smith, Inc.'s name on the notice. Typically the exclusive license agreement will expressly state that ABC Corp. may use its name in the copyright notice. However, even if the contract is silent, ABC Corp. can list itself as the owner. Also note that ABC Corp. can, and should, record its exclusive license with the U.S. Copyright Office; the procedure is discussed in Appendix A.

Assume that Jack Smith, Inc. has licensed to ABC Corp. a *non-exclusive* right to reproduce the program for sale worldwide. In this case, ABC Corp. may not list itself on the copyright notice.

Form of Notice for Software that Includes Software Owned by Others

Suppose that ABC Corporation's program includes code owned by Jane Doe and used by permission. The notice would read:

Copyright © 1993 ABC Corporation
Copyright © 1988 Jane Doe
All rights reserved

However, should ABC Corporation fail to give Jane this attribution, Jane need not worry; her copyright cannot be lost by ABC Corporation's omission in labeling its own software.

Form of Notice for Software Based on Other Works

A similar practice applies for software based on a novel or another pre-existing copyrighted work that applies for a derivative work. Again the notice would normally include both the software copyright and the copyright notice from the earlier work. For example, if Jack Smith, Inc. based its computer game on a movie owned by Magnum Studios, Inc., the notice would read:

Form of Notice for Jointly Owned Software

If Jane Doe and Jack Smith, Inc. jointly develop (or jointly purchase all rights in or jointly get an exclusive license for) software, the notice would be this form:

Form of Notice for a New Version of Software

If the software has gone through various versions or releases, the notice normally gives each publication date in this form:

Or, if the number of publications are too numerous, use this form, giving the first and the most recent dates:

Form of Notice for Unpublished Software

If the work is not yet published and is still in development, you should nonetheless include a copyright notice. Use this form:

Form of Notice for Software Documentation

In placing a copyright notice on computer documentation, it is a good idea to expressly mention both the program and the documentation. For example,

Copyright © 1986, 1990 Jack Smith, Inc. (Program)
Copyright © 1990 Jack Smith, Inc. (Documentation)
All rights reserved

Using the Symbol "(c)" Instead of "©"

Sometimes people want to create a copyright notice, but do not have access to the "©" symbol. This can occur when a copyright notice needs to be uploaded to a bulletin board. Or it may occur when a programmer wants to embed a notice in source code but the character-based environment does not include the "©" symbol. It is then customary to substitute "(c)", as for example:

Copyright (c) 1986, 1990 Jack Smith

Is this concoction "(c)" really a legally valid substitute for "©"? No one knows whether "(c)" actually works, because Congress didn't mention it in the copyright statute and the issue is hardly mentioned in the case law. But you needn't lose sleep over this issue. Under the Copyright Act, your use of the word "Copyright" in the notice cures any problem about the symbol.

Where Does the Copyright Notice Go?

There is a consistent practice in the software industry regarding the use of copyright notices. I recommend that you follow this practice and put the copyright notice on *all* of the following:

- The label on the diskette, CD-ROM disk, or other media on which the software is sold.

- The first screen that the user sees. (If the copyrighted material is accessed by modem or over a network, the terminal should display the notice upon sign-on at the user's terminal.)

- On the face and back of the package in which the software is sold.

- On the "shrink-wrap" license included with the software.

- On any computer documentation supplied with the program.

This is more than the law requires. Where notice is legally required (on software published before March 1, 1989), it is technically sufficient under the Copyright Act if the notice is placed on the media containing the software *or* on the first screen that appears. (When notice is legally required, it is also acceptable to have a notice in the "machine readable form," i.e., in the object code, so that "on printouts it appears either with or near the title or at the end of the work.") However, as I noted, most companies use the notice much more liberally—and you should too.

Even if you do not license your source code, it is a good idea to put a copyright notice on the first page of the source code, at or near the top of the page, and at the end. That way if anyone should get hold of a copy of your source code, they will be on notice that it is copyrighted.

Registration of Your Copyright

To best protect your computer programs, you should register your copyright with the United States Copyright Office *as soon as you start sending a program out into the PC software world*—at the time of first commercial sale or even earlier. The reasons that you should register early in the life of your computer program are:

- Registering your software is *very* easy.

- Registering your software is an incredible bargain. The application fee is only $20.00. This is a small fraction of what it costs the government to examine your application and store your deposit of computer code.

- Timely registration, as discussed shortly, gives you *important litigation advantages*, including access to "statutory damages," and a good shot at an award of attorneys' fees. These advantages are extremely valuable if you need to threaten or sue an infringer. If you wait too long to register, these advantages are irretrievably lost.

The Simple Process of Registering

The copyright registration system is based on the proposition that all works are created equal and all are worthy of registration. As long as the (rather simple) formalities are done correctly, every software work is accepted.

The United States Copyright Office is a branch of the Library of Congress set up by Congress to run the copyright registration system. Its knowledgeable staff members examine applications, issue certificates of registration, classify and maintain materials sent to the office, and aid the public in the registration process.

To register a copyright you send an application, a "deposit" of copyrighted material (usually part of the source code), and the modest $20.00 fee to the Copyright Office. Most software companies do their own copyright registrations without using their attorney.

There are a few wrinkles and rules that you have to know when you fill out the application, but they are not difficult. To be sure you do the application right the first time, however, it is important that *before* filling out your first copyright application, you read Appendix A of this book, which includes a simple step-by-step explanation of what you need to do. Also included in this book is a full-size tear-out copy of Form TX, the copyright registration application itself. If you have unregistered copyrights, photocopy Form TX and get those applications in! (If the program is primarily visual or audiovisual (such as an arcade-style game), you should use Form PA; Appendix A gives the number of the Copyright Office Form Hotline where you can order that form for free.)

The Advantages of Timely Registration

Some software companies never bother to file a copyright registration until they are faced with infringement. However, waiting until the time of suit to file the application is very unwise. My advice is that for every new version of any significant software product, including every significant revision (beyond minor repairs and bug fixes), you should file another copyright registration as a matter of routine, for the following reasons.

Statutory Damages Under the Copyright Act

In most lawsuits you need to prove "actual damages" in order to recover money. Actual damages usually will mean what you lost due to wrongdoing or what the malefactor gained. Under copyright law, however, you can get monetary damages even if you do not or cannot prove actual damages. These damages without proof are called "statutory damages." The amount you get under this provision is set by the judge in his or her discretion; the award can be as high as $20,000 and, if the infringement was intentional, as high as $100,000.

The right to claim statutory damages gives you the option of a simpler and less costly lawsuit. However, the judge can grant you these "statutory damages" *only* if you have made a timely registration. If you file your application too late, then in order to get an award of money in your suit, you will need to prove actual monetary damages.

Getting a Good Shot at Attorneys' Fees   Even more important than statutory damages is the opportunity, that comes from timely registration, to seek an award of attorneys' fees after trial. An award of attorneys' fees under this provision again is discretionary; that is, the judge can freely decide whether or not to award fees. In practice, attorneys' fees are granted quite often to prevailing plaintiffs. The clearer and more blatant the infringement is, the more likely you are to get an award of attorneys' fees, the amount of which can be *very* substantial. Even the availability of the remedy gives you important settlement leverage. But if you don't register your copyright in a timely way, the judge has no power to award you *any* attorneys' fees at all.

What is "Timely" Filing?

Statutory damages and attorneys' fees are available only if you sue under the following circumstances:

- **For Infringement of Unpublished Programs:** If you registered your program *before the infringement began.*
- **For Infringement of Published Programs:** If you registered *before the infringement began or within three months of publication.*

In calculating whether you filed in time, the key date is the *effective date* of registration, which is the date on which the Copyright Office *receives* your properly prepared application, together with the appropriate fee and your deposit of program code (all as described in Appendix A). The date the Copyright Office finally issues the Copyright Certificate, which may be months later, is irrelevant.

Copyright Before Publication

You may wonder why the law has rules for registration *before* publication. Actually, the risk of such infringement definitely exists for software. This is because of two common prepublication practices found in the software business: distributing copies widely for beta testing and distributing evaluation copies to numerous potential publishers or prospective investors. These practices and the tendency of people to copy and share interesting new software can cause copies of your software to travel far and wide before publication. The best practice is to register before substantial prepublication distribution. If you make only minor changes after registration, such as fixing bugs, you need not register again.

Beta test agreements (discussed in Chapter 5) and confidential disclosure agreements (discussed in Chapter 6) are designed to help control unauthorized disclosure and distribution. However, it is impossible to give programs 100 percent protection from unauthorized copying and distribution.

Presumption of Validity of Your Copyright   If you have registered your copyright either *before* publication or *within five years* of publication, the law also gives you another procedural benefit. In a copyright lawsuit, until proven otherwise, your copyright is presumed valid; and until proven otherwise, all the statements in your copyright registration are taken as true.

These presumptions can simplify proof somewhat at trial and are meant to be another incentive to prompt registration. However, the matters that are the subject of this rule are really not very difficult to prove in litigation. This is therefore a less important advantage than statutory damages and attorneys' fees.

Making Copyright Registration a Regular Practice

As you can see, you can be sure to get the legal advantages outlined above, and strengthen your hand against an infringer, only by registering early. As a practical matter, you should register your software product, and any new release or substantial revision, before circulating it widely. At the latest, registration should take place during the three-month window allowed by the Copyright Act that we discussed earlier in the chapter.

Recording Assignments and Exclusive Licenses

In the chapters that follow we will look at transactions in which a copyright holder transfers rights in a copyright (for example, software assignments in Chapter 7, software development agreements in Chapter 8, and software publishing agreements in Chapter 10). If you have received an assignment of a copyright or obtained an exclusive license to software, you should get on record at the Copyright Office.

You should promptly *register* the copyright if it is unregistered, using the steps spelled out in Appendix A. If the copyright has been previously registered, you should *record* at the Copyright Office the contract or other instrument that granted you your interest. The procedures (which are quite simple and inexpensive) for recording an assignment or exclusive license are described in detail in Appendix A.

Why is it important to to record an exclusive license or assignment? The reason is that recording early can protect your priority rights. Recording too late can cost you the rights you bargained for. You have 30 days after the transfer or license grant to get on file (60 days if the transfer took place outside the United States). If you miss that window, your rights are subject to any assignee or exclusive licensees who files in good faith before you do.

> **Example:** You pay Smith $1,000,000 for a license to the exclusive worldwide rights to a software program. You fail to record the license within the next 30 days. Next, Smith grants the same worldwide rights to the program to Jones for another $1,000,000. Jones records his license at the Copyright Office before you do. The result: Jones has licensed the copyright to the program exclusively, and you own nothing.

> **Example:** You pay Smith $1,000,000 for an exclusive license to a software program throughout the United States. You fail to record the license within the next 30 days. Next, Smith grants Jones an exclusive license to copy and sell the program in the states of California, Oregon, and Washington. Jones records

his license before you do. The result: You have no right to market the software in those three states; only Jones has the right to market there.

Example: You pay Smith $1,000,000 for an exclusive license of the worldwide rights to a software program. Next, Smith grants the same worldwide rights to the program to Jones for another $1,000,000. Smith records his license before you, but you record your license *within* 30 days of the date it was granted. The result: You have licensed the program exclusively, and Jones owns nothing.

Most often when there are priority conflicts in license grants, it is a matter of accident rather than deliberate fraud. But whatever the cause, it is best to get the law on your side by recording your assignment or exclusive license. Follow the procedures in Appendix A, and make your rights a matter of record at the Copyright Office. Also note that any transfer of any exclusive right in a copyright must be in writing and signed by the transferor (or the transferor's agent) in order to be legally binding.

Enforcing Your Copyright When It Is Infringed

When your copyright has been infringed, you must take prompt steps to protect your rights. In this section, we will look at how your rights might be violated, how to respond, and what will happen in litigation if it occurs.

What Constitutes Software Copyright Infringement?

Infringement of your copyright occurs when someone duplicates, sell, uses, or makes derivative works from your copyrighted program without permission.

The following are examples of infringement:

- **Pirating.** You develop Katmandoo, a fantasy adventure program, and begin marketing it. A software pirate, Smith, buys one copy. In Taiwan, he has 100,000 copies made, including imitation packaging and instructions. Smith sells the Katmandoo copies through a New York broker to retailers in the United States, England, and Canada. Smith and the broker have both infringed your copyright. The retailers in the United States, England, and Canada have also infringed your copyright, albeit innocently.

- **Cloning.** You develop Dragon Fire, an arcade game program, and begin marketing it. Smith, a "cloner," sees it and then copies all of your game's features: its plot, screens, sequence, characters, appearance, and sound, in a new game called Inferno, which he sells. If the differences between the two games are insubstantial, Smith has infringed your copyright.

- **Creating Unauthorized Derivative Works**. You write Canals of Mars, an outer-space adventure game that runs on a Macintosh computer, and begin marketing it. You grant a non-exclusive license to Brown to reproduce and sell the game for Macintosh computers, but grant no rights to create derivative works. Without your permission, Brown writes and sells a Windows version of your game. Brown has infringed your copyright.

- **Going Beyond the Market Restrictions of the License.** You develop Home Run, a program for pricing baseball card collections. You give Smith a license to reproduce the program and sell only to a specified mail-order list of sports magazine subscribers. Smith makes thousands of copies of the program to sell through retail dealers. Smith has infringed your copyright.

- **Selling More Rights Than You Own.** You develop Trade-Up, a program for picking stocks. You give an exclusive license to Jones, who records the license with the U.S. Copyright Office. Desperate for money and losing your moral compass, you grant another "exclusive" license to Smith, who begins selling the program. Smith has infringed Jones' right as the exclusive licensee. You are liable to Smith for fraud.

Your First Step: Investigation and Consultation with Counsel

If your software copyright is infringed, your first step is to find out as much as you can as quickly as you can about the infringement. Phone calls to customers and distributors may yield valuable information. If you can buy a copy of the infringing product, you should. You should also get copies of any advertising or promotional material for the infringing product. Take this information to your lawyer so that counsel can help you work out a strategy. You need legal advice before playing out this game.

The Second Step: The Cease-and-Desist Letter

After gathering information, your next move normally will be to rush out a "cease-and-desist" letter. The letter should use firm language and notify the infringer that he is violating your rights. It should demand that the infringer cease marketing the infringing product immediately and that he confirm in writing that the infringing product is off the market. The letter should be sent by certified mail with return receipt requested so that you can prove receipt. You should send such a letter only after discussing with your attorney the merits of your case against the infringer, your options, and the text of the letter. A sample cease-and-desist letter is included in Appendix C as Form 1-1 and on diskette as C&D-LTR.W51.

You can send the letter yourself, or you can have your software lawyer send it. It is better to have your lawyer send the letter. Why? Because the *threat* of a imminent lawsuit will be more palpable to the infringer if he receives the letter from an attorney. The lawyer's letter will make it sound like you mean business, and increase your chances of a negotiated solution.

There is one risk in sending a cease-and-desist letter; the accused infringer may beat you to the courthouse and file a *declaratory judgment* lawsuit against you. In essence, such a filing turns the lawsuit around; in it the accused asks the court to declare that there was no infringement. Why would the alleged infringer rush to court? The reason is to pick a court in a location that is inconvenient for your company. For example, if your company is in California and the alleged infringer is in central Georgia, the declaratory suit could be filed in federal court in Atlanta. For this reason, sometimes the victim of copyright infringement will skip the cease-and-desist letter and simply file a lawsuit. Again, this is a tactical question that you must discuss with counsel.

What Will Happen Next

After receiving your cease-and-desist letter, the accused infringing company has some tactical choices:

- **Playing Hardball.** If the opposing side believes that it can stare you down or that it can wage a legal struggle and win, it may take a hard line. Typically, it will write back a strident letter denying any infringement and defiantly continue its actions.

- **Negotiation Strategy.** If the infringer believes your claim has some merit and wishes to avoid the cost of a litigation struggle, it will want to talk seriously. Once again, you will receive a letter denying any infringement, but in this case, the other side will contact you and suggest a settlement dialogue. Meanwhile, it may well continue its infringing actions. The infringer's usual tactic is to delay as long as possible and then make the best deal it can.

- **Capitulation**. Every once in a while an infringer just gives in and agrees to quit wrongdoing. This could occur if the infringer has copied your software in a very blatant way, is easily intimidated, or has a readily available alternative source of suitable software. Even when the infringer is ready to abandon the infringing product, it will usually be difficult to get it to discuss paying you monetary compensation.

Negotiation Opportunities

Whether there is litigation or not, it may be possible to settle with the other side. To settle a dispute takes a willingness on both sides to compromise and sober realism. As the holder of the copyright, what you want in a settlement is:

- Recognition of the validity of your copyright.

- Admission that your copyright was infringed.

- Compensation for past wrongful use of your copyright.

- An agreement on what will happen in the future, either (a) that infringement will stop, or (b) that the infringer will pay a generous royalty on sales of the infringing product.

Of course, you can't get everything that you want all of the time. Negotiation, however, may get you a deal that you can live with, without the cost of litigation. It's usually worth a try. Your attorney should be involved in documenting any settlement.

It is also a good idea to push for a quick negotiated settlement. Don't let negotiations drag on for months. You can prejudice your legal case if it looks like you "slept on your rights."

Litigate When You Need to

Litigation is a process to invoke the power of the judicial branch of government to enforce your legal rights. Litigation skillfully employed has been an important weapon for established and well-capitalized software companies. Lawsuits can be used as a tool to protect a copyright and to fend off illegal competition. Sometimes you cannot settle a dispute, either because the opposition is being unrealistic in your discussions, or because your stake in protecting your copyright is too important to allow you to compromise. Then you have to sue.

There are a number of times when litigation comes up in this book. For example I will discuss trade secret litigation, contract litigation, trademark litigation, and patent litigation. Each variety of lawsuit has its own wrinkles. For example, copyright cases are heard in federal court, but most contract cases are heard in state court. However, the process is basically the same throughout. This discussion of litigation in the copyright context therefore will also serve as an overall introduction to the subject of lawsuits. I will draw on this discussion as we revisit this topic of litigation from time to time.

There is an old saying: "The wheels of justice grind slowly, but they grind exceedingly fine." The justice process sometimes seems to move at a glacial pace and can burn up an awful lot of money, but the process in the end can be very powerful, and the impact of a victory can be profound. Moreover, sometimes just initiating the litigation process raises the stakes high enough to force a settlement.

Litigation can, however, be a crisis for a young and undercapitalized company. A fight in court over intellectual property early in a company's life may scare off investors and venture capitalists, and it may drain the time and money of a young business. It is a fact of life that a young company may have a great legal case, but be too poor to assert it effectively. Young companies should pick up the sword of litigation only after exploration of all alternatives.

Most people start their first lawsuit without knowing what the process is like. I will be describing the process in enough detail that you can get the general idea of what you and your litigation opponent are in for.

The Nature of Modern Litigation

Modern litigation for high-technology businesses is sophisticated and complex, filled with arcane court rules and procedures. If you think you might be able to do it yourself, forget it. You need someone who knows how to play the game. Parties that are *pro se*, that is, who represent themselves, get eaten alive.

There definitely is a lot of "sticker shock" in litigation. The only solace is that it is usually costing the other side as much as it costs you. Because of the cost, it is common that litigation ends after the preliminary skirmishing that focuses the attention of the parties on settling the dispute. Studies have shown that about 95 percent of all litigation cases settle. Many settle soon after they are filed. Some cases settle "on the courthouse steps" just before trial, and a few are fought right through to the bitter end.

Don't give one of these cases to just any lawyer—or to just any litigator. To pursue one of these cases properly, you need counsel that understands your technology *and* the tactics of litigation. A major part of winning the case is presenting technology in simple terms that even a judge can understand. You need counsel that understands your technology well enough to do that.

Asserting and Proving Your Claim

Let us return for a moment to the case that we discussed earlier in this chapter: your innovative game Hercules and your opponent's very similar game Thor. Let's say that you are sure that Thor is a copy and you have decided to sue for copyright infringement. How do you proceed?

Whom to Sue   The first question is: Whom do you sue? Generally litigation is brought against the publisher of the infringing work. The author may be sued as well, but the publisher is the main target because it controls whether copies are made and it hopefully has the "deep pockets" to pay monetary damages. Others may in theory be liable as well, for example distributors and end-users, but they are not commonly the targets.

What You Need to Prove   Assuming that you have decided to sue the author and publisher, the next question is: What do you have to prove in the presentation of your infringement case?

In order to prevail in copyright infringement litigation, first you have to show that you have a valid copyright. We discussed earlier reasons why your copyright might not be valid—for example if your Hercules program is not an original work or if it was published before March 1, 1989, without a proper copyright notice. In most cases, however, it will be easy to prove that you have a valid copyright.

Assuming you have a valid copyright, it is necessary to prove copying took place. There are two ways to prove this. The first method is direct: You produce a witness who saw or participated in the act of copying. For example, a former employee of the defendant's business might admit that he and his co-workers created Thor by running Hercules repeatedly on their computer and copying its visual and thematic elements one by one. That would be very powerful direct evidence of copying.

The second, and much more common, method of proving copying is indirect: You prove (1) that the author of Thor had *access* to your program and (2) that Thor is *substantially similar* to your Hercules game. From these subsidiary conclusions, the court can conclude that copying occurred.

To prove access, you need to present evidence from which it is reasonable to conclude that the defendant obtained a copy of the Hercules game. For example, it may suffice to prove that Hercules was on sale in nationwide distribution. Of course, if the author of Thor denies that he or she had access to Hercules, it is up to the jury (or the judge if case is being tried without a jury) to decide whether the denial is credible. In a case where a plaintiff is trying to prove infringement of an unpublished program, the need for proof that the defendant had access to the allegedly copied program can be a major stumbling block.

Proof of substantial similarity is, as we discussed, based on an element-by-element comparison. Then a conclusion is based on whether according to that comparison, copying has taken place. In deciding similarity, the analysis would *exclude* elements that are merely functional or are in the public domain. For example, some elements of the story of Hercules are part of a 2000-year-old myth that is definitely in the public domain. What is relevant is your game's *original expression:* its sound, pictures, dialogue, sequence, plot elements, its portrayal of characters, etc.

There is another factor that you must take account of in deciding if you have a strong case: the "feel" of the case. This factor, which we will revisit in Chapter 2 in the context of trade secret litigation, is not written in any statute book, but it is extremely important. A common factor affecting the "feel" of a copyright infringement case is how blatant the copying is. No one likes plagiarism. In addition, any infringement case is better if the alleged infringer has done something that sounds devious or wrong. Here are some examples of misconduct that would make a copyright infringement case easier to prove:

> **Example:** The accused infringer was a trusted former employee that learned all about the product by working on it and then faithlessly exploited that knowledge to create a "clone" of the game.

> **Example:** The accused infringer is a publisher that evaluated your product and considered publishing it, but wouldn't pay the price. It used a demonstration copy of your game, which you sent for evaluation purposes, to create its "knock-off" version.

> **Example:** The alleged infringer is a giant company that dominates the market. After creating its imitation version of your product, it used its purchasing power and marketing clout to underprice and cripple your smaller company.

Needless to say, calculating the strength of your case and the likelihood of success is something that you need legal advice for. And remember that *nothing* is certain in litigation.

A Blitzkrieg Opening Gambit: Motion for a Preliminary Injunction

In many copyright cases, the plaintiff (the party that files suit) will try to get a forceful remedy that comes not in years but in just days or weeks after the case begins. The plaintiff will try to get the judge to order the defendant (the party accused in the suit) *to take its infringing product off the market immediately*. The court order implementing this preemptive strike is called a "preliminary injunction."

While the preliminary injunction formally lasts only until the date of trial (which typically is about two years after the case is filed), in fact the preliminary injunction is often a blast that shatters the defendant's position in one blow. After the preliminary injunction is issued, the defendant has suddenly lost its product revenues and in a few weeks irrevocably loses all its customers for the banned product. Unless its other resources are vast, the defendant is often forced to capitulate and seek peace on whatever terms it can get.

Why not get a preliminary injunction in every case? Well, a preliminary injunction is what we lawyers call "an extraordinary writ"; it is granted sparingly precisely because it is so powerful and can be decisive of the whole case. The judge will usually give you a preliminary injunction (1) if the violation of your rights is quite overt, (2) if you are suffering present harm, and (3) if you sued soon after learning of the violation. Moreover, preliminary injunctions are usually sought on the basis of *affidavits*, which are written statements of witnesses under oath, and legal briefs. The judge therefore rules on these motions with only an incomplete understanding of the facts and without having the credibility of statements tested by cross-examination. The judge's ruling on preliminary injunctions is often "rough justice" and never a certainty. Whether or not to seek this preemptive relief is a complex tactical question calling for a skilled litigator's advice.

When you get a preliminary injunction, you almost always have to post a bond to pay damages to the defendant in case the injunction turns out be wrongful. As a practical matter, this may require you to put $5,000 or more aside (sometimes much more) in the custody of a bonding company, until the case is resolved.

There is another consideration in moving for a preliminary injunction. If you lose the motion, it may have a devastating effect on your case. You may not wish to spend the money to take the case to trial and you may lose much of your settlement leverage because the other side has won the first-round. Often plaintiffs give up after a first round loss.

The Cost of Litigation

If you ask a litigation lawyer how much a case will cost to file and take through trial, he or she will invariably say: "It all depends." The lawyer isn't being evasive, it's just that there are many variables that can affect cost. Here are some broad "ballpark" generalizations.

- A case that can be settled in its early stages could cost from $5,000 to $25,000. Typically the more clear cut the case of infringement, the less the cost.

- A case that is contested and has some genuine issues could cost from $75,000 to $300,000 in legal and expert witness fees to take through trial. Expenses mount especially fast just before and during trial.

Some cases can cost millions of dollars. An example of an incredibly expensive litigation is Apple Computer's titanic legal struggle against Microsoft. As you may know, Apple claimed that the Windows graphical user interface infringes Apple's copyright on the Macintosh interface. The judge rejected Apple's arguments and dismissed Apple's case, and Apple's huge investment in this litigation has borne no fruit. As of the writing of this book, Apple had said it would appeal.

Possible Defenses

The defendant in an infringement suit may try to establish one of the common defenses listed below. Whether any one of these defenses will work will depend on the facts of the case.

Copyright Invalidity　　The defendant may claim that your program was itself an illegal copy of someone else's software or is in the public domain.

Permission or License　　The defendant may claim that it had valid permission to create or sell the challenged product.

Lack of Similarity　　The defendant may claim that its program is sufficiently different from yours and that its program is not a copy.

Separate Creation　　The defendant may claim that its program was not copied at all, but simply an independent creation of its own.

"Fair Use"　　The defendant may claim that its use of your program was limited to "fair use." As you learned earlier, "fair use" has been invoked to defend reverse engineering of software.

Statute of Limitations　　Normally infringement that took place more than three years before the date of suit cannot be pursued. However, you can sue for infringement that *occurred within the three-year period* even if it started before that period.

Through Trial and Beyond

If the case does not settle early, the parties will then press on through the rest of the litigation process, until a settlement is achieved or until the process grinds to a final conclusion. The stages of this process are as follows.

Discovery   In this stage of litigation, the parties gather and exchange hundreds and sometimes thousands of pages of documents. Witnesses, including the plaintiff, the defendant, and the experts for both sides, are examined under oath in attorneys' well-appointed offices, sometimes for several days. The lawyers fight about who gets what information, but usually the essential facts are on the table by the end of the process.

Motions   Litigators file a variety of motions, some of them quite routine. The important ones are those that ask the judge to decide the case or an important part of the case without a trial—as, for example, when the essential facts are not disputed and the case turns only on an issue of law.

Trial   This is the part that looks a bit like trials that you see on TV—only much slower and *much* more boring. In this portion of the case, the witnesses testify, and the exhibits are admitted into evidence. If there is question of whether there is substantial similarity of two software products, expert testimony will be required. Experts may also testify on monetary damages. Finally, the judge or jury decides the case. (In most copyright cases, either party can chose a jury trial. If neither party opts for a jury, then the judge decides.)

Appeal   Sometimes the loser in the trial court will seek an appeal. The rule is that if you don't like the result in the trial court, you can ask a three-judge panel of the Court of Appeals to review the record and see if the trial judge did something wrong. The majority of appeals do not succeed, and the losing party in many cases does not bother to appeal. Sometimes, however, a case is reversed on appeal; the party that lost at trial may suddenly be declared the winner, or there may be a new trial.

The Relief Granted When You Win in Litigation

If you win in copyright infringement litigation, what do you get? There are three things that you want: a final end to infringement, monetary damages, and attorneys fees' and costs.

- **Final Injunctive Relief**. Often, in a case that goes to trial, the infringer will have abandoned the offending product. If not, the Court will usually award a permanent injunction to stop the infringement. The injunction may require that copies of the offending product be destroyed.

- **Monetary Damages.** In copyright cases, you get a choice, statutory damages (if you have filed your registration application in time as I have advised you to do) or actual damages. Actual damages mean your lost profits due to the infringement *and* the profits that the malefactor gained (to the extent that they do not duplicate your lost profits). Proving actual damages normally requires a substantial amount of analytical work by an expert accountant, and therefore an additional expense. Of course, after you get the court to award judgment, you have to *collect* it—which can be a problem if the defendant has fallen into financial difficulty.

- **Attorneys' Fees and Costs**. If the plaintiff has registered the copyright in a timely manner, the Court may—and often does—award attorneys' fees. Some of the costs of litigation, including transcript cost, photocopying, and the like may also be granted, again in the discretion of the Court.

A Final Word on Software Copyright Law

The protection of software under the Copyright Act is of great significance for the industry. Copyright protection is far from perfect. Nonetheless it is vitally important because it rewards originality and deters unauthorized copying. It allows our system of commercial software creation, distribution, and sale to exist.

CHAPTER 2

Software Trade Secrets and Confidentiality Agreements

Trade Secrets and the Case of Eugene Wang

In September 1992, Eugene Wang, a top executive of Borland International, Inc., announced that he would soon be resigning from his post as head of Borland's language software group. He was going to join Borland's archrival, Symantec Corp.—a move that raised eyebrows throughout Silicon Valley.

But the real surprise was on Mr. Wang. In the weeks preceding his departure announcement, Borland had become suspicious of Wang. Borland had secretly used a little-known feature of MCI Mail to capture and store Wang's E-Mail messages. According to Borland's allegations, Wang had been passing highly sensitive information about Borland's business plans and operations to Symantec.

Borland executives had gone to the Santa Cruz County District Attorney, charging that Wang was stealing Borland's trade secrets. The District Attorney's Office obtained a search warrant from the Santa Clara Municipal Court. As soon as Wang resigned from his high-level job at Borland, the police moved in. After serving the warrant, they searched Wang's Silicon Valley home and Symantec's offices in Cupertino, California. The police seized disks and documents from Symantec and Wang—which Borland says contained confidential Borland information. The police also questioned Wang. Borland immediately filed a civil trade secret lawsuit against Wang and Symantec, who publicly denied any wrongdoing.

The other shoe dropped in March 1993, when criminal indictments were handed down against Wang and Symantec Chief Executive Officer Gordon Eubanks, charging violation of California trade secret statute. Both contend that no violation of law occurred. The possible penalties, if there is a conviction, include a prison sentence. As of this writing, neither the civil trial nor the criminal trial have taken place.

The remarkable tale of Mr. Wang and the two companies is, to be sure, a sensational example of trade secret law at work. But the events serve to underline the fact that trade secrets should be a matter of serious concern at every software business. Trade secrets are important intellectual property, and they generate a lot of litigation.

In this chapter I will address some bottom-line questions about trade secret protection: How do you make sure that confidential information used in your business will be legally protected under trade secret law? What do you do if your trade secrets are wrongfully used by someone else?

I will also discuss documents that help to protect trade secrets and confidential information (and provide samples in text and on diskette). These documents include:

- Written confidentiality policies
- Exit interview forms
- Confidentiality agreements

I will explain how employees who are leaving jobs, and companies that are hiring new employees, can avoid trade secret problems.

In Chapter 3, I will discuss some additional topics related to employer-employee relationships:

- How non-competition agreements can be used to restrict an employee's freedom to take a job at competing companies.
- How employees can plan to change jobs, and how employers can hire, without being sued under non-competition agreements.
- "Rules of the game" that apply to employees who wish to leave their jobs—governing what they can and cannot do before departure.

What is a "Trade Secret"?

Trade secret issues arise under state law. That means that the fine points and gray areas of trade secret law will vary from state to state. On the whole, though, the principles are the same all over the United States.

The words "trade secret" may bring to mind an image of a wizened scientist in his white coat crafting complex and nearly magical chemical formulas. In reality, the definition of a trade secret is much broader than that image would suggest. A trade secret is:

> Information used in a business that is held in confidence and gives the business an advantage over its competitors.

In the software field, there are generally two kinds of trade secrets: (1) technology, and (2) customer and other confidential commercial information.

Technology as a Trade Secret

Many different software technologies could classify as trade secrets, for example, methods of data storage, graphics display techniques, character recognition methods, encryption and compression techniques, speed optimization methods, etc. The list is endless.

Some trade secrets are more valuable than others. If you make a quantum leap ahead of the competition, if you solve a problem that others have tried to solve in vain, yours will be a much more *valuable* trade secret. But on the whole, the level of originality required for a trade secret is not high. A modest advance that confers a six-month advantage in the market has value. The test is a pragmatic one: is the secret information of genuine value to the competition—will the company be hurt if the competition gets it?

Legal protection for a technological trade secret protects the secret in all its various forms. Say, for example, that you have a novel algorithm for high-speed data transmission. Trade secret law would cover the algorithm itself, flow charts that describe it, and the computer code that implements it.

Confidential Business Information

Software firms have another type of trade secret that can be equally valuable: customer and commercial information. Examples are confidential customer databases and contact lists, prospect lists, mailing lists, product development and acquisition plans, profit margin information, contract bids, business plans, etc. Is all this material really trade secret information? Again, the test is the pragmatic one: Does the confidential information provide an advantage over a competitor?

Sometimes courts claim to make a distinction between "trade secrets," which are technological, and "confidential information," which describes customer data and other business information. This is a distinction without a difference; in most cases the legal rules that apply to both categories of secret information are the same.

Limits to Trade Secrets

Trade secrets do not include information that is not really secret, such as:

- Techniques or information generally known to skilled personnel in the field—even if they were taught to an employee at great expense to the employer.
- Sales and marketing techniques generally used in the computer business.

Sometimes in trade secret litigation, clever lawyers will try to make rather mundane techniques and information look like high-tech secrets, and opposing lawyers will try to portray genuine secrets as common knowledge. Most often the courts see through all this legal sleight-of-hand—but not always.

Some Basics of Trade Secret Protection

The following are some of the nuts and bolts of trade secret law.

Trade Secret Protection Is Not Automatic

Trade secret protection is not automatic; trade secrets don't exist unless they are protected by reasonable security measures. The measures required are explained later in this chapter.

What Trade Secrets Are Protected Against

The law protects trade secrets against wrongful disclosure and use. When trade secrets are taken, the culprit is often a recently departed employee. Less frequently, trade secrets are taken by a current employee, by industrial espionage or bribery, or by a faithless joint venture partner. When trade secret rights are violated, the law grants the owner of the trade secret a litigation remedy. (Trade secret litigation is discussed below.)

How Long Trade Secrets Last

Trade secrets last as long as the information remains secret and valuable. For some trade secrets—like the Coca-Cola formula—that can mean a very long time. But for software technology, the period of protection is likely to be rather short. The reason, of course, is that computer technology changes so quickly. Techniques that are considered "advanced" quickly become passé. "Hot" technologies cool.

Some technical trade secrets are broken like a bursting bubble for a different reason—they are reverse engineered by the competition or by "hackers" who diffuse the technology throughout the programming community. Trade secret law generally thinks that reverse engineering is perfectly OK. As we discussed in Chapter 1, however, reverse engineering of computer software can raise serious *copyright law* issues. Therefore you should get legal advice before you decompile and reverse engineer another's software as part of your product development efforts.

If Trade Secrets Are Disclosed

If trade secrets are *wrongfully* disclosed and if the disclosure is *limited*, trade secret protection will usually not be lost.

Example: Lexington Software Ltd. sells software that guides the breeding and feeding of thoroughbreds. Boone, a worker at Lexington, has developed a trade secret program that selects just the right sire and the right mare to breed Kentucky Derby contenders. Lexington's archrival, Blue Grass Programming, then hires away Boone to write a competing breeder program. Right after resigning from Lexington, in breach of a confidentiality agreement, Boone discloses the trade secret to Blue Grass. Lexington discovers the breach, and immediately sues and obtains a preliminary injunction to stop Boone or Blue Grass from disclosure or use of the trade secret. Lexington's trade secret will remain intact and keep its protected status.

On the other hand, lawful publication disclosure will destroy any trade secret. Even illegal disclosure, if broad enough, will shatter trade secret status.

Example: Boone, in breach of a confidentiality agreement, publishes Lexington's trade secrets in an "technical tips" article in *Horse World* magazine. Lexington's "trade secret" program is a secret no more. The technology is now public information and has lost its protected status. Lexington's only remedy would be a suit for damages against its former employee Boone. *Horse World* magazine would not be liable unless it was on notice, from the text of the article or otherwise, that the material was proprietary.

Is Taking Trade Secrets a Crime?

In a number of states, it is a crime to take a trade secret. State criminal statutes against theft of trade secrets usually protect only scientific and technical data—not marketing information and the like. The California criminal investigation and indictment in the case of Eugene Wang is by no means the only criminal prosecution that has resulted from allegations that trade secrets were stolen. In 1991, the Texas Court of Criminal Appeals affirmed the felony convictions of two men who took a trade secret computer program from their employer, Texas Instruments. The criminal defendants were hardly common criminals; they were both Ph.D.s who specialized in speech synthesis. Nonetheless, the sentence imposed on the two was imprisonment for five years.

In spite of these cases, the fact remains that criminal prosecutions in trade secret cases are uncommon. Most trade secret litigation is civil, not criminal. In a routine trade secret case, you will probably be wasting your breath to complain to a district attorney about someone taking your trade secrets. The criminal justice system is focused on street crime, drugs, and fraud; in most areas, outside of Santa Cruz County at least, trade secret protection is not a top law enforcement priority.

Criminal prosecutions in trade secret cases are most likely to occur when there is a truly egregious violation that causes major harm and when the victim has economic and political clout in the community and the sense of outrage to press for a criminal prosecution. Criminal prosecution is also much more likely if there is other criminal activity involved as well. For example, if there was an illegal wire tap or a break-in or bribe to steal trade secret materials, then a prosecutor might become very interested.

Can More Than One Company Have the Same Trade Secret?

More than one company *can* have the same piece of trade secret technology. This could happen through independent development of the same technology. Unlike patents (discussed in Chapter 15), trade secret protection does not provide the owner any ability to halt the use of technology by another company unless the other company obtained the trade secret from the owner by improper means.

As long as the technique is not generally known in the industry, and as long as all of the trade secret owners takes reasonable security measures (of the type discussed the next section) to preserve confidentiality, the trade secret can continue to exist in several companies.

Care and Protection of Trade Secrets

If you have trade secrets, you must establish and maintain reasonable security measures to protect them. Here's why you need security measures:

- The law will not protect your trade secrets unless you have taken security measures.

- Unless you protect confidential information, your employees will simply take your secrets. Soon there will be no secrets to protect.

- Venture capitalists and other investors often *insist* that trade secrets be protected as a condition of their investment.

The bottom line: Every software company that wants the benefits of trade secret protection must make security a matter of routine.

The law expects "reasonable security measures." What does that mean? You don't have to build Fort Knox and you don't need guards with automatic rifles. What is "reasonable" is defined by the culture of America's high-technology enterprises. Businesses, large and small, use a fairly standard collection of safeguards. Reasonableness is also a matter of common sense: a company with three employees will obviously need fewer formal procedures than a business with a thousand employees. The following is a summary of what needs to be done.

One Person in Charge of Confidentiality Measures   The first step to adequate security is to put a single responsible person in charge of security measures. There needs to be implementation and follow-up on a consistent basis.

Controls on Access to Confidential Data   The company must control access to confidential information within the company. The methods are straightforward:

- **Computer Password Protection.** Where confidential information is accessed by computer, whether in a single machine or on a network, use password protection. Access should be limited for directories where source code, product plans, customer lists, or other confidential data is stored. Access should be on a need-to-know basis. Passwords should be changed frequently, and passwords for departing employees should be deleted promptly.

- **Permanent copies.** Where confidential data is stored on tape, CD-ROM, or hard copy, access to the information should be controlled. It may be sufficient to be sure that all copies are kept and used only in one location. Or there can be a sign-out arrangement. Trade secret information should be placed in a locked file cabinet or other secure storage place at the end of the day.

Entry Control and Badges   You do not want any stranger to saunter in to your shop and start copying secret information. It is standard procedure at high-technology companies to monitor who comes in and out. Visitors sign in and out, and should be issued "Visitor" badges which they surrender on leaving. Visitors should always be escorted.

As soon as the company is large enough that all employees are not known to one another, the employees should get numbered identification badges that include a photo. Systems to generate the badges are commercially available.

There should also be reasonable security protection for the job site as a whole. After-hours access should be controlled by a security system, and there should be an intruder alarm.

Confidentiality Legends on Documents, Code, and Other Data   Trade secrets must be marked. All trade secrets should have a clearly visible "legend" or notice. The legend alerts anyone who sees the document—employees and non-employees alike—that trade secret protection is claimed.

Your confidentiality legend should normally be typed in all capital letters (in order to be more conspicuous) and read like this:

> **NOTICE: THIS [PROGRAM, DATABASE, DOCUMENT] CONSISTS OF TRADE SECRETS THAT ARE THE PROPERTY OF [NAME OF COMPANY]. THE CONTENTS MAY NOT BE USED OR DISCLOSED WITHOUT EXPRESS WRITTEN PERMISSION OF THE OWNER.**

Confidentiality legends should be used regardless of the form in which confidential information is maintained. For example, the legend should be placed conspicuously in or on:

- Every source code file (written several times into the source code, including at the top and the end)
- Every propriety database
- Product plans, specifications, market research results, etc.
- Every printout or other hard copy of every type of confidential information

If in doubt, mark the information with the legend.
It is also a good idea to get a rubber stamp reading

> **CONFIDENTIAL TRADE SECRET:**
> **PROPERTY OF [NAME OF COMPANY]**

and use it to mark documents, diskettes, and other media that contain trade secret matter.

While use of a confidentiality legend is very important for secret information used within a business, the notice is even more important for information provided in confidence to someone outside. I have seen a judge deny trade secret protection to a graphics enhancement video board design based on the distribution of a single blueprint with no confidentiality legend to a potential business partner.

Confidentiality Agreements for Employees   Employers have two concerns about employees. First, the company wants employees not to use or disclose confidential information while they remain employed. Second, the company wants these same restrictions to remain in effect after employees resign and go on to their next job. Most high-technology employers therefore require all employees who have access to confidential information to sign a confidentiality agreement that binds the employees to keep secrets during and after employment. (These agreements are discussed in more detail below.)

Posted Policy on Confidentiality   A company should have a written policy on protection of intellectual property which includes a discussion of trade secret protection posted in the office and made part of the employee manual. A sample is included in Appendix C as Form 2-1 and is found on diskette as POLICY.W51. Of course, you may need to customize this form to make it fit your business.

New Employee Orientation   When new employees or officers are hired, an explanation of the company's trade secret policies and protections should be part of their introduction to the company. On or before the first day of employment, they should sign the company's confidentiality agreement and receive a copy of the company's policy on protection of intellectual property.

Exit Interviews   When employees leave, whether they resign or are laid off, there should be an exit interview, where trade secret matters are covered. In many companies, departing employees are asked to sign a written statement that they have returned all materials belonging to the company, and that they will maintain trade secrets and confidential information in confidence after leaving. A sample of such a document is included in Appendix C as Form 5-2 and on diskette as EXIT.W51.

Restrictions on Code and Other Data Kept Out of the Office   Sometimes, programmers download code to their computers at home (or bring it home on diskette). Many programmers are "telecommuters"; they spend days or weeks without setting their eyes on the office.

Confidentiality agreements should include the employee's express commitment to protect information kept at home. Employees should also promise, in the text of the confidentiality agreement, to return all copies of company software that are kept on diskette and to erase all copies from the computer hard disk at home—when they are through using the programs or when they leave employment at the company.

Measures for Confidential Disclosure to Other Companies Often a company wants to share trade secret software code or technology in confidence. For example a company may disclose software to a prospective publisher or to a proposed "strategic alliance" partner.

Before showing the family jewels, the disclosing company should get the other side to sign a form of confidential disclosure agreement that *expressly acknowledges* that trade secret or confidential information is being provided and provides for appropriate measures to preserve confidentiality. In Chapter 6 we will see that some confidential disclosure forms include provisions for protection of trade secrets—*and some do not.*

Be very circumspect about this type of disclosure. You can easily lose trade secret protection if you disclose confidential information outside your company without proper contractual safeguards. You should be especially careful about disclosing information that gives away the design of the software, such as flow charts or any source code. As is noted above, even after you get the proper confidential disclosure agreement in place, all data and information provided to any other company should still have a prominent trade secret legend.

Any company that will be disclosing trade secret matters orally—in a meeting with a prospective partner or customer for instance—should carefully plan in advance what will be discussed and what will not. A suitable confidential disclosure agreement should always be signed in advance. The disclosing party should prepare and present a written outline (with a confidentiality legend) that summarizes in general terms what will be discussed. In the case of a dispute, this document will help the disclosing party prove that various matters were in fact revealed. It will also help the party receiving the trade secret information prove what was *not* discussed.

Special Provisions for Licensing of Source Code   The usual rule for licensing computer code is simple: You should only license *object code* and you should keep *source code* secret. But one does not always have that choice. Publishers often get source code and many end-users do as well.

> **Example.** Applications Unlimited develops a computer program for tracking video rentals in 50 states for Monster Video Stores Ltd. In order to be sure that it can maintain the system if Applications fails to do so, Monster Video demands that it receive a copy of the source code. Under its contract with Applications, Monster Video will receive the program source code, but must keep its copy under adequate confidentiality safeguards.

When one is licensing "large ticket" software, the customer will often demand a copy of the supplier's source code as part of the deal. When that happens, the software license agreement should contain terms requiring the customer to safeguard the supplier's source code and to restrict access. Such contractual arrangements should also require that the customer provide similar protection for any user documentation that refers to the source code or other confidential matters. Again, an owner of software can easily lose trade secret protection unless confidentiality safeguards are in place.

When a supplier licenses object code to a user, the end-user agreement (see Chapter 12) should provide that the customer may not decompile or reverse engineer the object code. Developers should seek similar provisions in software publishing agreements (see Chapter 9) and in so-called "shrink-wrap licenses" in mass-market software (see Chapter 11). Even though it is not clear that these contractual clauses are always enforceable, they can aid trade secret protection.

Can Software Trade Secrets Be Licensed?

Where a company is selling technology, rather than just a software application, it is not unusual that trade secret techniques (or confidential "know-how") are licensed. And trade secret technology is often shared under a joint venture agreement.

To protect trade secrets you need to share the technology but keep it confidential nonetheless. Again, the agreement involved should mandate that the trade secret licensee provide security for confidential technology. Drafting these agreements can be subtle. If you are interested in licensing your trade secrets and confidential know-how, you should see an attorney.

Confidentiality Agreements for Employees

A crucial aspect of trade secret protection is the use of confidentiality agreements.

The Nature of Confidentiality Agreements

In a confidentiality agreement, employees acknowledge their access to trade secrets and confidential data and promise not to use or disclose it during or after employment. These agreements usually also provide that intellectual property developed on the job, trade secrets, software copyrights, patentable inventions, etc., are the property of the employer.

Every well-organized high-technology company requires each employee with access to sensitive information sign a confidentiality agreement at the time that the employee begins employment. The purpose of a confidentiality agreement is to enhance the legal protection of the employer's confidential information by defining explicitly the employee's obligation to protect confidentiality during and after employment.

A sample of an employee confidentiality agreement is included in Appendix C as Form 2-3 and on diskette as CONFID.W51. This is a relatively simple document, but an employer should have an attorney review it to be sure that it fully accords with local law. Provisions similar to those in the form should be placed in all agreements with suppliers and consultants.

The Effect of a Confidentiality Agreement

The company that holds a signed confidentiality agreement has more leverage in dealing with an apparent trade secret violation by a former employee.

The presence of a confidentiality agreement is only one factor in proving a trade secret case—but it is a very important one. Getting a preliminary injunction for a trade secret violation is never a sure thing (as is discussed further below). But having a confidentiality agreement in hand gives the employer a better shot, because the agreement is explicit evidence that the employee knew that he or she was dealing with secret materials.

The confidentiality agreement *adds* to trade secret remedies an *attorneys fee' clause*—the employee's promise to pay the employer's legal fees incurred because of any trade secret violation. The clause gives the employer some extra leverage because it raises the potential cost of a trade secret violation. Because legal fees can be substantial, this factor alone may encourage present and former employees not to reveal or use confidential information.

A confidentiality agreement also adds a legal weapon against an employer who is hiring an employee away to obtain his current employer's trade secrets. The former employer can sue the new employer for *interfering* in the confidentiality agreement between the former employer and employee.

A Word to Employees About Leaving a Company

In order to avoid suit on trade secret grounds or under a confidentiality agreement, an employee ought to take a few simple precautions when leaving one employer and going to another.

- **Leave "Clean."** A departing employee should not take or keep property that belongs to the former employer. Programmers take a risk when they retain diskettes and programs from their last job. Remember that code written by the employee for the employer belongs to the *employer*. The more information, documents, code, or other data an employee takes, the worse it will look. In one case that I was involved with, the judge got very angry that a group of departing sales employees had taken their Rolodexes (which contained customer names.) Most employees may think that the Rolodex on their desk is their own—but chances are that it's not. (If the employer paid for the time to fill in the Rolodex, then the information belongs to the employer.) Where there is doubt about a departing employee's right to remove any item of property, the employee should get permission to take the item.

- **Avoid Taking a Job that Looks "Bad."** Although it may mean missing opportunities, the employee should avoid a job so directly competitive that it appears to call for use of the former employer's trade secrets. The employee, and the new employer, will be better off if the field of work for the new employee is different, so that the apparent danger of misuse of trade secrets is slight.

A Word to Employers About Hiring

A prospective employer also needs to be concerned about confidentiality agreements with other companies that an applicant may have signed. These agreements may be a warning that hiring the applicant will lead to a trade secret lawsuit. They may also be a warning that the applicant may deliver technology that actually belongs to a former employer. In general, a would-be employer needs to take these precautions:

- **Ask About Contracts Signed by the Job Applicant.** Before hiring a new employee, a company should find out what agreements the applicant has signed with former employers. If there is a confidentiality agreement or a non-competition agreement (see Chapter 3) currently in effect, the document should be reviewed with legal counsel before the employee is hired.

- **Ask About the Existence of Trade Secrets at the Applicant's Past Employer.** Before hiring an applicant, it is also a good idea to ask the applicant whether there were trade secrets at the former employer that might be applicable to the new job. (Of course, the prospective new employer must not ask about the details of the trade secrets.) Again, this inquiry should be part of the application process. If the answer is yes, it would be smart to consult legal counsel to see if there is a potential problem.

- **Advise the Employee to Leave the Old Job in a Proper Way.** The employee should be instructed to leave the old job "clean," to take nothing, and not to use any proprietary technology of any other company on the new job.

A hiring employer should also be aware that the larger the group of employees hired away from another company at one time, the more suspect the hiring will be, and the more likely that litigation will result. "Raiding" of rivals (discussed further in Chapter 3) is dangerous and invites litigation.

Dealing with Violations of Trade Secrets

The Need to Enforce Trade Secrets Rights

When you know or strongly suspect that someone has violated your trade secret rights, you must take immediate steps to stop the violation, including litigation if necessary.

Delay can be dangerous. If you do nothing, you risk letting your secrets circulate—and once they circulate, they are not secret anymore. Moreover, judges will likely rule later that if you didn't care enough about your "secrets" to enforce your rights promptly, the "secrets" probably did not deserve protection.

Two Types of Trade Secret Cases

There are two ways in which trade secrets violations normally occur. The first and most common situation involves employees who leave a company and take trade secrets with them. The culprit could be a single employee hired by a rival company, or a group of technicians and/or marketing personnel who depart and found their own competitive business. Or a rival business might conduct a "raid" and hire away an entire technical or marketing group. In these situations, the company that seeks to protect its trade secrets must move quickly. Its goal is to cut the enemy off at the pass—to prevent wrongful use of its trade secrets.

The second situation arises when an owner of trade secrets discovers unauthorized use months or years after the theft itself, usually when competing products appear on the market. This situation might arise when a former employee has passed on the secrets to a new employer, or when a company has received trade secret information in confidence and then has used it without permission. In this case, the owner of the trade secrets will not only seek to regain control of the technology, but to recover substantial monetary damages.

Departing Employees Who Take Trade Secrets

In theory American business is about rational decisions to increase revenues and maximize profits. But when it comes to trusted employees departing with trade secrets, it is often the emotions rather than rational analysis that take command.

It is a fact of life that employees look for their next job in secret, then suddenly announce a resignation. When a trusted employee announces the decision to go to a competitor, in the employer's eyes he or she suddenly goes from being "one of us" to "one of them." In an instant, warm feelings of trust toward the employee are replaced by feelings of hurt, betrayal, anger, and suspicion. The employee's loyalty shifts just as quickly to the new company. And it is in this emotionally charged atmosphere that most employee departure trade secret litigation is played out.

The risk to a high-tech company that trade secrets will be taken by a departing employee is very real. But to deal with the situation successfully, it is important to have a rational assessment of the legal options and the risks. For that reason, counsel should be involved as early as possible when such a problem arises.

Remedies Short of Litigation   What can an employer do, without the expense of litigation, to stop former employees from delivering trade secrets to a new employer? There are steps that the employer can take (with the advice of an attorney), although none of them provide absolute assurance that the trade secrets will be safe:

- **Notice to Respect Trade Secrets**. If the threat of a trade secret violation is moderate, a pointed reminder of the employee's obligations may suffice. The employer may give the employee a written reminder of his or her trade secret obligation as a routine part of the exit interview process. Then the employer can follow up with a letter to the former employee and the new employer stating the areas of trade secrets information involved, and insisting that the confidentiality agreement be adhered to. In either case, it is best to supply both the employee and the new employer with a copy of the confidentiality agreement signed by the employee so that the new employer will understand that a wrongful disclosure will violate a contractual duty.

- **Demand for Measures to Prevent Disclosure.** If the disclosure risk is high, a more forceful letter is called for. This sort of letter is strong medicine and is meant to be part of a strategy in which litigation is a possible outcome. The preferred goal is a negotiated solution in which the employer can get reasonable assurance that trade secrets will not be disclosed. Such a letter might state:

  - That procedures should be put in place immediately at the new employer's business to prevent use or disclosure of trade secrets.

- That employees at the new company must be instructed not to discuss the subject matter of the trade secrets technology with the employee.

- That the employee should be assigned only to work areas and to projects that are technologically distinct from and physically separate from any work area that might want to use any relevant trade secret information.

- That the new employer confirm in writing that these safeguards will be put in place immediately and will remain in place for an agreed-upon period.

- That the employee and the new employer confirm in writing that no trade secrets have been or will be revealed.

- That litigation will result if suitable assurances are not received. (Note, however, that you should never threaten litigation unless you are prepared to follow through on the threat.)

The employer needs to discuss an overall strategy with counsel before sending any letter concerning a suspected trade secret violation.

When non-litigation methods fail, the employer must seriously consider a prompt litigation approach.

The Preliminary Injunction Struggle   Trade secret litigation against a recently departed employee tends to be a rather quick affair.

The goal of these suits is to stop the wrongful disclosure of trade secrets before it begins. In almost every case, the holder of the trade secrets (the plaintiff) will ask the court for a preliminary injunction—a court order requiring the former employee and new employer (the defendants) not to use the trade secrets. (Preliminary injunctions in general, and the role they play in litigation, are discussed in Chapter 1). One key consideration in deciding whether to bring litigation is deciding if you are likely to win the preliminary injunction motion—a judgment call that obviously requires a lawyer's advice.

The preliminary injunction motion creates an early and critical decision point. In many cases, the dispute is actually resolved by agreement just before a hearing on the motion. In most cases, if the injunction is granted, the plaintiff will have the leverage to force a favorable settlement. If the injunction is denied, the defendants will usually obtain a settlement favorable to their side. Rarely do these cases go to trial.

Because most cases turn on a preliminary injunction, they are also most often relatively inexpensive as litigation goes—the cost is usually in the range of $7,500 to $20,000. Of course, if the parties do not settle after the preliminary injunction is decided, the cost can go considerably higher.

Making a Case: Direct and Indirect Evidence　When key technical and sales employees depart and begin work for a rival company, there is often no direct evidence of theft of trade secrets. On occasion, to be sure, the employer gets some direct evidence by luck: a conversation overheard at the office or at a local bar, a piece of paper carelessly left behind, or an erased document recovered by use of a utility program. Most often, however, a trade secret case is based on inference and circumstantial evidence—and often that indirect evidence may be good enough.

> **Example.** An employee, the technical director of a software project, is using unique methods to develop a neural net program to be used for stock market simulations. The technical director abruptly quits and joins a rival company where she becomes director of a project to create a directly competitive product. The former employer— as well as a judge—is likely to conclude that she must *inevitably* disclose and use her first employer's trade secret technology. It is farfetched to believe that she will discard all the secrets that she learned and use an entirely different technological approach. The chance of getting a preliminary injunction is good.

Analysis of the strength of a trade secret case against a recently departed employee will usually be based on a variety of factors, such as:

- **Identification of the "Secrets."** It is essential that former employers point to a concrete set of data, documents, techniques, or solutions as the "secrets" that are being taken. Generalized claims of unspecified secrets are a prescription for losing a case.

- **The Employee's Level of Responsibility and Access to Secrets.** The case will be more powerful if the former employee or employees had been trusted with full access to secret material. Betrayal of trust can be a powerful theme in these cases.

- **Value of the Trade Secrets.** The case is stronger if the trade secrets involved have substantial monetary value or potential. The plaintiff's case will also be more powerful if the trade secrets resulted from a large investment of time, effort, and money.

- **Adequacy of Security Measures.** The former employer's claim to have trade secrets will be credible only if its procedures for protection of trade secrets have been diligent.

- **Hiring for Direct Competition.** The case is stronger if the defendant employee or employees were hired by a competitor to work on a directly competitive product.

- **Confidentiality Agreement.** While a confidentiality agreement is not an absolute requirement to protect trade secrets, the case is much stronger if the defendant employee has signed a well-drafted agreement acknowledging his or her obligations.

- **Non-Competition Agreement.** As is discussed in the next chapter, the plaintiff company may get much more leverage if it has a enforceable non-competition agreement, which may prevent the defendant employee from working for the new employer for a period of time.

- **Number of Persons Who Left.** The case will be stronger if a group of persons have left the former employer together, because then it will be much more likely that the group will continue to use the trade secrets that it used before.

In assessing a trade secret suit against a departed employee, a final, very important factor is the "feel" of the case—or perhaps it would be more accurate to refer to the "smell." It is *much* easier to get an injunction if the departed employee has done something that sounds low or dirty or wrong. Here are some examples:

- The employee has surreptitiously taken the company's technical or business documents (or tapes or disks) containing data or computer code

- The employee has versions of the company's source code or unreleased object code at home on diskettes and fails to return them when leaving the firm
- The employee spent a weekend photocopying documents just before leaving
- Before leaving, the employee tried to recruit key technical employees to join in the departure
- The employee logged onto the company computer from home and downloaded many files just before announcing his or her departure

The case of Eugene Wang (discussed earlier in this chapter) presents an example of how the appearance of skullduggery can provide high octane fuel for a trade secret case.

Many companies have computer systems that monitor who enters the premises after hours, who logs on to the network, etc. These systems often generate important evidence for trade secret cases. An aggrieved employer should move quickly to see that this evidence is preserved.

Remedies in Suits Against Recently Departed Employees   If the court issues a preliminary injunction after a hearing, what will the court require? The court has broad discretion in framing relief, but normally it will order:

- That the departed employee refrain from disclosing the trade secrets
- That the new employer refrain from using the trade secrets

The court may also order that measures be put in place to separate the former employee from work on a directly competitive project where the trade secrets would be most relevant and most likely to be disclosed.

The court might order that the employee be separated from the new job altogether, but this would be a rather unusual order, unless the former employee has signed an enforceable non-competition agreement (discussed in Chapter 3).

Preliminary relief will normally be ordered into effect for the duration of the litigation, but the judge can order a shortened period of relief if the trade secret has a limited time value.

As I noted, these cases tend to settle soon after a preliminary injunction is issued or denied. Preliminary injunction orders are *appealable*, and sometimes an appellate court has its say before the matter is put to bed. It is possible, but uncommon, that these cases can drag on and even go to trial.

Litigation Over Products Based on Stolen Trade Secrets

Trade secret litigation is quite different where the wrongful use of trade secrets is discovered only *after* a rival product appears.

Example. TECH-MED Corporation develops a trade secret software data and telecommunications system that enables insurance-related information from doctors, clinics, and hospitals to be gathered and processed inexpensively with no paperwork. TECH-MED signs a confidential disclosure agreement with Bigco, a large computer software publisher. Bigco studies TECH-MED's trade secrets in the course of the confidential disclosure, then declines to do business with TECH-MED. A year later, the managers of TECH-MED are shocked to see that Bigco has introduced a system that uses the TECH-MED trade secrets.

In a case like this, a preliminary injunction may also be a potent weapon for the plaintiff (TECH-MED in this case). However, where a preliminary injunction will stop a rival's business (and put people out of work), it is likely to be issued only if the violation is very clear-cut. If there have been substantial sales of the defendant's product, the plaintiff may have a good shot at large monetary damages.

If the stakes are high, the litigation can be very expensive unless it is settled quickly. Discovery (see the discussion of the role of discovery in litigation in Chapter 1) could go on for a year or more. Attorneys' fees will be very substantial. A technical expert may be necessary to prove that trade secrets were taken. A accounting expert may be necessary to prove damages.

Taking a case like this from the start of litigation to trial could easily cost $100,000 to $150,000 or more. (Some lawyers may agree to take a percentage of the recovery in lieu of legal fees, which could reduce the out-of-pocket cost.) If there is a trial, it will often be with a jury.

What can the plaintiff win through this litigation? If the plaintiff prevails, it could be awarded the following:

- **Damages.** Normally the measure of many damages would be the greater of the profits made by the defendant by wrongful use of the trade secrets or the profits lost by the defendant. In some states, additional punitive damages or attorneys' fees may be available.

- **Injunction.** In most cases, the court will also order that wrongful use of the trade secrets terminate—for a designated time or permanently.

Obviously, you should not file such an action without thoroughly discussing with your counsel both the potential benefits and the costs of the lawsuit.

CHAPTER 3

Employee Non-Competition Agreements and Other Employee Issues

If you are an employer, you may be able to use a contract to stop many of your key employees from taking a job at a competitor.

If you are a skilled technician or salesperson, your next career move could be blocked by a contract; the threat of litigation may stand between you and a company that wants to hire you.

If your company is hiring technical or sales personnel, attempting to hire an experienced employee might result in a bitter legal brawl—and in the end your company would gain nothing.

All of these consequences come from non-competition agreements, employee contracts that curb an employee's ability to move from one job to another. In this chapter, we examine the law affecting these contracts and address some important related questions:

- When and how are these non-competition agreements enforceable?

- How can employees change jobs after signing a non-competition agreement?

- How can companies hire without being sued because of non-competition agreements?

In addition, this chapter covers another important topic: the "rules of the game" that apply to departing employees—what employees can and cannot do before they are out the door.

What is a Non-Competition Agreement?

Non-competition agreements are also commonly known as "restrictive covenants," "covenants not to compete," or simply "non-comps." Employees who sign them make a promise that if they leave their current job, they will not work for a competitor for a specified period of time. The agreements are written to apply whether the departure is voluntary or not. These agreements are usually combined with a confidentiality agreement as a single contract document.

Non-competition agreements are controversial. (One attorney in Palo Alto that I know—perhaps reflecting the view of California law—described them as "barbaric.") They impede employees' power to take the job of their choice. These documents are often resented by employees, who feel trapped and pressured into signing them. They can generate bitter litigation. Employers, however, see these agreements as a powerful device to protect their secret technology and relations with their customers—and this is a view that many venture capitalists and sophisticated investors subscribe to.

In many states, non-competition agreements are enforceable against technical and sales personnel. In those states, it is normal business practice at some high-tech companies to *require* employees to sign non-competition agreements.

A Word About State Law

The law governing non-competition agreements is state law. Under the law of some states, notably software powerhouse California, non-competition agreements restricting employees are unenforceable.[1]

In addition, state law varies on whether an employee must be given *extra pay* at the time that he or she signs a non-competition agreement. In some states, particularly

---

1   Different rules apply for non-competition agreements that are part of the sale of business. Even in California, these agreements are generally enforceable

if an employee has already begun work *before* signing a non-competition agreement, the agreement will be *invalid* unless extra compensation has been paid. As a matter of practice, the best time to resolve the issue of whether a non-competition agreement will be required is *before* an employee begins work. It makes no sense to leave this potentially divisive issue open while an employee settles into a job.

The law of the state involved is crucial. Before an employer asks its employees to sign a non-competition agreement, it must consult a lawyer and determine that what it wants to do is legal.

A Further Twist on State Law

Employees too need a word of caution about state law. Let's say you are an employee itching to leave your present job in the frigid Northeast and head to sunny California. Perhaps you think that if you signed a non-competition agreement in say, New Hampshire (where these agreements are enforced) you can get free of the agreement by taking a job in California—just as the fugitive slaves before the Civil War fled to Canada for their freedom.

It's not that simple. To begin with, even though you have moved to California, your former employer may sue you in New Hampshire, and the orders issued by the New Hampshire court may be enforced in California. Even if you are sued in California, the court might decide that New Hampshire law applies. The bottom line: If you have a potential problem with a non-competition agreement, you need to get a lawyer's advice.

Enforceable Non-Competition Agreements

Even in states that tolerate non-competition agreements, the courts refuse to enforce many of them. Two factors generally determine whether a restriction is enforceable: (1) the nature of the employment, and (2) the reasonableness of the restrictions.

The Nature of the Employment   Generally the law assumes that competition is a good thing, and that people should be free to take whatever job they want. And judges certainly don't like to throw people out of a job. For these reasons, non-competition agreements are enforced (even in states that permit them) only if a company has a good reason to keep its former employees from competing.

There are basically only two categories of employees who may be restricted by means of non-competition agreements:

1. **Employees who have access to trade secrets or confidential information— usually technical employees.** The rationale is that the restraint preserves legitimate trade secrets. To enforce a non-competition agreement on this theory requires proof (1) that the employer really has trade secrets, (2) that the employee knows the secrets, and (3) that the employer protects trade secrets with reasonable security measures.

2. **Sales employees who have gained customer loyalty.** The rationale is that the restraint allows the employer to protect its customer relationships. In this case, enforcement of the non-competition agreement requires proof (1) that customer contacts are important in the employer's business, and (2) that the employee had frequent and significant customer contact on the job.

Requirement of Reasonable Scope and Duration   There is another important restriction on non-competition agreements. The courts enforce agreements only if they are reasonable in duration and geographic scope. This rule is a "balancing test"—pitting the employer's need for protection against the employee's interest in employment freedom. Some general rules on duration and geographic scope follow:

- **Duration of Non-Competition Agreements.** Normally a one year restraint is considered reasonable. In many states, when good reason is shown, two year restraints are enforced. A three year restraint is a stretch but will be allowed for good cause in some states. In general, the shorter the restraint, the more likely that it will be enforced.

- **Geographic Scope for Employees Holding Trade Secret Information.** A reasonable geographic area of restraint is the area where the trade secret information might aid a competitive business. Some secret information has only local value. Most software technology has value without regard to boundaries, so that restrictions that are national or even international in scope might be considered fair.

- **Geographic Scope for Sales Employees.** A "non-comp" will usually be considered "reasonable" if it is tailored to the area in which a salesperson has developed customer relationships. A common restriction is to prohibit salespeople for a specified period from making sales in the territory where they were assigned by the employer. Some sales employees sign a version in which they promise for a defined period after departure not to solicit the customers and prospects of the employer.

The terms of a non-competition agreement are often negotiable. Employees who are esteemed by a company often have substantial leverage for negotiating changes in a proposed non-competition agreement, and may be able to reduce the duration or geographic scope or both.

For information purposes, I have included a sample non-competition agreement in Appendix C as Form 3-1. However, *you should not just copy the form and use it.* Because the law on these agreements varies so much from state to state, *an employer must have an attorney examine any non-competition agreement it wishes to use.*

The "Blue Pencil"　What happens if a non-competition agreement goes too far? What if the restraint on an employee is too broad in geographic scope or lasts too long? Is the agreement then null and void—just a meaningless scrap paper filled with legalese?

Again state law controls. In some states, the rule is that the employer who overreaches gets no protection at all. The court just throws the offending agreement out. In other states, the judge has the power to "blue pencil" the agreement—to rewrite it to make it more reasonable, and then enforce it as redrawn. Even where the courts have this power to "blue pencil," if an agreement is too grossly unreasonable, the judge has the power to refuse to enforce it at all.

These rules governing non-competition agreements act as a kind of self-enforcing constraint on employers. The less burdensome the restriction, the more likely it will be upheld in a court of law. The more onerous and unreasonable the restraint, the more likely that it will be thrown out of court.

Enforcement of Non-Competition Agreements by Employers

Let's look at enforcement of the non-competition agreements from an employer's point of view. In this discussion, I am assuming that the restraint involved is legal under state law, is reasonable in scope, and is otherwise enforceable.

When to Involve Counsel

If the employer finds that a departing employee is breaching a non-competition agreement, it needs to contact an attorney who knows software litigation *right away*. The legal remedies may evaporate if the employer waits too long. How long is "too long"? There is no fixed rule, but even a few weeks delay can weaken the case.

Remedies Short of Litigation

What can an employer do without litigation to stop the employee from violating the non-competition agreement? Generally speaking, the best bet is a demand letter insisting that the former employee and the new employer observe the restraint.

Sometimes it will be sufficient if the new employer promises, for example, that a salesperson will be given a territory different from that which is forbidden in the agreement. Sometimes the former employer will have to demand that the former employee be suspended or terminated from the new job for the duration of the non-competition agreement.

Any demand letter should be written by or approved by an attorney before it is sent. Together with the letter, the former employer should send both the employee and the new employer a copy of the non-competition agreement.

A demand letter will normally state that litigation will result if the demands are not met. Of course, a company should never threaten litigation unless it prepared to follow through.

The Fight Over the Preliminary Injunction

Like trade secret cases (with which they are often combined), litigation on the basis of a non-competition agreement normally turns on a preliminary injunction hearing. (Trade secret litigation is discussed in Chapter 2.) For this reason, these cases may be relatively inexpensive as litigation goes—typical litigation costs might be in the $7,500 to $20,000 range. An expensive and prolonged litigation struggle is possible, but quite uncommon in these cases. In most cases, the decision on the preliminary injunction (or an expedited appeal of a preliminary injunction decision) is effectively the end of the case, one way or the other. The party that won the opening round usually has a strong advantage in settlement talks.

In these cases as well, the "feel" of the case plays an important role. If the employee has walked away with papers, disks or other property of the former employer, or has otherwise failed to leave "clean," a preliminary injunction will be easier for a former employer to get.

Remedies in Suits Against Recently Departed Employees

If the court issues a preliminary injunction, what will the injunction require? Normally the court will order, in quite specific terms, that the non-competition restraint must be complied with. The court has great discretion in fashioning relief, but it is common that the employee be ordered not to work for the new employer for the duration of the restraint in the non-competition agreement.

Leaving a Job Without Being Sued Under a Non-Competition Agreement

Employees who have signed non-competition agreements often want to know how to "get out." Sometimes there is no escape from the terms of the agreement. There is no magic bullet that "kills" them. On the other hand, sometimes the agreement is completely unenforceable. And sometimes enforceability will be unclear, which itself can be a problem. Much turns on the particular facts of each case.

Example. Smith has worked for several years as a chief programmer at Super Graphics Software where her specialty is image compression products. Super Graphics uses trade secret compression algorithms. Smith has signed a one-year non-competition agreement, and Super Graphics is located in Massachusetts, a state that enforces these contracts. Ultra Visual Programming, a competitor of Super Graphics in image compression software, offers Smith a job at a higher salary, and Smith takes the position at Ultra. Super Graphics Software promptly sues Smith in a Massachusetts court.

In this case, Super Graphics is likely to get a preliminary injunction preventing Smith from working for Ultra Visual Programming for the duration of the non-competition agreement. In fact, when Ultra learns of the non-competition agreement, it may well decide that hiring Smith is not worth the risk and expense of a lawsuit. Smith may end up leaving Super Graphics and find herself with no job at Ultra either.

However, Smith's chances of "beating" the preliminary injunction— and holding onto her job with Ultra—are better if:

- The supposed "trade secrets" at Super Graphics are public information and Smith can prove it.

- Super Graphics has clearly failed to take adequate security measures to protect trade secrets.

- The non-competition agreement is overbroad and unreasonable.

Checking Out the Agreement   The employee who has signed an entangling non-competition agreement and wishes to move to another job needs early legal advice on whether it is enforceable. The attorney will read the agreement, evaluate the employee's work situation, and perhaps do some legal research. The cost should be about $500 to $1000 to get an opinion on enforceability. The attorney can also provide insight on how likely it is that litigation will follow a contemplated career move, and how much a lawsuit is likely to cost.

Avoiding the Problem by Avoiding Competition   Often the employees' best strategy to deal with a non-competition agreement is to try to find a new job that allows them to use their technical skills without competing with their current employer. A technical employee can look for a new job where the trade secret technology used in the current job is not applicable. A salesperson can get a job that serves a different software market.

This strategy makes litigation less likely for two reasons. First, an employer is not likely to undertake the cost and hassle of litigation without a good reason. If the new job is no threat to the employer, there is nothing to provoke a litigation response. Second, if the job is not competitive, the employer will be more likely to lose any suit it might file—and no company wants to initiate a lawsuit that it is going to lose.

Hiring an Employee Who Has Signed a Non-Competition Agreement

A would-be employer must find out what agreements the applicant has signed that might affect employment. This inquiry should be a routine part of the application process.

If the employee has signed a non-competition agreement with a competitor, and if the agreement appears enforceable, the new employer runs a significant risk that it will be sued for "inducing" the employee to breach the non-competition agreement.

If a job applicant is potentially valuable and if there is a problem with a contract that the applicant has signed with a past employer, the prospective new employer needs the advice of legal counsel. Counsel will do the requisite analysis—looking at the agreement itself, at the facts, and at the law—and determine the legal risk. Needless to say, this should be done *before* offering the applicant a job.

Employee Behavior Before Departure

It is a fact of life that key software employees—often groups of key employees—leave their employer either to join a rival company or to found their own software business.

Whether employees are subject to confidentiality agreements or non-competition agreements or no agreement at all, there are certain "rules of the game" that govern departing employees *before* they leave. These are not rules of etiquette, but rules of law. State law is involved, and there are variations from state to state, but the general principles are the same. Unfortunately the "rules" are rather fuzzy, and this is another situation where the "feel" of the case can count for a lot.

Departing from a high-tech company is a matter to be treated with care. As I mentioned in Chapter 2, the departure of trusted employees generates anger and feelings of betrayal. For this reason, breaching the rules can risk passionate (and expensive) litigation, where punishment and revenge are goals as much as compensation.

Some general rules for employee behavior before leaving a job are as follows:

- **Prepare to Compete but Don't Compete.** It is generally all right for employees to *prepare* to compete—on their own time. For example, they can arrange for office space for a new venture, or print announcements to be issued when they move to their new job. However, they *cannot* actually compete before they leave.

- **Don't Solicit Business.** Before leaving, employees *may not solicit business* for a new venture or for a new employer. Some states permit employees to tell customers that they will soon be leaving; other states do not allow even this.

- **Beware of Soliciting Other Employees.** It may be dangerous for departing employees to solicit a group of their fellow employees to leave with them. In most states, this can be a violation of law if the impact on the employer would be "sudden" and "substantial." Group departures are more likely to be permitted when there is a history of dissatisfaction or where others leave out of loyalty to the departing employees. The law in this area is unclear, and caution is advised.

- **Beware of "Raiding."** There is a similar risk when a new employer, acting in cooperation with one or more of a rival's employees, arranges to solicit and hire a group of the rival's personnel. If this results in significant damage to the rival's business, this agreement to "raid" may be deemed an illegal "conspiracy." Again the limits of what is permissible are unclear. Simply hiring a rival's employee is normally perfectly legal, as long as the employee has not signed a contract that would be violated by the new employment. Caution is advised in group hiring, because of the risk of litigation.

Employees who violate these rules—and new employers who encourage or participate in violations—are very likely to find themselves sued. Employers who are injured by violations may have a legal remedy, including a claim for lost profits reaped by the violations. Departures should be in modest numbers and done fast and "clean." When in doubt about what is permitted, get the advice of counsel.

CHAPTER 4

Introduction to Commercial
Software Negotiations

We now turn to the subject of commercial software agreements, the array of contractual tools that are used to transfer, buy, sell, and license software. Over the next eight chapters, we will discuss the various deals by which software rights are licensed and transferred. These deals involve developers, publishers, distributors, dealers, and end-users—a constellation of agreements for creating software products and exploiting them. Each type of deal has its characteristic issues and documentation.

Your tour of commercial software transactions begins in this chapter with the negotiating tactics that apply to all of these various software deals. In addition, in this chapter you will learn about the dangers of oral agreements and pre-agreement "letters of intent." You will learn about the role of legal counsel in the contract negotiation process.

The Need for Preparation and Care in Negotiation

The negotiation of an agreement or contract (the terms are interchangeable) is a process that requires time and attention as well as business savvy. Some entrepreneurs whose background is in computer science or other technical fields feel that they can't be bothered with the legalese and mumbo-jumbo of contracts, and sign the boilerplate contracts presented to them. Some think that because they are very bright, they can negotiate against the pros—even though they have little or no experience with the issues raised by contract negotiations. And some think they can turn over their contract negotiations to an attorney and walk away, without educating the lawyer about special problems and business or technical issues. All of these are deeply flawed approaches. When an agreement is poorly conceived or one party has overreached; financial troubles, conflict, and litigation wait in the wings.

Contract negotiations require the same degree of careful planning and skillful execution that is needed to write software or to develop and execute a marketing plan. Effective negotiations also require knowledge about how these software contracts work. This book will not free you from the need for a lawyer, but over the following chapters, it will give you basic knowledge you need to bargain effectively.

In the following sections of this chapter, I discuss the tactics and methods of negotiating software agreements. These methods are not new. Although software agreements provide a new business context, the basics of contract negotiation are probably unchanged from the days of the first written contracts in ancient Egypt. If you are a veteran of many negotiations, the discussion in this section may be old hat. If you are new to the process, it will definitely help you.

Preparation for Negotiation: The Overall Strategy

As all veterans of negotiations know, a good agreement comes together as the result of a sound overall strategy and a lot of hard work. Contract negotiation must be seen as a process. First, there is a period of selling. Then there is serious negotiation on terms—the most important issues first, then all the others. Finally, a deal is documented. The process can take weeks or months.

Before any negotiation, you need to formulate your bargaining position and strategy. As the negotiating process goes forward, of course, your plan for the negotiation should be constantly re-evaluated and adjusted. Consider doing the following as you prepare to negotiate:

Get the Background Information You Need

If possible, you should use your network of contacts to get information about the company that you are dealing with—and what its needs are. You should find out what the other side has done on similar deals. How much has it paid or charged? On what terms has it insisted, and on which issues has it been flexible?

It is also important to find out who are the key decision-makers for the other side. To make that key deal with another company, you will usually need an advocate on the inside of the other company. It is important to find out who inside the other side's organization has the clout to sell your product to management or to conclude a deal.

Figure Out What You Can Deliver to the Other Side

You need to analyze realistically how your product can help the other side. If you want to license software to a publisher, for example, you need to analyze how your software will help sell the *other* products the publisher has. How will your product fit into the other side's existing product line? The better you can sell the benefits that you can provide, the more likely it is that there will be a deal.

Assess Your Credibility

An important quality in software negotiations is credibility. The history of software is full of long delays and "vaporware" (promised software that never appears). Many software products have failed to perform adequately. Much custom software is delivered with unacceptable amounts of bugs and errors.

If you will be supplying software or software-related services, you need to prove your ability to deliver as promised, on the basis of your past achievements or by presenting a demonstration of the software you want to market.

Look for a Deal that Works for Both Sides

Before negotiating, you should have a fairly good idea of the deal that ought to come out of the process—and it ought to make economic sense for both sides. This means having a sound grasp of your own costs and margins and an understanding of the economic value of your goods and services to the other side. If you can't see how the dollars work for both sides, it may not make sense to negotiate in the first place.

Negotiation Tactics

While every successful negotiator has his or her own style, the following are some accepted techniques to use in the give and take of negotiations.

Negotiating in the Right Setting

Negotiations are more likely to succeed in a setting—such as a conference room—where there will be no distractions. It is important to get everyone to set aside enough time to explore the full set of issues. A meeting that is constantly interrupted by telephone calls will not accomplish anything.

Adopt the Right Demeanor

The best demeanor for negotiations is calm and polite, but firm. Even if you receive disappointing proposals, don't show anger. Often you will be negotiating for a relationship that will last months or years—and no one wants to deal with someone who flies off the handle.

Act as if you have full confidence in your position. Even if your bargaining position is weak—and even if the other side knows it—you should not show fear and anxiety or your position may be steamrollered.

Deal With the Most Important Terms First

It is best to focus on the key issues first. In negotiations involving software, the most important terms are usually features, time of availability, and price. If those terms come into place, the parties will have a substantial incentive to resolve all the other terms.

Develop Justifications for Your Positions

To negotiate effectively, you need to develop justifications for the positions that you take. Be prepared to sell your positions just as you might sell a product. In reaching for agreement on open items, try to emphasize the ways in which your proposals for terms are to the benefit of the other side—or advance the mutual aims of both parties.

Make Trades Rather than Concessions

Don't be quick to offer concessions. Negotiations are like a ratchet mechanism—once you've made a concession, you cannot take it back without putting the negotiating process at risk. It is much better to propose trade-offs, in which you give up something in exchange for some concession on the other side.

Negotiate Price Terms with Firmness

Price negotiation is usually a process of give and take. It is best to position yourself for price negotiations by starting out with a figure that leaves room for bargaining to get to, or even well above your "real" figure.

Don't be quick to drop your position on price. You want to avoid bidding against yourself. Often disagreements on the price terms can be closed with an offer of something extra—an additional program or function—rather than a price concession. When opposing positions on price are very close, then it is often the right time to "split the difference" and arrive at the final price.

Understand Every Clause of the Contract Draft

Typically, when the main issues are decided, one side or the other will put a contract draft on the table. This is the time that all the remaining issues emerge.

It is a major error to ignore these "other issues." As we will discuss in the following chapters, there are issues in the text of the contract that can be *very* important because they involve potentially huge liabilities. Many companies have suffered large losses because they failed to take the time to understand and negotiate important contract terms.

Be sure that you understand *every* clause of the contract draft proposed by the other side. Determine which provisions are threatening to your interests.

When the other side has sent a proposed agreement, a common and effective response is to send back a marked-up copy of the draft with suggested changes and an "addendum" containing the additional language that you want in the agreement. You can also raise disagreements that you have with the other side's draft by sending a list of issues for discussion. In any case, it is best to meet and go through the issues one by one.

Understand "Standard" Agreements

The rule on standard software agreements is simple: *There is no objective standard as to what should be in an agreement.* There are only agreements that favor one side or another.

If the negotiators for the other side propose the first draft and say; "This is a standard agreement," what they are really is saying is: "This is a form of agreement that is favorable to us, and we try to use it a lot." You should study it carefully, then negotiate to modify the draft with clauses and provisions that make the bargain more balanced. It is not enough simply to react to what is *in* the other side's draft; you also have to pay attention to the important issues that have been *left out*. The chapters that follow in this book will assist in that process. If you need an attorney to understand the issues fully and form an appropriate response, you should get one.

Sometimes a party has a bargaining position so weak that it is forced to accept a one-sided agreement. But in the overwhelming majority of negotiations there is room for bargaining and pressure on both sides to compromise. It is a poor idea to sign a so-called "standard agreement" without a genuine attempt at negotiation on the unfavorable points.

A word of warning about negotiating changes in "standard form" contracts: Some form contracts have language that say that the sales staff cannot vary terms, and that any changes have to be signed by headquarters. Those clauses are often enforced and can *invalidate* "side letters" or additions grafted on by salespersons who are negotiating without authority. If you negotiate to modify such a form, get the changes in writing in the text, or an addendum to the original agreement, and get the agreement, with its modifications, signed by the right person.

Prepare for the Normal Set of Issues

Even though there are no "standard" software contracts, there are sets of issues that are commonly raised in software contract negotiation. There is a general understanding among attorneys and software executives, for example, about the *topics* that will be found in most software development agreements.

To be prepared for hard commercial bargaining, you need to know what the issues will be and what it is reasonable to ask for. The following chapters in this book will help you through that process.

Refuse to Accept Unwritten Promises

Don't accept or rely on any promise made that is not in the written agreement. Insist that every point in the deal be made part of the written contract. This is true no matter how honorable you find the person that you are negotiating with. Don't forget that the other side's employees or owners can change at any time. Make sure that the deal is completely documented.

Avoid Oral Contracts

A contract can be written or oral. Many, but not all, oral contracts are enforceable. *Your* contracts should *always* be in writing. You should avoid making bargains orally—and that means that you should be very cautious about *saying* that you have a deal.

Oral contracts are a fertile field for litigation. Where there are no records of a bargain, either side is free to invent or elaborate on the facts. Even well-meaning people may have their recollection of a conversation colored by their self-interest.

Oral contracts are also dangerous for what they leave out. For example, most written contracts to license software will disclaim warranties and seek to limit liability for any damage to the user's business. Informal oral contracts invariably leave such matters out. Every contract you make, from a transfer of a single piece of software to the sale of your software business, should be documented in writing. This applies to contracts with friends as well as strangers. Many a friendship has foundered on an oral contract.

I also suggest that you abolish from your negotiating vocabulary (and from that of any negotiator acting for you) the words "We have a deal" or "We've agreed on the essential terms" or the like—until you *sign* the contract. If you are not careful, if you "shake hands" on a deal before the contract is drafted, if you suggest that a "deal" has been made, you may make an oral contract without knowing it. After you've made this type of statement—and after you have refused to sign the "confirming" contract draft the other side sent—it is easy to spend a great deal of money litigating whether you have a contract or not. In the meanwhile, the ownership of the rights to the software may be placed in doubt.

Rather than making categorical declarations of agreement, it is best to move the negotiations to the contract stage by saying: "We've made great progress, and we're ready to work out the written contract."

Be Careful with Letters of Intent

Often, in the course of complex negotiations, parties sign "Letters of Intent" to outline a proposed contract. Letters of intent typically have a short summary of the contract terms that will be included in a more formal contract. The problem is the same as that we saw above: after you've signed a letter of intent—and after you have refused to sign the contract draft the other side sent—you can be sued on the claim that the letter of intent *is* a contract! I recently handled litigation over a letter of intent between a software developer and a publisher. It took me more than two years to finally establish that the poorly drafted letter of intent was not a contract.

To prevent this problem, any letter of intent that you sign should follow the format of Form 4-1 in Appendix C. This text makes it very clear that "Neither party is now bound and neither will be bound in any way until the formal written contract is signed." With this form signed by both parties, the negotiations may be called off at any time.

Contract Litigation and Arbitration

The wording of a contract has two functions. First, it is a set of rules for the parties—to guide their performance and their dealings with one another. Second, it is a guide for the judge, jury, or arbitrators who will intervene to enforce the contract in the light of the applicable law if there is a dispute. When negotiating an agreement, it is important to remember that the document may end up before a twelve-member jury or a panel of arbitrators. This is an important reason why the bargain should be well considered and carefully drafted.

Contract Litigation

The stages and the course of contract litigation are very much like the copyright litigation that is discussed in Chapter 1. Most often contract litigation is in state court rather federal court, but somes cases are tried in federal court. Contract cases are usually tried to a jury, but again there are exceptions. In most contract cases, the plaintiff (the party filing the suit), seeks money damages as the primary or exclusive remedy. Most contract litigation is settled before trial.

The cost of contract litigation is high, although the final cost depends on the complexity of the facts, the legal issues, the tactics of the parties, whether expert testimony is required, and a variety of other factors. Obviously, the sooner the case settles, the less it will cost. It is not unusual for a contract case to take two or three years to reach trial and to cost over $100,000. After a case is decided, it can be appealed. It is not unusual for fees on an appeal to be $15,000 or $25,000 or more.

Of course, even after you win in litigation, you still may have to *enforce* the judgment of the court. If the other side is bankrupt or in financial distress, you may recover nothing. On the other hand, if the other side has ample cash flow or valuable assets, it will usually be possible to enforce the judgment and collect money damages.

Arbitration

It is very common for software agreements to have an arbitration clause. The clause requires that most disputes be resolved by a hearing before one or more arbitrators, rather than in a court of law.

The arbitrators can be chosen by any procedure agreed to by the parties. They are often attorneys, but may be computer professionals if the parties wish. Often parties use the American Arbitration Association, which arranges commercial arbitrations. Most cases are heard by panels of one or three arbitrators. Compared to litigation, arbitration is a streamlined process. The parties usually exchange documents and proceed to the hearing of the merits in a matter of months rather than years. Rules of evidence are relaxed to make it easier and cheaper to present one's case.

The parties pay arbitration fees, which include the cost of paying the arbitrators for their time and are therefore usually substantial. Nonetheless, because of the expedited process, arbitration usually costs substantially less than litigation—often the savings are 50 percent or more.

Arbitration awards are almost always final. They are normally enforceable in court, and difficult to appeal, reverse, or alter in the courts. Of course, you still need a solvent defendant before you can collect damages.

Documenting Your Own Deal

You *can* do a complex deal from start to finish without a lawyer, and you *can* create your own form agreements, but I do not recommend it. If you create "do-it-yourself" agreements, there is a real risk that you will do it wrong.

No agreement can completely eliminate business risk. Even the best software agreements are inherently ambiguous, because they deal with terminology and concepts that are "fuzzy." It is often unclear, for example, what is a trade secret as opposed to technology commonly used in the industry. It may be uncertain what is a "competitive product." It may be unclear whether software has functionality that "substantially conforms to product documentation" and so forth. Language is an imperfect tool, and no contract can cover every possible contingency that might arise. It follows that even using a lawyer will not ensure a perfect agreement.

Why then is counsel often required? The answer is simple. Good attorneys understand how to draft agreements that better fit a particular business context, even if the fit is not perfect. They know what clauses and language are normally found in agreements for a particular type of transaction or relationship. They also know how the use of certain terms will shift the risk of certain contingencies from one party to the other in the transaction. Having an attorney involved will therefore give you a higher degree of confidence that you understood the issues correctly, avoided errors about the legal effect of a proposed agreement, and made the best deal you could.

Sometimes parties create do-it-yourself contracts by patching together clauses from a grab-bag of all the contracts that they have signed in the past. The problem with this approach is that it's like taking pieces from several different jigsaw puzzles and trying to ram them together. It's a fair bet that the pieces won't fit, and that you won't get a coherent picture of anything. Often the contract terms are inconsistent, there are ambiguities, the risks are misunderstood, and important items are left out altogether. These mix-and-match contracts sometimes may be unenforceable and usually lead to misunderstandings—and misunderstandings can generate expensive litigation.

In addition, to make sure that all the clauses are properly drafted can be hard work. A change in one part of the contract often has an effect on provisions elsewhere in the text. Therefore, it is essential that the deal as a whole works and that all the parts of the contract fit together in a way that makes business sense. This is another reason why getting the perspective provided by a lawyer may make very good sense.

If you use the contract forms in Appendix C of this book (all of which are also on diskette) and vary them to fit your needs, you will get closer to a deal that does make sense. You can print out these forms, mark them up, have the draft typed up, and use them as working drafts of agreement documents. Nonetheless, I recommend that, for any important contract or contract form, you have a computer lawyer review it before it is signed. The relatively modest cost will be money well spent.

Carrying Off the Details

If the parties choose to conclude a contract without counsel, they should attend to the details and create a workmanlike product, considering the following:

- Word usage should be consistent and important terminology should be defined.

- All important terms of the agreement should be included in the writing.

- The draft should be proofread to eliminate typos, misspellings, and accidental omissions.

- Every page should be numbered.

- If last-minute changes are made, they should be put in the draft in pen and each change should be initialed by both sides.

- Each page should be initialed in the upper righthand corner by both sides.

- The contract should be dated.

- The contract should be signed in duplicate and each side should get an original copy.

CHAPTER 5

Beta Test Agreements

When a developer (or publisher) has a new or revised software product, the product often is the programmer's "almost final" commercial version which is not yet ready for prime time. All known bugs are fixed, but undiscovered glitches and gremlins are lurking in the code. The software has been tested, but not with the range of PC hardware and software out there in the "real world."

To get the bugs out and put the final touches on the software, developers or publishers often provide copies of the not-quite-ready software to users without charge for a tryout. The trial user often is promised a free or discounted copy of the final released version when it comes out on the market. In exchange, the trial users provide reports on bugs and problems in the software and suggest needed improvements. The trial users also provide a valuable advance look at whether the software is easy to use and whether users like the product.

The software released to volunteer testers is the *beta* version (the prototype was *alpha* and the final released version presumably will be *gamma*). The trial users are known as *beta testers*. Before the software is released to a best tester, it is customary (and *very* important) that the tester sign a *beta test agreement*.

Goals of the Beta Test Agreement

A beta test agreement is designed to serve several important goals.

- **Limiting Liability.** It is possible that due to unknown bugs, the software in beta testing may fail and may ruin data. The developer wants the tester to assume the risk that this might happen.

- **Defining the Roles of the Parties.** The beta test agreement establishes the obligation of the tester to report problems. The agreement may also offer a reduced cost or free version of the final released product.

- **Limiting the Rights of the Tester to the Program.** The agreement establishes that the tester does not own the program, has the right to use it only for the test period, and then must return it.

- **Establishing Proprietary Rights in the Program.** The agreement acknowledges the developer's ownership of the program, its copyright, and trademarks.

- **Keeping the Software and Its Features Confidential.** The agreement pledges the tester to secrecy about the product and its features during the test. This is hardly a perfect barrier. Information from beta tests (and copies of beta software) are often "leaked." Nonetheless, this provision may give some help in keeping the new product and information about it out of the hands of the competition.

- **Coping with Unsolicited Advice.** Sometimes a beta tester will send you detailed ideas for improvements in your product, or even provide a flow chart for additional functions and features that the tester thinks should be added to your software. If you make a change that looks like one of the tester's ideas, he will want to be paid for his contribution. If he is not paid, he may sue. To head off this type of problem before it happens, it is best to make it clear in advance that there will be no compensation paid for any contribution made and that the developer does not want proprietary information from the tester or anyone else. It is also a good idea to return promptly any unsolicited material that arrives.

The Importance of the Beta Test Agreement

If you are running a beta test, you should be sure to get the beta test agreement signed before giving out the software for the test. Of all the various legal purposes of the beta test agreement, the most important provision is limiting your liability. If some catastrophic accident happens at the beta tester's company and vital data is lost—for example billing or accounts receivable data—the tester's first reaction will be to blame the beta test software. To avoid a damage lawsuit, it is best to have a clear and documented disclosure of the risks and of the lack of any warranty.

You should *not* send the software with the beta test agreement. Rather, you should send the beta test agreement out first; and when it comes back signed, *then* send the software. If your tester won't sign the agreement, the tester should not get the software. The process of getting the agreement signed can be done by fax if it needs to be done quickly.

Following Up on a Beta Test

It is a good idea, from a business and a legal perspective, to follow up on the beta testers (including making contact with those testers who never call or report)—to see if they had trouble with the software and whether there were problems (such as impaired data) that might raise liability issues. Obviously, the problems that they report, of all kinds, should be fixed to the maximum extent possible before a product is released for commercial sale.

Often a beta test agreement is sent with a report form which the tester is encouraged to fill out and return at the end of the test period. The report form asks for the tester's overall impression of the software, how the software ranks against other products, whether the tester would buy the product, additional features needed, etc.

Marketing Uses of Beta Test Agreements

In addition to testing functions, beta test agreements often serve a vital marketing agenda. The marketing functions including the following:

1. **Getting a Foot in the Door.** If the product fits the needs of a large corporation, the beta test stage may be a chance to expose the users in the corporation to the software and its advantages. The beta test agreement thus can be a prelude to a major sale. This is a particularly important function if the software is a "big ticket" item, such as, software that fetches and organizes data from dozens or hundreds of users on a network.

2. **Establishing a Pedigree.** If the beta tester is a prestigious company, and if its personnel *like* the new product, the developer can use the approval of the big company's personnel to establish instant credibility for a software product.

3. **Carrying Out a Demonstration.** If a developer contends that the software will save the user thousands of dollars—or accomplish some other positive goal, he may be able to arrange to use the beta test site to demonstrate and prove the effectiveness of the software.

Of course, the developer and publisher should be sure that the programs are reasonably bug-free *before* this type of beta testing if these marketing strategies are to work. Delivering programs that crash or destroy data is not the way to win customers or influence corporate users. If the software publisher wishes to use the name of the tester and the results of the test in advertising and promotions, the beta test agreement should grant the publisher the right to do so.

More Elaborate Beta Tests and Beta Test Plans

Let's say that a publisher has worked out a plan with a major potential user/customer to do a more elaborate beta test with a sophisticated product supporting many workstations—a project that requires software installation, training, and technical support. In that case, the form of the beta test agreement is very similar, but with a few changes to adapt it to the more sophisticated test format. To carry out such a beta test, the publisher needs first to create a separate document called the *beta test plan*, after discussions with the tester. (In this case, the corporate customer, rather than an individual, will be the beta tester.)

The beta test plan is not really a legal document at all. It is a business document that spells out pragmatically the intended working relationship of the two parties. The details of the plan will be largely dictated by the product and its business setting. Generally, a beta test plan should cover the following items:

- **Equipment and Scale of the Test:** The number of computers or workstations to be involved and the hardware and software platforms to be used.

- **Test Sites:** The business locations where the software will be installed and used.

- **Installation Details:** The timing and sequencing of installation, and the work needed from both sides to set up for and carry out installation.

- **Training and Technical Support:** Provision for how and when the supplier will make available training and technical support for users, often including a "hot line."

- **Contact Persons:** The personnel at the tester company who will be in charge of coordinating the beta test, and the contact persons for the supplier.

- **"Bug" Reports:** The method and format of reporting on problems and bugs.

- **Meetings:** The scheduling of regular meetings with the tester's staff to access problems and progress.

- **Final or Periodic Evaluation of the Software:** Evaluation procedures in which the software is compared to projected results or to the competition, and user satisfaction is rated.

When a beta test agreement incorporates such a beta test plan, the parties normally agree to use "reasonable efforts" to carry out the agreed-upon plan. However, the beta test plan is a document that will never be enforced in a court of law—it is designed to give structure to a voluntary cooperative effort.

Two Forms of Beta Test Agreement

Included in Appendix C (and in the diskette included in the book) are two forms for a beta test agreement.

Form 5-1 (on diskette as BETA1.W51) is suitable for use for a simple beta test. This document is for a software product that will be sent to the end-user to install and use—for the type of software product, for example, that will eventually be sold in boxes at retail.

Form 5-2 (on diskette as BETA2.W51) is for a cooperative beta test, where the software will require installation, training, and support from the supplier, and where a beta test plan has been agreed upon. This is the form of agreement that would typically be used for more complex software applications.

CHAPTER 6

Software Evaluation Agreements

The purpose of a software evaluation agreement, also known as a confidential disclosure agreement, is to define the legal rules for sharing information about software and software technology. These agreements are commonly used in software business transactions.

The party disclosing information about software is typically the developer or the holder of an exclusive license to the software. The party that receives the information is usually a prospective publisher, joint venture partner, or investor. The technology and ideas to be disclosed are usually unpublished and confidential. I will call the party providing the confidential information the "disclosing party" and the party receiving this information the "recipient."

It is common (and prudent) that disclosure of software and software technology take place in stages. When the recipient is just taking a first look, only object code should be disclosed, and little if anything should be disclosed about the underlying technology. Later on, when serious evaluation of the software is under way, the disclosing party may give technical details about its program and even the source code, pursuant to the terms of an appropriate software evaluation agreement.

Divergent Perspectives on Disclosure

Software evaluation agreements are really simple documents used to advance a dialogue that may benefit all concerned. But, as you will see, the perceived interests of the disclosing party and the recipient often diverge substantially. There are therefore very different versions of this type of agreement—depending on which side prepared the form agreement.

The Disclosing Party's Perspective:
Concern About the Risks of Disclosure

While eager to make the sale, the disclosing party is concerned that it might lose the technology that it discloses.

Even disclosing object code in the initial stages of disclosure could conceivably be risky for the disclosing party. As you learned in the discussion of copyright law in Chapter 1, the copyright of a program generally does not protect the general idea of the program or its collection of features. The fear is that the recipient could reject the disclosing party's software, and then develop its own software based on the same general idea and features. The disclosing party would be left in the cold.

Disclosure of technical details and source code raises more serious risks for the disclosing party. As we discussed in Chapter 2, there is a danger that revealing confidential information without a prior written agreement of confidentiality may destroy trade secret protection. In addition, the disclosing party needs assurance that the recipient will not use or disclose any of the technical information that it receives.

The Recipient's Perspective:
Concern About Continuing Obligations

The recipient also wants to encourage disclosure, but it has a different set of concerns. The recipient fears that after it rejects the software, it will have a lingering obligation to the disclosing party that will inhibit its freedom of action. The following example illustrates the point.

> **Example.** SoftGame, Inc., is a publisher of software games. SoftGame receives an average of 20 personal computer arcade-style games to evaluate a year. SoftGame evaluates a war game programmed by Storm Software, Inc., and rejects it. A few months later, with demand for war games expected to go

up because of imminent American intervention in Armenia, SoftGame pays for the development of a similar game by American War Games, Inc., which SoftGame brings to market. Storm Software immediately sues SoftGame; it alleges that SoftGame stole the ideas that Storm Software revealed in confidence.

The recipient's fear is that receiving information might expose it to claims later on that it has wrongfully taken any product concepts that it rejected. The recipient's interest, therefore, focuses on preserving its freedom to develop or purchase other technology.

The Two Basic Types of Evaluation Agreements

Given the difference in perspective of the developer and publisher, you won't be surprised to learn that lawyers have evolved two basic types of software evaluation agreements.

1. The disclosing parties' form—often entitled "confidentiality agreement"—emphasizes that the disclosed information consists of the disclosing party's proprietary trade secret and copyrighted information and the recipient's promise that confidentiality will be maintained for all information disclosed.

2. The recipients' form—often entitled "evaluation agreement"—emphasizes the publishers' freedom to use or disclose information sent by the disclosing party as long as the copyright is not infringed. These forms expressly give the recipient the right to develop products similar to those submitted for evaluation. Some of these forms promise confidentiality, and some do not. They hardly ever mention trade secrets.

Included in Appendix C as Forms 6-1 and 6-2 are samples of software evaluation agreements. Both are based on commonly used forms. Form 6-1 (on diskette as EVAL-DIS.W51) is the disclosing party's format, structured to put firm legal safeguards in place to protect software and technology disclosed in the course of negotiations. Form 6-2 (on diskette as EVAL-REC.W51) is the recipient's preferred format designed to maximize the recipient's freedom of action.

Most substantial software companies use both types of forms. They use the one that fits the situation of the moment. When disclosing information to others for evaluation, they use a form that guards trade secrets and other confidential information. When evaluating software that comes from others, they use the form that does not mention trade secrets and gives them maximum freedom of action.

When IBM receives information, it sometimes uses another variation that goes one step further. It's form states: "The Recipient [i.e. IBM] may use information for any purpose which does not violate [its] obligation of confidentiality." Any disclosure party that signs this form grants IBM the right to use the ideas and concepts in any way IBM wishes, so long as the ideas are held in confidence. Any developer should be very wary of signing such an agreement, and should negotiate to avoid granting to the recipient any rights to use technology. Even IBM would surely agree to modify this unreasonable language if it really wanted to see a significant new product or technology.

Pragmatic Negotiation of Software Evaluation Agreements

In my experience, the conflict of viewpoints regarding software evaluation agreements is more apparent than real and it is usually possible to bridge the gaps in this battle of forms. My advice to both sides is to be flexible and deal with the conditions of disclosure one step at a time.

At the onset of negotiation—where all that is being revealed is object code for initial evaluation—the stakes for the disclosing party are not that high. Revealing the object code will not disclose the trade secrets. There is no guarantee that the concept of its program won't be used by the recipient, but that risk is normally quite low. After all, it takes a lot of time and money to write complex software. If the idea or features of the program are themselves a valuable secret, then the disclosing party may want to try to negotiate a disclosure agreement that is more restrictive. In any case, the disclosing party should be careful not to reveal confidential technical information (orally or in writing) without a firm written agreement of confidentiality.

The time when a more restrictive form of the software evaluation agreement should be insisted upon is normally later on, when the recipient is looking for technical disclosure. Then the disclosing party should require that firm contractual protections (like those in Form 6-1) be provided to preserve the status of trade secrets and confidential information. A suitable agreement should be signed *before* the technical disclosure is made. In short, when the parties are seriously discussing the details of the technology and trying to work toward a deal, they can handle this issue in a serious way. (For further information on confidential disclosure and protection of trade secrets, please refer to Chapter 2.)

CHAPTER 7

Software Assignments

Transferring a Computer Program

A software assignment is the transfer of a software owner's interest in a computer program. Although some might dispute whether an assignment is technically a sale, for convenience I will call the parties to this type of transaction the "buyer" and "seller." (It is technically more accurate to use the more formal terms "assignor" and "assignee.") In this chapter, I will be discussing software assignments of the most basic type; that is, the simple transfer of ownership rights to a software program in exchange for a price, by means of a document simply entitled "Assignment" or sometimes "Transfer of Title Agreement."

It is quite possible to have a software assignment that is part of a more complex transaction. For example, in many software development agreements (see Chapter 8), the developer writes a program and then transfers rights in the program to the buyer upon acceptance and payment. In most software publishing agreements (see Chapter 9), the developer licenses the program to a publisher. However, it is possible to draft a software publishing agreement that features the absolute assignment of rights to the publisher. It is also possible to make an assignment as part of a larger transaction that governs many other assets, for example, the sale of a business.

In the simple form of assignment discussed in this chapter, payment is not contingent on sales or revenues from the program. The seller undertakes no obligation to fix bugs or offer any other software support. Rather, the rights are sold and the transaction is over.

One can assign all rights in a software program or only part of them. For example, one could assign the rights to copy or sell the program in Europe. Or one could assign the rights for use of the program in a specified application. One could assign the rights to derivative works. And so forth. The point is that each variation of an assignment would be absolute and irrevocable when made. In subsequent chapters we will discuss licensing transactions, in which the rights that are licensed revert back to the owner when and if the license is terminated. In an assignment, there is no provision for the rights to revert back.

When a Software Assignment Makes Business Sense

A software assignment in the simple form discussed here will normally be the transaction of choice only if the buyer perceives that the program is valuable just the way it is. Either the program needs no modification or the buyer thinks that modifications and software support can be done without help from the seller. The following are examples of situations where this would be appropriate:

> **Example.** The seller has developed a business software program that the buyer, a software vendor, wants to market. In the buyer's opinion, the program needs very minor modifications, such as adding the buyer's name and trademark on several screens and adding other visual elements. The buyer obtains the right to the program through a software assignment, gets a copy of the well-documented source code, and has its own engineers make the modifications and provide any necessary software maintenance.

> **Example.** The buyer sees that the seller's program, which runs as a single-user application under MS-DOS, has useful data processing features, but believes that only a version that runs on a Novell network will be commercially viable. The seller is not interested in making the necessary modifications for a network version. The buyer obtains the rights to the program

through an assignment, and obtains the source code; then the buyer's programmers modify the source code to make a network-ready version of the program.

Example. Jack and Jill jointly develop a software program, and Jill wants to sell out all her interest in the program to Jack. They use a software assignment to accomplish the transfer.

What to Watch for When Transferring Rights to Software

The party selling rights in software in the straightforward transaction discussed here should be sure that all the money or other consideration is paid at the time of the transfer. If the seller transfers the program rights based on the promise of payment later on, there is risk that the buyer will fail to pay, perhaps because of lack of funds. The seller might wind up filing a lawsuit in hopes of collecting payment, or end up with a claim in a bankruptcy proceeding.

If the agreement calls for payment over time, the buyer should consider whether he should be signing a simple assignment at all. The better course would be to negotiate a license agreement (a variant of the publishing agreements discussed in Chapter 9) that provides for transfer of the program *after* all payments are made, and also provides that the license can be terminated if payment is not made. A lawyer can help the seller make sure that the transaction is done properly.

The buyer of rights in software should take care to evaluate the software thoroughly. It is a good idea for the buyer to have someone with sophistication use the program and put it through its paces. Getting well-documented source code is a necessity—otherwise the program may be impossible to maintain or upgrade. Therefore preassignment evaluation of the source code (which normally should be done under a software evaluation agreement of the sort discussed in Chapter 5) is important. If there are existing users or beta testers, the buyer should talk to them about the program and how well it works. If there are many bugs, it will be the buyer's burden to fix them.

The buyer should do its best to be sure that the software is in fact totally original—that it does not incorporate software owned by others and that it is not a derivative work. There is no foolproof way to do this, of course. At the least, the buyer may inquire thoroughly as to the origin of the code and the seller's prior licensing or transfer of computer programs. One focus of the inquiry is to determine if the seller will be conveying a software product that includes pieces of code that are also contained in earlier programs that the seller has transferred or exclusively licensed to others. If so, the seller might have to deliver to the buyer written licenses from each of the earlier licensees, in order to allow the buyer to use the code without fear of an copyright infringement claim.

In the bargaining of the parties for an assignment, the main issue, of course, is price. The seller will come to the table armed with arguments about why the price for the program should be high, and the buyer will offer reasons to the contrary. If in the end the price gap is too large, the parties may want to try another concept, perhaps a publishing deal (see Chapter 9), where both the risks and the upside are shared.

If the seller is a software developer, it may seek to include in the language of the assignment a provision that reserves the right for the seller to use some of the same source code in future programs, if the code is of a kind that is commonly used in the software industry. The buyer may resist the inclusion of such a provision, arguing that the provision makes the assignment less than total. Indeed, there will certainly be some ambiguity as to what technology and techniques are in fact "commonly used" in the industry. On the other hand, a developer does not want to "reinvent the wheel" every time it writes a program, nor does it want to sign away all right to use routine code for memory management, screen displays, and the like. The inclusion of such language is a matter for negotiation.

Form of Software Assignment

I have included in Appendix C. Form 7-1 (found on diskette as ASSIGN.W51), a sample software assignment agreement. Form 7-1 is a straightforward document, but it still probably makes sense for the parties to have their legal counsel give any important assignment transaction a once-over before it is finalized and signed. The buyer may want to ask counsel to make sure that the assignment document includes all rights and all property that should be transferred. The buyer and seller may want legal advice on the seller's representations and indemnities concerning non-infringement (discussed in Chapter 8) that are a common feature of these documents.

Software Development Agreements

The software development agreement is one of the basic transactions of the computer business: An independent developer or programmer promises to write or modify a program to specifications for an agreed-upon price and to transfer the program to a customer.

In exchange for payment, the developer often transfers to the customer the source code, the object code, and the ownership of the software copyright. Other approaches are possible. For example, the customer could get an exclusive license to use the software in a particular field, with developer retaining certain rights to use the code in fields that do not compete with the customer. In general, however, when the customer has software written at its sole (and rather considerable) expense, it will expect quite broad rights in the software that results. Frequently, the customer will expect to receive the source code it paid to have created.

Software development agreements are used whenever a company pays for the outside creation of software.

Example: Electric Accounting Corp. licenses accounting programs to business and industry. It wants to add new functions to its receivables and payroll programs. It does not have sufficient staff for such a large job, so it contacts CPA Programmers, Inc. CPA Programmers express a willingness to do the work for a fixed price based on written specifications. CPA Programmers delivers documented source code and object code to Electric Accounting.

Example: Pacific Machinery Corp. has an in-house DEC mini-computer-based system that handles its sales, including customer order entry, shipping and billing. Pacific wants to add a data and market analysis systems to project failure needs for preventive maintenance and spare parts—and it wants the system to run on the existing hardware and operating system. Pacific's MIS Department retains System Developers, Inc. to write the software to its written specifications, and to deliver the documented source code. A work and payment schedule is agreed upon.

The developer in a software development agreement is typically a business, small or large, that has a high level of expertise in software design. The customer can be anyone who has a business use for software: a publisher, a computer service bureau, the MIS department of a large corporation, a government agency, or a variety of other user types. (Some aspects of contracting with the federal government are discussed in Chapter 12.)

An agreement for developing software can have a variety of names: software development agreement, software programming agreement, agreement to write software to specifications, or software modification agreement. Some forms for these agreements are titled work-for-hire agreements, and may use the term "work-for-hire" in the text. However, the contractual relationship between the developer and the customer usually does not qualify as "work-for-hire" under the strict definition of the term in the Copyright Act. (See Chapter 1 for a discussion of the concept of work-for-hire.) This is because the company or person doing the programming is almost always an *independent contractor* who is not subject to the customer's day-to-day control. Therefore, it is important that the software development agreement should expressly assign or license the copyright to the customer.

Forms to Use with This Chapter

In this chapter, we will review the main issues that arise in software development agreements. Included in Appendix C are additional tools to help you negotiate these agreements.

Form 8-1 (on diskette as DEV-CHK.W51) is a software development agreement checklist—intended as a quick overview of all the sections of these agreements and as an aid in covering the bases in negotiation. Form 8-2 (On diskette as DEV-AGR.W51) is an annotated software development agreement. Form 8-2 presents sample language for these agreements, including alternatives and options. Commentary included in Form 8-2 provides an explanation for many of the provisions and choices that are available. Of course the sample agreement cannot cover every possible variation—and your deal may well require options that are not covered. Together with this chapter, these forms are intended to guide you through the nuts and bolts of these documents. In drafting the sample contract, I have used contract language that, as much as possible, is in layman's terms. But I admit that reading through Form 8-2 and its commentary is hard work. I suggest that if you are not engaged in negotiations now, that you skim Form 8-2. When you are negotiating a deal and you have a need to get into the details, that is the time to read thoroughly Form 8-2 and its commentary.

These materials will help you use an attorney efficiently (because you will understand the issues much better) and will also help you draw up a first draft of your own software development agreement. However, I caution you that these agreements may have consequences that you might miss. Therefore, it is best to negotiate these agreements subject to review by counsel.

Negotiating a Software Development Agreement

As is true with most contract negotiations, the negotiation and performance of a software development agreement come in stages. First, the parties come to a general understanding about the deal—an overview of what is to be done and a general estimate of the price. Next, the parties come to a more detailed understanding and work out specifications, the work schedule, and the contract price. Finally, the parties try to put down on paper the language of an agreement that reflects their expectations. They need satisfactory provisions for what happens if things go wrong, for example, the customer's remedy if the developer fails to deliver the software, the developer's remedy if the customer fails to pay, correction of defects, indemnification for copyright infringement, termination of the agreement, and the like. Let's first take a further look at the first stage of this process.

Before Negotiating the Agreement

It is important for each party to know who they are dealing with before an agreement is negotiated. The developer's first task is to assess its potential customer's sophistication and its needs. Often an important part of the selling process is education—informing a customer about what it reasonable to expect from the proposed custom-written software and what costs and problems to expect.

The developer may be concerned about being paid during or at the end of the work. In some cases, the customer may be able to contact other developers who have worked with the customer and find out if receiving payment has been a problem. If the agreement price is substantial and the customer is a small company, the developer may want to increase the up-front payment and may want to ask for assurance, such as bank or financial statements, showing that the customer can afford to pay.

From the customer's point of view, the key issue is the credibility of the developer. Does the developer have a record of delivering good products reasonably close to the time specified? If the developer has not worked for the customer before, the customer should check references.

Negotiating the Specifications, Work Schedule, and Price

As you surely know, the three most important terms in the agreement are the specifications, the time for performance, and the price. The parties to a software development agreement are much more likely to avoid trouble if both sides have realistic expectations about all these items.

The Right Specifications   It is very important that the specifications, attached as a schedule to the agreement, sometimes called the "Statement of Work," be done accurately and comprehensively. Poorly written specifications cause trouble because they make the proposed job unclear to both sides. An unsophisticated customer will not know what it really wants, and its set of specifications may be a bare-bones description—which would allow the developer to price and deliver a bare-bones system the customer will hate.

A few years ago, two developers I know signed a contract with a game publisher to convert a MS-DOS arcade-style game to run on an Amiga computer. The specification called for the Amiga version to use the MS-DOS version screens (which were CGA graphics) and sound. The price agreed upon was $30,000.

But there was a problem: the Amiga machine had graphics and sound capability far superior to the MS-DOS machines. CGA graphics and PC style sound were going to look and sound crude on the sleek Amiga machine, and the two developers knew it. But they needed the money and they feared that the game company would not pay the much higher price of developing new art and sound for the Amiga.

At the end of several months, the developers delivered the game, which worked exactly as specified. When the officers of the game publisher saw the game, they were bitterly disappointed and mad as hell—and they refused to pay for the work. Eventually the matter was resolved, but it left a legacy of bitterness.

It is in everyone's interest that the specifications describe a system that will satisfy the customer. If the product is to be sold commercially, it should be suitable for the market. If the product is business software, the developer should talk directly to the system users to see what is required. Everyone's expectations should be in sync. Remember that there can be a lot of repeat business in this field.

Where the software is to be used for transaction processing—such as retail sales or order entry—there should be a thorough discussion of issues relating to the volume of transactions, so that the software will have acceptable throughput capacity and response time. (Response time is the number of seconds from the time the user presses the key to initiate a transaction until the cursor comes back on the screen. For most transaction processing function, an end-of-transaction response time of more than a few seconds will irritate users.) Performance issues should also be carefully addressed in any contract concerning software that manages large networks or may substantially add to the load on a large network.

The Right Schedule Another issue that is a perennial problem is the time allowed for the programming work to be done. Other times it is possible to estimate the amount of effort required with reasonable accuracy, because the task is routine. Sometimes estimating the effort is nearly impossible. For example, the team that wrote the first Windows word processor couldn't have known in advance how many months of work would be required.

It is best that the schedule for delivery of new software be as realistic as possible. It is a common perception that software development is *always* late. Developers sometimes promise delivery when the customer wants it, fearing to tell the customer about probable delays. Lack of realism and candor in the beginning may lead to frustration and anger later on—particularly if the software is needed to serve an important corporate purpose for the customer.

If there are delays, the timeframes can be extended by mutual agreement in writing (usually by a letter). But if the customer is looking for an excuse to terminate the contract or force a price reduction, late delivery will often provide it. Under contract law a modest delay in delivery is not always fatal. Sometimes a court of law will rule that payment in full is due in spite of some tardiness in delivery. However, where the fine print of the agreement states that "time is of the essence," any delay past the stated deadline will probably be ruled a material breach of the contract. Some software development agreements are written to provide the developer an option to extend the time for delivery by a specified time if the development pace is slower than expected.

Developers who are late in their delivery run other risks. If completion of the software is behind schedule, the developer must incur costly expenses for programming work not provided for in the budget. In addition, delay in producing the software means delays in payment—and this too may cause financial strains on the developer. Customers hate it when developers come asking for more money. Again the moral is that realism in time and cost estimates is very important.

The Right Price and Payment Terms   The parties have to select price payment terms that make business sense for both sides. The issues here are *how much* will be paid and *when* payment will be due.

Even after negotiating the final price, the parties may have very different viewpoints on the right timing for payment. For example, developers are often undercapitalized and are eager for money up front or generous progress payments. Customers will try to delay most payments until delivery of product.

The parties that enter into a software development agreement have many options for prices and terms. Here are some common price terms:

- **Payment on Acceptance.** The simplest provision is to have the payment due on acceptance of the program, which is based on delivery on a specified date of a program that conforms to the specifications. The problem is that the developer may be unable or unwilling to do all the work without up-front or progress payments.

- **Up-front Payment Plus Payment on Acceptance.** A common variant is to have a substantial payment on signing and a final payment due on acceptance.

- **Level of Effort Agreement.** If the project is one that is technically innovative and of uncertain duration, the only option may be a "level of effort" agreement. Such an agreement would provide, for example, that a certain number of technicians are to work full time on the program and be paid at an agreed-upon hourly rate. Monthly or other periodic payments are also possible. The customer reviews progress periodically and has an option to stop. In this type of agreement, the delivery date for the final product is left open. In most cases, however, customers will reject an ongoing payment obligation without a cap.

- **Limited Periodic Payment and Final Payment.** A variant of the level of effort agreement provides regular payments for a period, then requires work without further payment until the work is done, with a final lump sum payable on completion.

- **Milestone Schedule.** A common option is to have an agreed-upon set of "milestones," such as the example in Form 8-2. At the date of each milestone, the developer must deliver a defined version or portion of the program, known as a "deliverable," to the customer. Typical deliverables are prototypes, code for critical functions to demonstrate feasibility, alpha or preliminary versions, beta versions, and the final program with documentation.

Using a milestone schedule has several advantages. From the customer's viewpoint, this choice provides early warning of trouble. If the early deliverables are defective or late, the customer can terminate the agreement and cut its losses. The advantage to the developer is that it provides cash during the course of the work as the milestones are met. The main disadvantage for the developer of the milestone format is its rigidity: the dates for deliverables are set, and usually there is no provision for extensions of time. Of course the parties can negotiate provisions that provide flexibility in milestone dates.

Negotiating the Written Agreement

When the parties have dealt with the specifications, the time for performance, and the price, it is time to turn to all the other issues that go into the software development agreement. These issues—the tedious fine print—matter very much. Some of these provisions can directly affect the parties' pocketbooks, such as the terms for acceptance criteria and obligations for software maintenance. Some are important matters of risk allocation, such as who is responsible for infringement claims.

Your tools for working through the details are Forms 8-1 and 8-2 in Appendix C, which cover many optional provisions and alternatives together with this chapter. I suggest that you dissect the other side's draft clause by clause using these tools.

In addition, the following are some general words of advice about working through the details of a draft of a written software development agreement. To understand how the following items translate into the text of an agreement, you may wish to skim through Form 8-2 before you read the following sections.

Delivery, Acceptance, and Opportunity for Cure

Almost every software development agreement contains a mechanism for the customer to evaluate each software deliverable. In order for the developer to get the payment for the deliverable, the customer must accept it. The agreement sets an acceptance standard, and the customer can reject any deliverable that fails to measure up. The customer typically has a given amount of time to accept or reject. If the deliverable is rejected, the developer usually has an opportunity to cure the defect but a second failure to deliver an acceptable deliverable will give the customer the right to terminate the contract.

A common standard for the customer's acceptance is that the program must "meet all specifications" and "perform consistently and without failure." Literally, this means that the software will perform all functions perfectly and be bug-free—and it is a fair bet that no software of any sophistication was ever written and delivered bug-free. Developers who sign these agreements are taking a calculated risk, expecting that the customer will be more flexible than the agreement requires at the time of acceptance.

Sometimes the customer is successful in having the acceptance criteria softened to read that the program must *substantially* meet all specifications." The use of the word "substantially" here makes the acceptance criteria unclear, because the word means something like "for the most part." It allows the developer to argue that it has complied with the criteria, and thus deserves payment, even if there are some bugs discovered in acceptance testing.

It is common for acceptance procedures to require that the customer give the developer a list of the defects, bugs, and errors that can cause rejection of a deliverable. But there is risk that even when those listed bugs are fixed, still more bugs will appear, and that the customer will continue to withhold payment.

As a practical matter, a sophisticated customer will not make a final payment until it is satisfied with the software. This normally means that the software is stable and satisfactorily carries out its business or technical function in normal use, and that any known bugs are minor and do not interfere with its use.

Transferring the Object Code, Source Code, and Intellectual Property

A very important consideration is what rights the customer is to receive in the software. As I noted earlier, when the customer has funded development of software, it will normally want broad rights in the software that results. Often the agreement provides that the developer will assign all rights in the software to the customer. Sometimes the buyer will get an exclusive license covering a particular field of use. Sometimes the buyer gets a non-exclusive license and a royalty on any further sales of the software by the developer. If you are interested in drafting a royalty provision, please see Chapter 9 on software publishing agreements, where software royalties are addressed in considerable detail.

Developers often include provisions in software development agreements that allow them to retain some limited rights in the code they create for others. For example, developers may reserve the right to reuse the code supplied to the customer in other non-competing programs written for other customers. Or developers may want the right to reuse commonly used code—such as code that displays images, drives a printer, manages memory, etc.

There is also an issue as to *when* the legal rights to the software transfer to the customer. Generally, the customer will want its rights in the copyright (and other intellectual property) to pass into the customer's ownership the moment the software is delivered. However, the developer gets the most leverage if the copyright remains the developer's property until and unless timely final payment is made. Some software development agreements provide that right to the program goes to the customer immediately, but reverts to the developer if payment is not made.

The agreement will often state that the customer will have the right to register the copyright. The customer may wish to register the copyright soon after delivery and acceptance. (See discussion of copyright registration and recording assignments in Chapter 1 and Appendix A.)

Product Warranties and Remedies

A warranty is the same thing as a guaranty, an assurance about the nature, the quality, or performance of goods. In software there are two types of warranties: the first relates to the quality of the software product, what the software will do and whether it is free of errors or defects; the second relates to whether the software does or does not infringe intellectual property rights (primarily copyrights, and patents) of another person. I will first discuss warranties of product quality.

Limiting Product Warranties and Liability   Every software development agreement ought to have clauses in which the developer disclaims product warranties and limits damage claims. (If use of the software might affect human health or safety, careful consideration should be given to these broader liability issues. See the discussion of liability issues in Chapter 13.)

The need to disclaim warranties and limit liability comes from the provisions of the Uniform Commercial Code (UCC) that control sale and warranties. (Most courts have found that the UCC, which covers sale of "goods," applies to software licensing and transfers.) The UCC, which governs sales in every state except Louisiana, provides certain default warranty provisions that take effect *unless otherwise agreed*, as follows:

- **Express Warranties.** Under the UCC, any description of goods, in a written agreement or in a letter or advertisement, even in an oral statement, is a *warranty*—a binding warranty about the quality and performance of the software product.

- **Implied Warranty of Merchantability.** The UCC imposes an "implied" (imposed by law) warranty of "merchantability"—which means that the product is of adequate quality and will do what it is supposed to do reasonably well.

- **Implied Warranty of Fitness for a Purpose.** If the customer states a purpose for which the software is being bought, orally or in writing, the UCC imposes an implied warranty that the software in fact fulfill the particular need.

In addition, the UCC has provisions for the monetary damage remedy that the customer will get in litigation if the software is defective or falls short of an express or implied warranty. Again these are the provisions that apply *unless otherwise agreed*.

Under these UCC provisions, the customer may sue and recover the cost of replacing the original software with software that works as warranted. The UCC also provides that the customer may recover *consequential damages*—which means money damages for interruption of business, lost of production, or lost profits due to software errors. If the software creates havoc in a customer's business, ruins vital data, or fails to deliver projected cost savings, the developer could face huge liability in litigation—without any contractual limitation. Under the UCC provisions that apply *unless modified*, the liability risk to the developer is effectively *unlimited*.

Because of this liability threat, software development contracts almost always have provisions designed to modify these UCC default provisions and to provide a large measure of contractual protection to the developer. These provisions are extremely important from the developer's point of view. In summary, these contract provisions are the following:

Limiting Express Warranties.   As I will discuss below, the developer normally includes weak express warranties in the text of the agreement—or provides no warranty at all.

The "Integration Clause"   Developers want to prevent customers from asserting warranty claims based on oral promises or writings that pre-date the written agreement. Any well-written development agreement therefore has a clause limiting enforceable contract provisions to those expressly stated in the text of the Agreement. This type of provision is known as an "integration clause" or an "entire agreement" clause. (For its part, the customer should be sure that the text of the agreement actually incorporates what the developer has promised. Promises not included in the written agreement are likely to be unenforceable).

Disclaiming Implied Warranties   Almost always, a software development agreement "disclaims" or "excludes" the implied warranties of merchantability and the implied warranty of fitness for a purpose. Under the UCC, to be effective, these disclaimers must be "conspicuous," that is, IN ALL UPPER CASE LETTERS.

Strict Limitation of Remedies   The UCC allows parties to agree on limited remedies—so long as the limitation is not unreasonable. Often the agreement provides that if the software is defective or fails to meet a warranty, the developer may either fix the error, replace the software, or refund the customer's money, at the developer's choice. Consequential damages, including lost profits or damages for lost data, and incidental damages are excluded. The agreements also commonly provide that even if the customer recovers money damages, the amount is limited. Typically the maximum is the license fee paid by the customer or some designated dollar limit. The agreements also provide (and this is important) that these are the *exclusive* remedies available. These limitations are also normally in upper case type, although technically this is not required.

Express Warranty Provisions

Express warranties that commonly appear in software development agreements are quite limited. The developer often warrants in the agreement that the software will "perform substantially in accordance with the specifications." Where such an express warranty is given, its duration (usually beginning at acceptance) is normally quite short—often the warranty ends on the same date as the developer's bug-fixing obligation discussed in the next section. This makes sense; after all, the limitation of remedy provision makes bug-fixing a remedy for software defects or failure to conform to the warranty.

In many software development agreements, the developer excludes all warranties. Those agreements provide that the software is sold "AS IS." (Again conspicuous upper case letters are called for.) In some cases, the agreements actually provide that the parties agree that software bugs are inevitable.

Self-Protection Obligations

Often software development agreements include requirements that the customer take measure to back up programs and data every business day and use anti-virus software. Instructions to do these tasks are also included in the user documentation.

These provisions are designed to shift to the customer any blame for a large loss of important data.

The Bottom Line on Warranties

What is the net affect of all these modifications of the default UCC warranty and damage provisions? The bottom line is that most of the risk of bad software is shifted to the user—if these provisions are enforced. (In egregious cases involving very bad software and/or unsophisticated customers, the exclusions and limitations may be ineffective. See the discussion of litigation of end-user agreements in Chapter 12.) Under these very common provisions, the *customer* takes the risk that bad software will result in lost data, lost profits or lost business opportunities. If the software fails to work right or fails to work at all, the customer's remedy is limited. Usually, the only remedy is bug fixing—a process that sometimes can take months. And normally, even if the bug fixing effort fails, the customer can only get his money back—although some customers are smart enough to negotiate higher damage limits.

At first glance, from a customer's point of view at least, this shift of economic risk may seem to be unfair. But it's really not. From an economic perspective, requiring more extensive warranties and remedies would only impose more costs on the software developers of the world—costs that ultimately have to be passed back to the customer in increased software prices. In software, like everything else, there is no free lunch.

The Obligation to Fix Errors

The developer normally assumes an obligation to fix errors and bugs—often a specified number of hours of work or to a specified number of months. Thereafter the customer will agree to pay for the service of fixing bugs either for a yearly (or often periodic) maintenance fee, or on an hourly bases. How much bug fixing is included in the price, and how long the developer must fix bugs, for free or at a cost, are items that must be negotiated.

Non-Infringement Warranties and Indemnification

Software development agreements normally have two provisions that deal with the developer's right to transfer intellectual property rights to the customer. The first is an *intellectual property warranty* and the second is an *indemnification clause*.

Limiting the Intellectual Property Warranty   In an intellectual property warranty clause, the developer warrants that its program does not infringe anyone's intellectual property rights. Or, in a milder version, the developer warrants only that it *knows* of no such infringement.

For their own protection, developers should try to limit the intellectual property warranty they give. They should warrant only that they *know* of no infringement. Or at the most, the developer could warrant only that there is no *copyright* infringement. (As we discussed in Chapter 1, if the program is not copied from some other program, there is no copyright infringement.) It is difficult or impossible to know whether any software program infringes a patent, and therefore the developer certainly should always try to avoid any warranty on the absence of patent infringement. (See the discussion of software patents in Chapter 15.) Under the UCC, there is a broad non-infringement warranty that automatically applies unless the parties agree otherwise. For this reason, it is important that the developer get a narrower warranty clause in the text.

Limiting the Indemnification Clauses   The indemnification clause in a software development agreement deals with what happens if someone files a suit against the customer for copyright or patent infringement. Such suits are rather rare, but they are potentially devastating when they occur, because of the huge expense and risk of intellectual property litigation. Often the customer will want the developer to "hold it harmless," that is, for the developer to agree to pay all costs to defend any infringement suit, and to pay any judgment or settlement that results.

The scope of the indemnification clause is usually related to the scope of the intellectual property warranty that we just discussed:

- If the developer has broadly warranted that there is no infringement, then the agreement will usually place the entire cost of defending any infringement claim *and* the cost of paying any settlement or judgment on the developer.

- If the developer has warranted only that it *knows* of no infringement, then only if that warranty is *false* should it be required to indemnify or defend the customer or pay a settlement or a judgment.

Again, it is advisable for the developer to *limit* its exposure to liability. As I noted earlier, the developer is normally a small or medium-size business. It will typically not have either the resources or the practical know-how to defend a major infringement claim. Many software developer agreements have a stated limit or "cap" on the amount of potential indemnification liability.

In some cases, agreements are negotiated in which the patent infringement indemnification is *reversed*, that is, the *customer indemnifies the developer* from patent infringement liability. These reverse provisions are sometimes negotiated when a large company is seeking to develop a new area of software technology and has contracted with a small specialized developer. When the small company balks at taking the unknown legal risk of jumping into a new field, the customer agrees to protect the smaller company if the venture results in a patent infringement claim.

Limiting Potential Losses from Infringement   When the developer agrees to grant a broad intellectual property indemnification, there is often a provision that deals with ways the developer may be able to reduce the impact of an infringement problem. Often the developer is permitted to control and settle a suit and is allowed either to get the customer a license for use of the infringing technology or to "design around" the problem. Under many agreements, as a last resort, the developer can refund the purchase price paid by the customer, wholly or in part, as full compensation for the customer's loss of the right to use the program. These clauses also require the customer to cooperate with the developer in defending the claim in order to get the benefit of indemnification.

Negotiation of Remedies for Failure to Perform the Agreement

The software development agreement will have provisions that govern what happens in the case of a failure of one of the parties to perform its obligations under the agreement.

Suppose that the customer terminates the contract because the developer fails to deliver the beta version of the program. Does the customer then own the prototype version that was previously delivered (and paid for)? Can the customer stop the developer from selling a final version of the program to someone else—and the copyright as well? The parties may negotiate a provision that restricts the defaulting developer from selling any similar program to competitors. Many agreements simply let the parties go their own ways if the agreement is breached.

Suppose that the developer delivers the final version and the customer simply fails to pay for it. Is the developer then free to sell the final version and the copyright to someone else? At a minimum, the developer has the right to sue the customer for the price, but some agreements allow the developer to sell the software and thereby reduce the amount of damages it can claim. Some agreements give the developer the rights to the program in lieu of any claim for damages or the price. All of these items are open to negotiation.

Other Agreement Provisions

There are additional clauses that should be considered. For example, the parties most decide whether there will be an arbitration clause. There should be provision on how notices are given, what state's law will govern, and what happens if there are delays due to "acts of God." These rather routine matters are covered in the annotations to Form 8-2.

Unequal "Standard" Agreements and Poorly Conceived Agreements

As you read in Chapter 4, it quite common that one side of the negotiation simply signs the "standard" agreement form proposed by the other side. This occurs, for example, when a sophisticated programming company sends its standard form to an unsophisticated customer, such as a small business or a local hospital. Or it could happen when a savvy software publisher sends its standard form to a small programming outfit.

Standard form software development agreements—usually drafted by a lawyer for one side or the other—are very one-sided. The ones drafted by the developer will set unreasonably short periods for acceptance and will impose the cost of fixing all bugs on the customer. The ones drafted by the customer may require payment only if the program meets the customer's subjective satisfaction.

What is the result of these unequal contracts? Sometimes there is no effect at all, if the software is delivered on time and works right the first time. Payment is made and everyone is happy. The problems arise when things go wrong.

Take, for example, the contract that unreasonably favors the developer. Suppose that customer receives software so full of bugs that it is unusable. But suppose that the customer fails to reject the delivery in the time allotted under the agreement, and the language of the agreement says that the customer is then required to pay the full contract price. The developer may then press for payment for unusable software.

Or consider the contract that unreasonably favors the customer. The developer may find that the customer is entitled to withhold final payment until the program is made to run to its subjective satisfaction—a moment that never comes even though the customer is using the software. The developer will have to sue to get paid.

The moral is that it is worth working through the nitty-gritty details of a software development agreement, using this text and Forms 8-1 and 8-2. You will find that in most cases it is possible to arrive at an even-handed agreement.

"Mix-and-Match" Software Development Agreements

A related problem is that sometimes neither party has any contract sophistication and neither gets the advice of counsel. Then the resultant agreement may be a hodge-podge of language taken from other contracts, full of ambiguities and contradictions and often simply omitting important subjects. The point is that you should be sure that you know what you are doing, and seriously consider getting a lawyer to review a software development agreement before it is signed.

CHAPTER 9

Software Publishing Agreements

A software publishing agreement is an agreement between a company or person who already owns or is going to develop software (the "developer") and a company that is going to produce and market it (the "publisher"). Under a software publishing agreement, the developer not only creates the program, but also retains an ongoing interest in future earnings generated by the work—in the form of *royalties* on sales. The developer and the publisher thus share in the risks and potential rewards of the marketing of program.

This chapter will aid you in understanding the negotiation of a software publishing agreement, a document that may be the foundation of a commercial relationship that lasts for years. If the agreement contract is done well, the foundation will be solid. If not, one side or the other—or both—may be very unhappy.

Uses of Software Publishing Agreements

Following are some examples of circumstances in which a software publishing agreement might be used:

Example: ABC Corp. markets a line of small business order entry, shipping, billing, and accounting software programs that run on local area networks. Jack Smith, Inc. has a program that prepares state sales tax returns for small businesses. ABC decides that the program, with a few modifications, can be incorporated in its own product and will add value to its line. Jack Smith agrees to do the modifications in four months' time and to license the modified version to ABC for a modest up-front fee, plus a royalty of $100 per sale.

Example: XYZ Corp. has brought out a successful software game based on the action adventure movie "Eliminator II" that runs under Windows. XYZ contracts Game Developers, Inc. to write a Macintosh version. A work schedule covering 250 days and a progress payment schedule are also agreed upon. The parties agree that Game Developers will receive a royalty of 12 percent of sales.

Example: New American Software, Inc. develops a visual applications development environment that runs under Windows NT. Japan Micro, Ltd. of Tokyo wants to bring out a Japanese version of the program to run under the NEC operating system. Japan Micro signs a license agreement that gives it a copy of the source code and exclusive rights to the Japanese market. Japan Micro converts all text and functions into Japanese and publishes the new version in Japan. Japan Micro agrees to pay New American a one-time fee of $100,000 plus a royalty of $5 for each copy of the software program sold.

Commercial Settings for Software Publishing Agreements

There are two different settings in which parties negotiate publishing deals. In the first, the software has already been written, perhaps needing minor modifications by the developer, but it is essentially a complete product. Even for software that already exists, a software publishing agreement is quite a complex document, which must address a variety of issues that we will examine in this chapter.

In the second setting, the software that is being bargained for does not yet exist. The publishing agreement will provide for *both* the *creation* of the software and for its *publication*. In Chapter 8, in the context of software development agreements, I reviewed in some depth the legal issues involved in the creation of software. Many of those issues—for example, specifications, scheduling and timeliness of performance, acceptance and rejection of deliverables, product maintenance, and warranty and indemnification—also apply to software publishing agreements. I will touch on these issues, but I will not repeat that discussion. If you are negotiating an agreement for software that is to be written *and* published, you should reread Chapter 8 in conjunction with this chapter.

Tools for Use with This Chapter

This chapter covers key issues that arise in the negotiation of a software publishing agreement. Additional significant issues are covered in Forms 9-1 and 9-2 in Appendix C and on the diskette that accompanies this book.

Form 9-1 (on diskette as PUB-CHK.W51) is a software publishing agreement checklist that provides an outline of the sections of these agreements and issues typically covered in negotiation.

Form 9-2 (on diskette as PUB-AGR.W51) is an annotated software publishing agreement. Form 9-2 presents sample language for these agreements, including alternatives, options, and commentary. Of course these forms do not cover every possible issue, and your deals may include options that are not covered.

Software publishing agreements are quite complex, and may have consequences that you will miss without the assistance of counsel. It is best, therefore, to negotiate these agreements "subject to review by counsel" and have your attorney review them before the terms become cast in concrete.

About Software Publishers

The first step in a publishing deal is for the developer and the publisher to find one another. Software publishing companies come in all sorts—with different interests, serving different markets, and with different skills. Some are large, and some are small. Some are well-capitalized, and some live hand-to-mouth.

Software is a highly differentiated market. Publishers have a variety of different market strategies and specialties. For example:

- **Hardware and/or Software Platforms.** Some publishers specialize in software for UNIX or for DEC computers. Some publishers specialize in such narrow specialties as Lotus 1-2-3 or Microsoft Excel templates and macros. Some publishers focus on applications that can be easily ported across many platforms.

- **Price Range.** Some publishers specialize in business, industrial, or scientific products that are high-priced, need support, and require a sophisticated "sell." Others specialize in "shrink-wrap" products for the mass market.

- **Line of Commerce.** Some publishers are in markets defined by a profession or branch of commerce such as engineering, education, medicine, law, defense, religion, etc.

- **Computer Technology Markets.** Some publishers focus on fields defined by particular computer technologies. A very active field is networking products and middleware that bridges applications and systems in network environments. Other examples of such specialized markets are computer-assisted design, computer-controlled industrial processing, laboratory data acquisition and analysis, computer-assisted software engineering, computer languages, and programming tools.

- **"Niche Markets."** Some publishers have the expertise to sell to "niche markets," that is, markets for software that have been adapted for particular uses. There is indeed a process of evolution by which products, particularly database, transaction, and network products, become increasingly adapted to niche applications. One publisher might, for example, license and sell a generalized multiuser relational business database. A second publisher might market the same product in a modified version adapted for management of group medical practices. A third publisher might take this modified version and adapt it further for the niche market of Medicaid-funded medical practices for lower-income patients. A fourth publisher could adapt the product further to serve Medicaid-funded clinics operating under the special reporting requirements of California law. This process of software evolution and differentiation can profoundly extend the market penetration of the original product.

- **Geographic Focus.** Some publishers distribute only in the United States. Some have overseas affiliates. Some have expertise in adapting products for foreign markets.

The first step in this process of commercializing software is for the developer to clearly conceptualize all the ways that its programs and technologies can be used, and to find the publisher that fits that market focus. Publishers often help developers to identify and serve target markets and refine their products.

Negotiating a Software Publishing Agreement

Software publishing agreements are typically the result of a series of meetings, stretching over weeks or even months. The following is a survey of some of the major issues that will be covered. It may be helpful for you to skim the provisions of Form 9-2 before you read the following text. This will allow you to see how negotiating considerations translate into agreement provisions.

Development of the Software

If the software that is to be published is not yet written, there are a host of issues that flow from this fact. Specifications have to be agreed upon. There is normally a milestone schedule, tying payment to deliveries of portions or versions of the program; these payments are usually advances on royalties rather than payment for the program. Provisions for acceptance of deliverables need to be worked out. There needs to be provision for termination of the agreement upon failure to deliver. As noted above, we looked at many of these issues in Chapter 8 in the context of software development agreements.

Scope of the License

In a software publishing agreement, a fundamental consideration is *what kind* of license the publisher is to receive. Ownership of the program can be seen as a bundle of rights. The developer often will grant only a part of those rights to any one publisher—the rights can be sliced up in an endless variety of ways. Following are some of the issues for the parties to ponder in deciding the scope of the license:

Exclusive or Non-Exclusive License   Any license, broad or narrow, can be exclusive or non-exclusive. If a developer grants an exclusive license, it cannot grant the same rights to anyone else. And if it grants any non-exclusive rights to a market, it no longer has the option of granting anyone exclusive rights in that market.

Most publishing agreements feature a broad exclusive license, which puts a lot of the developer's eggs in one basket. If the publisher fails to market the program aggressively, the developer is stuck, at least for the duration of the license.

On the other hand, an exclusive license often is necessary to give the publisher the incentive it needs to exploit a product fully. In many cases, the publisher will insist on exclusive rights as the price of accepting the product.

Of course, if the publisher is going to modify the program and sell it in a narrow niche market, it will be more likely to take exclusive rights only for its target market. The developer should try not to give any broader exclusive rights than the publisher will use.

Duration of the License   A license, exclusive or non-exclusive, can be for any duration that the parties might agree upon, and it can be permanent. The publisher will typically be looking for a substantial license period, three years or more. In addition, the publisher will want the right to renew the license repeatedly for as long as sales of the product or royalties attain a specified minimum level.

Territory Covered by the License   Software can be licensed for a territory as broad or narrow as the parties might decide. In theory, you may set up any territory that you wish; the agreement can permit the publisher to sell the software worldwide or only in Chicago.

Practically speaking, the publisher's territory will usually be defined by national borders, or perhaps, as in the case of the European Economic Community, by a free-trade zone. The publisher will therefore normally get rights to sell in a country, in a group of countries, in a defined trade area, or worldwide. It is also possible to license the right to sell a version of the program in a particular language for a defined area. (For a further discussion of international licensing arrangements, see Chapter 16.)

From the developer's viewpoint, it makes the most sense to grant a license to the publisher only where (1) it has a distribution network, and (2) it has an intention of publishing of the product. For example, the developer should resist granting exclusive worldwide rights to a company that has no ability to distribute products outside the United States.

Field of Use, Platform, and Market Restricted License   It is possible to license a program for use only for a particular application, platform or market. Say, for example, that a company has a program for computer memory management that can speed up many kinds of programs. The company can license its program to a word processing company on a non-exclusive basis for use only in the licensee's word processing products. This leaves the owner of the program free to license the same program to many others for the same and different uses.

Sublicensing Restrictions   The publisher must be able to grant end-users a license to use the program, but it does not normally need the right to sublicense the product to other publishers. From a developer's viewpoint, the danger of granting sublicensing rights to a publisher is that the developer may not get a fair share of the sublicensing revenue.

Suppose, for example, that the developer grants an exclusive worldwide license for a program to its American-based publisher for a royalty of 10 percent of all net revenues including all sublicensing revenue. The publisher then sublicenses the program to a German publisher at a 10-percent royalty. This means that the American publisher would get 10 percent of the German publisher's sales revenue and the developer would get *10 percent of 10 percent*, that is, *one percent.* For every sale by the German distributor of $1,000 worth of product (at that the German distributor's wholesale prices), the developer's share is only $10. If the developer had licensed the German publisher itself, its share would have been $100.

The publisher may maintain that if the developer fails to use foreign distribution rights, the publisher should use them. The publisher should get *something* for finding a good foreign publisher, but certainly much less than it would for actually publishing in the foreign market.

In general, foreign distribution rights should be granted to a publisher only when there is a plan to use them and where there is a fair sharing of the benefits.

Source Code Delivery and the Right to Modify the Program   It is quite common that the developer will deliver the source code to the publisher. The publisher wants to be able to get bugs and errors fixed if the developer fails to do so, and the publisher also wants to be able to modify the code to add features or otherwise change the program.

Giving up the source code is always a danger for a developer. If the source code is delivered, the developer should insist that there be reasonable measures for its security. (See Chapter 2 on security measures to preserve trade secrets.)

Sometimes the publisher wants the right to require the developer to alter the program. The publisher may also demand the right to hire other programmers to do modification work if the developer refuses, and to deduct the cost of this work from royalties otherwise payable to the developer. This arrangement might make sense if there is a limit to how many dollars can be spent at the developer's expense and there are adequate security safeguards for the developer's trade secret source code.

A possible alternative to delivery of the source code to the publisher is to create a *source code escrow*. In this arrangement, a neutral third party holds the source code under a *source code escrow agreement*. The third party agrees to release the source code to the publisher if the developer fails to fix or modify the program as agreed. (A more detailed discussion of source code escrows can be found in Chapter 12.)

Derivative Products   Often the publisher will want the rights to derivative software (or non-software) products—for example, the rights to versions for other hardware platforms. Again this may be reasonable, if the publisher has a plan for *using* those rights and it the developer will be compensated fairly for their use. The developer may wish to negotiate a clause that provides that rights to other platforms reverts to the developer if not used within a specified amount of time.

Improvements and New Releases   Often the publisher will want the agreement to provide access to any new and improved versions of the program for free. And in fact it may be best for both parties to have the publisher selling the most competitive version of the product. However, as a practical matter, there are not going to be major new versions of the program until the parties decide what they will contain or how their creation will be financed. Realistically, the developer and publisher will have to negotiate specifications, work schedules, and new financial arrangements before a developer will undertake a major revision of the product. The effect of this type of provision may be primarily to insure that the new version does not go to the publisher's competitors.

Payment Terms

Of course, the payment terms will always be at the core of the negotiations. There are a variety of types of payment terms for software publishing agreements:

- **Percentage of Sales.** Most software publishing agreements grant a royalty of a percentage of publisher's "net sales." (We discuss later just *how* "net sales" may be calculated.) One could also have a "sliding scale" royalty that changes with the volume of sales. An example would be a royalty at 10 percent of net sales until 25,000 units have shipped and then 15 percent thereafter.

- **Payment per Unit.** It is favorable to the developer to have a fixed amount of royalties due per software unit shipped, or alternatively a minimum royalty per unit shipped. This option makes royalty calculation, or the minimum royalty calculation, very simple and straightforward.

- **Minimum Royalties.** Another provision that favors developers is to have a set total minimum royalty payable each quarter or each year.

- **Lump Sum Royalty.** It is possible—but not common—to have royalties paid only once and up-front. This single lump sum payment would make the agreement similar to the software development agreements that we discussed in Chapter 8. Some agreements provide the publisher with an *option* to get a permanent paid-up license, in essence to buy out its future royalty obligations, by making a large lump sum payment.

- **Advance Royalties.** As noted above, publishers often fund development of software. Normally, advance payments are deductible from product royalties. One matter for negotiation is how the advances will be recouped. For example, will the deductions reduce royalties to zero or only cut them, say to one-half of the normal rate, until the publisher recoups the advance payments? Normally the developer will get to keep the advances they have been paid during the development stage, no matter how poorly the product sells.

Royalty Calculation and Sales Reporting Issues

Determining a percentage royalty is simple, right? Wrong. It can be a slippery business, and there are several issues that need to be looked at with care by both developer and publisher. This is fine print that both sides should read very carefully.

The Definition of "Net Sales"   Every percentage royalty agreement states royalties as a percentage of "net sales." But there is no standard definition of what net sales are. Some of the issues are:

- **Bundling and Allocation.** Often a publisher will sell several pieces of software in one package or for a combined price, a practice known as "bundling." The publisher will then allocate the revenue among the products in the bundle. The publisher may be tempted to allocate less of the price to the product with the highest royalty. A publisher that also sells hardware could offer a "bundle" of hardware and software priced so that the hardware price tag is high and the software quite low. Where bundling is an issue, the parties should reach an understanding as to how the price allocation will be done. One common but not fully tamper-proof rule is to allocate the revenue by the ratio of the list prices of the goods in the bundle. It is possible to specify a minimum dollar value to be used for such an allocation.

- **Deduction for Credits.** Deducting promotional costs, such as advertising credits or promotional incentives paid to distributors and dealers, may also be reasonable. The developer should be sure to have an understanding as to what the policy is for such credits and how the costs will be allocated between the developer's products and the rest of the publisher's product line. It may be advisable for a developer to negotiate a percentage "cap" or limit for such deductions. The goal should be to keep the deductions reasonable and the calculation of the final figure reasonably simple.

- **Deduction for Routine Returns.** The publisher can make a legitimate case for deducting dealer returns of the product made in accordance with its standard return policy. Some types of software products, notably game software, are plagued by high return rates. For other products, it is much less of an issue. Sometimes new versions of the software will trigger returns of the old one. Sometimes the publisher will encourage distributors and dealers to "swap out" existing slow-selling inventory for new "hot" products; this too can lead to high returns. The developer may want to try to negotiate a "cap" on deductions due to return rights granted to distributors and dealers.

- **Deduction for Returns Due to Defects.** Sometimes a software product will be returned because of defects. Usually minor bugs and errors can be cured by sending registered users a replacement diskette, at a relatively minor cost to the publisher. However, if the defect impairs the usefulness of the program significantly, a large number of returns can result. Some reduction of net sales due to returns of defective software may be legitimate—but what if the defect that caused the returns was due to a modification that the *publisher* made?

- **Deduction for Bad Credit Losses.** Most software publishing agreements are based on revenues, not on shipments. This means that if the publisher ships large quantities but the customers pay very slowly, fail to pay, or go bankrupt, revenue goes down and the developer loses out as well. Bad debt reserves can have a major negative impact on net sales of a product. It can be argued that most of the risk of bad credit should be on the publisher, who picks the customers. The developer may want to negotiate a "cap" on these deductions, as well. Or the developer can seek a royalty deal based on the volume of products shipped rather than net sales. Of course, if the publisher has high enough bad-debt losses, the developer may face a problem of a different kind, the possible insolvency of the publisher.

- **Deduction of Operating Costs; Royalties Based on Profits.** Should costs associated with the product, such as production, advertising, and salaries for salespeople, be deducted? Generally speaking, it is *unreasonable* to suggest that operating costs should be deducted. The similar suggestion that royalties be based on product *profits* is also unreasonable. Deducting costs of operation is likely to cut drastically into the royalty payments to the developer. Costs are easy to inflate and notoriously difficult to allocate among products. Any cost-based or profit-based calculation will generate complex accounting that is very difficult and expensive to check out.

Setting Royalties   How do a developer and publisher set a royalty percentage or sliding scale? Where do the numbers come from? Often there are prevailing rates for similar programs. Royalties in the 10- to 20-percent range are common for many types of products. But in the final analysis it depends on the value of the program, the needs of the parties, and how badly they want to make a deal.

Assuming that the developer had a sufficiently hot product or enough leverage that it could get a "minimum per product shipped" royalty, how could such an royalty amount be set? The following is a rough example that illustrates the concept and approach.

Suppose that a program is to be published of a type normally listing for $200. Distributors might pay roughly half of list or about $100. Allowances and returns might reduce average revenue to the publisher to $90.00 per unit sold. If a 20-percent royalty is being discussed, that would mean $18.00 revenue to the developer on average from each product sold. On those numbers, a publisher might agree to pay $10.00 to $14.00 as a minimum per shipment royalty for the product.

When Payments are Calculated and Due   Normally a software publishing agreement calls for royalties to be calculated each quarter and paid to the developer within 30 days after the end of the quarter. This means, of course, that the publisher gets the use of the funds due to the developer for a considerable time—a range of 30 to 120 days before payment—or, on the average, 75 days each quarter. This system is, in effect, an interest-free loan of these funds to the publisher. More frequent payments are possible, although publishers consider more frequent payments administratively cumbersome. Less frequent payments are unreasonable and raise the risk that they will never be paid.

Auditing: Checking Up On the Publisher   Nearly all software publishing agreements contain a provision for the developer to inspect and audit the publisher's books to verify royalty calculations. Invariably the audit is at the developer's own expense and usually the audit must be done by a certified public accountant. The more complex the formula and numerous the deductions, the more likely that errors in calculating the royalty will be made.

If you are a developer and if the amount of sales under an agreement is significant, it may make sense, from time to time, to conduct an audit. You need an auditor who is smart, knows something about software, and is efficient. Unless you get a special price break, you will not want someone from an expensive accounting firm. If you have the right auditor, he or she will often discover enough to pay for the audit. Usually the problems uncovered are sloppy practices or departures from agreed-upon procedures. Outright cheating is not common, but it does happen (and when it does happen, alas, the accountant may not always ferret it out).

The Publisher's Obligation to Promote a Program and Sell It

After the developer delivers the program, the publisher has to try to promote and market it. The developer wants the publisher to make a vigorous sales and promotion effort: advertisements, direct mail, magazine reviews, assignment of marketing personnel, telemarketing, sales to dealers and distributors, etc. The developer's nightmare is that the publisher will favor other products and neglect the program that the developer has supplied. Usually, the publisher will make a reasonable effort to sell the program. After all, the publisher only makes money if it makes sales. And the publisher has a strong incentive to recoup its up-front costs and investment in the program. However, it is certainly true that many developers have been disappointed at the effort put into marketing their software products.

Many agreements proposed by publishers state no affirmative marketing obligation at all. Some state blandly that the publisher may sell the product. Some agreements simply set a royalty rate and say nothing about an obligation of the publisher to do anything. A developer can reasonably expect the publisher to undertake some kind of written commitment to action to promote the product.

Best Efforts Obligation A common, but not very rigorous, standard is for the contract to state that the publisher will use its best efforts to sell. In reality this means only that the publisher must do something significant—some sales effort that is within the realm of reason. But there are no specific requirements as to what must be done. While a developer would prefer a detailed marketing plan, often this best efforts language is the most a developer can get, and it is better than no commitment at all.

Promotional Spending Requirements If the publisher has promised a definite level of promotional effort, that commitment should be in the agreement. Sometimes a publisher will make a commitment to a defined level for spending on advertisements in national magazines, for the hiring of a sales manager for the program, and for other promotional activities. Such a provision will allow the developer to terminate the agreement if spending falls materially short of the agreed-upon level.

Option to Terminate If Sales Goals Are Not Met From a developer's viewpoint, one common safeguard is an option to terminate the license if a specified level of sales is not made by a particular point in time. The measuring date is often at the second anniversary of the agreement. This provision may act as an incentive for the publisher to expend a significant level of effort to market the program.

Enforcement of Proprietary Rights in the Program

When both the publisher and the developer share an interest in the program, they both have a vested interest in protecting the intellectual property that the program represents. What happens, then, if a third party infringes the program's copyright? Does the publisher have to sue the infringer or does the developer bear this litigation burden? Who pays for the legal cost? Who decides if the litigation is worth bringing? There are various possible provisions. Often the publisher wants the *option* of deciding whether to sue. Commonly, the agreement will provide that if the publisher declines to bring the lawsuit, the developer can bring it.

Warranty and Indemnification Issues

The considerations on warranty and indemnification issues are very much the same as those discussed in Chapter 8 (which I suggest you review). The developer should urge that implied warranties under the UCC and consequential damages be disclaimed. With regard to potential infringement claims, a developer should seek to warrant only that it *knows* of no infringement; it should not warrant that none exists. The developer should also seek to avoid broad infringement indemnification language.

It is reasonable that the developer should continue to have an ongoing obligation to fix bugs and errors in the program—and in fact it is in the developer's interest to do so, because errors that impair the program are likely to cripple sales.

Publishers may seek to include a clause in the agreement that states that if there are bugs or defects in the code, the costs of replacing defective disks will be *deducted* from net sales or from royalty payments. Developers may resist such a clause, arguing that the publisher has accepted the product after inspection and therefore should assume the risk of such returns. If such a clause is included, the developer may want to negotiate a limit or cap on such deductions and may wish to bargain for a provision that there will be no other charges or deductions for alleged defects in the program.

Termination Issues

A topic that must be addressed is termination of the software publishing agreement. Here are some issues that must be discussed and resolved:

What Triggers Termination?   Both sides in a software publishing agreement have an interest in having an exit from the relationship if things go wrong. Usually the agreement will have a term of years, and the publisher will normally have renewal options based upon the publisher's maintaining a designated level of yearly sales or royalties paid.

In many contracts, either party can terminate when the other side has committed a material breach that is not cured after notice of the breach. Some publishers' standard form contracts make this a one-way street: They provide that, after publication, the developer cannot terminate no matter what breach of contract is committed by the publisher. It is better and fairer if termination rights are given to each side if the other side commits a material breach of the agreement.

What Obligations and Rights Survive?   Software publishing agreements usually contain provisions allowing end users to continue to use the program indefinitely, even after the publishing agreement has been terminated. There are also usually terms allowing the publisher to sell off existing inventory, subject to paying normal royalties. There is often a clause requiring each side to keep the other's confidential information secret.

Other Provisions of the Agreement

As in the software development agreements discussed in Chapter 8, there are additional clauses of a software development agreement that should be considered, including a possible arbitration clause, a clause on how notice is given when required under the agreement, the choice of what state's law will govern, etc. These matters are covered in Form 9-2.

CHAPTER 10

Distribution Arrangements and Dealer Agreements

Over the past 20 years, a major industry consisting of thousands of large and small businesses across the United States has evolved to profit from the software distribution process. There is a wide variety of companies in this diverse system.

This chapter will provide you with an overview of the types of arrangements used for software distribution. You will also learn in detail about one of the most important marketing vehicles for many small and medium-size software companies: software dealerships, and about the negotiation of software dealer agreements.

Software Distribution Channels

The following is an outline of the main ways in which software is distributed in the United States. (In this chapter, I will use the term "supplier" to refer to the software publisher or manufacturer that creates the software product at the start of the distribution chain.)

Many software suppliers use a variety of channels of distribution for their products. A key part of software marketing is determining what mix of distribution systems to use and how to manage them all.

Direct Sales Operations

In direct sales distribution, the supplier's employees deal directly with end-users. Direct sales (of course, it is really *licensing* transactions we are discussing) include the following:

Customer Contact Sales   Many software products can be sold only through direct contact with customers. The software products that are suitable for this type of distribution are relatively complex and costly—products that require substantial customization, installation, and training. These products are often sold together with computer hardware. To make these sales, the supplier hires a sales force, often on salary or salary plus commission. To obtain nationwide distribution, the supplier must establish a national network of branch locations.

Telemarketing   In telemarketing, employees of the supplier market by telephone calls to preselected prospects and to existing customers. Sometimes calls are made "cold" to targeted names. (There are list vendors that sell telephone and address lists of prospects.) More often calls are to companies that have indicated some interest in the software products by answering advertisements or by requesting information at trade shows.

Software products sold through this form of distribution are often niche market products that command a higher price than mass-market software, but that nonetheless are sufficiently easy for end-users to install and use.

Niche markets served by telemarketing are often defined by professions or groups that have specialized software needs. Examples are software for architects, accountants, attorneys, medical practices, banks, and retail stores. Also included would be software for special functions, such as CAD systems, manufacturing control, high-resolution graphics, or laboratory data acquisition and analysis, etc.

Direct Mail   In a direct mail operation, the supplier markets software—often mass-market products—by mailings of material to a selected list of names. Mailing lists can be purchased, or mailing can be done to registered users of the supplier's products. New versions or upgrades of mass-market software are often sold by direct mail. Orders are taken by mail or phone. Delivery is usually by an express service or the postal service. A supplier may have its own direct mail operation, or it may contract with a company that specializes in providing direct mail selling services.

For small companies with relatively inexpensive software products and low cash flow, direct mail is often the only available form of distribution. Until a product has achieved market acceptance, distributors will often be reluctant to buy. Direct mail is a way of building demand for a newly introduced product by contacting end-users directly. Success in direct mail requires the right product, the right mailing list, and careful control of costs.

Distributors

Distributors are software wholesalers. The largest software distributors in the United States are Ingram Micro Inc. and Merisel Inc. (Both companies handle foreign sales as well.) These two companies sell huge volumes of software and dominate much of the distribution of mass market software (and hardware) to retail stores, small retail chains, and to many dealers. There are many other smaller distributors, many of which specialize in niche markets.

Dealers and Sales Representatives

Dealers and sales representatives (or "sales reps") are independent businesses that provide marketing for products to end-users. Most dealers and sales reps are small businesses that have at most a handful of locations and sell to customers located in their area. Suppliers that use dealers have to establish a far-flung dealer network to obtain broad distribution.

A dealer is normally a *reseller*—that is, a company that "buys" software products from a supplier or distributor and then "resells" the software. (As we discussed in Chapter 1, these transactions are actually licensing, rather than sales, of software.) A dealer will most often arrange delivery and provide installation and end-user support if required. A dealer gets its revenue from the difference between the wholesale price it pays and what it gets from the end-user. In addition, the dealer may gain revenue from selling services to the end-user, such as technical advice, troubleshooting, and training.

The essence of dealer selling is niche marketing. A typical price for applications software sold by a dealer might be anywhere from $2,000 to $50,000 or more. Software that commands prices in this range will be for specialized market segments.

A sales representative's role is much more limited than a dealer's. The sales representative is fundamentally an order taker. The sales representative's mission is accomplished by getting suitable order and a downpayment from an end-user. The supplier—not the sales representative—ships the product and arranges for installation and support. Sales representatives normally work on commission.

From a lawyer's perspective, the key difference between a dealer and a sales representative is that a supplier can legally control the price that a sales representative offers to customers. However, as is explained in the section on federal and state antitrust law (later in this chapter), suppliers are forbidden from setting resale prices for dealers.

Sometimes, the legal distinction between dealers and sales representatives is not so simple or clear. Some dealers, for example, work under arrangements in which they market software products, but do not resell them. Instead the dealer gets an order and the software is then shipped and licensed directly from the supplier to the end-user. Sometimes, software updates and support are provided directly by the supplier. In this arrangement, the software products are not resold (or relicensed) at all. Nonetheless, if the local company that made the sale also provides other services to the end-user, such as installing or customizing the product, or integrating it with hardware or other software, it is customary to call the company the "dealer" or "reseller." Because of the risks and uncertainties involved, both the supplier and the dealer should consult an attorney about the use of any scheme for setting mandatory resale prices.

VARs

"VAR" stands for *value-added reseller*—a term that could probably be applied to the majority of software dealers. A VAR usually adds value to software products by customizing the software, providing consultation, supplying training, etc.

VARs often sell software and hardware together as a complete or turnkey system. An example would be a customized retail transaction processing system. The delivery might include operating system, network, and database software; custom programming of the database product; installation; user training and maintenance; as well as computer and network hardware. Of course, VARs also sell, customize, and install systems designed to run on the end-user's existing computer hardware.

OEMs

The term "OEM" stands for *original equipment manufacturer*, but this is a misnomer. What an OEM arrangement means in business is private labeling—the OEM puts its own label on another company's software product or markets a system under its own name that includes the software product. OEMs obtain products directly from the supplier or from distributors.

In some cases, the OEM may do nothing to the supplier's software other than change the name. In other cases, the OEM may make substantial additions or alterations to the supplier's software. Most often the OEM is also responsible for providing support and technical advice to end-users. An OEM can also supply the end-user with customization or other valuable services.

System Integrators

A system integrator is a company that assembles and integrates a variety of hardware, software, and telecommunication components to create complex computer systems. Most system integrators work on large contracts for large corporations, government agencies, or the military. System integrators are typically not tied to any one source or supplier, but obtain products from many hardware and software suppliers.

Mass-Market Sellers

Mass-market sellers are the large and small companies that sell mass-market software products, from Microsoft, Lotus, Borland and the like, to businesses, consumers, and other end-users.

Retailers   Retailers are the many shops and small chains that sell mass-market software products. These companies normally obtain products from distributors, and therefore must pay higher prices for software than large chains that get software directly from suppliers. In recent years, retailers have had difficulty competing with discount retailers who often can charge lower prices.

Discount Retailers   Discount retailers are large-scale sellers of mass-market software who get software directly from suppliers. They include discount stores such as Egghead or CompUSA and large telephone order operations such as PC Connection. Discount retailers also use catalogs sent by mail to build sales.

Shareware

An low-cost alternative for distributing microcomputer software is "shareware" distribution—distribution mainly through computer bulletin boards or services such as America Online, GEnie, and CompuServe. A few companies create shareware disks and sell them by catalogs mailed to users.

The pattern of shareware distribution has evolved over the years. In the early 1980s, shareware products were simply uploaded to bulletin boards. As a practical matter, anyone who used the program had only a moral obligation to pay for it. In fact, a small percentage of users paid anything to shareware authors. Because morality proved a weak incentive for payment, shareware distribution has changed. Now the typical shareware version uploaded to a bulletin board is not fully featured. Rather it is usually a crippled or incomplete version. The uploaded version invites the end-user to pay the supplier for the "real" working version of the software. What has not changed is the ease of getting into the shareware business. The author of a new program simply uploads his or her new software product—or a version of the product—to a bulletin board.

All shareware authors dream that their software product will go "big time." They dream that their creation will be grabbed up by a publisher or that it will generate money to fund an entry into the mass market. Shareware distribution may in fact expose the software to thousands of potential buyers. However, the hard fact is that shareware products rarely generate large financial rewards for authors.

Doing Your Own Distribution

If your company is planning to write or acquire rights to new software, a threshold question is whether *you* wish to distribute it using any of the alternatives, rather than arranging for a publisher to take care of distribution.

In the late 1970s and even in the early 1980s, in the glory days of the Apple II and the TRS-80, the creation and distribution of software was almost a folk industry. Successful products were written at home or in university computer labs, had under 100K of code, and were distributed in clear plastic bags with photocopied documentation. Some of those products grew into successful businesses. But those heady days are now long gone.

Today, to write and successfully introduce a software product takes sophistication and lots of money. The level of skill, sophistication, and funding required for packaging, promotion, advertising, and sales is dramatically higher. One software marketing consultant that I know advises that to start a dealer network (with a good product in hand) can take $200,000 to $500,000, and to launch a mass-market product costs well over $1,000,000. The costs and risks (and the potential rewards) of software distribution are high. Companies should choose to distribute rather than publish only when they have the financial and human resources to succeed in this endeavor.

The need to be aware of the costs and sophistication required by software marketing applies with even greater force to distribution outside the United States. Many companies that have successfully distributed their own software products in the United States have nonetheless turned to local distributors for sales in Europe, Japan and other countries. (For further discussion of foreign distribution, see Chapter 16.)

Contracts for Software Distribution

Each of the distribution arrangements that we have discussed has its associated appropriate contract documentation. A supplier's direct dealings with an end-user, for example, will normally require an end-user agreement (discussed in Chapter 12) or a shrink-wrap license (discussed Chapter 11). Direct mail selling and shareware distribution also feature the use of a shrink-wrap license.

Even simpler documentation may apply for a supplier's sales of mass-market software to a large distributor or to a discount retailer. In these cases, the legal relationship may be documented by little more than a series of purchase orders, sales confirmations, and invoices. When a small supplier deals with a retailing giant, the detailed conditions of sale may often be decided for the buyer in the terms stated in a preprinted purchase order form.

When a supplier establishes a relationship with a dealer, however, a written software dealer agreement is most often negotiated by the parties. In negotiation of these agreements, there is often room for give and take. There are thousands of companies in this country that sell software though dealers and there are tens of thousands of dealers. Many of the readers of this book no doubt participate in some way in distribution through a dealership system. For this reason, this chapter examines dealer agreements in greater depth.

Tools for Use with This Chapter

Software dealer agreements come in a great many forms. All of them grant a dealer a license to market a software product—but beyond that, there are an endless number of permutations and combinations of provisions and terms.

This chapter covers the main issues that often arise in the negotiation of a software dealer agreement. Included in Appendix C are two forms that cover these and some additional issues. Form 10-1 (on diskette as DEAL-CHK.W51) is a software dealer agreement checklist, for use as a negotiation guide. Form 10-2 (on diskette as DEAL-AGR.W51) is an annotated software dealer agreement. Form 10-2 presents sample language for an agreement, including some alternatives and options. The commentary in Form 10-2 provides an explanation for a number of the provisions. Of course, these forms cannot cover every possible variation—your deal may well require provisions and options that are not covered.

Both sides need legal assistance before one of these agreements is signed. These agreements are complex, they may have consequences that a non-lawyer may miss, and they are designed to last a long time. The enclosed forms can be used to structure and advance the negotiations. However, each party should arrange for a review by their legal counsel before the issues for negotiation are closed.

Software Dealer Agreements

A software dealer agreement is a contract that governs the relationship between a software supplier and a dealer. We will examine issues that arise when parties negotiate or renegotiate such an agreement. We will also look at franchise laws and antitrust laws that may affect supplier-dealer relationships. Many of the issues that we will discuss apply as well to the agreement between a supplier and a sales representative, or to an agreement between a supplier and a small or medium-size distributor.

Suppliers' and Sellers' Viewpoints

From the supplier's viewpoint, the goal of a software dealer agreement is to build distribution without incurring huge costs. Recruiting and supporting a dealership network is not cheap—but it costs the supplier far less than opening its own offices and hiring staff in cities throughout the country.

Software sellers have their own goals in becoming dealers. They want a "cutting edge" product in a market segment where margins are high and demand is growing. And they want a profitable and stable long term relationship with an innovative supplier who will keep the software product line up-to-date.

The dealer is the proverbial "middle-man," and that position can involve risk and anxiety. To fix defective products, for example, the dealer is dependent on the supplier for support. Keeping the dealership usually depends on making a specified number of product purchases from the supplier, and discounts from the supplier also often depend on purchase volume. On one hand, this system puts constant pressure on the dealer to make sales. On the other hand, suppliers need their dealers and cannot themselves succeed unless the dealers do well.

The Negotiation Dynamic for Software Dealer Agreements

A critical factor in establishing the terms of a dealer agreement is usually the relative leverage of the parties. If a software supplier has a strong product with an established reputation and proven customer demand, the prospective dealer may have little leverage in contract negotiations.

On the other hand, it may be hard for some suppliers to get good software dealers. This is particularly true for suppliers promoting new software or novel technology. To get a qualified and proven dealer to adopt a new product line, the supplier may have to make important concessions on price and other terms.

The Scope of the License

Every software dealer agreement must specify the scope of the license and the products that the dealer will distribute. The agreement will normally permit the dealer to market the licensed products to end-users and to display the supplier's trademark on the premises and in promotional material. The dealer will usually be forbidden to license the software to anyone other than a bona fide end-user or to modify the software code.

The products included in a software dealer agreement may be all the products that the supplier markets, or only designated products or lines of products. Often future software products are included as well. The agreement may be limited to products designed for a particular user type or for a specified hardware and software platform. The products that are covered are normally listed in a schedule attached to the agreement.

There is often a provision that new releases of the licensed software products will come under the agreement. A prospective dealer may want a provision that compatibility of data and file structure with existing versions of the software will be maintained in future versions and that the supplier will continue to supply technical assistance and bug fixes for superceded versions of the software products for a specified time.

Exclusive Dealer Territories

On occasion, dealers are granted exclusive territories, where they alone have the right to market the licensed software products. The defined geographic territory may be a country, a specified region, a state, part of a state, or any other area the parties designate. The theory is that exclusivity is an incentive for the dealer to commit itself to the product, secure in the knowledge that no rival dealers in the territory will try to woo its customers away. Dealers are understandably eager for exclusives.

Practical Difficulties   Many suppliers resist granting exclusive territories, in part because exclusive rights give dealers too much leverage, and in part because exclusive territories give rise to practical problems.

One type of problem with exclusive territory arises because software sales and installations span geographic borders.

Example: Branch-Net Systems, Inc. makes a software product that gathers retail sales data from transaction processing systems and analyzes the data by customer profile and area. Branch-Net grants each of its dealers an exclusive territory: the state where the dealer is located. The Colorado dealer installs Branch-Net software at the Denver office of National Corp., a large conglomerate with several regional operations. National Corp. likes the product so much that it asks the Denver dealer to install a similar system at its New York City headquarters. To allow the system to gather the requisite nationwide data, the

Denver dealer installs Branch-Net software at National Corp.'s offices in New York, Denver, Los Angeles, and Dallas. As a result of the Denver dealer's work, the Branch-Net dealers in New York, California, and Texas complain to Branch-Net about the "invasion" of their respective territories, demand compensation, and threaten to switch to the product line of a competitor that will provide protection against such invasions.

Branch-Net probably could have avoided these "turf" issues altogether if the dealerships had been non-exclusive. Having said this, it is fair to point out that these issues are not insuperable. Any system of exclusive dealerships needs to have arrangements for cooperation on deals that span territories or deals that are referred from one dealer to another.

Non-Exclusive Dealer Territories

Most commonly, software dealer agreements grant a non-exclusive territory. This arrangement is much more flexible from a supplier's viewpoint. Typically, in a non-exclusive agreement, there is still a grant of rights for a territory, but it is usually very broad, such as the entire United States. As a legal matter, any dealer can seek any sale within the territory.

There are alternatives within the framework of a non-exclusive dealership agreement that allow the dealer considerable incentive to develop sales in a given market area. For example, a supplier may have a policy of establishing one dealer per metropolitan area and allowing each dealership to make whatever sales it can. Sometimes such a policy will be the subject of negotiations and may be written into the terms of a dealer agreement. Often, the dealer must take the risk that the supplier's policy will change.

Multiple Marketing Channels

As noted earlier, many suppliers use a mixture of direct marketing and dealers. Sometimes suppliers will reserve the right to market directly to *national accounts*, the large businesses whose operations spans numerous territories or to other customers. Such mixed systems can generate tension in dealer networks. Problems may arise, for example, when the supplier's price cutting or aggressive selling tactics begin to harm dealer sales. This type of friction between suppliers and their dealers and distributors is known as "channel conflict." A modest amount of channel conflict is not necessarily bad. Managing a company's various marketing channels so that all of them remain productive is an important part of the marketing process.

As a negotiating matter, prospective dealers should ask that the software dealer agreement make it clear whether the dealer will or will not be competing against its own supplier for end-user sales.

Pricing

Every software dealer agreement has a provision for the prices that the dealer pays for software products. There are a variety of ways that pricing can be specified in the agreement. The following are some of the choices and issues.

Specified Prices   One option for pricing is to simply have the Software Dealer Agreement specify the software prices for the term of the agreement—normally in an addendum to the contract.

While this is a straightforward way to set prices, there are potential problems with this arrangement. It allows very little flexibility; the prices set may turn out to be too high if the competition begins price cutting, or they may turn out to be too low to permit the supplier a fair return. It is difficult or impossible to set fixed prices for a period of years.

Percentage of List   More commonly, the prices that the dealer pays are set by the supplier from time to time at its discretion. Often the supplier will have a wholesale price list or grant the dealer an agreed-upon discount off "list price," which the supplier can change from time to time. In this system, only competition in the marketplace places a lid on price increases. Often the discount from list price increases if the dealer achieves specified levels of products ordered and paid for.

Under some dealer agreements, the supplier grants a discount based on the projected volume of dealer orders, with a provision that removes the discount retroactively (and therefore requires the dealer to pay additional amounts for the software products) if the required volume levels are not met.

Price Protection   When the supplier has the power to raise prices, the dealer agreement may include a "price protection" provision, that is, a promise that price increases during any year will be limited to a specified percentage. In some cases, minimum and maximum wholesale prices may be set in the agreement.

Price Discrimination   As is discussed below, in the discussion of antitrust law, it may be illegal to give some dealers better prices than others.

Ordering, Delivery, and Payment

The terms of the software dealer agreement specify a process for ordering and delivery. These provisions may include dealer sales forecasts so that the supplier can plan its production. Often there is a provision that the supplier can allocate production or cut back orders if demand for the software products outstrips the available supply.

Duplication of Product   In some cases, the supplier does not actually ship the product to the dealer. Rather, it allows the dealer to duplicate the product and ship copies to customers. Under this system, the supplier provides the dealer with a software "master diskette," which contains the object code of the program, and camera-ready documentation. It is then the dealer's job to reproduce both diskettes and documentation. When this system is used, the dealer agreement usually provides that the payment obligation to the supplier is triggered whenever the software is shipped to a customer. Under this system, the dealer agreement will have clauses granting the supplier the right to audit the dealer's books to make sure that the payment obligation is being observed.

When Payment is Due   Normally when a supplier is shipping software to a dealer, the supplier issues an invoice upon shipment. Payment is then due as specified, normally in 30 days, but a longer period can be negotiated. When payment is due and the amount of credit extended to the dealer may be crucial in providing cash flow to the dealer. It is common for dealer agreements to allow the supplier to restrict dealer credit if the payment history or the financial condition of the dealer make such steps appropriate. Other types of payment arrangements are possible, but less common. For example, payment to the supplier could be due when the software is delivered to the customer, or when the customer accepts the software and pays for it.

Minimum Product Orders

It is common for a software dealer agreement to have provisions that permit the supplier to terminate the agreement if the dealer fails to achieve specified yearly sales goals. For example, the agreement may require the dealer to make a specified minimum level of payments for software products to the supplier every year, a provision sometimes called a "purchase commitment schedule." The requirement could be a minimum number of new customers each year, or the agreement might provide that the dealer submit a sales goal each year and commit to fulfilling it. In addition, there may be a specified minimum initial order at the time the dealership agreement is signed.

Where exclusive territories are granted, the dealer agreement commonly includes a quota of product orders as a condition for continued exclusivity.

Dividing the "Follow-on" Revenue Flow

The terms of the software dealer agreement set the rules for dividing up the "follow-on" revenue—revenue that comes from each end-user during the months and years that follow the original software licensing transaction.

The license for sophisticated business, engineering or scientific software to an end-user typically includes provisions for software support. The end-user pays a monthly, yearly, or other periodic fee and receives technical advice, bug fixes, and enhancements for the program. (End-user agreements governing these follow-on services are reviewed in Chapter 12.) One matter for negotiation is whether the end-user gets support only from the dealer, or directly from the supplier, or from both? Who gets the revenue from software support?

Suppliers often want to capture a significant part of the revenue from end-user software support. Why? First, because profits from this support are often high. Second, because software can often be delivered by modem or mail, and most technical support is by telephone. In fact, most dealers cannot provide software support without the aid of the supplier, because most often the dealer does not have the source code for the software products. Therefore, even if the dealer provides support to the end-user, providing service and support to customers must be a cooperative effort between the dealer and the supplier. For this reason, support is a matter that is often the subject of negotiates between supplier and dealer.

There are additional sources of follow-on revenue. One example is the licensing of major revisions of the software product. The supplier will often draw a distinction between a minor update (provided under the software support provisions of the end-user agreement) and a major revision that will be provided to the end-user for a significant additional licensing fee. In addition, the end-user may decide to license additional software to add to its existing system. An example would be adding new modules to an accounting program, such as modules for payroll and tax returns. The supplier may want to set prices so that the dealer gets a high margin for licensing to *new customers*, and a lower margin for licensing to *existing customers*. Again, the division of these types of follow-on revenue can be the subject of negotiation.

Many dealer agreements impose a requirement that the dealer report information about end-users. Some agreements provide that the supplier must be given copies of all agreements between the dealer and end-users. Some require the dealer periodically to supply an updated list of licensed users, including their address, phone numbers, contact persons, and the products used. This provision helps the supplier track the identity of all end-users, and allows the supplier to contact them directly if necessary.

Dealer Marketing Obligations

It is quite common for software dealer agreements to require that the dealer undertake certain marketing obligations. Examples are:

- The dealer must maintain a specified level of inventory.

- The dealer must provide an office location where the software products will be demonstrated.

- The dealer must provide a specified level of sales staff and technical staff.

- The dealer must provide customization, installation, and/or training for end-users.

- The dealer must maintain books and records concerning its revenues and make these materials available (on request) for audit by the supplier.

- The dealer must not make sales to other dealers—a practice known as "gray market" selling.

- The dealer must submit a marketing plan every year or on some other periodic basis.

It is also common to require a dealer to use its best efforts to promote the product. In addition, dealers often agree not to market products that serve the same market or function during the term of the agreement and for a specified amount of time after termination of the agreement.

Supplier Support Commitments

Software dealer agreements may also impose obligations upon the supplier to use best efforts or reasonable efforts to provide support for the dealers, including requirements like the following:

- The supplier will supply reasonable quantities of sales literature for its software product line.

- The supplier will provide technical advice and support on the use of the software and on coping with technical problems.

- The supplier will provide technical assistance to aid the dealer in responding to requests for proposals received from prospective customers.

Trademark Issues

A software dealer agreement will usually include a license for the dealer to use the supplier's trademark on signs and in advertising and promotional pieces. The dealer will be permitted to identify itself as an authorized dealer. Other uses of the trademark normally will not be permitted.

Under some OEM arrangements, an OEM may put its private label on the software, and the dealer agreement with an OEM will include a provision that permits this.

Product Warranties and Remedies

Warranty Disclaimers   A software dealer agreement will normally have a section in which the supplier disclaims product warranties and limits damage claims. (The legal background for this type of provision under the Uniform Commercial Code (UCC) is discussed in Chapter 8.) To summarize briefly, the need to *disclaim* warranties and *limit* liability comes from provisions of the UCC which impose broad product warranty and damage obligations on the supplier that take effect *unless otherwise agreed*. Therefore broad product warranties are disclaimed. It is also normal for the supplier's liability for defects in any copy of the software to be limited to replacing the defective software or, at the supplier's option, refunding the price of the defective software. Both the warranty disclaimer and the limitation of damages should be in conspicuous large type, as shown in Form 10-2 in Appendix C.

Reasonable Obligation to Fix Errors   In lieu of a broad warranty, the supplier normally assumes an on-going obligation to use its reasonable efforts to fix errors and bugs in the software for a certain period after delivery. This means that it promises attempt to supply bug fixes or patches to the software either to the end-users or to the dealers as soon as possible after a problem is reported. Of course, fixing the software is essential to maintaining end-user loyalty. The dealer will therefore have an incentive to report bugs, errors, and problems quickly, and the supplier will have an incentive to fix them as soon as possible.

Terms of License to End-Users

The software dealer agreement will determine the mechanics of the dealing between suppliers and dealers, for example, whether the dealer resells software or merely acts as an order taker. The agreement will often specify license terms that must be used in the dealer's agreements with end-users, know as "flow-down provisions." Many dealer agreements require that the dealer use an end-user agreement form specified by the supplier. These flow-down provisions and required end-user agreement forms always contain damage limitation language that parallels that in the dealer agreement. The purpose of these provisions is to ensure that the dealer takes steps that will minimize the risk, both to dealer and supplier, of potential liability for software defects or copyright or trade secret infringement problems. There may be other flow-down provisions as well. For example, if the supplier finds out that its software infringes a third-party patent and if the supplier cannot get a patent licence or design around the problem, the supplier may need to terminate all end-user licenses. Or, if an end-user violates the intellectual property rights of the supplier, the supplier may wish to sue the end-user directly.

Non-Infringement Warranties and Indemnification

Software dealer agreements also have clauses that deal with the rather rare contingency of a copyright or patent infringement suit filed against the dealer. Normally the supplier will be responsible for infringement claims based on its source or object code. Any infringement claim due to code or functions added by the dealer will be the dealer's responsibility.

Term and Termination

The term of these agreements is commonly two or three years, although they could be longer or shorter if the parties so desire. Normally there are provisions that the agreement will be automatically renewed for another additional term unless one or the other party gives notice of non-renewal a specified number of days before the expiration.

Dealer agreements usually provide that they may be terminated for material breaches of the agreement. They also normally provide that even if the agreement is terminated, the end-user licenses for the product stay in place, and that the dealer must cooperate in turning the customers over the to supplier or a new dealer appointed by the supplier. The goal is to be sure that end-users are not inconvenienced by any dealership termination.

The Risk that the Supplier Will "Go Direct"

A software dealer's nightmare is that the supplier will "go direct"—that is, that the supplier will replace its dealer operations with a direct sales force. Because dealers almost always have contracts for a fixed term, they are usually vulnerable to this type of changes in a supplier's distribution strategy.

As a practical matter, it is not common that software distributors eliminate their dealers, in part because customer loyalty may be to the dealer as much as to the supplier, and in part because the cost of going direct is high. But the risk of such a change remains—and may be increased as software prices fall and supplier margins fall with them. There is also a risk that the supplier will open new channels of distribution to the same market. For example, the supplier may begin direct marketing or direct mail solicitation in the area where the dealer operates. Aside from the protection afforded by franchising statutes in some states (discussed on the next page), dealers have little or no legal protection from a supplier's decision to make these changes. In the final analysis, the dealer's protection against change depends on the value that it brings to the supplier, on the dealer's personal relationship with the supplier's officers and staff, and on the expense and risk to the supplier of change.

Federal and State Franchise Laws

One important aspect of the law that may affect software dealerships is federal and state franchise law. This body of law is important because a software dealer *might* be deemed to be a *franchisee*, entitled to the protection of federal regulations and state laws. This body of law may impose strict pre-contract disclosure rules on companies that recruit dealers. Even more important, this body of law may make it difficult or impossible to terminate a dealer contract in some states.

The Background of Franchise Regulation

Classic examples of franchise operations are fast food operations or operator-owned gasoline location, but franchises have also covered a great variety of other enterprises: income tax preparation, real estate brokerages, dental offices, optician shops, and many others. In the 1970s there were many abusive and dishonest franchising schemes that promised riches and delivered heartaches. After these schemes consumed the life savings of many unsuspecting owner-investors, franchising became something of a national disgrace, and federal and state franchise regulation followed.

Although a software dealership may seem far removed from the world of fast food, the courts have on occasion ruled that software dealerships are covered by franchise law.

Pre-Contract Disclosure and Registration

The Federal Trade Commission (FTC), an agency of the United States government, reacted to the public outcry against franchise abuses by adopting regulations requiring extensive financial and business disclosure to prospective franchisees. Similar laws requiring disclosure have been enacted by 14 states including California, Illinois, Michigan, and New York. Many of these states require that any offer of a franchise be registered and approved in advance by the state regulatory authorities—after a filing a disclosure form with the state that includes specified financial and business information about the franchisor. Failure to comply with the FTC regulations or these state statutes can result in fines, may permit the franchisee to rescind its agreement, and may result in other liabilities to the franchisee. Willful noncompliance may be a criminal violation.

Restrictions on Termination

In addition, 16 states have statutes that regulate a franchisor's ability to *terminate* a franchisee. States with such statutes include California, Connecticut, Illinois, Michigan, and New Jersey. Generally, these statutes mandate that the dealer cannot be terminated except *for cause*—and "cause" usually means for the failure of the franchisee to perform the requirements of its agreement. In these states, a franchisor *cannot* get rid of a troublesome or unproductive franchisee by simply letting the franchise agreement expire—because *the agreement will never expire*. When the supplier tries to terminate the franchisee without cause, the franchisee can file a lawsuit and get an injunction forbidding the termination.

A Software Dealership May Be a Franchise

How does one determine whether a software dealer is, as a legal matter, also a franchisee? This is not an easy subject. The federal government and the states use slightly differing rules, and this is therefore a matter where counsel's advice is a necessity. As you might expect, the fact that a software dealer agreement *says* that it is not a franchise agreement carries little or no weight. Generally speaking, these are the elements that the court looks at in deciding whether there is a franchise relationship:

- **Licensing of a Trademark.** A franchise arrangement must include permission for a dealer to use the trademark of another company. Most software dealers fit this test because most are granted the right to use the supplier's trademark. Those OEM dealers that do not use the vendor's trademark cannot be franchisees.

- **Franchise Fee.** Franchise arrangements include a franchise fee, which is money paid by the dealer at the start of the relationship. Under the FTC regulations, a franchise fee may be as little as $500 paid as much as six months before or after the agreement is signed. Any amounts paid to a supplier other than the bona fide retail price of goods may be deemed a franchise fee. A franchise fee can be a payment that is mandatory under a contract or a payment that is required as a practical matter, even if the payment is ostensibly voluntary. Many software dealer agreements have up-front license fees or other payments that might be found to be franchise fees.

- **Some Element of Common Interest, Association, or Control.** The final element of a franchise agreement is phrased differently by the FTC and by various states—but the essential element is *control or influence* over the purported franchisee's business by the supplier. This element might include sales training, operation and marketing manuals or guides, management advice or training sessions, flow-down licensing provisions, marketing plans from the supplier, control of dealer locations, or control of advertising and promotion.

There is also a fourth, unwritten factor: the treatment of the dealer. The more it looks like the dealer was unfairly treated, the more likely it is that a court will find that franchise law protection applies.

How Software Suppliers Cope with Franchise Laws

Every software supplier with a dealership network takes the position that its dealers are *not* franchisees. Nonetheless, if they are prudent, suppliers take steps to reduce with the risk that franchise laws might apply.

- They get the advice of counsel. In each state where they wish to establish a dealership, a prudent supplier learns of the applicable franchise laws and other relevant restrictions. Sometimes, suppliers will require, as a condition of the dealer agreement, that prospective dealers get an written opinion of local counsel that the contract does *not* create a franchise under state or federal law.

- Suppliers can draft the software dealer agreement in a way to minimize risks that it will be deemed a franchise agreement. For example, up-front fees that might be deemed franchise fees can be eliminated. Mandatory controls of the dealers can be kept to a minimum.

■ The suppliers include in the dealership agreements a requirement for a minimum yearly level of purchases from the supplier or sales to end-users. Such a provision often allows the supplier to terminate an unproductive dealer *even if* franchise law restrictions apply, because the dealer will have failed to fulfill the requirements of the agreement.

State and Federal Antitrust Laws

There are also some risks to any company that engages in the licensing or distribution of products under state and federal *antitrust* laws. These principles apply to *all* of the varieties of distribution that we have discussed. Both dealers *and* suppliers can be at risk for antitrust violations.

The most important federal antitrust statute, the Sherman Act, was passed at the turn of the century to prevent unlawful monopolies and forbid certain anti-competitive contracts. Most states have very similar statutes. Antitrust suits are serious business, because if a company files a federal antitrust lawsuit and wins, it automatically gets judgment against the loser for triple damages and attorneys' fees.

What is important to most software businesses is the antitrust rule on *how companies may set prices and terms*. (Unless you dominate a market, suits alleging monopolization are not an issue for your business.) Here are a few very simple guidelines:

Price Fixing

A company cannot fix prices by agreement with its competitors. Price fixing is a classic antitrust violation that can easily result in a triple damage suit by the overcharged customers. Price fixing can also lead to *criminal prosecution* by the United States Justice Department or by state governments. A supplier cannot make a price fixing agreement with another supplier. Dealers cannot fix prices with other dealers.

Informal price fixing agreements are as illegal as formal ones. Nothing stops a company from matching a competitor's price. However, if a company sends its competitors its new price list so that the competitors can follow those prices, the practice is illegal and very dangerous.

License Terms

A company may not fix non-price terms of licenses with its competitors. Fixing non-price terms can be as injurious to customers as fixing prices. For example, it would likely be a violation of the law for a company to agree with its competitors on the minimum configuration of software or on credit or warranty terms to be offered.

A Supplier May Not Set Distributor or Dealer Prices

Under the antitrust laws, it is illegal for a supplier to set mandatory pricing for its dealers. *Suggested* resale prices are all right. So are packages with pre-marked pricing. And it is perfectly all right for a supplier to grant *end-users* a rebate coupon that the end-user may redeem directly from the supplier. But the supplier must not make resale prices mandatory. Again there is a risk of triple damage suits by overcharged customers.

Termination of Price Cutting Dealers May Be Dangerous

If a number of dealers request their supplier to terminate another dealer who is low-balling prices, the supplier should *seek legal advice before acting*. It may face an expensive and risky antitrust claim if it complies with this request.

Restrictions on Pricing to Dealers

There is another federal antitrust statute that may apply to software, called the Robinson-Patman Act. This statute forbids a company from giving one dealer better prices or terms than those made available to others. The intent of the law is to protect small businesses against the economic power of large dealerships or distribution operations.

It is unclear whether the Robinson-Patman Act applies to software dealerships and distribution—but it might. The act applies to "commodities," and it is not clear whether the term "commodity" includes software. In a legal database search, I couldn't find a single reported software case under the Robinson-Patman Act (although there may be unreported cases). But the fact that coverage is unclear does not mean that it is safe to ignore the act. There is a risk to suppliers that the law will be applied to software.

If it does apply, the act has exceptions where price discrimination is permitted, such as meeting competitive prices and genuine cost-based quantity discounts. Many computer hardware and software vendors are careful about the Robinson-Patman Act, and avoid giving special discounts to favored customers. Instead, they build revenues by having a standard list of quantity discounts available to all dealers and by running special "limited-time only" discounts available to all dealers or distributors. Certainly the safest course, from a legal perspective, is to apply pricing and discounts equally to all dealers. If you are concerned about the possibility of liability under the Robinson-Patman Act, you should contact legal counsel.

Litigation Between Suppliers and Dealers

Litigation between suppliers and dealers is rare, until the relationship breaks down and one party or the other seeks to terminate an agreement. In a way, the relationship is rather like a marriage. Even when the relationship between the two parties is troubled, as long as the dealership is in place, both parties have an incentive to learn to live with one another. But when the relationship is coming to an end, then the lawyers and the courts frequently get involved.

Litigation filed by suppliers against dealers is normally to collect debt. Typically, the dealer has failed to pay for its final shipments of goods. Slow payment, in fact, is a common cause of dealer termination.

In most lawsuits filed by dealers, the goal is to get an injunction to stop the termination of the dealership or to seek monetary damages allegedly caused by the termination. Dealers often file suits accusing the supplier of unfair business practices, of antitrust violations, and franchise law violations. Usually the supplier wins these contests, but there have been dealer successes.

CHAPTER 11

Shrink-Wrap
Licenses and Warranties

Shrink-Wrap Licenses for Mass Market Software

A shrink-wrap license is an end-user license agreement for software sold in the mass market. You've seen these shrink-wrap licenses dozens of times. When you buy software, you open the box and find that the diskettes are sealed in a large white paper envelope. The envelope contains a notice in capital letters across the top that says:

> BY OPENING THIS SEALED DISK PACKAGE YOU ARE AGREEING TO BE BOUND BY THE TERMS OF THIS AGREEMENT. IF YOU DO NOT AGREE TO THE TERMS OF THIS AGREEMENT, RETURN THIS PRODUCT TO THE PLACE OF PURCHASE PROMPTLY FOR A FULL REFUND.

Following this notice is a page of legalese, which is the shrink-wrap license itself. The shrink-wrap license states the terms and conditions of the software sale—written, of course, in a way that strongly favors the software company.

The name "shrink-wrap license" comes from the clear plastic "shrink-wrap" that is used as a protective covering for retail software products. Another common term for it is "Tear-off License." Because the text is sometimes printed on the software package, another name is "Boxtop License."

A variety of companies use shrink-wrap licenses. They include manufacturers of software, software publishers, programmers who distribute their own software, and OEMs who put their own label on another company's software.

For convenience, I will refer to all the companies that use shrink- wrap licenses by the general (if rather formal) term "licensor."

When Do Companies Use a Shrink-Wrap License?

Companies include a shrink-wrap license with their software product *every time they sell a software product for which they can't get a signed contract from the end-user in advance*. A shrink-wrap license is used with software that is sold for as little as $10 or as much as $2,000 or more. Of course, a great deal of software is sold through contracts signed *before* the delivery and sale—and as we will see, this is preferable from a legal point of view. But as marketing costs for software climb, companies are using shrink-wrap licenses on more expensive and sophisticated products.

Shrink-wrap licenses are used with software sold through a variety of distribution methods including retail sales, telemarketing, direct mail, and shareware distribution.

Let me add a note on terminology. As we discussed in Chapter 1, while we may speak of "sales" of software, usually it is licensing transactions that are taking place. With packaged software the distinction is less clear. When someone goes to a software store, puts down her money and gets packaged software in return, the transaction looks very much like a sale of a product. It is unclear whether dealings in package software are sales or licensing or something in between. For convenience, however, we will speak of sales and selling of software.

The Terms of a Shrink-Wrap License

Each company's version of a shrink-wrap license uses a slightly different text, but the substance is basically the same. A typical shrink-wrap license has the following provisions:

> **Specification of Program Ownership.** The license says that the seller retains ownership of the program. The user has only a license and may use the program only in the limited manner that the license provides.

Hardware Limitation on Use of the Program. Typically use is permitted on one computer or workstation. Sometimes the license allows installation on one network server and requires that an additional license be purchased for each workstation. (There is a more comprehensive discussion of scope of use limitation in licenses in Chapter 12.)

Restriction of Copying and Transfer. Unauthorized copying is forbidden, with the exception of a single backup copy. (The right to make a single copy for archive purposes is granted by federal copyright law.) Transferring or selling the software to another user is not allowed.

No Reverse Engineering. The license states that decompiling, disassembling, and reverse engineering are forbidden. The purpose of this provision is to help safeguard the trade secrets in the program.

Limited Warranty. The license contains a warranty[1] "that the software will perform substantially in accordance with the accompanying written materials" for a short period, typically 60 or 90 days. Some warranties promise that the program is "free of defects materials and workmanship"—which means that it is completely bug-free. (It is probably better to offer the more modest warranty.) All other warranties are "disclaimed" in large type.

Limitation of Remedies. The license says that the user's sole remedy for any complaint is replacement or a refund (at the licensor's choice).

Notice About State Law. For "consumer software" (discussed in detail later in this chapter), the license includes notice that

---

1   The term "warranty" means the same thing as "guaranty." This book generally uses the term "warranty" because it is the term most commonly found in statutes and legal texts relating to licensing of software and sale of goods.

state law might give the user better rights and remedies than the text of the license itself.

How Effective Are Shrink-Wrap Licenses?

For most licensors, the most important provisions of a shrink-wrap license are often those that disclaim liability. No doubt you've seen this kind of warranty disclaimer in a shrink-wrap license many times. The language seems very broad and it looks very impressive. The following is typical:

> LICENSOR DISCLAIMS ALL OTHER WARRANTIES, EITHER EXPRESS OR IMPLIED, INCLUDING BUT NOT LIMITED TO IMPLIED WARRANTIES OF MERCHANTABILITY, FITNESS FOR A PARTICULAR PURPOSE AND ANY WARRANTY OF NON-INFRINGEMENT WITH RESPECT TO THE SOFTWARE AND THE ACCOMPANYING WRITTEN MATERIALS.
>
> YOU AGREE THAT LICENSOR'S ENTIRE LIABILITY AND YOUR EXCLUSIVE REMEDY SHALL BE, AT LICENSOR'S CHOICE, EITHER (A) RETURN OF THE PRICE PAID OR (B) REPLACEMENT OF THE SOFTWARE THAT DOES NOT MEET LICENSOR'S LIMITED WARRANTY AND WHICH IS RETURNED TO LICENSOR WITH A COPY OF YOUR RECEIPT.
>
> IN NO EVENT WILL LICENSOR BE LIABLE TO YOU FOR DAMAGES, INCLUDING ANY LOSS OF PROFITS, LOST SAVINGS, OR OTHER INCIDENTAL OR CONSEQUENTIAL DAMAGES ARISING OUT OF YOUR USE OR INABILITY TO USE THE PROGRAM

Is this type of language legally effective? What if the software trashes the user's hard disk—destroying months of work and valuable data? What if it generates incorrect data? What if the user files a lawsuit? It is easy to imagine circumstances where a great deal of money turns on the answer. (Of course, in most situations where software goes wrong, even when data is destroyed or a disk is trashed, the monetary damages are too low to justify a lawsuit. Only exceptional situations result in litigation.)

> **Example.** Valu-Stock Software, Inc. makes and sells a software program to value securities, including bonds. Lynch Brothers Brokerage, Inc. buys three copies of the program at retail for $500 each and gives them to its top bond traders. There is an undetected bug in the program that causes it to overvalue any bond with an interest rate of exactly 12.25 percent. Due solely to misinformation generated by the defective Valu-Stock software, Lynch Brothers loses $5,000,000 in bond trading, and sues Valu-Stock for this loss. Valu-Stock admits that the program has an error, but denies that it is liable. Its defense is based on the disclaimer of warranties and the limitation of remedies in the shrink-wrap license. Lynch Brothers asserts that the disclaimer and warranty are null and void.

If the limitation of damage clause in the shrink-wrap license is *effective*, Valu-Stock at most has to replace the defective software or refund the $500 purchase price. Under no circumstances would it be liable for the $5,000,000 in monetary damages. (As a practical matter, every software firm will want to replace defective software, in order to maintain customer good will. Sometime minor bugs are fixed in a subsequent release, but software with major bugs will usually be replaced quickly and for free.)

On the other hand, if the shrink-wrap license is *ineffective*, then the Uniform Commercial Code (UCC) controls. As I mentioned in Chapter 8, the UCC is a set of laws that has been adopted (with a few variations) to govern sales in every American state and territory except Louisiana. Under the UCC, the licensor is quite often *liable for all damages* caused by a defective product. Therefore, if the shrink-wrap license is ineffective, there is a risk that in litigation Valu-Stock would be tagged for the $5,000,000.

If you are simply looking for a reasonable form of a shrink-wrap license, a typical form is included in Appendix C as Form 11-1. However, if you want to know (and you *should* want to know) what the shrink-wrap license actually *means* in terms of protection from your business, read on. You will see that these very simple agreements are embedded in some very fuzzy law. You will also see that the shrink-wrap license, though used universally, is an awfully weak shield.

Rulings on Shrink-Wrap Licenses and Liability

The central concept of a shrink-wrap license is its system of acceptance or rejection: If you accept the contract, you tear open the envelope; if you reject it, you return the package for a refund. But does this "tear open" concept work? Does the law really allow the licensor to force the user to abide by this choice?

When you look at the shrink-wrap licenses used by Microsoft, Lotus, Claris, Digital, and many other companies, you realize that these documents are written by company lawyers—some of the most sophisticated software lawyers in the United States. And it is obvious that the software industry has had time to work out the most effective language possible for these shrink-wrap licenses. So, no one could deny that these documents are legally binding and effective. Right? Worng.

The fact is that for more than a decade software lawyers have had grave doubts about the legal effectiveness of shrink-wrap licenses. For years there were no court decisions on the issue, but every company dreaded what the courts would say. Finally, a few cases have been decided. These cases have come out as everyone in the industry feared, supporting the consensus of software lawyers that shrink-wrap licenses are *not binding!* That's right. According to the case law so far, the disclaimers of liability in most shrink-wrap licenses are probably not worth the paper they are printed on.

Why Are Shrink-Wrap Licenses Likely to Be Ineffective?

The rationale for the grave doubts about shrink-wrap licenses comes from basic contract law. A fundamental idea in contract law, from its eighteenth century roots to the present, is the *bargain*—what lawyers sometimes call a "meeting of the minds." In a classic contract, the terms are bargained out, *then* the sale takes place as agreed. Although the sale of goods is now governed by a state statute (the UCC), the same concept has carried over. The contract is completed before or at time of the sale.

The problem with a shrink-wrap license is that the retail software sale is over *before* the customer is presented with the one-sided terms of the shrink-wrap license. After the sale is already made, it is too late to try to impose adverse terms.

However, any express warranty that the *licensor* makes to the buyer in a shrink-wrap license is almost certainly *enforceable!* There is some logic to this result. The end-users are not bound to terms they never agreed to, but the licensor is held to its written word.

Shrink-Wrap Licenses Placed On the Outside of Software Packages May Fare Better

Some software companies have tried a different approach in an attempt to make the shrink-wrap license legally binding. *They place the license on the outside of the software box.* The purpose is to give the buyer notice of the terms of the shrink-wrap license *before* the purchase of the software. This lets the licensor argue that there *was* a "meeting of the minds" before the sale.

There is resistance by marketers to this approach. The software box is the licensor's advertising space; many companies do not want to fill a large part of it with legalese. Nonetheless, some companies are placing the license on the side or back of the packaging, in hopes of making the license stick.

It is unlikely that the software industry can really solve its legal shrink-wrap license dilemma by putting an extra copy of the license on the outside of the box. Only a fraction of software is sold in retail stores. The majority of mass-market software is sold by direct mail solicitation and telephone orders. In these sales, the terms of a shrink-wrap license (inside the box or outside) are not mentioned before the sale is completed. It is most unlikely that mail and telephone buyers would be bound by terms they never heard about until their software arrived.

Even in a retail store sale, it is uncertain whether the shrink-wrap license on the side of the box is effective. A judge might find that the license was too inconspicuous, or that its effect is overridden by the affirmative promises also contained on the box. Moreover, as we discuss below, there are state and federal law limitations on how much warranties and remedies can be limited for goods normally sold to consumers.

The result is that for many—perhaps most—software sales, the shrink-wrap license is probably not legally effective in a court of law, even if it is on the outside of the box. Still, if you are selling software products and want to have the highest chance of having an effective shrink-wrap license, consider putting it on the outside of the box as well as on the diskette package inside.

When one is selling shareware, it is common to upload a demo version of the program to a bulletin board, and then let buyers order the full-featured version by phone or mail. It is a good idea to include a shrink-wrap license with the demo version, along with a notice that all sales of the full-featured version are subject to the license terms. This procedure could give you a pretty good argument that the user assented to the terms of license *before* the sale and that therefore the terms should be held legally effective.

Liability if the Shrink-Wrap License Does Not Control

As we have discussed earlier (in Chapter 8), the UCC provides certain default warranty provisions that take effect unless otherwise agreed. If the shrink-wrap license is ineffective, then nothing is "otherwise agreed," and these default provisions of the UCC apply:

> **Statements by the Licensor as Warranty.** Under the UCC, any description of goods—in the documentation, in advertisement, in the sales pitch by a telemarketer—is a warranty, a binding promise.
>
> **Implied Warranty of Merchantability.** The UCC imposes a warranty of "merchantability"—a fancy term that means that the product will do what it is supposed to do reasonably well. For example, software that crashes all the time is not merchantable.
>
> **Implied Warranty of Fitness for a Purpose.** Under the UCC, if the buyer says: "I need software to do my taxes" and you sell him Jiffy Tax, then he has your warranty that it will *do* his taxes. If the buyer expresses a need, say over the phone to your phone order operation, and you sell him a product to meet it, a warranty is created.
>
> **Liability for Damages.** Under the UCC, damage liability includes consequential damages—which means damages for interruption of business, loss of production, or lost profits. These could be big-ticket items. (The UCC also provides for

incidental damages—cost "incidental" to replacement of defective software—such as shipping and installation costs. This will usually be a relatively modest amount.)

Does this then mean, in our hypothetical example, that Lynch Brothers Brokerage, Inc. will be able to recover $5,000,000 from Valu-Stock Software on account of a $500 software product? Perhaps it will—you cannot be sure. Many judges probably would refuse to allow a jury to impose such disproportionate liability, but some might just let the jury decide. And what if the loss is $100,000? What if the software cost $1,000? The fact is that there is a substantial risk that a liability case is going to stick in this type of case—and that a shrink-wrap license will fail to limit liability.

A New Approach to the Problem

It is becoming more important for the software industry to come to grips with the shrink-wrap license dilemma. This is because of the fact, noted above, that shrink-wrap licenses are being used on more and more expensive software. The higher the price of the software, the more likely the application is critical for a business. And where the application is critical, it is more likely that bad software will cause a large loss. It is thus more important than ever before that software vendors find a way effectively to limit contract damages.

There have been suggestions for new measures to make shrink-wrap licenses effective, but they are untested and therefore by no means guaranteed to work. For example one knowledgeable California lawyer, David Hays,[2] recommends that every software package prominently display the following legend:

> **Notice:** [NAME OF COMPANY] IS WILLING TO LICENSE THE ENCLOSED SOFTWARE ONLY UPON THE TERMS OF THE LICENSE AGREEMENT THAT IS ENCLOSED. You can obtain a full copy by calling **(xxx) xxx-xxxx**. IF YOU DO NOT AGREE TO SUCH TERMS AFTER READING THE LICENSE,

---

2   David Hays is an attorney at Fenwick & West in Palo Alto. This section is drawn from David's article, "Shrink-Wrap License Agreement: New Light on a Vexing Problem," Hastings Commercial and Entertainment Law Journal, Vol. 15, No. 3, with the author's kind permission.

YOU MAY RETURN THIS SOFTWARE FOR A FULL REFUND. EXCEPT FOR THE LIMITED WARRANTY EXPRESSLY STATED IN THE LICENSE AGREEMENT, [NAME OF COMPANY] DISCLAIMS ALL OTHER WARRANTIES, INCLUDING ANY IMPLIED WARRANTIES OF MERCHANTABILITY, FITNESS FOR A PARTICULAR PURPOSE, OR NON-INFRINGEMENT. IN NO EVENT WILL [NAME OF COMPANY] BE LIABLE FOR ANY DAMAGES, LOST PROFITS, LOST DATA OR INCIDENTAL OR CONSEQUENTIAL DAMAGES ARISING FROM OF USE OR ANY INABILITY TO USE THE SOFTWARE.

This legend is designed to give conspicuous notice of the crucial clauses in the shrink-wrap license before sale, yet take up less of the precious advertising space on the box than the entire license agreement. I have included this suggested language in the sample shrink-wrap license, Form 11-1 (in Appendix C).

Of course this proposal does not deal with the legal dilemma for telemarketing sales that we discussed above: The customer never sees the box or any legend on it until after the sale is completed—and then it is probably too late. To deal with this issue, Hays recommends that each telephone sales person's "selling script" include a mention of the shrink-wrap license that will come with the software and a statement to the customer that if the customer does not accept the terms of the license, the customer should return the software. I know of no company that now follows this practice. Most companies would probably rather simply pitch the product over the phone and leave the license terms to later. Whether a warning about the shrink-wrap license will chill sales is something I will leave for you to decide. However no one has suggested any other means of telemarketing that might *cure* the shrink-wrap problem.

These suggested measures are unproven and by no means certain to work. But they have a better chance to work than the standard shrink-wrap practice used in the software industry, which seems almost certain to fail.

Legal Constraints on Shrink-Wrap Licenses on Consumer Products

As if all of this wasn't complicated enough, there is a federal statute and state law provisions (which vary from state to state) that regulate what a warranty clause may provide in sales of consumer products.

The Magnuson-Moss Act

The federal statute that regulates warranties for consumer products is the Magnuson-Moss Act ("the Act"). There is also a set of federal regulations under the Act written by the Federal Trade Commission.

The Act was passed during a period of concern about deceptive warranties. It was a classic political compromise, created by a Congress taking heat from hard-pressing consumer advocates on one side and tough industry lobbyists on the other. So the law came out with a series of half-measures. The Act—and regulations under it—are not meant to supplant state law; rather they enhance state law provisions in limited ways and provide some measure of "truth-in-warranties."

Note that the Magneson-Moss Act does nothing to resolve the questions of whether the disclaimers and limitations of shrink-wrap licenses are effective in the first place. That is left to state law. For the most part the Act governs what consumer product warranties must *say*. In a few, rather limited ways, it adds to consumer rights. But it does nothing to solve the licensors' problems with shrink-wrap licenses.

The Act applies to "consumer products"—which means goods "normally used for personal, family, or household purposes." Software with both personal and business use, such as a word processor or a spreadsheet, would be covered under the Act. Other software that has only a professional use, for example CAD/CAM or CASE products, would probably not be governed by the Act. If there is any doubt about how to categorize a product, it is safest to assume that the product will be in the "consumer product" category. If it is a "consumer product," the Act applies—whether the benefit goes to Jane Q. Citizen or to General Motors.

For software shrink-wrap licenses, the following are the most important things to know about the way the Act works in practice.

Granting a Warranty: Optional in Theory, Mandatory in Reality.   Under the Act, the licensor is not *required* to give *any* warranty on consumer software. It is theoretically legal to sell consumer software with a notice saying that the product is licensed "AS IS" and to disclaim all warranties. However, almost all software licensors *do* give a warranty.

The reason to give the warranty is half marketing savvy and half facing up to the law. Offering the warranty has definite sales, customer relations, and promotion value. In any case, it is very unlikely that the courts will take much notice of a disclaimer that a product is sold "AS IS." This is because normally the product's package, documentation, and advertisements all say how much the product will do, and the courts will usually hold the licensor to its word. There is a further reason not to use an "AS IS" disclaimer on consumer software. Judges and juries are all consumers, and it is unlikely that you will win their hearts and minds with such scrooge-like license terms.

The "Limited Warranty"   Shrink-wrap licenses for most mass market products are normally entitled something like "License Agreement and Limited Warranty?" Why "limited warranty"? Unless the licensor is willing to give what the Act calls a "full warranty" (which no one ever gives), the warranty must be called a "limited warranty."

One difficulty with the "full warranty" is that it permits *no time limitation* on state law UCC warranties—which can last as long as *six years*. This puts companies in the position of officially supporting software long after it is superceded. Note, however, that in several states, any limitation on the duration of implied warranties for consumer goods is null and void.

Restricting the Duration of the Warranty   It is allowed under the Act to place a restriction on the duration of a limited warranty as long as the restriction is reasonable in view of the time it would take a normal user to find defects (although, as noted above, the laws of some states may invalidate the restriction). Most mass-market software licensors give 60- to 90-day warranties that the software will perform substantially in accordance with the accompanying documentation. A California consumer statute (the Song-Beverly Act) provides that the duration of consumer product implied warranties cannot be limited to less than 60 days. California is the state with the largest mass-market software sales, and this statute is another reason why most companies give warranties of no less than 60 days.

Implied Warranties   During the duration of the stated warranty, the UCC implied warranties (discussed earlier) of merchantability and fitness for a purpose cannot be disclaimed.

Limiting Remedies   Most software shrink-wrap licenses limit remedies to the licensor's choice of replacing defective software or refunding the purchase price. Consequential and incidental damages are normally disclaimed. Nothing in the Act prevents such a limitation of remedies. In some states, however, an attempt to limit remedies for defects in consumer goods may be ineffective.

Notice of State Law Remedies   State consumer law often gives buyers a better deal than the Act. In fact, for reasons that I have explained, all disclaimers and limitations in consumer product warranties may well be ineffective. Regulations under the Act require the following three notices be given in nearly every limited warranty:

- "Some states do not allow limitation of how long an implied warranty lasts, so the above limitation may not apply to you."

- "Some states do not allow exclusion or limitation of incidental or consequential damages, so the above limitation or exclusion may not apply to you."

- "This Warranty gives you specific legal rights, and you may also have other rights which vary from state to state."

The sample shrink-wrap license included in Appendix C as Form 11-1 is written to comply with the current formal requirements of the Act and the regulations. Failure to comply with the Act can result in suits by consumers or by the Federal Trade Commission.

"Warranty Registration" Card   Sometimes consumer product warranties are conditioned on the customer's returning a warranty registration card. While the Act does not ban this type of restriction for a limited warranty sale, the law in most states will grant a warranty whether the card is returned or not.

The best practice is to provide support to customers with defective software whether the warranty card is returned or not. Many customer don't bother to return the cards. And most licensors want to be able to keep their customers happy by solving problems in the software. In fact the real reason that software companies want the cards is for marketing purposes—for selling upgrades and related products.

The best course, therefore, is to make it as easy as possible for the customers to return the cards (they should be postage-free business reply forms). It is all right to have a legend on the registration card that says: "IMPORTANT: MAIL IN THIS CARD IMMEDIATELY." But it is a bad idea to say that the warranty won't apply unless the card is returned.

The Validity of Other Clauses in the Shrink-Wrap License

As we have seen, the warranty limitations on the shrink-wrap license may not count for much. That raises a question about the other provisions of the license. What about the clause that says you cannot decompile or reverse engineer the software—is that valid? What about the clause that says that copying (other than one archival copy) is forbidden?

The Reverse Engineering Issue

A clause in virtually every shrink-wrap license expressly forbids decompiling and reverse engineering of the software. This is a very important issue. Every licensor wants to stop the buyer from decompiling and reverse engineering its product.

There was a well-known court case in the mid-1980s that tested this issue of shrink-wrap licenses and reverse engineering. Vault Corporation made ProLok, a then-widely-used copy protection system for MS-DOS software. Quaid Software Limited made a piece of software that permitted computers to cheat the Vault scheme and to *copy* software that had Vault's protection. In short, Quaid's product defeated Vault's product, and the people at Vault were mad as hell.

Vault sued Quaid in federal court in New Orleans. Why did Vault, a California corporation sue, Quaid, a Canadian corporation, in cajun country? I'll answer that question after discussing the background a bit more.

In order to make its product, Quaid had decompiled and reverse engineered the Vault copy protection code. Vault claimed that this was a copyright violation. Quaid argued that decompiling to determine how the Vault software worked was permitted under the Copyright Act. The judge agreed with Quaid, and held that the reverse engineering was permissible under federal copyright law. (As I noted in Chapter 1, under some circumstances the Copyright Act *permits* reverse engineering of software and in others it does not.)

But Vault had another argument. Vault claimed that when Quaid bought the ProLok software, Quaid had accepted a shrink-wrap license that *forbade reverse engineering*. As I have stated, there is grave doubt that a shrink-wrap license is effective, but Louisiana has a state statute that provides specifically that restrictions on copying and reverse engineering in shrink-wrap licenses are effective. This was why Vault chose to sue in New Orleans, because it was *relying on an exceptional Louisiana law*. Unfortunately for Vault, the court ruled that in this case, the Copyright Act, which is federal law, trumps (or as lawyers say, preempts) Louisiana law on the reverse engineering issue. So Vault lost the case on all fronts. (Illinois has a statute similar to Louisiana's; the effect of the Illinois statute has not yet been tested in court.)

Based on the result in the Quaid litigation, it appears most likely that any attempt to use the shrink-wrap license to stop reverse engineering is not going to work and that the Copyright Act will govern whether mass-market software can be reverse engineered or not.

Usage and Copying Restrictions

What about the clauses in shrink-wrap licenses that state that the user cannot make copies of the software (except one archival copy), and restrict the number of machines that the software can be used on—are these clauses valid?

Most likely these restrictions *are* binding on the user—not so much because they are in the shrink-wrap license, but because of the Copyright Act, which *forbids* copying except as expressly permitted by the copyright holder. (See the discussion of the Copyright Act in Chapter 1.)

A Final Word on Shrink-Wrap Licenses

From a legal perspective, a contract that is *signed before the purchase* is likely to be considered a binding bargain between the parties. If you are in a business that lends itself to contracting in advance, you can avoid the shrink-wrap license conundrum altogether.

But when you are selling through large-scale distribution, use a shrink-wrap license. It is not perfect—and may not be legally effective—but it surely doesn't hurt. It may help to deter claims and suits, and who knows, some judge might enforce it. (For further discussion of coping with potential liabilities from software, see Chapter 13.)

CHAPTER 12

End-User Agreements

Software end-user agreements are the documents used to license software to customers in business and industry. The party that licenses software to the end-user under one of these agreements could be a publisher, a developer, a distributor, or a dealer. For convenience, we will refer to the party supplying the software as the "vendor" and end-user as the "customer." In most transactions, both the vendor and the customer are corporations, rather than individuals.

End-user agreements include a variety of deals. At the modest end of that range might be an agreement for, say, a time and billing package installed on the computer system for a modest-size accounting or law firm or an inventory control system for a shoe store. At the other end of the spectrum are agreements for sophisticated systems that run on mainframe computers and nationwide and international networks, for example, systems to manage international currency transactions or to manage air traffic and navigation systems.

The vast majority of end-user agreements, however, are for commercial software products that serve day-to-day needs in commercial, industrial, scientific and professional firms. It is these agreements with which we are concerned here.

Settings for Software End-User Agreements

An end-user agreement is often entitled simply "license agreement," "software user agreement," or the like. Most end-user agreements are created for the following kinds of business settings:

- The agreement is signed by both parties after a negotiation process; typical pricing for the deal is $5,000 and up.

- The vendor provides a software solution by using one or more "off-the-shelf" software products. The solution may require using several products together and may require customization or database programming, but the work is usually much less than programming a new application.

- The technical risk is relatively low, because pre-existing software products are used. The vendor's work usually consists of such tasks as setting up data files, creating forms and screens, creating report formats, adapting the product to the user's network, and some code writing.

- The software runs on widely available hardware and software platforms that are standard products, rather than on hardware created for the application.

- The customer needs installation services and (often) pays for training.

- The customer needs continued services after the software is installed.

Tools for Negotiating Software End-User Agreements

In this chapter, you will find a discussion of some of the most common issues that arise in the negotiation of a software end-user agreement. Additional aids for negotiating these agreements are a software end-user agreement checklist, Form 12-1 (on diskette as USER-CHK.W51), and an annotated software end-user agreement, Form 12-2 (on diskette as USER-AGR.W51), both in Appendix C.

End-user agreements are not the most complex contracts, but they do have some subtleties and raise issues that you might miss. If licensing software systems is your business, you will need one or more standard form agreements to use as the basis of negotiations. It is smart to have your counsel's assistance in creating these forms or negotiating major modifications. Similarly, an end-user who is investing substantial funds in a important software system should not sign or agree to an end-user agreement for a significant transaction until the document has been reviewed by counsel.

Agreements for Software with Hardware

Often customers will buy or lease their own hardware and use a vendor for the applications software. The computer hardware—particularly if it is microcomputer hardware—is commonly considered a "commodity item" and is often obtained through mass-market channels. For networked systems, however, it is common for a vendor to provide the microcomputer network, including cabling, network hardware, network operating system software, and the applications software. Or sometimes the vendor will provide the customer with a complete system (sometimes called a turnkey system) with both computer hardware and application software.

When the transaction involves minicomputer or mainframe solutions, customers may want a single agreement to cover both the hardware and software, so that if the system is defective, the customer can return the entire system, or if there are problems with the system, one vendor is responsible for fixing it. This is not a book about hardware sales, but I note in passing that sophisticated hardware agreements raise their own series of issues about delivery, installation, acceptance, warranties, remedies for defective equipment, replacements and returns, upgrades, useful life of components, service, and support. If you are either providing or acquiring a hardware and software system, it is even more important that you have a qualified attorney check out the agreement before it is signed.

Bargaining Between Vendor and Customer

The bargaining process for software end-user agreements usually depends to a large degree on these three factors:

- The amount of revenue to be generated by the software license and by follow-on revenues from support fees and possible additional software licenses.
- The competition (or lack of competition) for the customer's business.
- The sophistication of the customer about computers and contract negotiations.

The vendor will usually go into discussions with the customer with a form contract in hand (which is one reason why the form should be carefully drafted). Some large vendors have a policy that its sales representatives cannot vary their form agreements without approval from headquarters—and language to that effect is included in the forms. Such contract language should be taken seriously; it is often upheld by the courts. The more money that is at stake, and the hotter the competition, however, the more likely it is that vendors—large and small—will have to negotiate changes and concessions in the terms. The customer should make sure that all promises made actually end up in the contract—rather than in side letters signed by sales persons who may lack authority to bind their corporation.

For better or worse, many software customers are not sophisticated enough to know what to bargain for in a computer software contract. For this reason, there are many one-sided end-user agreements signed every day. Where the customer is sophisticated or has sophisticated counsel, it will normally seek to alter the form contract and to get the vendor to agree to an addendum to the agreement that modifies a number of terms and conditions. (See "Common Issues in Negotiating End-User Agreements," later in this chapter.)

Corporate customers who understand software negotiations commonly turn the standard form contract strategy around and use it against the vendor. Large corporate customers often have their own standard forms for *purchasing* software. These forms may well put vendors to hard choices about whether to accept unfavorable terms to win large contracts. However, as in any negotiation, there will usually be room for bargaining and give and take in any substantial and important transaction.

Vendor and Customer Goals

The vendor normally has the following goals in the negotiation of an end-user agreement:

- To get a price with a reasonable profit margin and to get an adequate amount of cash early in the transaction
- To secure a continuing revenue stream for software support and services
- To maintain flexibility in future performance requirements and prices
- To limit potential liability

The vendor maximizes its up-front revenue by the software license fee payment required by the agreement. Some of the license fee typically is a downpayment when the contract is signed. More is paid at the time the software is delivered. An additional payment (or none) may remain to be paid when the customer tries out the software and accepts it.

The sophisticated customer's goals should be:

- To obtain a software product that genuinely meets its needs
- To obtain a favorable price on the software license fee and to set reasonable fees for software support in the future
- To get a firm commitment on the delivery date and a right to cancel if the software is not delivered within a specified time
- To have the opportunity to test the software for a reasonable period with real data under real conditions before paying the major part of the price, and to have the right to return it if dissatisfied
- To incorporate in the agreement flexibility for future needs, including options for increasing overall system size and capacity, adding functions, enhancing performance, "downsizing" to smaller microcomputer-based systems, etc.

The customer naturally will be in the best position to get a favorable deal before the contract is signed. The customer's leverage diminishes after delivery, because most often the customer is dependent on the vendor for software upgrades and support. Therefore it is important for the customer to know what it wants in advance of the negotiation of an agreement.

It is in the interest of both parties that the customer know all the costs that result from obtaining new software, which include many costs in addition to the software license fee. When a major new software system is obtained, there may be substantial expenditures for training, employee overtime (to compensate for hours that employees spend in training), data conversion, parallel operation tests, and software support fees. In many cases these additional costs equal or exceed the license fee for the software.

Many customers initiate the process of a major software or computer system acquisition with a Request for Proposal (RFP). The RFP states what the customer's needs are, what tasks the software will be required to perform, what volume of data the software will need to process, and the like. RFPs are circulated to vendors to elicit bids. Some RFPs are very tightly drafted, but many are quite vague about what is really required of the software. Where the required system is complex and performs a crucial business function, smart customers will often hire a computer consultant to write a carefully considered RFP. The Request for Proposal and the vendor's response are sometimes incorporated into the specifications of end-user agreements.

Common Issues in Negotiating End-User Agreements

The following are some of the issues and provisions that come up in the negotiation of an end-user agreement. Further materials on many of these matters are found in the software end-user agreement checklist (Form 12-1) and the annotated software end-user agreement (Form 12-2) found in Appendix C.

Fees Due to the Vendor

As is noted earlier, under the terms of the agreement, the customer pays a license fee to obtain the software. Installation, if required, is typically included in the license fee. The fee typically also includes "software support" for a limited period—often 90 days, six months, or one year. Software support means that the vendor resolves software malfunctions and fixes bugs, delivers enhancements for the program, and provides technical advice to the customer on the use of the software. After the initial period of support is over, the customer will need to pay a monthly, yearly, or other periodic software support fee to obtain software support.

To keep its customer making payments for support month after month or year after year, the vendor has a carrot and a stick. The "carrot" is knowledgeable product advice and genuine improvements in releases of the software, all supplied for the periodic "support fee" (also known as the "maintenance fee"). The vendor needs to keep improving the software: (1) to keep the software equal or better to the competition and (2) to convince the customer that paying for support provides value. The "stick" is that the vendor usually makes technical support, bug fixes, and other services available *only* to customers "on support." Because sophisticated software is never completely bug-free, software support may be essential just to keep the program performing its normal business function. Indeed the process of improving software will itself create new bugs that make support essential.

Software support fees can be due yearly, quarterly, or monthly, and are normally due in advance. The support fee may be a specified amount or may be stated as a function of the license fee charged for software, often 10 to 20 percent of the price per year. The vendor is better off if it has flexibility in setting future prices for support. For example, vendors' form contracts often state that yearly support fees will be "at the price set in vendor's then current price list." Such provisions allow the vendor to increase (or lower) prices in response to market conditions.

When software prices are falling, which is common when competition is heating up, vendors will offer "price protection." This is a promise that if the license fee for the software falls during a specified period (which may be, for example, 90 days from the date the agreement is signed), the customer will get the benefit of the price reduction.

The Scope of the License

One especially important aspect of end-user agreements is the scope of the license that is granted to the customer.

Non-Exclusive License   Except in unusual circumstances, the customer will get a non-exclusive license. This license will normally provide that the vendor retains ownership of the program and all rights except those specifically granted in the license.

Ownership of Modifications   Where the customer pays the vendor to modify or customize the program, the customer may ask for ownership of or an exclusive license to the modifications. If the agreement does grant the customer exclusive rights to the modifications, the vendor must be careful that the same code is not licensed to other customers. Sometimes the agreement will provide that the vendor will own the modifications, but that the customer will be paid a royalty if the modifications are licensed to another customer. And sometimes, unfortunately, the agreement is ambiguous as to who actually owns the modifications, creating a situation that can lead to conflict. Obviously this type of ambiguity can be avoided by careful drafting. It is very important that vendor companies track carefully which computer code belongs to whom. Selling code that belongs to someone else can lead to both breach of contract and copyright infringement litigation.

Scope of Use

The following are some of the choices for defining the scope of use permitted to the customer in an end-user agreement (we touched on some of these choices in Chapter 11 in the context of shrink-wrap licenses):

- Site license

- Single user (a single individual)

- Single corporation (and perhaps subsidiaries and affiliates)

- Single server and a specified number of users

- Single server and a specified number of workstations

- Single server and a specified number of concurrent users

These choices require some discussion.

Site License   It is common for end-user agreements to be limited to a single location or "site." For mainframe or minicomputer software, this usually means that the software will be installed in the CPU and serve as many terminals as may be installed at the site currently or in the future. For microcomputer software, a site license may include the right to copy software and to install copies on however many microcomputers the customer installs at the site. More commonly, a microcomputer site license allows the customer to install the software on a single network server and make it available to client microcomputers throughout the network.

To define the "site" for a small to medium-size business, simply stating the address of the customer may be enough. For a customer with a growing business or with several facilities, however, it may be necessary to define more carefully what site is intended and to draft the agreement so that it may be renegotiated if the site grows beyond a specified size.

It is possible to create a multisite license, with a relatively large license fee for the first site, and the option to add additional sites at lower prices. Alternatively, license fees can be charged on per-user or per-workstation basis after the system grows beyond a specified size.

Corporate License   Sometimes a license simply grants a corporation use of the software in its operations. An example would be a system that is used to manage inventory and sales for a retailer with five store locations.

A corporation-wide license may give unexpected results, however. What happens, for example, if the customer corporation does a merger deal and suddenly grows to 50 stores? Can the customer fairly take the position that its existing license now covers all 50 stores because the customer, while bigger, is still legally the same corporation? Does the software support fee set out in the agreement (and negotiated for support of only five locations) require service for all 50 locations?

The moral: It is best to think through the business problems that will come when the customer grows (or shrinks) or alters its use of the computer system. Where a license is granted to a corporation as a whole, the agreement should carefully define who and what the customer is. In addition the agreement can place limitations on usage or tie the fees to the size of the system.

Subsidiaries and Affiliates   Often a corporate customer will ask that a license be granted to the corporation and its "subsidiaries and affiliates." These terms make the scope of the software license uncertain, because they are very vague. Subsidiaries are companies owned, wholly or in part, by another corporation; the term thus can include 100-percent ownership, 51-percent ownership, or perhaps even 30-percent ownership. Affiliates are companies that share some or all of the same owners—but the degree of common ownership required is undefined.

The better practice in many cases is to negotiate the particular subsidiaries and affiliates that will be using the software, or to link the fees to the size of the system, as it may grow.

License for Use on a Specified Number of Workstations   It is common that a license is not only restricted to a particular site, but to a specific number of network workstations. Often the documentation requires the customer to obtain a license for the software installed on the server and a separate workstation license for each network workstation. This scheme makes the most sense when every workstation in the system is using the same software, for example operating system software, or in the case of many offices, word processing software.

License for Use By a Specified Number of Users   Licenses may be granted that permit installation on a network server, but restrict access to a specified number of individual users. Such software requires the customer's network manager to maintain a file on the program server that lists each user. The program will usually limit the number of users that can be listed. In order to call up the program, an individual user must enter his or her name or initials. Only if the name or initials match the user of a given file can the user access it.

License for a Specified Number of Concurrent Users   An increasingly common option is to grant a license that allows installation on a single network server with a specified number of concurrent users. In such systems, a software metering system is included in the program installed on the server. The metering system monitors the number of workstations that are using the software. When the maximum number is reached, the metering system shuts out any additional workstation that attempts to access and load the program. These systems have provisions for vendors to increase the number of simultaneous users (which they will do for a fee) and usually allow network managers to monitor and keep a log of usage.

Other Scope-of-Use Issues

For microcomputer software, the grant of the license may address other matters concerning scope of use, including the following:

Home Use of Office Software   If a vendor has granted a site license for a microcomputer program, are employees of the customer allowed to install a copy of the program on their home computers? If the license has a specified license fee per workstation, must the company pay an additional fee for a copy of the software on the machine at home?

Some vendors' software agreements permit their customers' employees to install the program on a home computer—without extra charge if the at-home use of the program is no more than 20 percent of the employee's total use of the software.

Laptop and Notebook Computer Use   A very similar issue is the following: May employees install copies of the program on portable computers to use on the job? Some vendors permit a portable computer and a desktop computer to be counted as a single installation, so long as only one person has sole use of both machines.

"Customer's Own Data" Restrictions   End-user agreements commonly restrict the scope of a software license to the "customer's own data" or the "customer's own use." The purpose of this provision to prevent "service bureau" use of the vendor's software; that is, the vendor does not want its software to be used by the customer to process data for a variety of *other* businesses.

While this sounds simple enough, in fact the question of what is a software customer's "own data" or its "own use" may be unclear. Take, for example, a bank that licenses software from a vendor to keep its customer account records where the end-user agreement signed by the bank contains these restrictions. Suppose the bank later modifies the program to allow depositors to log in to the bank's computer, examine their own accounts, check market yields for certificates of deposit and other investments, and to transfer funds or pay bills. Is it the bank's "own data" that is being accessed by depositors or is it the data of the depositors? Is the bank breaching its contract with the software vendor by offering this service to its depositors? Can the software vendor terminate the agreement unless the bank agrees to pay a higher licensing fee? The answer to all these questions is unclear. This is another situation where thinking through the issues and being specific in the licensing provisions can avoid disputes later on.

The "Non-Transferable" Provision   Software end-user agreements state that the license is non-assignable and non-transferable. This provision is normally a reasonable requirement and is usually accepted by the customer without quibble. The customer understands that the vendor wants new customers to license their software from the vendor, *not* from the customer.

But there is one situation where the "no-assignment" provision can cause a customer an unpleasant surprise: That is when the customer tries to assign the software license, together with all the other assets of customer's business, as part of the sale of all the customer's business operations. Relying on the "non-transferable" clause of the agreement, the vendor might refuse to permit the transfer of the license to the new owner, and demand that the new owner pay a new license fee.

For a vendor to play hardball like this with the buyer of its customer's business might be risky. In a recent case in Florida, a court ruled that an unreasonable refusal to consent to a software assignment, in the context of a sale of a business, was an illegal unfair business practice by the vendor.

Smart customers will often negotiate assignability of the license before the agreement is signed.

Limitation to Specified Hardware and Software Platforms   It is common for an end-user agreement to specify the type of hardware and software that the software will be running on. An important reason for this provision is that the vendor will be able to verify that the software will be installed on computers and operating systems that the software is known to work with. Many vendors have lists of "supported platforms" for their products. In many end-user agreements, the software vendor reserves the right to require that the customer upgrade its operating system or its hardware as a condition for software support or the delivery of new versions of the software program.

In the case of mainframe and minicomputer software, the agreement may license the software only for use on a particular CPU identified by model and serial number.

A Word About Linked Networks

It is increasingly common for customers with sophisticated data systems to have hardware and software that lets one network link to another. These links may be local, combining several local area networks (LANs) within a few hundred or thousand feet of one another. Or the links may create a wide area network (WAN), in which one LAN is linked with others hundreds or thousands of miles away.

When LANs are linked, a user at one location may suddenly get access to programs and data that are somewhere else. When remote users exploit access, they may violate end-user agreement provisions that restrict use of the program to a particular site or to particular hardware.

As with so many scope-of-use issues, the best approach is to anticipate this issue in negotiation, so that usage is proper and fees are based on actual usage by all users no matter how they access the program. Of course, it may be difficult for vendors to monitor customer's usage and therefore to some degree scope-of-use restriction are based on good faith and truth.

Purchasing Additional Software Components or Capacity

Customers' software needs may evolve as their businesses grow or change. An important feature of many end-user agreements is the option to add new software or to add to program capacity or functionality. Often the agreement is phrased in general terms so that it covers all additional programs that may be licensed from the vendor in the future. Agreements normally provide that to obtain support for any additional software, the customer must pay additional software support fees.

Adding Additional Terminals or More Users   When the license is limited to a certain number of terminals or concurrent users, the agreement will normally include an opportunity for the customer to increase the scope of the license for a price. Also often included is provision for additional user manuals, and, if needed, additional software diskettes.

Modules for New Functions   Often software is licensed in "modules" that allow the vendor to sell additional functions separately. An example would be an accounting program that licenses separate modules for general ledger, payroll, and tax returns. An end-user agreement can specify the terms for adding such modules.

Regulatory or Industry Changes   Sometimes software will change to meet new requirements issued by government or by business. For example, doctors, hospitals, and clinics may have to provide claims on new forms required by insurers or federal or state government. The end-user agreement can specify that the vendor will write or obtain software for the customer that will meet changing requirements for a specified fee.

Delivery and Acceptance

Important provisions of the end-user agreement relate to the delivery, installation, and acceptance of the software.

Delivery   The agreement will specify *what* has to be delivered, and sometimes will also say *when*. If no delivery time is specified, the vendor must deliver in a "reasonable" time. As a legal matter, "reasonable" means what is normal in the industry and meets any special time constraints stated by the customer. As a practical matter, vendors must deliver in a time frame that keeps its customer reasonably happy or the customer may seek to cancel the agreement.

Installation   Some software is sufficiently easy to install so the vendor just sends it to the customer with installation instructions. When installation is more complex, installation services will be provided. Such installation is usually included in the licensing fee. Data conversion (conversion of data stored in the file format of the customer's old software into a new format) may be needed as part of the installation process, and is often supplied for an additional fee.

Acceptance   In many agreements, a portion of the license fee is due on "acceptance." There are several types of provisions for acceptance commonly found in
end-user agreements:

1. **Performance Criteria.** This type of provision says that the customer must accept
   the software if it substantially performs according to specified criteria: Commonly the specified criteria is that it runs the functions described in the user
   manual. Because the manual is based on the software, only the worst software
   will fail this test. However, the fact that software carries out the functions listed
   in the manual does not mean that the software will do what the customer's
   business requires. Before signing this type of contract, the customer should be
   sure that software has all the functions and capabilities needed—including
   those capabilities that the customer anticipates in the foreseeable future.

2. **Specified Corrections.** Under this kind of provision, the customer must list any
   bugs or other needed corrections in a specified number of days after delivery. If
   these are fixed, the customer must accept the software.

3. **Customer-Specified Acceptance Criteria.** In many cases, the customer may
   define the acceptance criteria—which may include using actual data and running real reports. One common form of acceptance criterion is a "parallel" test,
   in which the same function is performed on the customer's old software and on
   the new software from the vendor. A parallel test allows the customer to verify
   the accuracy of the new computer code. Acceptance criteria may also include a
   performance standard, that is, the throughput capacity of the software when
   installed on specified hardware or the speed with which it response to a command, known as the response time.

4. **Free Trial—Optional Acceptance.** Under this alternative the customer makes
   the up-front payments and then obtains and tests the software. If it chooses, the
   customer may accept or reject it. If the software is not rejected in a specified
   number of days, the software is automatically accepted. If the customer does
   reject the software, the agreement may provide that the vendor keeps the downpayment as compensation for its work to customize and install the software.
   This "try-before-you-buy" provision has marketing advantages, but it also
   gives the customer an easy way out of the agreement if there are problems with
   the software. Any vendor that uses such a right-to-return provision should be

sure that the end-user agreement states that if the customer returns the software within the stated time period, the return of the software is the customer's sole and exclusive remedy for any breach of the contract or product defect.

Whatever the criteria, a careful vendor documents the date of acceptance. The best evidence of acceptance is a document that the customer signs stating that the acceptance criteria have been met. Many vendors simply send a letter confirming that acceptance criteria have been met and that the program is therefore accepted.

Protection of Intellectual Property

End-user agreements often have clauses forbidding decompiling, reverse engineering, and/or use of the code in other products. When source code is delivered to the customer (which is quite rare), there are often additional protections, including restriction of access to source code to certain individuals whose names are supplied to the vendor, and provisions for confidentiality. In licensing software that is not in mass distribution, it is common for the vendor to include a provision that the user manuals and other user information supplied to the customer are trade secrets and the customer must preserve the confidentiality of such information.

Prevention of Illegal Copying

Standard vendor end-user agreement forms commonly require that the customer prevent unauthorized copying of the software. This obligation sounds innocuous, but it is possible to imagine situations where the clause could impose liability on the customer. This provision may make the customer liable if, for example, an employee passes a copy of the software on to someone who sells hundreds of illegal copies. The risk is higher when source code has been delivered to the customer, because then the vendor's technology and trade secrets are easier to steal.

Sometimes a vendor will soften the language of this clause to say that the customer agrees to take reasonable efforts to prevent copying of the software. Of course, this may still leave the customer exposed and liable if it fails to take reasonable efforts. A sophisticated customer may be able to negotiate a limit to this potential liability, say a few thousand dollars.

Term and Termination

In the great majority of cases, in exchange for the initial license fee, the agreement grants the customer a license to the software that has no stated end, that is, a perpetual license. This means that in theory the license to use the software lasts forever; it is the duration of software support and of the warranty that are limited. Because software is frequently upgraded to add features, and to take advantage of changing computer technology, software programs change frequently. As a practical matter, therefore, software has a rather short life; a program written five years ago is old, and one written ten years ago is ancient. Therefore as a practical matter, the license has a limited life, even if technically it is perpetual. Some attorneys think that it is best for a software license to have a termination date, even if it is far in the future. There are exceptions to the perpetual format. On occasion, a license agreement will grant a limited term, a year or two, and require additional fees for renewal.

Agreements also provide for termination of the license under specified circumstances. An agreement will provide the vendor the option to terminate the license if required payments are not made or the customer otherwise materially breaches the agreement. Upon termination, the agreement usually provides that the customer must erase the software from the hard disk, tape, or other storage media, destroy any archival copies, and return the original diskettes or other media and documentation to the vendor, and the vendor has the right to inspect the customer's premises to verify that these steps have taken place.

Training Employees to Use the Program

New software often requires training, which may be addressed in the end-user agreement. A certain number of person-days of training may be included in the license fee, or training may be separately priced. The agreement (or a schedule to the agreement) may specify the number of trainers and trainees, the days or hours of training to be provided, the qualification of trainers, the curriculum, the place where the training will be provided, the hardware to be used, the sample data to be used, etc. Some customers want to obtain training materials several days in advance of training sessions. Some vendors offer videotape training material and tutorial software. Vendors also offer, on an ongoing basis (and at additional charge), training on advanced use of its programs or on features of new releases of its software products.

Software Support Provisions

Continuing software support is essential for complex computer systems. As a practical matter, most customers will feel that it is necessary to pay for software support for any sophisticated or complex software.

When Support Provisions Become Effective The support provision usually "kicks in" after the end of an initial period of support provided under the agreement, which may also be called the warranty period. This initial period is most often 90 days, six months, or one year. Obviously, the shorter the initial period of support, the sooner the revenue from software support will begin. For marketing reasons, however, it is quite common for vendors to include six months or one year of software support in the license fee.

Diagnosis and Response Time When a problem arises, the vendor's first task is to diagnose the problem. Many vendors agree to respond promptly. In some agreements there is a specified number of hours within which a technician will respond. If the software is used at a site far from the vendor's location, the customer may have to pay travel and other out-of-pocket costs for on-site service. Many vendors offer a service in which vendor's technicians log in to the customer's system by modem and run diagnostic programs to help find the problem.

Of course rapid response does not guarantee immediate cure. If the problem has been seen before, there may be an available software patch. Otherwise, a software engineer may have to find the problem and fix it.

Bug Fixes An important part of the support service provided under the agreement is providing bug fixes and patches. When bugs are reported, the vendor obtains a new release that fixes them, sometimes known as a "maintenance release," and sends it free of charge to all customers who are on support. Often the solution does not actually eliminate the bug, but just works around it by providing a alternative way to accomplish the functions involved without triggering the bug.

In many cases, the vendor is a dealer who does not have access to the source code of the software. In those cases, getting the right patch or work around for the customer requires the dealer to contact the manufacturer of the software. An important aspect of dealer service to customers is to have a smoothly function system for getting technical data on problems up to the manufacturer and getting solutions back down to the customers. Some end-user agreements have provisions for the situation when the vendor is unable to fix the software. These provisions allow the vendor to "pull the plug," that is, to discontinue support, refund some or all of the license fee or support fee, terminate the license, and cease further obligation to the customer. These provisions, which obviously do not help with software marketing, are most common in situations where the software requires considerable development before delivery and there is a high degree of technical risk.

New Versions of the Software   It is normal for the vendor (or the publisher that supplies the vendor) to release improved versions of the software from time to time—versions with faster operation, greater ease-of-use, more functionality, or that take advantage of new features of hardware and operating systems. Often new versions are provided without additional charge as part of software support. Sometimes a vendor may draw a distinction between minor revisions and a major rewrite of the software: It will provide the revisions without additional charge, but require that the customer pay an additional license fee (usually a substantial discount from list price) to get the major rewrite.

Support Only for Current Versions   It is normal for the agreement to provide software support only if the customer is using the most recent release (or one of the two most recent releases). This policy to support only recent releases is born of necessity. No vendor can afford to be fixing and supporting obsolete versions of software used by only a few customers.

Continuing Technical Support   Under software support provisions, the vendor will provide technical advice on use of the program. Sometimes there is a limit to the number of hours included in the support fee, with additional hours available on a charge-per-hour basis. Some vendors offer the option of reduced support fees, with technical advice provided on a "900" telephone number at a $2 or $3 per-minute charge.

Disclaimer of Warranties

All software vendors should insist that the agreement contain language to limit potential damage claims for software defects. To limit claims, almost all end-user agreements contain the following provisions:

- The vendor has the option to replace or repair any defective software, and there is a provision that if this is done, it is the exclusive remedy.

- If the vendor fails to repair or replace the defective software, there are restrictions on the total dollar amount of damages that the customer can recover in a lawsuit. Typically the limit is the license fee that the customer paid for the system, although a higher amount can be negotiated.

- There is restriction on the *type* of injury to the customer that is compensable—usually only "direct damages," the cost of replacing the defective software or system.

In connection with the third item, end-user agreements *disclaim* liability for "incidental" or "consequential" damages. Incidental damages are costs incidental to replacement of defective software, such as expert consulting fees or shipping and installation costs. Consequential damages, usually by far the larger item, are damages for interruption of business, loss of production, or lost profits.

Customer claims for damages arise primarily under the Uniform Commercial Code (UCC), a statute that we discussed in Chapter 8 and Chapter 11. (See also the general discussion of software liability issues in Chapter 13.) As we have noted previously, under the UCC provisions, language that disclaims warranties needs to be "conspicuous" and is usually therefore printed in large capital letters.[1] It is customary (although not strictly required) that language limiting the total amount of damages also be in large type. Form 12-2 in Appendix C contains typical provisions on limitation of liability.

---

1   The products under end-user agreements that we are discussing normally have only business, industrial, or professional applications. Therefore they will usually not come under the Magnuson-Moss Act, a federal statute governing warranties which applies to products "normally" used for "personal, family or household" purposes. The warranty requirements of the Magnuson-Moss Act are discussed in Chapter 11.

In most cases, it is a mistake for a vendor to try to eliminate *all* liability for software errors or to reduce damage below the price paid by the customer. There is a high risk that the courts will find such a limitation to be unreasonable and nullify it. The effect will be to expose the vendor to unlimited damage liability.

The customer, for its part, cannot reasonably expect the vendor to eliminate limitations on warranties and contractual remedies, because the vendor simply cannot afford the risk of an unlimited damage claim. However, some upward adjustment may be made in the limit of potential damage claims.

The Customer's Obligation to Protect Its Data

When something goes wrong with software, important data can be lost or garbled. The damage will be minimized, however, if the data has been backed up to tape or other storage media. As an additional line of defense against damage claims, many end-user agreements require that the customer regularly back up all data. Then, if data is lost, it will be because the customer did not comply with the requirements of the agreement. Such a clause may also require the customer to install and maintain anti-virus software. The vendor's user manual should also include advice to the customer that these safe data management practices should be followed.

Intellectual Property Indemnification

Most end-user agreements contain language indemnifying the customer if it turns out that the program infringes another party's rights under patent or copyright law. These provisions raise the same issues that we discussed in Chapter 8 and in Chapter 10 regarding indemnification. In such a provision, the vendor agrees to defend the customer against infringement claims arising from the software. The vendor typically has the right to procure a license for any infringing technology or to supply non-infringing code and to require that the customer switch to the non-infringing version. The customer is obliged to cooperate in defending any infringement claim. It is also common that the vendor maintains, as a last resort, the right to pull the plug and terminate the customer's use of the program, if the vendor cannot find a suitable and cost-effective way to allow the customer to use the program without infringement.

General Provisions

Most end-user agreements have general provisions of the types that we have seen earlier in this book on choice of law, notices, etc.; examples of which are found in Form 12-2 in Appendix C. Another common provision is an arbitration clause. In addition, vendors' forms commonly provide that the vendor may recover attorneys' fees for collection of unpaid invoices. The customer may seek to modify this clause to provide that in the case a suit or arbitration, the prevailing party—whether vendor or customer—will recover attorneys' fees.

Escrow Agreements for Crucial Software

For software that plays an essential role in a customer's business, software support is absolutely critical. If the software has a bug that cannot be fixed, or renders the data inaccurate or crashes the system, the customer's business may be paralyzed. Or it may be critical for a company to get functions updated. Accounting systems are a prime example. When accounting rules change or the tax law is amended, the customer *has* to be able to get its accounting system changed.

What happens if a vendor fails to render support, perhaps because it loses its key employees or because the owner closes shop and becomes a beachcomber? What happens if the vendor goes bankrupt? Often the customer needs to be *sure* that critical changes and fixes for the software are available no matter what.

One answer to the dilemma is to give the customer a copy of the source code of each version of the software that is delivered. Then, if needed, the customer can hire a programmer to fix and add new functions to the code. The problem here is that most customers find that source code is hard to get. Sometimes the vendor does not even *have* the source code, but has obtained the program in object code from a supplier. Even if the vendor has the source code, it will not want to give up control of crucial trade secrets.

A common solution to this dilemma is a *source code escrow*. The vendor and customer enter into a source code escrow agreement as part of the commercial relationship. When the vendor is not the manufacturer, it will normally be the manufacturer that puts the source code into escrow and enters into the escrow agreement with the customer. In that case, the provisions discussed in the following pages would be modified accordingly) The escrow agreement provides for a copy of the source code for the product to be placed in the hands of a third party, known as an *escrow agent* or *escrowee*. Under the terms of the escrow agreement, the escrow agent will release the source code to the customer under specified conditions. Often the escrow agent is a specialized company whose business is to hold source code, known as an *escrow house*. (A list of some of the escrow houses is included in Appendix D.)

One issue that must be negotiated is *verification*. The customer should be able to verify that each time that the vendor releases a new version or update of the program, the corresponding source code goes to the escrow agent. The escrow agreement may provide that the vendor certify each year, or on some other periodic basis, that the current source code is in escrow. In addition, the escrow house will provide verification of the contents of the escrow on request, for a fee. To perform this service, the escrow house will compile the escrowed source code and compare the compiled program to the object code supplied by the vendor. This is one reason why other possible escrow agents (a bank or an attorney), are usually not a good choice—they rarely have the expertise to verify source code contents.

In spite of the requirements of the escrow agreement, some vendors neglect to make the deposits of software required to keep an escrowed source code current. When the object code for software is changed frequently, the version of the source code in escrow may become completely obsolete. Many customers sign the escrow agreement and then forget it. That is a mistake. The customer must check periodically that the latest version of the source code has been deposited as required. Moreover, a vendor in financial trouble is more likely to neglect updating software escrow deposits. Therefore, if the vendor is financially unstable, the customer should be even more vigilant to press the vendor to update the escrow deposit.

The parties must also negotiate the *release conditions*, that is, the conditions under which the escrow agent will give the source code to the customer. Normally, these will include the vendor's termination of business, its bankruptcy, its failure to maintain the software, and the like.

In addition, the parties must agree on the *release mechanism*, that is the procedures for releasing source code to the customer. Normally the escrow agent does not want to get in the middle of a fight between the vendor and the customer. Many escrow agreements provide therefore that if the customer and the vendor disagree on whether a release condition exists, the escrow agent will continue to hold the source code until a court of law or an arbitrator orders that the source code be released to the customer. Some escrow agreements provide the reverse—that the code will be released to the customer unless a court orders, within a specified number of days, that it remain in escrow.

Finally, the parties must agree on *escrow fees*, because the escrow will terminate (and the source code will be sent back to the vendor) unless yearly escrow fees are paid. Usually the customer pays the escrow fees because it seeks the benefit of the escrow agreement. It usually costs roughly $1,000 to set up a software escrow at an escrow house and about $500 to $600 per year to maintain it, not including the cost of any verification services supplied by the escrow house.

For marketing purposes, some vendors set up a single, multi-customer escrow. The escrow agreement provides that if the release condition exists, the source code will be released to all customers who have arranged for source code escrow protection.

Escrow houses have their own form contracts. These forms can be modified to allow the parties to supply the specifics about what software must be deposited, what verification will be done, what the release condition and release mechanism will be, etc. So that you can become familiar with the language and terms of a source code agreement, a sample is provided as Form 12-3 (on diskette as ESCROW.W51). Any customer relying on a software escrow for important software should have an attorney review and approve the escrow agreement before it becomes final.

Software "Time Bombs" and Locking Devices

Recently the courts have dealt with a new phenomenon—software that self-destructs or shuts down when the vendor's bills are unpaid. The courts have given these ploys a chilly reception.

Normally an unpaid vendor's remedy is litigation, but in some cases, vendors have used a quicker and more powerful remedy: software "time bombs" and "locks." Software time bombs are routines, hidden in the program code, that cripple or destroy the software at a specified date and time or under specified conditions. A software lock is a routine that shuts down all program functions when triggered by the vendor, who can access the customer's computer system though a modem.

Time bombs and software locks are used for leverage in fee disputes. Sometimes when a vendor provides extensive programming services, serious disputes can arise over how much money is due to the vendor. For example, the programming work required for a job may have exceeded the vendor's original estimate, and the customer may balk at the final price. Or acceptance testing may uncover bugs and the customer may refuse to pay until all the bugs are fixed—even if the remaining bugs are not serious and the program is in fact in use. You can guess the scenario that follows: The customer refuses to pay. The bomb or lock shuts down the customer's operations. Then the vendor offers to restore the software to working order—*if* the customer pays the bills.

The results in lawsuits over these devices have been totally one-sided: the vendors always lose. Judges hate software locks and time bombs if they are surreptitious. In several cases, judges have not only ordered that program function be immediately restored, but have imposed *punitive damages* against vendors that have used these devices.

The only time that locks and bombs should be used is if they are agreed to by the customer *in advance* in the text of the agreement. Of course, many customers will resist agreement provisions that permit the vendor to shut the customer down. It is more common for vendors to include clauses that permit a software lock to be activated on any copy of the program that is wrongfully transferred to a company other than the customer. The bottom line is that you cannot use these bombs and locks unless the agreement expressly says that they may be used. In fact, a careful customer will ask for written assurance in the agreement that no bombs or locks will be included in any software that it receives from the vendor.

End-User Agreements in Litigation

Disputes between vendors and their customers have frequently generated litigation over the years. Usually the cases have erupted because the software has just not worked or has been so full of bugs that it has little value to the customer.

The litigation process that follows is essentially the same as the one that I described in Chapter 1, except that in many cases the process will be in state court or in arbitration rather than in federal court. In most cases, the customer will be seeking money damages as the main or sole remedy to compensate for poor software. As we have discussed previously, the process in arbitration will likely be faster and less expensive than in the courts.

Litigation and arbitration cases make it clear that contract language often protects vendors, but that the protection is not 100 percent guaranteed. The law provides ways around agreement provisions. For example, we have discussed the fact that some agreements have acceptance criteria that are easy for vendors to meet. But if the software has never worked right on the customer's actual data, there is a risk that a court will allow the customer to *revoke* acceptance and get its money back. The court has the power to decide that the time allowed for evaluation was unfairly short or that there were "latent defects" that the customer could not have discovered earlier. In addition, courts sometimes invalidate liability limitations as unreasonable or "unconscionable." And if the court finds that the customer was deceived in some way, it may find the vendor (and the vendors' officers or employees) liable for fraud. No contract clause can eliminate or limit the amount of fraud liability.

Judges, juries, and arbitrators are all human, and their judgments may be swayed by emotion. A limitation of damages clause that is perfectly valid in a case against General Motors, may be held "unconscionable" when asserted against a small town community hospital. The more naïve the customer, and the worse the software has performed, the more likely the court is going to try to find some legal theory that helps the customer in spite of disclaimers and damage limitations. There is no "bulletproof" language that protects against all litigation risk.

If, soon after the software is installed, it becomes clear to the vendor that the software is bad, it often makes sense for the vendor to try to find a way to accommodate the customer—even if it means concessions, the application of considerable labor, or a refund.

A Note on Licensing Software to the Government

One of the largest customers for software is the United States government, which buys commercially available software for managing governmental operations and has software written for special applications. A major government purchaser of standard and special-purpose software is the Department of Defense (DOD).

Software companies dealing with the government must become thoroughly familiar with the procedures of the Federal Acquisition Regulations (FAR) and the Department of Defense FAR Supplement (DFAR). These procedures are administered by the General Services Administration (GSA), by DOD, or by various federal agencies that need software. Generally speaking, there is a solicitation of vendor proposals and a selection process carried out by the GSA or other agency involved, in a process replete with forms and red tape.

One important aspect of dealing with the federal government is the scope of the license granted to the government. Under FAR and DFAR, the federal government can have either unlimited rights or restricted rights. Unlimited rights mean what they sound like: the government gets a license to "use, duplicate, release or disclose . . . computer software in whole or in part or in any manner and for any purpose whatsoever." If the government has unlimited rights, a vendor can sell a single copy to the government and the government could make 10,000 copies for its own use.

Most often, when the government buys software that was not created under a government contract, the government will agree to receive only restricted rights, which are quite narrow. Restricted rights can be expanded by contract, but at a minimum the government gets: (1) the right to use the software for the computer for which it was acquired; (2) the right to use the software with a backup computer if the original hardware is disabled; (3) the right to make backup and archival copies of the software; and (4) the ability to modify the software and to use it with other software products. Restricted rights do not include the right to duplicate the software for the purpose of using additional copies.

FAR and DFAR contain provisions that spell out how the federal government obtains restricted rights to software. With some exceptions, the regulations require that the written agreement between the vendor and the government expressly state that only restricted rights are being granted. (In many cases, absent express agreement, the government gets unlimited rights.) The regulations also require that legends be put on software referring to the relevant contract and stating that only restricted rights are granted. Software vendors should be sure to comply with these regulations.

Very often vendors of mass-market software include restricted rights legends in their shrink-wrap licenses included on software packages. An example of such a provision is included in Form 11-1 in Appendix C. It is prudent to use this language in shrink-wrap forms. However, it is unclear whether a shrink-wrap legend alone is sufficient to limit the government's rights.

Restricted rights generally apply only to software that was developed or acquired by the developer independently of the government contract. If the government is buying software and funds its development, the regulations provide that the government obtains all rights to it.

The FAR and DFAR are important regulations that any company selling software to the government must become very familiar with. Vendors can get further information from the GSA about procedures for dealing with the government. Vendors can also get advice on the regulations from attorneys specializing in government contracts.

State and local governments also have regulations concerning contracts and purchase that may apply to software. The vendor should learn applicable regulations before doing business with state and local government agencies.

CHAPTER 13

Software Liability Issues

Managing the risk of large liabilities is an essential part of operating a software company. We all know that software can go wrong—and that the consequences of software problems can range from trivial to catastrophic. Software is said to be the most complex object ever created by humankind. It is common for personal computer software to have half a million lines of code; mainframe software programs can be many times larger. Errors in software are often caught and fixed, but there is no scientifically proven methodology for finding *all* errors in program logic. No one has a method for proving that a program is error-free. Software errors and software failures can be reduced, but they cannot be eliminated.

Enormous social responsibilities now rest on software. Virtually all telecommunication is software operated. Software manages the transactions of every bank and brokerage house. International currency transactions are managed by software. "Program trading" on Wall Street executes billions of dollars of trades without human intervention. Businesses large and small rely every day on software for essential ordering, shipping, billing, and inventory control functions. Businesses have been destroyed by computer failures.

Human lives also depend on software every day. Software is used to schedule trains, to operate commercial airliners, and to monitor nuclear reactors. Software is used to design bridges and skyscrapers. When this software fails, people may die.

We also live in the most litigious society in the history of the world. In the United States, when systems fail and something bad happens, people expect compensation and the lawyers swing into action. When software goes wrong, the damage awards can be great.

Software-related liabilities can crush a software business. In this chapter, I will discuss some of the threats, and the ways that the software business can cope with them. It does not cover everything a software business can do to get into hot water, but is a discussion of common ways in which software writing, sales, and distribution can cause trouble—and the most important means to avoid this crushing type of liability.

Liability for Personal Injury

An area of acute concern is software that can impact human health and safety. Errors in this type of software can lead to huge personal injury claims. The preferred strategies to deal with this threat are (1) quality control, (2) a well-planned rapid notification and recall program, and (3) liability insurance or a contractual allocation of the product liability risk to a party that can afford to bear it.

The Risk of Personal Injury Claims

There have been a number of reported cases in which defective software has caused personal injury. A well-known example involved a company called Atomic Energy of Canada, Ltd. Beginning in 1983, the company made a computer-controlled linear electron accelerator, known as Therac-25, used for cancer therapy. In its low-power beam mode, Therac-25 generated mild electron beams used to treat tumors at or near the surface of the skin. In its high-energy mode, the beam was ramped up to 25 million electron volts, a tungsten target swung into the path of the beam, and the unit generated x-rays used to kill cancer deep in the body.

The software program that controlled Therac-25 had a bug. The bug was triggered when a rather rare sequence of instructions was fed into the machine. When the bug was triggered, the machine switched to its highest power when it should have been generating a low-power beam—but without the tungsten target in place. The machine then blasted a searing beam of 25 million electron volts into the patient, scorching a cylinder of burned flesh right through the patient's body. In the first accident caused by the software bug, a woman endured years of excruciating pain and suffered permanent loss of the use of her shoulder and arm. The next two accidents resulted in ghastly deaths. Only after three major accidents was the software error discovered. As you can appreciate, all three accidents resulted in major lawsuits and substantial liability.

Human safety is on the line in a great variety of medical programs. Software programs control therapeutic machines, diagnostics, patient records, processing and testing of medicine, etc. Software is in control of every heart monitor and every blood analyzer. Blood banks use computer programs to match (or perhaps mismatch) blood donors with positive AIDS tests. The liability issues here are legion.

Note that products used for human therapy require prior approval from the Food and Drug Administration (FDA) before they can be marketed in the United States. However, a number of FDA-approved devices have proven to contain critical software errors. FDA regulation may nonetheless in some circumstances provide protection from liability suits for software devices. If you have questions about the nature and effect of FDA regulation of medical devices, you should see a qualified attorney.

Software in many other fields also crucially affects safety. Errors in software that control industrial machines and processing can cause serious injury or death on the assembly line. Some jet airplanes are controlled by "fly-by-wire" systems, in which software controls are major operating systems. Air traffic control systems are computer controlled. Errors in these complex systems could lead to hundreds of deaths. Computers in today's automobiles control the engines, and malfunctions could easily cause a fatal accident. The list of applications for software that could crucially affect human life grows every day.

In every state, the rule that generally governs defective products that injure people—including software—is simple: Everyone that made or sold the defective product is liable to the victim, and (unless otherwise agreed) the ultimate liability falls on the party that created the defect. It is not uncommon to see multimillion dollar awards in cases of injury or death.

Example: Admiral Motors makes an automobile known as the Madison Town Car. The car has a computer that controls the engine. Due to a software bug, the computer can cause the engine to race suddenly, causing a surge of acceleration. The software was written by Software Consulting, Inc. Smith buys a Madison, and due to the software bug, gets in an accident and is seriously injured. Smith can sue and collect monetary damages from everyone involved: the car dealer, Admiral Motors, and Software Consulting. If the car dealer pays Smith, it can get reimbursement from Admiral Motors. Unless otherwise agreed, if Admiral Motors pays Smith or the dealer, it can get reimbursement from Software Consulting.

In a serious accident, the plaintiff will normally sue everyone in sight. In this situation, Smith's right to recovery from everybody involved overrides any written contracts. It doesn't matter if Smith signed a contract saying that all warranties on the software were disclaimed or that software used in the car was sold "as is."

Managing the Risk of Personal Injury Claims

If your company is going to create or sell software that can affect health or safety, managing risk should be a fundamental part of your planning for the product. Indeed, all parties involved should agree upon the strategy for managing risk before signing any contract to write or sell the software.

In any well-planned system for distribution of products affecting health and safety, there must be mechanisms for immediately notifying users of any hazards and for safety recalls and upgrades. When supplying a manufacturer with a software program that serves such a critical function, the software company should get written assurances in the contract that all these necessary recall and upgrade systems will be in place. When a problem is discovered, users should, of course, be notified immediately, and replacement software that fixes the problem should be installed as quickly as is humanly possible. Preventing injury before it happens is the best way to deal with the potential liability issues.

Because not all mishaps can be prevented, a common strategy for managing risk is product liability insurance. A liability policy will normally include provisions for defense of any lawsuit brought by accident victims and for payments of settlements or monetary judgments. Insurance for potentially huge liabilities is expensive and may be hard to get. If insurance is the strategy you choose, then contact an insurance broker to shop for it. Be sure that both the scope of the protection and the amount of the insurance is adequate. Planning for insurance must be done early, before any contract to supply the software is signed, because the cost of insurance has to be taken into account before pricing the contract.

A second strategy for managing the risk of potential personal injury suits is to allocate the risk by contract. This strategy only works if the other party to the contract can actually afford to defend personal injury lawsuits and pay personal injury plaintiffs (or is willing to commit to buying the needed insurance protection). For example, if you are developing software for a well-capitalized customer, say a Fortune 500 corporation, your software development agreement can provide that your customer will take care of any personal injury claims or liability. In exchange for shouldering this burden, the customer will normally expect a price concession. If you are negotiating for this result, the issue should be on the table from the first day of negotiations.

Whenever you are going to supply software that has a critical function affecting health or safety, you need to have legal counsel involved in the contract negotiations to be sure that you get the protection that you need.

The Key Role of Quality Control and Beta Testing

The first and most important line of defense against product liability claims is to pay attention to software reliability and quality in product development and testing.

Admittedly, software quality is not a simple matter. There is often a rush to get software to market. No software product generates revenue until it is introduced, and there is a risk that the competition will jump ahead if a product introduction is delayed. Technology and competitive pressures force constant changes in products during the development cycle—features are added, functions are changed. All too often, products are released to the market full of hidden defects. My advice, in spite of these pressures, is to allow enough time for thorough testing and quality control.

The risk of liability issues increases if products are rushed. The need for adequate testing is especially acute for any product that serves a critical function. Beta testing in the "real world," rather than with canned data, is essential. While no complex software can be proven error-free, it is beyond cavil that testing can find and remove errors and improve reliability. The more that people depend on the software, the more time and attention should be given to improving the reliability of the program before release into the market.

Liability for Financial Harm to a Business

For most software applications, the liability risk is not loss of life or personal injury, but loss of money. Most potential liability is from software used to operate or manage the end-user's business. Software may seriously injure a user's business, or it may fail to deliver expected cost savings.

The preferred strategies to deal with this liability threat are (1) quality control, (2) swift replacement of defective software, (3) using contractual language to reduce liability, and (4) possible insurance protection.

Replacing Defective Software Without Delay

As I noted earlier, the best practice is to release software without critical bugs. However, if a critical problem is found, your company should implement a rapid response. If the defective program can cause serious losses or disruption in the user's business, it is best to arrange a quick replacement of the defective program.

If there are only a few users, the new version can be delivered to or installed at their work sites. If there are many users, the new release can be mailed or sent by modem to registered users, and the availability of the new version can be announced to the software trade press. There is of course a cost for this type of replacement. But fast action can fend off possible liability suits and earn a dividend in customer good will.

Using User Documentation to Limit Liability

One potentially devastating software failure is destruction of data—particularly valuable database or word processing files. A sensible way to reduce the risk of liability for lost or destroyed data is to tell the end-user to use reasonable measures to protect data. The user documentation should therefore preach the gospel of daily backups of data. Advice on this topic should come early in the documentation and should be stated prominently. Typical wording for such advice is the following:

> **IMPORTANT:** It is *essential* that you back up the data files created by [name of program] on a daily basis. The data stored on your hard disk can be corrupted by power surges, mechanical failures, unforeseen interactions of the various software on your computer system, computer virus, fire, or other unexpected causes. To prevent loss of your data, the only safe course is to back up the data at the end of every business day and to store the backed-up information off-site. That way, the most you can

lose is a single day's work. If you need more information on
software and hardware used in backing up data, see your computer retailer or a consultant.

A customer that *follows* this advice is much less likely to lose much data. Even if
the end-user has ignored this advice, a judge or jury may be reluctant to hold your
company liable for a loss of data that could have been prevented by taking the recommended measures.

In addition, it is prudent to advise the end-user to consider using commercially
available virus protection programs.

Using Contract Provisions to Reduce Liability

As we discussed in Chapter 11, shrink-wrap licenses may not be effective to fend
off liabilities. Therefore, the makers of mass-market software deal with potential liabilities mainly by the methods that we have discussed above.

However, for software businesses that routinely get signed end-user agreements
in advance, contractual provisions are a crucial line of defense. As I discussed earlier in Chapter 12, there are important items that a software vendor must secure in
negotiations with end-users:

1. It is most important that: *the agreement have a limitation on all damages.* Note also
   that the limitation must be reasonable; if it is too paltry, the courts will toss out
   the limitation on damages—and then there will be no cap on liability. Normally,
   the courts will consider that a limitation of damages equal to the original contract price is reasonable. In some cases, it may be more reasonable to limit liability to all amounts paid to the vendor over the life of the contract, which would
   include the price of the software plus maintenance payments.

2. *The agreement must disclaim liability for consequential damages.* Disclaiming consequential damages eliminates claims for lost profits or "lost cost savings" arising
   from problems in the software.

The following examples illustrate the type of financial damage claims that often
arise and how they are dealt with by these contract provisions.

Example: Smith Software creates a billing system for General Hospital for a licensing fee of $30,000. Errors in the software cause the software to not bill certain accounts. By the time the error is found, certain key insurance reimbursement deadlines have passed. As a result, General Hospital loses $1,000,000 in reimbursement payments. Labor costs for manual procedures to correct errors in the file system are $150,000. After the error is discovered, Smith Software fixes the error and the software functions properly. General Hospital sues Smith Software for $1,150,000. The agreement between General Hospital and Smith Software disclaims consequential damages and limits overall damages to the license fee.

Example: Software Systems, Inc. contracts to create an order entry, billing, and inventory management system for American Shoe Manufacturing for a licensing fee of $300,000 to replace existing manual systems. Based on the agreed-upon specifications, American Shoe reasonably expects $1,200,000 in labor savings over a three-year period. Software Systems has serious problems creating the system, but keeps working at it. One year after the scheduled delivery date, Software Systems is still unable to get the system to operate satisfactorily and abandons the job. American Shoe sues for the $1,200,000 in "lost" labor savings, plus the $400,000 cost of a new computer system, for a total of $1,600,000. The agreement between Software Systems and American Shoe Manufacturing disclaims consequential damages and limits overall damages to the license fee.

Let's look at the effect of end-user agreement provisions for damage limitation and disclaimer of consequential damages by applying them to these two hypothetical lawsuits. In the first example, these contract provisions would probably eliminate the entire claim by General Hospital. The hospital's only claim was for consequential damages, which are disclaimed in the contract. In the second example, these provisions would eliminate the entire claim of American Shoe to "labor savings," again because of the provision disclaiming consequential damages. American Shoe would still have its claim against Software Systems for the cost of a replacement computer system—but only up to $300,000. In both examples, having these protective provisions in place saves the vendor more than $1,000,000. The contractual provisions to accomplish this result are discussed in Chapter 12.

Like almost everything in the law, the protective provisions discussed above are not 100-percent foolproof. There is always risk that a judge will misapply the law or that some exception or loophole will be found. Nonetheless, these protective contract provisions work in court most of the time and are *essential* protection.

Liability Insurance

If your business seeks an extra measure of protection, you may want to consider product liability insurance coverage for this type of business loss. To investigate the costs, availability, and limitations of such coverage, you should see an insurance broker.

Liability for Fraud

Where software has performed very poorly, customers may assert claims of fraud, in litigation or arbitration. Fraud claims cannot be eliminated by even the most tightly worded warranty disclaimer, and fraud damages cannot be limited by contract. Therefore, claims of fraud must be taken very seriously.

Fraud is selling something or obtaining an advantage with a misrepresentation. Half-truths or misleading statements count as misrepresentations. In many states, the customer asserting fraud must prove that the misrepresentations were deliberately false or made with disregard to whether they were true or not. In some states, fraud claims can include an award of actual damages and punitive damages, that is, damages in the amount that the judge, jury, or arbitrator feels will deter and punish the defendant for its wrongful conduct.

Most of the case law about software fraud involves misrepresentations in the sale of computer systems—particularly deception by a software vendor about the reliability or state of development of software. For example, if a vendor has told the customer that software is tested and reliable, when in fact the system has failed frequently in testing, that may be fraud. If a customer is told that other customers are satisfied, when in fact they are not, that may be fraud. In many cases, the alleged fraud consists of oral statements and a main issue in these cases is whose version of the facts is believed.

Some frauds may also violate state laws against unfair business practices. A pattern of very egregious fraud may give rise to a claim against a vendor under the federal Racketeering Influenced and Corrupt Organizations Act (RICO), which provides for an award of triple damages against a wrongdoer, or under similar state law statutes. These claims as well cannot be eliminated by contract language.

If your business is threatened with any such claim, or if you are sued for fraud, you should contact counsel immediately. To avoid these claims, it is best to supervise sales staff and to eliminate "overselling" or misrepresenting products.

The Final Line of Defense

As a final line of defense against software liability under contracts law, every software business should be *incorporated* in order to protect its owners and officers. The time that you need this protection is when your other lines of defense have failed. If there is a huge liability, or if the business debts are overwhelming, the issue will be whether *your own personal assets* can be reached by injured parties or by business creditors. If the worst comes, you may lose the company, but if you are incorporated you have the best chance to hold on to your personal assets.

In general, there are several forms for doing business:

1. If you do business in your own name, or if you use a trade name but have not incorporated, your business is a *sole proprietorship*.

2. If you have partners with whom you share profits and losses, but you have not incorporated, you are in a *partnership*.

3. Your business can become a *corporation* only by filing formal incorporation papers with the state government. Most businesses incorporate in their home state or in the "mother of corporations" state Delaware.

If you do business either as a sole proprietorship or as partnership, you are taking a big and unnecessary risk, because your own personal assets are on the line for any contractual liability that arises from the business. If the business is unable to pay its debts, all your own personal assets—your home, your car, your bank accounts—are at risk.

The only prudent form for doing business is as a corporation, because in most states only incorporation provides *limited liability*. This means that in most contract related suits against the company, the assets of the corporation are at risk, but the shareholders' and officers' personal assets are not. In some states it is possible to form a *limited liability company*, in which one can have the limited liability advantages of incorporation without some of the formalities. You should check with your local lawyer to see if this option is available.

Incorporation is not a perfect protection for owners and officers. There are some exceptions to limited liability. Here are a few of the most common:

- The owners' and officers' own acts of negligence or fraud will often impose liability on them.

- To maintain a corporation requires certain formalities: paying a yearly corporate tax, making corporate filings, holding shareholder meetings and board of directors' meetings. Failure to observe the formalities can result in a failure of the protection against personal liability for the owners.

- Mixing personal and corporate assets, forming a business with inadequate assets, or removing too many assets from the company can result in personal liability for the owners.

Every corporate contract should always be signed by the corporation—not by an individual. Therefore, the signature line should read: "XYZ Corporation by Jack Smith, President." Failure to make it explicitly clear that an agreement is signed as an officer of the corporation can result in the personal liability of the signer.

If your software business is not incorporated, you should see a lawyer to arrange incorporation without delay. Ask about the requirements in your state to maintain limited liability protection. Incorporation also has important tax implications and requires some tax planning, so you also need to see your accountant. In most states, the process of incorporation for a small business will probably cost about $1,000 or less, plus applicable fees. The investment will be money well spent.

A Final Word About Liability Issues

Risk management—like quality management—is not something that you provide for and then forget. As your software business grows, you need to revisit these issues regularly—with staff, with counsel, and sometimes with customers as well. Planning for both quality and liability issues should be a routine part of your business.

CHAPTER 14

Protecting Your Trademarks

If you properly establish and protect your trademark, the law can be a powerful tool to stop competitors from stealing the name and reputation that you have painstakingly established. However, appalling things may happen if a trademark is not properly protected. For example:

- A company you never heard of could write to demand that you stop using your trademark—and sue you if you don't obey. You could be forced to stop using a trademark and even to destroy existing stocks of software goods and packaging—which could handicap or destroy your business.
- You could introduce a new product and be forced to withdraw it immediately.
- A competitor could start stealing your business by using your trademark or one that looks confusingly like yours. You might not be able to stop it from doing so.

There are several questions about your trademark that you will learn how to answer in this chapter: Are you secure in your right to use your existing trademark(s)? What legal criteria affect the choice of a new trademark? What kinds of trademarks can be protected? How can you protect a trademark? How are trademarks put to use? Do you have the right to stop someone else from using your trademark or a mark that is confusingly similar to yours?

You will also get an overview of trademark law, and learn what makes trademarks distinctive, how a trademark gets priority, how one does trademark searches, and how the trademark registration system works.

Trademark law is complex, but it is critical to any business that spends time, money or effort promoting its brand name. Therefore I urge you to read through the chapter, and consider how the concepts presented here apply to the trademarks used in your business. At the end of the chapter is a checklist to help you apply the concepts that are discussed here.

What is a Trademark?

You have an everyday sense of what is meant by a trademark like Microsoft, Lotus, or Borland. Trademarks apply to goods: for example a DEC printer, an Apple computer, a Digital Research operating system, an Oracle relational database. Trademarks for software appear on diskettes, on screen displays, on packaging, in advertising and in computer manuals.

A trademark can consist of:

- *A name* like "Microsoft."

- *A slogan* like the one used by DCA, "The Freedom to Communicate."

- *Letters and numbers* like "MS-DOS" and "OS/2."

- *A design* like the striped blue IBM logo or Apple Computer's multicolored apple.

Many software goods have more than one trademark on them; for example, "DESQview" and "Quarterdeck" are both trademarks of Quarterdeck Office Systems used on DESQview packages and diskettes. A trademark can also be used to show one company's endorsement of another. An example is the "Intel Inside" logo used by many computer makers.

Service marks are like trademarks, but apply to services. Computer businesses that use service marks include contract programmers, data recovery services, data and media conversion services, and system integrators. (For the sake of convenience, I will refer only to trademarks or just use the term "marks" in the discussion that follows; aside from some details of the procedure for registration, the rules for trademarks and service marks are very much the same.)

Marks for products may at first be chosen to be dramatic or informative or flashy. Over time, however, the mark takes on a life of its own. If the product succeeds, the trademark may come to connote quality and technical acumen, and help motivate the customer to buy new products and new versions of old ones. Trademark law is a means to protect a company's access to the powerful psychological effect these symbols can have on customers. However, trademark law does not protect every mark, and some marks get more protection than others. Moreover, there are things that you must do to obtain, extend, and preserve trademark protection.

Common Trademark Myths

Many companies unwisely fail to protect their marks, relying on trademark myths. Before we go further in this discussion, let's clear away some of the common misconceptions about trademarks which lead many businesses into a false sense of security.

Myth # 1: Safety with Incorporation

Many people believe that if they have incorporated a business in their home state (or in that "mother of corporations" state Delaware) they have protected its business name as a trademark. State incorporation requires a corporate name search, but incorporation nonetheless gives *no* protection to a trademark used on products, *none whatsoever*. Registering the name of the business at city hall likewise gives *no legal protection*.

Myth # 2: Safety from Use

Many people believe that if they have used a trademark for some months or years, no one else can use it. This belief is wrong for several reasons. First, others may already have rights to use the trademark. Second, someone else may already have a registration that grants the *exclusive* right to use the trademark. Third, someone that adopts it in the future and registers it with the federal government may be able to get exclusive rights to use it in most parts of the United States.

Myth # 3: Safety Without a Trademark Search

Many people feel free to adopt and use a trademark without making any search of marks in use. In fact, it is a mistake to make a substantial investment in marketing a product unless a trademark search has been done, because, as is explained later, the search may show that the mark is not available.

The Scope of Legal Protection

Trademark law generally protects the owner of a *distinctive* trademark who has *priority*. A distinctive trademark is one that is capable of distinguishing one company's goods from other similar goods made by someone else. Priority, generally speaking, goes to the first user of the mark in a market area or the owner of a mark registered with the federal government. The law gives the owner of a trademark that is distinctive and has priority a remedy in court when someone else uses the same mark or a mark so similar that customers are likely to be confused about the source of the goods.

Distinctiveness of Trademarks

Only distinctive marks are protected by trademark law. Broadly speaking, the more distinctive the mark, the better the legal protection. In this section, we will look at what makes trademarks distinctive.

Let's first consider why the law emphasizes distinctiveness. The reason is that the law seeks to balance trademark rights on one hand with the freedom to use ordinary language on the other. For example, only one software business needs to label its goods "Symantec," but many businesses legitimately need to label a program a "Utility." "Symantec" therefore is a "strong" mark, and "Utility" is a generic term that has no trademark protection at all.

In order to understand how to choose a trademark, or how much protection an existing mark can get, you have to understand what makes a mark more or less distinctive—what separates trademarks into "strong" marks and "weak" marks. We are talking here about *legal* strength, recognized in a court of law. Generally speaking the stronger, that is the more distinctive, the mark that you use on your goods, the easier it is to get strong legal protection for the mark in court and to get federal registration, through the process discussed later in this chapter.

Two Kinds of Distinctiveness   The law in fact recognizes two types of distinctiveness. The first is based on using words that *look and sound distinct* when applied to a particular kind of goods. "Lotus," for example, sounds distinctive when applied to software, but might not when applied to flowers.

The second type of distinctiveness is based on "secondary meaning"—that is, the power that a mark gets when many customers have come to recognize it. Secondary meaning is also called "acquired distinctiveness." A rule of thumb often used in the law is that a mark in continuous use for five years is presumed to have secondary meaning, but there are exceptions. In this mass-media age, recognition can possibly come in a few days or weeks through intensive advertising.

Strong and Weak Marks   When you go about choosing a mark or evaluating the strength of an existing mark, you need to know how the law classifies trademarks. There is a ranking based on how distinctive different types of marks are. The more distinctive are "strong" marks; the less distinctive are "weak" marks. These are the categories:

- **Arbitrary Marks.** An arbitrary mark is one that bears no logical relation to the goods that it labels. Examples are "coined" marks, like Corel or Symantec, or marks with meaning wholly unrelated to the function of the product, like Apple, Adobe, or Lotus. Arbitrary marks are the strongest.

- **Suggestive Marks.** A suggestive trademark is one that suggests but does not describe a product's function. Examples are WordPerfect, MathSoft, and Micrographx. None of these marks states what the products do, but each product mark suggests what the product does. Suggestive marks are also strong, but not as strong as arbitrary marks.

- **Descriptive Marks.** A descriptive mark primarily describes the characteristics of a product, such as its performance, function, features, quality, or capacity. Software examples are pcANYWHERE (remote access), PCKwik (disk cache), Virusafe (anti-virus), and Cursor Delux (custom cursors for Windows). Descriptive marks are weak, and trademark law protects them only if they have secondary meaning from public recognition.

- **Surnames as Marks.** Common family names as trademarks are weak, and like descriptive marks will often be protected only if they have secondary meaning. Surnames can be more distinctive if unusual or used in association with other words or in a distinctive design.

- **Place Name Marks.** Place names also make weak marks and normally will have protection only if they have "secondary meaning." The mark will be a bit stronger if the place name is less well known. Software examples are Harvard Graphics (named, incidently, for the town of Harvard, Massachusetts, not for the college) and Nantucket Software. Sometimes a place is known as a major source of a certain type of goods, like California wine, Maine lobsters, or perhaps Silicon Valley software. In such a case, the law may consider that such a mark is "primarily geographic" and grant no trademark protection at all.

- **Generic Marks.** Generic marks identify a category of goods recognized by an industry. For software, this would include the terms "Works," "Database," "Graphics," "Paint," "Draw," and "Utilities." These marks are the weakest. By themselves they have no protection at all. However it is possible sometimes to protect the combination of words that is generic in part but has a nongeneric component, for example: Microsoft Works, Norton Utilities, or CorelDRAW. Under trademark law, if a generic term is given a novel spelling, it is nonetheless generic.

Preventing "Genericide"   There are commonly quoted rules on use of trademarks that are designed to prevent them from *becoming generic*. As we have discussed, marks that are merely generic—such as the words "Draw" or "Works" as applied to software—are not protected by trademark law. Sometimes trademarks that were originally distinctive become generic because they come to be identified not as a mark for a product but with the product itself. Examples of common words that started out as trade names are "aspirin" and "dry ice." When a trademark becomes generic, it loses all protection, and then anyone can use it. Because the word "aspirin" is now generic, any company can call its brand of acetylsalicylic acid "aspirin." This type of death of a trademark is known to lawyers as *genericide*.

The following rules are often stated as means to help prevent genericide:

- Always use the trademark together with the product description and make the trademark look different, such as "**WordPerfect** Word Processing Program" or "WORDPERFECT Word Processing Program."

- Do not use the trademark in the possessive. Avoid "WordPerfect's features."

- Don't use the trademark as a noun or a verb; always use it as an adjective. For example, refer to "**Microsoft Excel** Spreadsheet Program" rather than "Microsoft Excel."

- Always use a trademark notice (see discussion later in this chapter on trademark notices).

There is a problem with these rules, however; they are often too cumbersome. For example, think how the Microsoft Excel user guide would read if Microsoft had to add the words "Spreadsheet Program" every time it used the word "Excel." What many companies do with these rules in real life is compromise. The first page of the Excel User Guide in fact has the words "Spreadsheet with Business Graphics and Database," but the text just refers to the product as Excel, using the mark as a noun. Most software companies reach the same type of compromises, and so far, seem to have avoided genericide. However, this more casual use of trademarks is a calculated risk.

The bottom line is that every advertisement, piece of packaging, and manual should follow these rules enough so as to make it absolutely clear to the reader that your trademark *is* a trademark.

The Use of the Term "Windows" In a Trademark

For several years, Microsoft has been conducting a legal campaign to establish its sole right to use the word "windows" in a computer product trademark. Microsoft lawyers have written stern letters to software developers and programmers demanding that they cease-and-desist from using "windows" in trademarks for their product. (According to Microsoft, "for Windows" was alright in a trademark, but "windows" was not.)

Microsoft's stratagem to capture the sole right to "windows" now appears to have abruptly collapsed. In the computer field, just like any other, trademarks may in fact be generic. A reminder of this fact came to Microsoft in the form of a recent decision on "windows" by a trademark examiner at the Patent and Trademark Office (PTO).

On February 25, 1993, the PTO examiner issued a decision on Microsoft's application to register "Microsoft Windows and Design" as a trademark for computer hardware and software in the graphical applications field. The examiner ruled that to register this trademark (I discuss federal trademark registration later) Microsoft will have to *disclaim* any exclusive right to the word "windows." In effect, the examiner has ruled that "windows" is a generic term in the computer industry and therefore is in the public domain.

In the decision, the examiner noted that the generic use of the word "windows," meaning windows on a computer screen, is found in dictionaries, patent applications, manuals and many other documents, including documents generated by Microsoft itself. This use of the word "windows" as a generic term in the computer field predated the introduction of Microsoft Windows by many years.

The examiner incorporated in the decision hundreds of pages of exhibits which illustrated this type of generic use. How did the examiner find all this documentary evidence about the use of the word "windows?" The not very surprising answer is that much of the evidence was filed at the PTO by Microsoft's rival, Borland International, Inc.

While the examiner's decision is not final and could be appealed, as a practical matter it will be very difficult to overturn. The effect of the examiner's decision is to make it very likely that no one has the exclusive right to use the word "windows" in a trademark. Microsoft will be able to prevent others from using the mark "Microsoft Windows" but probably cannot prevent the use of the word "windows" as part of an otherwise proper and non-infringing mark.

Microsoft is not the only company that has suffered this type of loss. A federal court in California ruled in 1991 that Intel's mark "386" is generic, and it is thus likely that no one has an exclusive right to this term either. This is the reason that Intel's most recent microprocessor has been named the "Pentium," rather than "80586."

"Confusingly Similar" Marks As I noted earlier, the law protects a distinctive mark with priority against other companies that are using marks that are "confusingly similar"—that is, marks that cause customer confusion about the source of the goods. This means that you may well be sued if you adopt or are using a mark confusingly similar to another distinctive mark that has priority over yours. (Priority is discussed later in this chapter.) Similarly, you may have a litigation remedy if someone else adopts a mark that is confusingly similar to yours and if you have priority.

Deciding whether a mark is confusingly similar to another is really a matter of common sense, based on the facts of the situation. If, for example, you use a software trademark that is very similar to an existing software product mark, people will be misled. For example, if you choose as your trademark "Lotis" or "Microsof," its a good bet that you will be sued and will lose. You also could run into a problem if you give your software product the same mark as a pre-existing computer hardware product. People could be confused and wrongly conclude that the source was the same.

The likelihood of confusion can be affected by scope of the use of a mark—which may be broad or narrow. Take, for example, a mark like Kodak, that is used for a variety of consumer and business products. Any other company that brought out a product named Kodak would surely confuse consumers if the mark was used in any field remotely related to Kodak's businesses.

On the other hand, if the field of use of two marks is very different, the same or similar marks are not confusingly similar. An example of this principle is the trademark LEXIS, which is the name of a database service for law firms owned by Mead Data. In 1989, Mead Data sued Toyota Motor Co., trying to prevent Toyota from using the trademark LEXUS for its luxury automobiles. Mead lost the case, because the judge decided that the uses of the two marks were too dissimilar to cause confusion.

In the software business, the way that these issues play out is sometimes not simple. An example is the Infocom text adventure game, popular in the mid-1980s, called Zork. After Zork was introduced, Zork Hardware Stores, a family-owned Texas retail chain, threatened to sue Infocom for trademark infringement. Infocom quite correctly judged that there was no danger of customer confusion. And in fact, Zork Hardware ultimately chose not to sue.

Infocom then tried another trademark tack. To promote its line of software games, Infocom started distributing *The New Zork Times*, a tongue-in-cheek newspaper about its products. The patrician New York Times Corporation was not amused, and its lawyers threatened to sue. This time, although the risk of confusion was still quite low, Infocom feared an expensive lawsuit, and changed its newspaper's name.

Distinctiveness in Selecting a Trademark Applying the concepts discussed above to selecting a trademark is straightforward. A mark will have the best legal protection if it is arbitrary or suggestive. Most of the marks that are powerful in the computer field have those characteristics. Strong marks such as Sun, Borland, Lotus, Paradox, Oracle, and Apple are examples.

Often new companies are inclined to choose marks that tell the consumer what the product does, which means that they will select a weak mark like "Virusafe." Perhaps marketing reasons support this type of choice. However, the price for picking a weak mark is that competitors may be able to enter the market with products bearing quite similar names. In general, it is best to choose a strong mark for any new product.

Even the most distinctive mark will not be protected, however, if the same or a confusingly similar mark already has priority. Therefore, before adopting a new product mark, you should understand how trademark priority works and learn how to investigate the other marks that are already out there. It is to these matters that we now turn.

Obtaining Priority Rights

As we have discussed, distinctive marks are protected if they have *priority*. Following are the three ways that distinctive marks get priority.

Priority from First and Continuing Use   Under state law, and to some extent under federal law as well, the user of a mark may obtain priority rights to use a mark just by using it first and continuously.

However, first and continuous use alone will grant protection only in the geographic market in which the mark is used. Moreover, use does not establish priority if there is a confusingly similar mark already in use in the area.

In addition, there can be no priority based on first and continuous use if the mark, or one that is confusingly similar, has already been registered by someone else in the federal Principal Register or in the trademark register of the user's state before the use began. (Most states have their own copyright registration statutes, which are of limited utility. Rights granted by state statutes are limited to the state's borders, and rights created by federal trademark registration override any state-created rights. The federal registration system is discussed below.) Due to these limitations, relying on use alone is not preferred.

Priority from Federal Registration After Use   If you are the first user, and your trademark meets the legal qualifications regarding distinctiveness, you can normally extend priority for your mark throughout the United States by registration on the federal Principal Register.

Priority from Obtaining Federal "Intent-to-Use" Registration Federal trademark law has a provision under which a trademark application can be filed even before first use—with the result that you normally get nationwide priority if the mark meets the legal requirements. Before making a heavy investment in a trademark, many companies take the precaution of filing an "intent-to-use" application for trademark registration on the federal Principal Register.

The Necessity of a Trademark Search

As we have just discussed, priority under state and federal law is dependent on *first use* or *federal registration*. Therefore, before you adopt a new mark, or before you can conclude whether you have the right to use your existing mark(s), you must find out whether anyone else is already using, or has already registered, a mark that is the same or confusingly similar to the one(s) you want to use. *It is your obligation to find out whether a mark that you wish to use is available.* It is no defense when you get sued for trademark infringement that you didn't know that you were infringing another owner's mark.

There are thousands of computer products and hundreds of thousands of trademarks used in other products. How are you to know if the mark you want to use is available? The answer is that you must do a *trademark search* for any trademark that you want to use.

The only prudent course is to do a search for every mark that you already use and for every new one that you plan to introduce. Otherwise, you may make a major investment in marks that you have no right to use. If, as a result of the search, you find that a mark you are already using is confusingly similar to an existing mark, you should see an attorney to decide the best strategy.

The Scope of the Trademark Search

If you are going to be selling your software or services nationwide, you need to conduct a trademark search that is nationwide in scope. You want to be sure that no one in the United States might stop you from using your chosen mark. (In some cases, an international search is appropriate as well.)

If you are going to be using a proposed trademark only for local or in-state use, you still need to do a nationwide search. Why? Because a company that already has the trademark or a very similar mark registered with the federal government will have nationwide priority. Even if another company is using the same or a similar unregistered mark and your area is within its zone of natural expansion, it may have priority over you.

Using a Trademark Search Service

There are two ways to have a search done. First, you can have a trademark lawyer arrange for it. The lawyer will usually contact a trademark search service and may also do additional searching. Or, you can contact a trademark search service yourself. A list of some of the major search services is included in Appendix D. The cost of the search (as of this writing) is about $200 to $500 per mark at a search service depending on the scope of the search. To search a proposed symbol or design, as opposed to words, may be more expensive.

What will a search service do? It normally will search:

- A computerized database of federal trademark registrations and applications.
- A computerized database of state trademark registrations and applications.
- Various legal databases (to see whether trademarks have shown up in litigation).
- Trade directories.

The search service will look for similarities in look, sound, impression, and use.

Doing Your Own Trademark Search

If you wish, you can do your own trademark search, although the search services will likely do a more thorough job than you can do yourself.

One source of information that you can use yourself is on-line trademark databases. One on-line service used for trademark searches is Dialog. To access Dialog you must become a subscriber. The cost is not cheap; it includes an annual fee, connect charges, and surcharges for database access. Dialog's trademark database, called Trademarkscan, includes state and federal registered marks, pending applications and expired registrations. There are also additional resources on Dialog that can be used to search for trademarks, including the Dun & Bradstreet Business Directory and a database called Trade Names. These services may allow you to find unregistered marks. The Dialog system allows some degree of sound-alike searching. Note that you can also access the Trademarkscan portion of Dialog through CompuServe; just type "GO TRADERC" at the system prompt.

Compu-Mark is another subscription service. Like Dialog, you must subscribe to Compu-Mark to use it. Compu-Mark also includes state and federal registered marks, pending applications and expired registrations. However, no other databases are offered, and therefore Compu-Mark offers no way to search for marks that are not within the registration system. Compu-Mark includes a sound-alike searching function. Compu-Mark is menu-driven and is designed to be more user-friendly than Dialog.

Included in Appendix D are the names and voice phone numbers for Dialog and Compu-Mark.

There are two drawbacks to on-line searching. One is the cost; it is not cheap, especially for inexperienced users that may spend time learning the system. A thorough search may well cost $200. The second drawback is that lack of experience may lead you to do an incomplete or inaccurate search.

Most major public libraries in the United States have federal trademark registration data in a CD-ROM database known as CASSIS. Using CASSIS is free, which certainly is a plus. CASSIS is a good tool for beginning a trademark search, but it has a number of limitations. First, it includes only federal registered marks and applications and provides no access to other sources. Second, it may be several months out-of-date. Third, it provides only alphabetical searching; there is no provision for sound-alike searching.

Also included in Appendix D is a list of trade directories and general trademark registers that you can examine to look for marks similar to the one you want to use. These books can be found at many major public libraries.

Limitations of a Trademark Search

A trademark search does not produce perfect information. It is possible that the search may miss current users of the name or a similar mark. Some businesses use unregistered marks that may not appear on any of the sources normally searched. It is also possible that someone will register a name or introduce a product with the same or a similar name after the date of your last search.

These imperfections mean that you could do all these searches, come to the conclusion that you have no trademark problems, introduce your product, and *still* get sued by a prior user. Nonetheless, the search is your best means of finding out what marks are in use. And most of the time, those who use the process get the information they need.

One more note about searches: If your search shows that a similar mark has been registered, it does not necessarily mean the mark is in use. It is possible that the user went bankrupt or gave up on the product line that used the mark. However, sometimes marks that are not currently used can be revived by their original owners. If you are uncertain as to whether a mark is available, you need to consult a trademark lawyer.

Evaluating the Results of a Trademark Search

Once the results of the search are in, they have to be evaluated. Look for the same or a confusingly similar mark in the same or related fields. If you have *any* doubt at all about what the search results mean, by all means see a trademark lawyer. Only a lawyer can give you a written opinion on the result of a search, and can explain the implications for the mark you want to use, for a fee of about $1,000 or so. That will often be money well spent.

Trademark Record Keeping

Because the time and manner of your usage of your trademark is a crucial factor in determining priority, and may sometimes become an issue in litigation (or important in registering a mark), you should, as a matter of routine practice, keep complete sales and shipment documentation for any new product.

Especially important is your documentation of the first use of the mark for *bona fide* commercial transactions and, in addition, the first use of the mark in interstate or United States foreign commerce. (See the section on the trademark registration process.)

It is also important to keep records of the promotional use of each mark, such as samples, advertisements, and direct mail materials, and copies of paid invoices for your promotion and advertising. These materials can help establish priority and secondary meaning.

The Advantage of Federal Registration

Let's say that you have chosen a distinctive mark, and that it has been cleared after a trademark search. Are you now done with your trademark labors? Can you relax and just use the mark? The answer is: Not quite. You should still seriously consider registering the trademark with the federal government on what is called the Principal Register.

Why register? Because federal registration extends the geographic scope of your copyright and makes the mark easier to enforce in a variety of ways. It does not give the mark 100-percent protection, but it makes it much harder to attack.

Major companies usually register all their important trademarks when they can. That does not mean that all trademarks of major companies are registered, however. Due to difficulties in obtaining registration or other reasons, some very common software trademarks are not registered. Examples of unregistered marks are "dBFast" of Computer Associates International and "Freelance Graphics" of Lotus Development Corporation. These unregistered marks nonetheless probably have substantial protection against others who would use or misuse these marks because the products are well known, have national distribution, are backed by vigorous advertising, and thus have "secondary meaning."

Nonetheless registration is by far the best way to get nationwide priority. If your trademark is important to your business, you should get federal registration on the Principal Register if you can.

The Federal Trademark Registration System

Under the federal trademark statute, known as the Lanham Act, the Patent and Trademark Office (PTO) maintains two lists of trademarks and service marks: the Principal Register and the Supplemental Register. Greater rights are granted by registration on the Principal Register, which is designed to protect *distinctive* trademarks, that is, the "strong" marks. The Supplemental Register, which allows registration of marks which are not distinctive, grants significant, but more limited benefits.

The Principal Register   Generally speaking, the PTO will put a mark on the Principal Register if the mark meets the following conditions:

- The mark has not become generic.

- The mark is distinctive: that is, it is arbitrary or suggestive, or descriptive, or has demonstrable secondary meaning.

- The mark is not primarily geographic.

- There is no likelihood of confusion with a mark already registered.

If your mark is enrolled on the Principal Register, you have the following very significant benefits:

- You can bring a federal infringement action in any federal court.

- Nationwide use of the mark is presumed to have occurred from the application date. (You can prove earlier use as well.) If this date precedes all other users, this date will usually establish a right of priority to the mark.

- Every user of the same or a similar mark is presumed to have notice of the mark (and therefore cannot claim to be an innocent infringer) from the registration date, that is, the date the trademark registration certificate is issued.

- In any lawsuit, during the five years after registration, there is a presumption that your use of the trademark is valid, that the mark is your property, and that your right to use it is exclusive. This is not absolute protection—a prior user can still challenge your right to priority during the five years after the registration—but it puts you ahead in litigation.

- After five years of continuous use after registration (and the filing of an affidavit at the PTO affirming this use), the right to use the mark becomes, with certain exceptions, "incontestable."

- You may use the "®" symbol with your trademark.

The Supplemental Register   The PTO also maintains a list of trademarks and service marks known as the Supplemental Register. The Supplemental Register was originally begun to allow non-distinctive marks to gain federal registration, which in turn helped owners get protection in foreign countries. Even if the PTO rejects your trademark for the Principal Register, the mark may qualify for the Supplemental Register. The benefits from such registration, while significant, are much more limited.

The PTO will approve an application for registration on the Supplemental Register if the PTO decides that the mark meets the applicable criteria:

- Generally the marks registered on the Supplemental Register are weak marks: descriptive, surname, or geographic marks without proven secondary meaning. Generic marks are not eligible for registration.

- The mark is not already registered for your field of use.

If your mark is on the Supplemental Register, you have the following rights:

- You can bring a federal infringement action in any federal court.

- The PTO will not grant the same mark to someone else in your field.

- You can file a later application for registration on the Principal Register, if, for example, you can prove secondary meaning at that later time.

- You can use the "®" symbol with your trademark.

Deciding Whether to Use a Trademark Lawyer

Before I introduce you to the process of trademark application, I will discuss *who* ought to file it, you or a trademark attorney.

I recognize that some people simply cannot or will not pay for trademark counsel's advice. It is also true that the PTO encourages small businesses to register their own trademarks by distributing "how-to" booklets and application forms (discussed later). I know software people that have gone through a trademark search and the federal registration process without counsel. You may choose to do the same.

My advice, however, is that you use an attorney for trademark matters. As you have seen in this chapter, federal trademark law is full of distinctions and rules. In addition, the discussion in this chapter is conceptual and certainly does not explain all the rules and exceptions. This field of law is complex and technical, and the amount of protection the law gives your mark—and even whether you have any protection at all—may not be evident to you. In the registration process, there are possible errors and traps that can prevent federal registration, limit the scope of protection, or even make the registration invalid later on.

I strongly suggest therefore that you consult a capable trademark lawyer to submit your trademark application and to advise you on trademark issues. Because this is a specialized field, lawyers skilled in the area have devoted considerable time to trademark practice. Having a lawyer bring the mark through the federal registration process normally costs less than $2,000, assuming that the process does not run into complications. (The registration process and its possible complications are discussed in the next section.)

Good trademark lawyers are admittedly not cheap—but then, how often do you introduce a new trademark or deal with a trademark infringement problem? If a trademark is an important asset in your business, it is worth protecting. Especially if your company is spending money on advertising and promotion, it should be willing to pay a reasonable sum to provide legal protection for the trademark.

The Trademark Registration Process

The registration process begins with an application. (You need to have the trademark search done before you decide whether to file an application.) An Examining Attorney at the PTO reviews the application, examining the mark's distinctiveness, searching for other similar marks, and scrutinizing evidence of "secondary meaning" if that is submitted.

You may recall that in my discussion of software copyrights, I said that virtually every program is copyrightable and that you can easily copyright your own software yourself. The trademark system is different; the PTO rejects a considerable proportion of the trademark applications that it receives. Many marks do not qualify for registration because they are not distinctive enough, and many are disallowed on the basis of other confusingly similar, previously registered marks or for other reasons. The registration process can bog down in red tape if the PTO raises questions about the application. Sometimes one can overcome the PTO's objections to registration, and sometimes not. It is best to have counsel's advice when dealing with these issues.

If the Examining Attorney judges that the mark passes muster, it is then published in the *Official Gazette*, a government publication. If you are lucky, after publication, no company will file an opposition to registration. Then the PTO will issue you a Certificate of Registration. As of this writing, the time from the filing of the application to the issuance of a certificate, absent any opposition, was running about 14 months.

If you are not so lucky, someone will file an objection to the registration. Then you will definitely need experienced counsel to aid you if you decide to press forward with the registration process, because the PTO may then conduct proceedings over a period of many months to resolve the objection. If there is a conflict over the right to use the mark between two companies that want to register it, the company that used the mark first usually prevails. A struggle over who gets registration can be prolonged and costly. Appeals to the federal court system seeking review of PTO decisions are also possible and will drive the legal costs higher still. If all objections are rejected, the PTO will register the mark.

Do-It-Yourself Registration

As I emphasized above, I do not think you should do your own trademark registration. However, I recognize that many small businesses file their own registration applications, because they are unwilling or unable to afford trademark counsel. If you want to go it alone (against my advice), here's what to do.

First, call the PTO's automated information line at 703-557-INFO (557-4636) and order a trademark booklet and application, which you can do by leaving a message on the voice mail system. In a week or so, the PTO will send out a book entitled "Basic Facts About Trademarks," which includes an explanation of the registration process. The booklet comes with the Principal Register application form, PTO Form 1478. The booklet in its current version contains two sample applications, one of which, coincidentally, is for a software product. The booklet explains how to fill out Form 1478. You should follow the instructions carefully.

Here are a few things to keep in mind if you do the registration yourself.

- You may only register one mark per application. If a mark is used in several distinct versions or formats, each one will require its own application.

- The application gives you an option of filing based on use or intent to use. You can only choose one of these two options.

- If you check the box for an application based on use, the application requires you to give a date for first use of the trademark in "in commerce which the U.S. Congress may regulate," also referred to on the form as the "commerce date." Generally speaking, Congress regulates transactions between states of the United States, between the United States and foreign countries, or involving a territory of the United States. Therefore the form is asking for the date of first use that fits one of these categories. The form also asks for the "date of first use anywhere." This date will differ from the "in commerce" date only if there were earlier transactions that were entirely within a single state. Transactions count to establish the date of first use only if the mark was in fact on the software goods involved or if the use was in connection with your software goods or services. Transactions must be for genuine commercial dealings not shipments made merely for the purpose of getting a trademark use date.

■ In specifying dates of use, be as accurate as possible. Check whatever records you have. If you are not absolutely sure of the exact dates of first use and first use in commerce, use phrases such as "no later than" or "on or about." Misrepresentations about the dates of use, even if inadvertent, may render the registration invalid later on.

■ Follow carefully the instructions in the booklet about the drawing of the mark and specimens showing use of the mark. The application requires three specimens. The PTO will accept three originals of the same specimen; it is not necessary to send three different ones.

Keeping Your Federal Registration In Effect

Once you have registered a trademark, if you want to keep your registration in effect, you must continue to use the trademark. Non-use for two years often is presumed to be abandonment of a trademark.

In addition, to keep your mark registered, you *must* submit an Affidavit of Use during the period of the sixth year after registration to certify that the mark is still in use. In addition, your mark gets "incontestible" status only if you also submit a Affidavit of Continuous Use during the same sixth year to certify that use since registration has been continuous. Normally both these requirements are met by filing a single form known as the Sections 8 and 15 Affidavit. You can get the required form from the PTO by calling the information number listed above. If you have any questions about the procedure involved, you should see an attorney. In addition, you *must* renew the registration during the tenth year and every tenth year after that. Again the required form is available from the PTO upon request. Timely compliance with these requirements is essential. If you have consulted a trademark lawyer, he or she will remind you to do these filings. Otherwise the burden is on you to be sure that it gets done. This is another good reason to use trademark counsel.

Essential Actions to Protect Your Trademarks

Whether you have registered your mark or not, there are certain essential steps that you should take to protect it.

Trademark Notices

Whenever you use your trademark (registered or not), you should use a trademark notice. The notice should appear together with the mark on every product, package, user manual, label, advertisement, and brochure for the product. The notice serves two functions. First, it puts all would-be trademark infringers on notice that you claim trademark protection. Second, it helps fend off claims that your mark has become generic. In many cases, failure to use a notice will impair your ability to sue for trademark infringement.

Notice for a Federally Registered Mark   If your mark is registered on either the Principal Register or the Supplemental Register, it is *very important* to give notice of federal registration. Usually, you will not be able to get monetary damages in a lawsuit for infringement unless there is such a trademark notice on your goods and on advertisements and promotional materials. To give notice of federal registration, the "®" symbol is used like this: Adobe®.

If you want, instead of the "®" symbol, you can use your mark with the words: "Registered in U.S. Patent and Trademark Office" or "Reg. U.S. Pat & Tm. Off." (You must use exactly these words.)

Notice for a Mark that is Not Federally Registered   If you have an unregistered trademark (including one for which there is a pending application for registration), it is still vitally important to give notice of your mark. For an unregistered trademark, you should use the "TM" symbol. For an unregistered service mark, use the "SM" or the "TM" symbol. These symbols are used like this: dBFast™.

Vigilant Defense of Your Trademark to Prevent Dilution

The protection given to a mark will be narrowed if you allow other companies to use the same or confusingly similar marks. A certain degree of vigilance is required. It is good practice to send cease-and-desist letters to infringers and to bring suit where necessary to stop blatant infringement. Most companies learn of infringement by chance, but it is possible (for a fee) to have one of the trademark search firms monitor all federal and state trademark filings and notify you when a similar name appears in an application.

To prevent dilution of the trademark, it is also a good idea to insist that when another company uses your trademark in an advertisement that the company acknowledge your ownership of the mark. This is the reason that advertisements in computer publications contain in fine print a listing of the trademarks referred to and the owners of each mark. If someone mentions your trademark in an advertisement without such an acknowledgment, and if it appears that there is a likelihood of confusion about the source of the goods or about whether your company has endorsed the advertised product, it would be a good idea to write to the advertiser and complain.

Trademark Assignments and Licenses

Trademarks can be assigned and licensed. Generally speaking, a trademark can be assigned only in the sale of a business or business operations. Trademarks are often licensed. For example, Intel licenses many hardware companies to use its "Intel Inside" symbol. In general, a trademark can be licensed only if the owner of the mark exercises control over the mark's use by the licensee. Control is often exercised through contractual restrictions on usage and often through inspection rights. The legal rules involved in these transactions are technical, and if the licensing is done wrong, trademark protection can be lost forever. You should consult a lawyer if you want to assign or license a trademark.

Trademark Infringement Litigation

Establishing Infringement

The owner of a mark can get a remedy in state or federal court if the owner proves that another person has infringed the mark. Needless to say, if you think someone has infringed your mark, or if you are accused of using someone else's mark, you should see an attorney immediately. Delay may hurt the trademark holder's case.

Generally, the owner of the mark has to prove these elements to establish infringement:

- That the owner has a valid trademark;

- That the mark is distinctive;

- That the mark has priority; and

- That there is a likelihood of confusion about the source of the goods bearing the marks.

The Litigation Process

The litigation process for trademark infringement is much like the copyright infringement litigation that we discussed at length in Chapter 1. (You may wish to review that discussion.) Pre-litigation tactics for a trademark infringement claim need to be carefully discussed with your counsel. The process normally begins with a cease-and-desist letter, and is followed up, if necessary, with litigation. As with copyright litigation, there is some risk that a party sending a cease-and-desist letter will be sued first by the alleged infringer in the infringer's jurisdiction.

When the infringement is clear, the dispute will often settle before litigation is filed. Quite commonly, the infringer simply agrees to stop using a mark after a few months' transition period. However, if the defendant has some hope of defending its trademark, and if it has had considerable success (and has earned real money) with the mark, litigation may be required.

Like copyright litigation, trademark cases often end soon after a decision on a motion for a preliminary injunction. (See the discussion of preliminary injunctions in Chapter 1.) If the judge grants a preliminary injunction early in the litigation, the defendant will lose the right to sell goods labeled with the challenged mark and must begin using a new trademark immediately. As a practical matter, the defendant may then be unable to save its trademark. A preliminary injunction therefore can force the defendant to sue for peace on whatever terms it can get.

On the other hand, if the plaintiff loses a preliminary injunction, its settlement leverage will often be gone because the other side has shown a strong hand. The cost of taking the case to trial may not be justified. Plaintiffs often give up after a first-round loss.

While most trademark cases end quite quickly, it is possible for seriously contested cases to cost substantial amounts. Proof of secondary meaning to establish a mark's distinctiveness or to establish the likelihood of confusion may be very expensive, because it can require customer survey evidence, which is costly to produce. Proof of distinctiveness, customer confusion, and damages all may require expert testimony. A contested case between two substantial firms can cost hundreds of thousands of dollars.

Infringement Remedies for Federally Registered Trademark

If you have a federally registered trademark and someone uses a confusingly similar mark, what happens when you *win* a trademark infringement trial in federal court? Remedies for infringement can include:

- Your lost profits due to the infringement or the profits wrongfully made by the infringer (whichever is greater).

- In egregious cases, three times the actual damages, or if that is inadequate, the amount of damages that the court deems "just."

- In egregious cases, an award of attorneys' fees.

- In addition, the court may order the destruction of the improperly labeled goods and of all copies of the improper labels and packaging.

If the violation is blatant "counterfeiting," that is, if the defendant was using an exact copy of your mark with the intent to deceive customers, the Court may also order seizure of the counterfeit goods by the United States Marshall at the beginning of the case. And where there is counterfeiting, the Court often will award three times the actual damages, and attorneys' fees.

As you can see, the remedies under federal law are powerful. Of course, winning a money judgment does not necessarily mean that the defendant will be have the ability to pay.

A holder of trademark on the Principal Register may also request the United States Customs Service to prevent the import of goods labeled with the mark. The Customs Service, unfortunately, does not have the resources to police all U.S. imports, and thus the amount of protection you can get from this system is uncertain.

Infringement Remedies for Unregistered Trademarks

Even if you don't have federal registration, state and federal law may give you protection if someone uses your trademark (or one confusingly similar) and harms your business. (But as noted above, federal registration can provide much better protection.)

There is a section of the Lanham Act that grants a remedy in federal court against anyone that damages another by using a name or mark that is likely to cause confusion or is deceptive. This statute has often been used to protect unregistered trademarks. In addition, state law is likely to protect unregistered marks against infringement.

Remedies under these provisions may include monetary damages and court orders (including preliminary relief early in the case) to stop the infringer's use of the mark.

Trademark Checklist

Here is a checklist to use to apply what you have learned in this chapter to your business—and to help determine if the protection of your mark is adequate.

First, make a list of all the marks you use, or plan to use, on your goods or with your services. Include all names, slogans, letters and numbers, and designs that you use to identify your products. Then ask:

1. Are these marks important for the business? Are they recognized by the customers? Are they significant sales tools? Are they important in obtaining new business? Is your business spending money to increase customer recognition of these marks?

2. How would the business be damaged if the use of the marks were lost? What would the injury be in terms of product recognition, marketing, customer relations, and prestige of the business?

3. Are any of the marks merely generic?

4. If the marks are generic, would the company be harmed if other companies used the same names—as they are free to do?

5. Should the company consider replacing the generic marks with marks that are more distinctive?

6. If the marks are not generic, has a trademark search been done to investigate the company's right to use the marks? Is the modest cost of trademark search justified?

7. Does the company use the marks only locally? Is expansion contemplated so that the right to use the mark in other areas would be valuable? If so, should federal registration be considered?

8. Are the marks distinctive, so that registration on the federal Principal Register might be available?

9. Are the marks sufficiently important to justify the cost of retaining trademark counsel to protect them?

10. Are the trademarks sufficiently well known that they can be exploited by licensing?

11. If trademarks are already licensed, was it done with legal advice and in a way that does not risk losing the trademark?

12. Has the company taken steps to deal with companies using confusingly similar marks, in order to avoid dilution of the mark?

CHAPTER 15

Software Patents

Software Patents: A New Factor

Until 1981, patents were not a factor in the software industry, but that has all changed. Patents are a particularly powerful form of intellectual property, which makes them a danger for some and an opportunity for others. Over the last decade, companies large and small have been developing software patent positions. Some small businesses have made very good money from enforcing software patents. Increasingly, however, fears are voiced by the programming community that patents will inhibit creativity and obstruct programmers and publishers.

From your point of view, there are two pertinent aspects of patent law. First, can other patent holders use their patent rights against you? Second, can you patent a new software technology or application and use the patent to make money? This chapter will give you guidance on both points. In addition, some aspects of patent protection in Europe and Japan are discussed in Chapter 16.

Introduction to United States Patents

A patent is a 17-year exclusive right, in essence a monopoly, granted by the federal government, to exploit an *invention*. Under federal statutes, patents can cover "any process, machine, manufacture or composition of matter." Modern patent law treats software running in a computer as a "process" or a "machine" (often referred to as an "apparatus" or "device") subject to patent protection. Typically, a software patent will grant a monopoly on certain functions and means to accomplish them using software on a computer. If someone makes, uses, or sells products incorporating the invention without the patent holder's permission after the patent has been issued, the law grants the patent holder a litigation remedy.

The right to exclude others is not necessarily the same thing as the right to use an invention. In many cases, a patent covers an improvement to other patented technology; in that situation, the patent holder may need a license from one or more other patent holders in order to have the right to use the invention.

Under United States law, patents are granted on an invention only after scrutiny by the United States Patent and Trademark Office (PTO), and only when the PTO finds that the software "process" or "device" is (1) useful, (2) novel, and (3) not obvious to a skilled practitioner in the field at the time of invention. There are no state law patents; only the federal government can issue a patent in the United States. (There are also foreign patents, of course.)

History of U.S. Software Patents

Software patents have a rather checkered history in this country. In the years before 1981, the PTO refused to grant software patents in most cases. The PTO's position was that programs were "mathematical algorithms," which are not patentable. Software algorithms, it argued, should be considered "basic tools of nature" that should not be owned by anyone.

Then in 1981, the United States Supreme Court decided that a patent *should* be granted for a computer controlled process to cure rubber. There followed a number of lower court decisions extending that ruling. As a result, the PTO did an about-face, and began issuing software patents in large numbers.

It is still the PTO's position that a patent should not be issued for pure mathematical algorithms implemented in software. To fit software into the statutory framework of U.S. law, patent lawyers often submit a patent application stating that the invention consists of or includes a "computer-implemented" process or device. But the reality is that the patents cover software. Here are some randomly selected examples of software or software-related patents that show how varied they are:

- IBM has a patent on an "Apparatus and Method for Synthesizing a Query for Accessing a Relational Data Base."
- Texas Instruments has a patent on a "Method of Generating and Displaying Tree Structures in a Limited Display Area."

- Hitachi holds a patent for an "Image Retrieval Method."

- Merrill, Lynch (the stockbrokers) own a patent for a "Securities Brokerage-Cash Management System."

- Wang Laboratories has a patent on a "Data Structure for a Document Processing System."

There are many United States software patents. One researcher estimated that by 1992, more than 9,000 software patents had been issued. There are pending applications for thousands more.

Major companies have built large software patent positions. IBM has the largest United States software patent position and reportedly gets about 200 new software patents every year. Apple Computer, for example, encourages its developers to submit software innovations so that Apple can obtain patents. Digital Equipment Corporation and Lotus do the same. Many software patents are held by Japanese companies.

Patents give the holder the right to exclude others from making, using, or selling devices that contain the invention. This right of exclusion potentially serves three purposes:

- **Royalty income.** By threat of infringement suits, the holder can force other companies to pay royalties for a patent license.

- **Exclusion of competition.** The holder attempts to prevent others from entering its market through threats of suits or through litigation.

- **As a bargaining chip.** The holder uses its patents as a "bargaining chip," an infringement threat it can use as a counterstrike when threatened by an infringement claim or as something to trade with other patent holders in a cross-licensing agreement.

The importance of software patents was underscored in a little-noticed term of a recent settlement between IBM and Microsoft. As you may recall, during 1991 and 1992, Microsoft and IBM, once partners in personal computers, fought a public battle over the future of the PC world. The main focus of this dispute of personal computer giants was the contest between Windows and OS/2. During June of 1992, Microsoft and IBM announced agreements that settled many of the issues between them. A little-noticed part of the settlement was on software patents: Microsoft paid *$20 million* for a permanent license to IBM's operating system patents. According to the *Wall Street Journal*, "IBM surprised Microsoft by brandishing a secret weapon: a portfolio of more than 1,000 patents relating to software." Of course, IBM's patents were not a "secret weapon" at all; they were a very public weapon. It's a sure bet that getting a license for the IBM patent portfolio was a key Microsoft goal in these negotiations.

A Concern to Programmers and Publishers

From the programmer's and publisher's point of view, software patents are the heavy artillery in the intellectual property field—and are a threat. Here are the reasons:

- **The breadth of patented software technology.** Software patents now cover discrete pieces of technology in a wide variety of software fields: operating environments, relational database management, CAD/CAM, financial data analysis, computer games, banking transactions, computer graphics, windowing in screen displays, networks, telecommunication, memory management, electronic mail, and many others. Whatever software field you are in, there are probably patents that cover some technology in that field. Software has thus become like many other technological fields in which a large body of patents has been created.

- **Independent creation is not a defense.** In patent law (unlike copyright law), independent creation is *not* a defense. In patent law, you are liable for infringement if you use patented technology, even if you didn't copy it and even if you never knew of the patent. Even if the patent was issued *after* you began using the technology, you still are liable.

- **The difficulty of patent infringement determinations.** Searching existing patent records to determine whether a large and complex program infringes one or more patents is very expensive, usually prohibitively expensive. This means that you could be infringing an existing patent and not know it. Of course, it also may be difficult for a patent holder to discover an infringing invention in another company's software code, and many acts of infringement probably go undiscovered.

- **Applications for patents are kept secret.** In the United States (unlike many other countries) patent applications are kept secret by the PTO until a patent is issued. This means that you could be using an invention in your software for years that is subject to a pending application and not know it, even if a patent search was done. As soon as the patent is issued, you will infringe the patent. The rationale for this United States practice of secrecy is that the patent is the incentive for disclosure, and that if the patent is never issued the applicant should be allowed to keep the technology a trade secret.

- **The expense of resisting claims.** If you are sued for patent infringement, it will be very expensive to resist. The litigation costs in patent cases are among the highest.

What it all means is this: any programmer or publisher might be ensnared at any time by a patent infringement claim that it was powerless to foresee or avoid. Many firms have been threatened and a considerable number are now paying royalties for patent licenses.

The Problem of Improperly Patented Software Technology

An additional problem with software patents is that the PTO has issued patents for software "inventions" that in the view of many, were not patentable in the first place, because the PTO has difficulty determining the state of the art in software technology. In the process of deciding whether a claimed "invention" is really new, a key factor that the PTO considers is the "prior art," the existing software technology at the time of the invention.

When dealing with mechanical inventions, the patent system itself presents well over 100 years of prior art. But software patents were rarely granted before 1981, so the patent system itself gives little guidance to software prior art. There is a lot of writing on computer programming, but it is not organized for easy accessibility, and many methods are not discussed in the literature. There are currently thousands of software programs on the market (and thousands more that were marketed in the past), but many are not extensively described in the published literature. Some of the prior art is found only in computer user manuals and other manufacturer documentation that is not collected or saved anywhere. A great deal of the history of software functions and programming techniques is not written down at all. The state of the art evolves as techniques and know-how passes through academia, government, and from one company to another, as technicians and scientists exchange information or move from job to job. The state of the art in software is therefore hard to find and sometimes invisible. This problem of hidden prior art is not unique to software patents, by the way; it is a feature of patent law that applies to any new technology. Many of the same comments can be made, for example, about patents in biotechnology.

Because the prior art for software is very difficult to find, the PTO patent examiners currently have neither the resources nor the time to hunt it down. Patent examiners work under a point system that gives them an incentive to increase the number of patents they process. Examiners are not rewarded if they spend day after day hunting down prior art that is obscure and difficult to find.

The amount of patented prior art in software is rapidly increasing, however, and this should help reduce the difficulty of discovering prior art in future years. Another source of computer prior art may be available soon from the Software Patent Institute (SPI) in Ann Arbor, Michigan. SPI is a non-profit organization founded by University of Michigan computer scientist Bernard Geller. SPI, which has "seed funding" from a number of major computer companies, plans to create a properly indexed computer database of software prior art. Its plan is to have a "testbed" version operational in 1993 and to have a fully functioning database in later years. SPI is asking people throughout the software industry, government, and academia to contribute descriptions of software techniques and processes to its prior art database. If you have relevant information on software prior art, I encourage you to contact the SPI and contribute to its database. You will help create a more rational and more accurate patent system. Information on contacting the SPI, by mail, phone or through Internet can be found in Exhibit D.

In addition, patent lawyers find that the ability of PTO examiners to deal with software issues varies considerably. Some are highly skilled in computer matters, and some are not. There is considerable turnover in examiners, and new examiners are required to deal with complex technology almost immediately. This circumstance may also lead to erroneous determinations.

Some contend that patent lawyers (and their clients) sometimes compound the problem. The rules of patent system require that the applicant provide the examiner with the relevant prior art known to the applicant. In order to get approval for broad claims of novelty in a patent, however, some applicants have been known to draft applications artfully and thereby omit what an objective observer would consider the most relevant prior art. (Any demonstrable cheating in a patent application makes the patent invalid if the deception is discovered.) Artful drafting may cause software patents to be issued for pre-existing technology.

All this means that companies may have been threatened and sued—and may now pay royalties—because they gave into demands based on patents that probably never should have been issued in the first place. The companies that pay are primarily those that did not want to undertake the financial and legal burden and risks of defending an infringement suit. This is indeed unfair, but software patents—proper and improper—are here to stay.

Who Is at Risk of Patent Claims?

The nightmare of software programmers and publishers is an assault by royalty-hunting patent holders and their lawyers. Are software patent holders roaming the United States looking for plunder? Are you yourself going to be threatened and sued due to a patent claim out of the blue?

Businesses in other computer fields have had to live with these anxieties for quite a few years. It has been quite common for makers of microchips, video boards, and other computer hardware to receive a call from an agent claiming infringement of one patent or another, seeking royalties and threatening an infringement suit. Many hardware businesses pay substantial patent royalties. Others make a lot of money from licensing patents. Texas Instruments, for example, gets a large percentage of its revenues from patent royalties.

The software industry's traditional freedom from these patent claims is now history. Most claims on software patents are now asserted by smaller companies that have comparatively modest numbers of patents. Most large companies have used software patents primarily for defensive purposes; but that too is beginning to change. Patent lawyers say that more and more companies are seeking software patents and aggressively asserting infringement claims.

Small programming firms and start-up software companies are largely untouched by patent infringement claims; they are too small and too poor for the patent holder to bother with. When a company has yearly sales of several million dollars or more and is showing products at the major trade shows, it is much more likely to be targeted with a demand for patent royalties. The more successful you are in software, the more you are at risk of a patent problem.

Companies that are on the cutting edge, using new methods and exploring new computer applications, are also at a higher risk. This is because there is a reasonable likelihood that other companies that are working in the same field are seeking patents. Companies with more mundane technologies are less likely to be bothered with patent claims.

It is also common for large companies to grant one another royalty-free cross-licenses of patents in a particular area of interest to both. The cross-license gives both large companies free rein to use the patented technology, but may force smaller companies to pay patent license fees to enter the area. The effect may be to exclude competition in a technological market.

If You Receive a Cease-and-Desist Letter from a Patent Holder

If you get a cease-and-desist letter from a patent holder, you should not panic. You need to carefully assess your position and then respond.

First you should get a good patent lawyer with expertise in software to advise you. After speaking with counsel, you may also need a software engineer or computer scientist to work with the attorney to read the patent and its claims, which are the formal statements of the method and technology that the patent holder claims to have invented, and then to look for prior art. You can work with the attorney yourself to do this analysis if you have sufficient grasp of the technology involved. However, you should not attempt to formulate a strategy or respond to a cease-and-desist letter unless you have first consulted with patent counsel, who will be better able than you to analyze the breadth of the claims in the patent and the significance of the prior art. Your attorney can also advise you of the steps that should be taken to keep your own investigation strictly confidential.

In your search for prior art, you are looking for proof that at the time of the alleged invention, the technology in the patent *was not novel* or *would have been obvious*. The best place to find computer literature is a good computer science library, such as are found in many major universities. Also try informal inquiries through discussions with other computer scientists and programmers on the phone or through bulletin boards or Internet. You should share the results of your investigation, whether good or bad, with patent counsel. If you find the right prior art, your attorney may be able to get the patent holder to settle cheaply—or even go away.

If your company is at risk because of an infringement claim and the problem looks like it is not going to go away, the company should discuss its options with patent counsel. The available options might include "designing around" the problem, licensing alternative technology (which will stop damages from accruing), paying for a license from the patent holder, or leaving the field.

A further note on patent-related letters: The beginning of the game is sometimes not a cease-and-desist letter, but rather an almost innocent sounding letter from a patent holder that expresses a wish to "draw your attention" to a particular patent. If you receive such a letter you should you should take it very seriously, and seek counsel immediately. Once you are on notice of a patent, if you continue to use the patented technology without permission, you may be found liable for *intentional infringement*—which (as I will discuss below) may result in very steep liability. The patent lawyer can study the situation, assist you in analysis, and give you a written opinion on whether the patent mentioned in the letter is valid and whether your product infringes the patent. (Of course the lawyer's best opinion is no guarantee that you will not be found liable for infringement.) The lawyer will counsel you on the risks and options in dealing with the threat of an infringement suit.

Patent Infringement Lawsuits

What happens if you are sued for patent infringement, or if you bring your own patent infringement suit?

A patent infringement claim begins with the usual pre-litigation maneuvering. The patent holder sends a cease-and-desist letter including a demand for money damages. Based on the advice received, the alleged infringer might capitulate and agree to pay a royalty. Or it might deny infringement and insist that the patent is invalid. Settlement before suit is always possible. Absent settlement, litigation usually follows. Litigation is in federal court and runs the general course that I described in Chapter 1 in the discussion of copyright law.

Patent litigation can be shockingly expensive. Patent litigation requires sophisticated expert testimony and skilled patent litigators. These cases can easily run $15,000 to $20,000 *per month* or more for the two years or so that the process takes. This level of cost, and the risks of litigation, pushes the parties on both sides to resolve these cases. For this reason, most patent suits settle before trial.

When a patent holder (the plaintiff) sues an alleged infringer (the defendant), the dispute focuses on two issues. Is the plaintiff's patent valid? (Patents are presumed valid, and the burden is on the alleged infringer to prove them otherwise.) Does the patent cover the defendant's software? If the court finds that the answer to both of these questions is yes, it must find that the patent was infringed.

Every time that the patent holder sues, it runs the risk that the court may find the patent invalid and render it worthless forever. Therefore if the patent is "weak"—if there is a danger that the court will find that the patent should not have been issued—the holder will be more likely to settle the case for a relatively small amount of money or a low royalty amount. If the patent is "strong"—if there is little risk that the court will invalidate the patent—then the defendant will be forced to settle at a higher price.

When the court finds patent infringement, it has the power to:

- Award damages to the patent holder equal to a reasonable royalty on the defendant's sales for the period of infringement, or in some cases, the profits made by the infringer by use of the patent holder's invention.

- Issue a court order to prevent further infringement (including a preliminary injunction stopping infringement early in the case if the infringement is clear).

In cases of intentional infringement, the court may also:

- Award damages equal to three times actual damages.
- Award attorneys' fees.

What the patent holder normally wants, of course, is money, together with recognition that the patent is valid and covers the defendant's product. Where the patent holder prevails or where there is a settlement, the most common result is that the defendant pays some amount for past use of the patent and a royalty on future sales.

The Difficulty of Anticipating Patent Problems

Let's say that you have a software product introduction planned for which you expect to spend large amounts of money. Can you determine beforehand whether there is a patent infringement problem? The answer is that you can obtain some information, but it will be incomplete, imperfect, and expensive to get.

The first problem is deciding what functions in your program should be the subject of a patent search. These days a typical personal computer application program has a megabyte or more of code and performs many functions, such as calculation, memory access, network communications, database storage, graphics, etc. Any of these functional areas might be the subject of a pre-existing patent. It would take an army of patent lawyers to search every claim in every patent that any portion of your program might infringe.

Assuming that, by some educated guesswork, your patent counsel could narrow down the functions of your program that require searching, the process of finding whether there is infringement is still difficult and expensive. For each function in question, for perhaps about $2,000, a patent lawyer could do a preliminary search for United States software patents that your program might infringe. For another $3,000 or so, you could hire a foreign attorney to do a similar search of patent filings in the European Patent Office (EPO). In the European patent system (unlike the American system), a patent application becomes public information 18 months after the European application (or a prior application upon which the European filing is based) is first filed. Often companies that apply for patents in the United States also file applications overseas; a foreign search therefore may give insight into pending United States patent applications.

These searches could give you some information on whether your product might infringe an existing United States patent or uses technology covered by a pending foreign application that is more than 18 months old. But the information gathered cannot be definitive or complete; the risk of a patent infringement claim remains. Moreover, as I noted earlier, United States patent applications are secret, and when there is no corresponding published foreign application, there is no way to learn of the contents of a U.S. patent application.

Because it is very difficult and expensive to search out potential software patent infringement claims, most software companies do not do patent infringement searches when they introduce a software product, except in the unusual circumstance where there is a particular reason to search a particular aspect of the program.

Rather they wait for the patent holder, if there is one, to come to them. Patent claims are a risk of doing business in software. This is the reason that companies should be cautious about indemnifying other companies for patent infringement claims.

How Companies Make Money with Patents

There is, of course, another side of the patent story: Software patents may be a source of financial success for individuals and small companies.

One publicized example of a company has that exploited software patents is CadTrak Corporation, a small California company that holds several patents for display technology commonly used in CAD programs. CadTrak makes a business out of enforcing its software patents. Its employees scan trade journals and patrol trade shows like Comdex, hunting for possible infringers. An article in the *Wall Street Journal* reported that, based on its patent enforcement strategy, CadTrak was receiving *nearly $5 million per year* in patent licensing fees from various computer and software developers and programmers. CadTrak is only one of a number of companies enforcing software patents as part of its business plan. Of course every dollar that CadTrak collects comes from some other software company that pays.

A well-known case of an individual programmer who made money with a patent is that of Paul Heckel. Heckel wrote an applications development program for the Atari ST computer called Zoomracks which featured a "card and rack" metaphor. Heckel obtained patents on his technology. When Apple brought out Hypercard, a similar "card" metaphor product that runs on Macintosh computers, Heckel sued Apple for patent infringement. Heckel did not claim that Apple copied Zoomracks. Apparently Apple independently came up with the same features as were covered by the patent. If Heckel had relied only on copyright protection of his software, he would have had no claim against Apple, because independent creation is a defense in a copyright infringement action. Heckel was able to sue Apple for infringement only because he held the more powerful rights granted by a patent. The case eventually settled; in the settlement, Apple agreed to pay for a license to Heckel's patent. As of 1992, the trade press reported that Heckel was asserting that IBM was bundling computers with software that infringed his Zoomracks patents.

Many patents earn little or no royalties, but the money from some patent licenses can be enormous. Magnavox Corporation received a patent that covers

"Pong" type games and other computer games where an object on a computer display "bounces" off another object. The patent was held to cover the ROM software in home video game cartridges sold by Atari and others. According to one court's finding in an infringement suit, by 1985, Magnavox had collected royalties on its patent from various manufacturers of *over $40 million*.

Deciding Whether to Seek a Software Patent

Patents are expensive to get, and they take a long time to issue. Therefore, you certainly don't want to try to patent every new technique, function, or application of software technology. You want to spend the money and the time required only if the patent is likely to be valuable.

In deciding whether you should try to obtain a patent, think about the following factors:

- **Originality.** Is your program truly new? Does it solve a problem that others have failed to solve? Does it meet a need that others have failed to perceive?

- **Marketability.** Does your software invention have a good chance to generate real money?

- **Advancement over prior solutions.** Does the software leapfrog the solutions currently available? If your program is only a small incremental improvement, it is less likely to result in a valuable patent.

- **Will the technology stand the test of time?** It takes two or three years or more to get a patent, and software technology changes quickly. Will your software technology still be useful when the patent is issued?

- **Are you willing to disclose the technology?** Much of software technology is kept as a trade secret. When a patent issues it must disclose the technology sufficiently to enable the invention to be practiced by anyone skilled in the art. You cannot get a patent without making some of your trade secrets public.

If your answer to all these questions is yes, a software patent might be useful to you.

How to Get a Software Patent

If you are interested in getting a software patent, what is the process? The following is a brief overview.

Get a Good Patent Lawyer or Patent Agent

Patent law is a highly specialized field, and if you wish to get a patent, you need a patent lawyer. Only lawyers that have passed a special federal examination can file a patent application or represent you before the PTO in patent-related proceedings. The fact that all other American lawyers (who are allowed to practice in all the other areas discussed in this book) are excluded from patent practice gives you some sense of the special complexity of this area of law. Most patent lawyers are engineers or have an extensive science background.

Although in theory you can represent yourself and prepare and file your own patent application, in reality most programmers and publishers (and indeed most lawyers) could not meet the highly technical requirements of the application. If you have large amounts of time on your hands, familiarity with patents, and good technical writing skills, you might give writing your own patent application a go. Otherwise you'd best forget it and get a good patent lawyer. If you hire a lawyer, you are more likely to get patent if one is obtainable—and to find out in advance whether applying would be a waste of time.

If you decide (in spite of my advice) that you want to try your hand at a patent application, there is one very well-written book on do-it-yourself patents, although it is not focused on software. The book is *Patent It Yourself* (Nolo Press, 1991), written by California patent lawyer David Pressman. Even Pressman agrees that the "claims" section of a patent application should be done by an attorney.

The PTO also permits applications by *patent agents*, non-lawyers who are legally qualified to prepare and prosecute patent applications. You will most likely get a broader view of the legal issues from a patent attorney, but patent agents are normally less expensive than patent attorneys. Whether you get a patent attorney or a patent agent, be sure to get one with software experience.

The government publishes a directory of patent attorneys and agents which can be purchased or ordered at any U.S. Government Bookstore. However, most people find patent lawyers and agents by asking an attorney who represents them in other matters.

Deciding Whether to Proceed with an Application

Your patent lawyer is able to help you decide whether it makes sense to proceed with a patent application. The first step is to determine whether your invention is truly a significant advance. Usually the inventor knows, at least in a general way, what the competition's software products can do. It will often help to assemble materials on the state of the art including articles and software manuals in the same field to show to patent counsel. Usually for under $2,000 an inventor can get an opinion on whether it is worthwhile to proceed with a patent application. A favorable opinion from an attorney, however, is by no means a guarantee that the PTO will issue a patent for your software invention.

The Application Process

Patent applications are highly technical. To prepare an application, the patent lawyer must understand the technology thoroughly and investigate the prior art to the extent that it can be found. Drafting the application requires skill, technical knowledge, and legal ability. The application itself includes:

- An "abstract" summarizing the invention.

- Technical drawings that illustrate the invention, which in the case of software would usually be detailed process flow diagrams.

- A discussion of the prior art and the ways in which the invention is an advance.

- A detailed discussion of the structure, operation, features, and advantages of the invention, including, in some cases, the actual source code used. The application must (1) describe the invention in sufficient detail that a person skilled in the field of the invention can make and use the invention, and (2) describe the best way to create and use the invention known to the inventor at the time of filing. (Failure to fulfill these two requirements render a patent subject to invalidation after it issues.)

- The "claims," a logical and precise statement of exactly what aspects of the technology in the application constitute the invention.

The cost for preparing a software patent application is usually in the $10,000 to $20,000 range, depending on the amount of prior art, the complexity of the invention, and other factors.

After the application is filed, the PTO does its own investigation to decide whether the purported invention is patentable. The PTO often raises questions and objections on patent applications. For example, if the examiner concludes that the invention is merely data gathering, a mathematical algorithm used to process the data to calculate a solution and insignificant post-solution activity, the examiner will conclude that there is no patentable subject matter. All the examiner's objections must be answered by written arguments. It is frequently necessary to amend or narrow the scope of claims. Even in the simplest cases, the applicant normally has to respond to at least two "actions" by the PTO requiring further information, amendment of claims, etc. The cost of "prosecuting" the patent, if things go relatively smoothly, could be about $5,000. If the examiner raises objections, the process can take much longer and be much more expensive.

It often happens that the PTO denies a patent application; then the applicant must appeal or abandon the attempt to get a patent. An appeal is an additional cost, with no guarantee how it will come out. More infrequently the PTO declares an "interference" between two persons who are both claiming the same invention, and may conduct hearings to determine who invented it first—at considerable expense to the parties.

To apply for a patent, you must pay a fee. Another fee is due if the application is granted. And the patent office also charges maintenance fees from time to time to keep the patent in effect. These costs, however, are comparatively modest. You should discuss these matters with your patent counsel or agent.

Assuming that your application is successful and faces no more than normal red tape, you can expect to get a patent in about two or three years. If appeals or other proceedings are necessary, it not only costs much more but it takes much longer. Some applications take as long as a decade before a patent is issued.

Tips for Those Interested in Getting a Patent

If you are thinking of seeking patent protection for a software method or application, here is some advice:

- This chapter provides only the briefest outline of a very complex field, and omits many of the details of the process. Consulting with a patent lawyer is therefore a necessity if you are interested in obtaining patent rights.

- In the case of a conflict over priority, United States law generally awards a patent to the first person to *invent* technology technology rather than the first to file an application. (Most other countries give "first-to-file" priority.) This means that *you must carefully document the time and details of the invention and have the documentation of the invention witnessed to be able to prove the invention date*. A patent lawyer can tell you how this is done.

- It is a good idea to seek the advice of a patent attorney *as soon as possible after the invention*. United States law requires that you apply for the patent within one year after the invention is available for sale or is published. Many patents have been lost under this rule. It is best to apply for the patent *before* commercialization or public disclosure; in fact it may be necessary to do so to preserve your rights to obtain foreign patent protection. Given the length of time between application and issuance of the patent, the earlier the application is made, the better.

CHAPTER 16

International Software Distribution

The United States is currently the world leader in software technology. United States software developers and publishers have made billions of dollars from distribution outside the United States. American software is distributed worldwide, but by far the largest markets are the 12 countries of the European Community (EC)[1] and Japan, and these markets are the main focus of this chapter.

There are many facets of international software distribution, and this chapter provides an overview of the subject—not a comprehensive discussion by any means, but enough to point you in the right direction. This chapter will discuss (1) some factors to consider in adapting products for foreign markets, (2) some aspects of international intellectual property protection, (3) some issues that arise in negotiations with foreign distributors, (4) a brief discussion of the problem of software piracy, and (5) an overview of United States export controls.

---

1   The EC consists of Belgium, Denmark, France, Germany, Greece, Ireland, Italy, Luxembourg, the Netherlands, Portugal, Spain, and the United Kingdom.

Foreign Distribution

Small and medium-size software companies distribute internationally through distributors. Large United States software vendors also use local distributors or create foreign subsidiaries. Most software that is distributed in foreign markets in quantity is not exported; rather, it is produced under license in or near the target foreign market. For reasons discussed in this chapter, U.S. companies rarely mass-produce French, German, Spanish, or Japanese language software domestically for export by sea or by air. When the software is manufactured and packaged in a foreign country, the only exporting involved for each product or version is the one-time shipment of computer source code or object code to the foreign distributor. Typically, the process of adapting software to foreign languages and markets and of production is done abroad.

Localization

When software is sold in a foreign country, it is usually translated and adapted to the local language and culture, a process known as *localization*. This process is a key part of international software marketing.

Even though the hardware and operating software used in Europe is generally the same as that used in computers in the United States, application software normally needs to be adapted for foreign markets. The work required for localization is often substantial, and the need to have it done knowledgeably is an important reason why local distributors are needed.

Some of the changes required for transferring the program into a foreign language are readily apparent. The character sets for German, Swedish, or French are obviously not the same as in English, and therefore characters used for screen displays, printer output, and telecommunication must be changed. The appropriate currency symbols for francs, lira, etc. must be put in place. The conventional manner for writing dates, for showing a decimal point, and marking the thousands place in numbers must also be changed to the European style. Inches must be changed to centimeters.

More subtle and less obvious changes are also required. Local markets may require different features. For example, a transaction processing system for banks may need to be adapted to local tax laws, to laws relating to bank secrecy, to local accounting practices, or to government reporting requirements. In addition, translations must be done with intelligence. Word-for-word translations will not do. The user interface should be idiomatic and easy to understand in its foreign version. The documentation normally must be extensively rewritten, as must tutorial programs. Examples given in documentation, for example, should be natural situations for the user.

Localization for Japan

The Japanese language and computer create a number of technical issues that must be addressed each time a computer program from the United States is adapted for Japan. Japanese uses two sets of syllables (each set has all the sounds of the language but with different syllables; it's like having two alphabets) plus about 1800 commonly used Chinese characters known as *kanji*. Japanese computers have ROM chips that store screen displays for these syllables and characters. Because there are so many symbols that the computer must display, a character in Japanese is typically two bytes on a Japanese computer, rather than one (as on U.S. machines), which means that managing these symbols is more complex. While books and newspapers have vertical columns that flow right to left, Japanese computers usually display text left to right like English. Nonetheless, printer interfaces are different and more complex because of the need to accommodate kanji. In addition, Japan has its own computer operating systems for mainframes, minicomputers, and micros. The most popular Japanese microcomputer operating system, for example, is a variant of MS-DOS manufactured by NEC.

The Japanese also have their own set of market-specific requirements and preferences. All these factors mean that substantial technical work must be done to revise software for Japan. However, distributors are familiar with the changes required, and major hardware manufacturers in Japan provide technical information and support concerning converting software to run on their computers and operating systems.

Foreign Marketing

To sell in foreign markets, it is necessary to understand local marketing practices and preferences. Basic marketing decisions have to be made on such matters as packaging and advertising. In some cases, the trademark of the product has to changed to make it sound better to the local consumer. It is crucial to know who the players are in the local distribution system: the resellers, the retailers, and the sales representatives. And it is vital to grasp what the customers want in terms of personal support, training, and service, and what they are willing to pay. The local distributor will be familiar with all these factors.

International Intellectual Property Protection

There are a series of international treaties that govern copyrights, trademarks, and patents. As you might imagine, there is great variation in the law of various countries on the protection of intellectual property rights. In some Third-World countries, for example, software piracy is common and legal protection is ineffective or non-existent. In a number of countries, there are excellent intellectual property protection laws on the books—that in practice are never enforced!

When dealing in any foreign markets, you will need to consult local counsel (or an American attorney overseas) to explore all local law issues, particularly if you expect any serious intellectual property problem. The following will provide a general overview and point out some of the issues to keep in mind.

Copyright Protection Abroad

Copyrights are governed by two international treaties that have been ratified by the United States, the EC countries, Japan, and most other countries: the Berne Convention and the Universal Copyright Convention. These two conventions differ somewhat in technical detail. The Berne Convention (like United States' law) requires no formalities to claim copyright protection; the Universal Copyright Convention requires a copyright notice with the "©" symbol, the name of the copyright holder, and the date of publication. In general, however, these treaties are both based on the principle of reciprocity, known formally as "national treatment". That is, the treaties require each country to give holders of copyrights of other signatory countries the same rights and privileges accorded to its own citizens who are holders of its own copyrights.

Your rights in a foreign copyright may arise directly out of foreign law, rather than under a treaty. For example, if you or your distributor develop a new localized version of your software and you publish it abroad, the new version of the software would gain copyright protection by virtue of the local law of the country or countries of publication.

However, knowing that you have the same protection as any holder of a German or Brazilian software copyright begs the question. You need to know what protection, if any, foreign law grants to its own software copyrights. Every country might have its own answer to a host of copyright questions: Is software covered by copyright law at all? Are software interfaces covered? Is reverse engineering forbidden? Are shrink-wrap licenses enforceable? And so on. These matters are often unclear.

Copyright Protection for Software in the EC

Even in the EC countries in recent years, the protection given to software copyrights in various countries has varied. For example, in some states, copyright protection has been rather strong, but in Germany, until recently, it was all but non-existent due to restrictive court decisions.

To create some uniformity among the EC countries, the Council of the European Community adopted the Directive on the Legal Protection of Software Programs, which was designed to bring some uniformity to software protection in the EC. The Directive did not directly change the law of the member countries; rather it directed the EC countries to include protection of software in their own law by 1993.

The Directive requires the EC countries "to protect computer programs, by copyright, as literary works." The copyright holder's exclusive rights include reproduction, translation, adaptation, and distribution. As in the United States, a licensee is permitted to make a backup copy of a program. Interface protection was left for the courts to decide on a case-by-case basis. Reverse engineering is allowed under the Directive's terms in certain limited circumstances. While some issues remain unclear, the thrust of the Directive is to give software in the EC protection roughly comparable to that provided in United States law.

It is too soon to say how the Directive and software protection in the EC will work in practice. However, it is likely that the courts of the EC counties will be granting more uniform protection to software copyrights. For details and to address particular problems, you still need to get advice on a country-by-country basis from counsel on the scene.

Software Copyrights in Japan

In 1985, Japan amended its copyright law to provide copyright protection for computer programs. Though there are only a few court decisions under the copyright law concerning software, those cases have generally enforced copyright protection. A 1987 case brought by Microsoft Corporation showed that a non-Japanese company could successfully assert copyright protection in a Japanese court. In part because there have been few decided cases, the limits of copyright protection for computer programs in Japan is still undecided. For advice on a particular situation, you should consult Japanese legal counsel or a specialist in Japanese law.

Patents

There have been software-related patents granted in other countries, including EC countries and Japan. The Paris Convention is a treaty that covers patent filings in the United States, the EC countries, Japan, and many other countries. An important feature of the Paris Convention is its one-year "window" for foreign patent filing. It works like this: If you file your patent application in the United States, and then file abroad in a Convention country within a year, you get the benefit of the United States application date. This is important because patent systems generally give priority to the first claimant to file. (An exception is the United States patent system which gives priority to the first to invent.) The Paris treaty is also based on a reciprocity or national treatment model; generally speaking, you get the same rights as a local citizen filing under the local patent system.

Most countries have their own process and criteria for patent examination. This means that the United States Patent and Trademark Office (PTO) may grant you a patent, while other countries may refuse to do so—or vice versa. European patent filing is simplified somewhat by the fact that there is a single filing center for many European states at the European Patent Office (EPO)[2] in Munich, Germany. But even after the EPO approves a patent application, the patent still must be registered with some or all of the countries separately (after translation into the national language) to be effective.

---

2   The EPO member states are the EC member countries plus Switzerland, Austria, Sweden, Liechtenstein, and Monaco.

Moreover, foreign patent applications in Europe, Japan, and elsewhere, are very expensive—much more so than in the United States. Foreign patent registration and maintenance fees (that is fees to keep the patent in effect) are very high. The EPO even charges high fees while a patent application is pending. The cost of applying for and maintaining a Japanese patent is also very high. It is easy to spend $50,000 to secure and maintain foreign patent protection for a single invention. Applying for foreign patent rights makes sense only where (1) the patent, if issued, will have substantial coverage and the ability to prevent competition, and (2) there is a very high likelihood of substantial foreign sales of the patented product or there is a licensee for the foreign patent rights who is willing to foot the bill for patent protection.

Trademarks

The Paris Convention also covers trademarks. Its provisions on trademarks are quite similar to those on patents. Trademarks are dealt with on a reciprocal basis. As with patents, there is a filing "window"—in the case of trademarks, it is generally six months. If you file your trademark application in the United States, and then file abroad in a Paris Convention country within the window period, you get the benefit of the United States application date. The same rule applies to foreign trademark holders from Convention countries that apply in the United States.

Currently every country has its own trademark system, with its own formalities, fees, scope of coverage, and requirements for protection. This means that getting trademark protection in a number of countries requires contacting competent local counsel in each country in which the company wishes to trade.

The EC has begun a process to bring its various trademark systems into accord, and it plans in the future to establish a central trademark authority that will function on an EC-wide basis for trademarks, just as the EPO does for patents. However, it may be years before this process of reform is completed.

There have been trademark abuses in some foreign states, often at the expense of American companies. In the United States, the rule until recently was that trademarks had to be based on use. But in most countries the rule is that the first to *file* becomes the owner of the trademark. In some countries, unscrupulous persons simply file applications for trademarks used by well-known foreign companies, then charge the companies a high fee to use their own marks. One major United States software vendor, for example, had to pay a considerable fee to use its own name in

Argentina. A company introducing a new trademark may need to move fast to protect it in all major foreign markets. Coordination and planning are required.

Agreements with Foreign Distributors

The nature of the bargain in a Foreign Distribution Agreement is very much like the Software Publishing Agreement that we discussed in Chapter 9. As in those agreements, the owner of the license grants rights to the product to the distributor, who is responsible for production and marketing. The owner in return gets a percentage of the revenue. As in those agreements, there are issues about the duration the license grant, the definition of "net sales" for royalty calculation purposes, auditing rights to verify royalties, minimum royalty payments, termination if a specified sales level is not achieved, rights to new products and new versions, technical support, etc. In fact you can use the Software Publishing Agreement Checklist (Form 9-1, Appendix C) as a guide to most of the issues that you will have to consider. However, there are also some additional things that you should consider in finding and negotiating with a foreign distributor.

Finding the Right Foreign Partner

Perhaps the most important aspect of an international distribution scheme is finding the right foreign distributors. The right contacts usually come from a process of networking and inquiry. Hardware and software vendors have an interest in increasing the number of software products that run on their systems, and they can provide guidance in choosing a partner in a foreign state. Companies that are already active in selling in foreign countries will also often share insights with other companies (except competitors). Guidance may also be available from the American Electronics Association (AEA) offices in Washington and Santa Clara (the AEA also has branch offices in Brussels and Tokyo), the Software Publishers Association (SPA), and the Department of Commerce's Office of Trade Information Services. Addresses for these organizations are included in Appendix D, this book's List of Software Business and Intellectual Property Resources. Businesses can also contact the American Chamber of Commerce in each country of interest. A number of consultants here in the United States are willing to guide companies looking for foreign partners, for a fee of course.

How Trustworthy Are Foreign Partners?

Some United States software owners fear that they will be cheated outright by their foreign partners, that sales will be under-reported, and that royalties will not be paid. In reality, there have been few problems of this sort in software-related dealings in Europe or Japan. Most software deals have been with foreign companies that are well established and financially healthy. These companies have a vested interest in maintaining a reputation as a good partner for U.S. companies. In the major industrialized states, the risk of outright cheating is no greater than it would be in dealing with a reputable United States company.

Allocating the Cost of Localization

As with any negotiation, issues in arranging foreign distribution involve bargaining about burdens and rewards. If the foreign partner shoulders the entire cost of localization and product introduction, the United States software owner can expect lower royalties than it would get if it shared in more of the risk.

The Scope of the License Grant

Most often the distributor will want an exclusive license. However, most United States companies resist granting an exclusive of more than one year or two at most. If a long term exclusive is granted to the wrong distributor, it may be a difficult mistake to undo. Some United States companies establish only one distributor in a country, but make no contractual commitment to maintain an exclusive.

Granting geographic exclusives may also create unintended problems. Consider, for example, what may happen if the version of the program marketed in the foreign state cannot read or write files created by the United States version. This can happen, for example, if the foreign program has different features that require a new format, or if the latest United States version of a program has not yet been localized for the country involved. The problem is that multinational companies, who are large software purchasers, want standardized software to use worldwide. In a multinational company, computer files created in New York must be usable in Paris, Rome, and Tokyo. Some multinational companies require their foreign subsidiaries to standardize on the United States version of the programs, and they buy the programs here for use by their operations in various foreign states. The problem is that sales of these United States versions of the product for use in foreign states may be a violation of the exclusive rights granted to foreign distributors. The distributors may demand compensation for what they consider stolen sales. These issues of standardization and multinational sales are best bargained out before an agreement is signed.

In western Europe, goods flow freely across national borders, and therefore, if short term exclusives are granted, it may make sense to consider licensing distributors by language rather than by country for the EC market.

Protection of Source Code

The process of localization of software almost always requires that the technicians performing the technical work have access to the program source code. Therefore, any agreement must have provisions for security and confidentiality, as well as provisions for return of confidential information when the relationship terminates.

Dealing with Local Regulation

It is part of the normal role of the distributor to be responsible for complying with all local regulation, including securing permits, paying any licensing fees or taxes, and so on. Normally it is also the obligation of the distributor to carry out the local process of copyright and trademark registration on behalf of the software owner. It is rare, however, that the distributor will undertake the burden and expense of patent filings.

Ownership Rights to Localized Software

When the foreign distributor creates a localized version of a program, who owns it? This issue becomes most pertinent if the agreement with the foreign distributor is terminated. The United States software owner should be sure that it either owns the foreign version of the software or can obtain all rights upon termination.

Ownership of Trademarks

It is also very important that the owner makes sure that it has ownership and control of all trademark rights in each country where it does business. If possible, trademark registration should be in the name of the owner, not the distributor. The owner should retain a right of control over the use of the trademark. And any distribution agreement should provide that, on termination, the distributor surrenders any right to use the owner's trademarks. Unless trademarks are handled correctly, the software owner may find that its valuable trademark is owned by a terminated dealer.

The Need to Consult Local Counsel or United States Attorneys Overseas

Most often the text of a Foreign Distribution Agreement will be in English, and will often have a clause calling for application of the law of a state of the United States and a specified country. Often there will even be provisions for arbitration in the English language in a United States city. Nonetheless, it is advisable to have the agreement examined by a reputable attorney in the distributor's country (either a local lawyer or a U.S. lawyer practicing overseas) to be sure that the agreement does not raise any unforeseen issues under local law. For example, local law may prohibit or restrict termination of sales agents or distributors under some circumstances. Local law may require pre-approval of certain distribution arrangements. Some countries restrict a company's ability to convert earnings into dollars or to export dollars or other hard currency. Local law may require licensing and fees for operations, and so forth. It is better to be informed than to be sorry.

Dealing with Software Piracy

Even in the industrialized world, including the United States, it is common for businesses and individuals to use illegally copied software. In developed countries, the remedy is normally civil litigation, or in egregious cases, a criminal complaint. The problem of illegal copying and illegal distribution is much worse, and much harder to deal with, in Third-World countries, where outright software counterfeiting is a frequent occurrence. Software piracy is notoriously common in Taiwan, China, India, Italy, Portugal, and other countries. In some cases, action against software pirates can be obtained from local authorities, particularly when encouraged by the local United States Embassy. In other cases, the local authorities will do nothing. Guidance on dealing with software piracy in the Third World is available from the SPA in Washington.

United States Export Controls

Even if the only software that an owner is sending out of the country is a single disk or tape containing source or object code, or if the owner is sending the software electronically, the owner is still *exporting* software. And any export of software or software technology is governed by and subject to United States export controls.

Export controls are part of the legacy of our 40 years of cold war with the Soviet Union and are based on concern for the military advantage that comes from technological superiority. The end of the struggle with soviet communism has led to a significant relaxation of export controls, a process of change that is ongoing. Nonetheless, the United States still has enemies, and the government still wishes to keep a technological lead in military affairs, and therefore substantial controls remain. In a world where software technology can be exported through international networks, controls largely depend on individual compliance and cooperation. It is important to note, however, that failure to comply with export control laws can result in substantial criminal penalties, including prison time and large fines.

There are in fact two export control systems, one administered by the Department of Commerce and the other by the Department of State. The Commerce Department's Bureau of Expert Administration (BXA), acting in cooperation with sister agencies in allied countries, has jurisdiction over dual-use technology, that is technology that has both civilian and military uses. While even the most humble computers can have some military uses, BXA's focus is on the more powerful and sophisticated equipment or equipment where military use predominates over civilian use. An example of the technology of concern to BXA is high-performance image enhancement systems and displays, which could have applications in publishing and medical diagnosis, but are also used for image processing for military intelligence. Also included are powerful computers, high capacity network systems, a variety of fast and powerful telecommunication devices, and other computer and telecommunication technology. Software designed specifically to drive or control these devices is likewise the object of BXA concern.

BXA issues detailed regulations that attempt to classify all computer technology export items. Most commonly available software comes under a general license, which means that it can be exported without prior approval simply by listing the applicable license category on a Customs export declaration (unless export is controlled by the State Department, as is discussed on the following page). Some items require a license issued by BXA on a case-by-case determination, known as a *validated license*. In many cases licensing is dependent on giving BXA written assurance that re-export will not occur—or in some cases that the technology will be given round-the-clock security. In other cases, export is forbidden altogether.

All countries are not the same to the BXA. A great deal of technology that can legally be exported to France cannot be exported to Iran or Syria. And from time to time, some countries are entirely embargoed, as are Serbia and Montenegro at the time of this writing. BXA will aid businesses in determining the applicable classification of software and the licensing policy that applies. The address and phone number of BXA in Washington are included in Appendix D.

The Department of State's Office of Defense Trade Controls (DTC) also regulates software exports; it has jurisdiction over equipment, including software, that consists of *munitions*, that is, weapons of war. For example, software used in guidance systems, military aircraft, fire control systems for artillery, and other military equipment can be exported only with a DTC license.

In addition, DTC has jurisdiction over encryption, and in particular regulates *any software that features full file encryption*. In exercising this jurisdiction over full file encryption, DTC works closely with the National Security Agency (NSA), which engages in electronic surveillance of foreign communications. DTC and NSA do not want enemy countries to obtain encryption techniques that the NSA cannot decipher. Generally, DTC is not concerned about software products that encrypt only passwords, or in software in which encryption is used only for copy protection, data compression, or in signal processing for cable television or mobile phones.

While DTC will permit export of some mass-market software with relatively simple encryption methods, there are even some mass-market products in the United States that normally cannot be shipped abroad due to their full file encryption features. Any company that wants to export any product with full file encryption, for example network e-mail products with an encryption option, should contact DTC for approval early in the process of setting up foreign distribution. The address and phone number of DTC are also included in Appendix D.

Because export control regulations are changing rapidly, the information in this section may become obsolete soon. It is therefore advisable to contact the government with regard to any planned export of software.

Dealing with Foreign Governments

If you are engaged in selling software to foreign governments, particularly in the third world, you need to be aware of the Foreign Corrupt Practices Act (FCPA), a law enacted by Congress. In many less developed countries, the government of the country is one of the largest customers for software. In some countries, such as China and Russia, many large enterprises are organs of the central government. In many cases unfortunately bribery—directly to a government official or indirectly though well-placed intermediaries—is necessary to get government business. Paying the bribe will violate the FCPA.

Under the FCPA, it is illegal to give or promise any money or anything of value to any foreign official, party, or politician to get business. It is also illegal to make such payments indirectly or through intermediaries. Willful blindness to the obvious purpose of a payment is no defense.

For violation of the FCPA, corporations may be fined up to $2 million. Individuals that violate the act may be subject to imprisonment of up to five year and to fines of $250,000 or more. Violation of FCPA can result in difficulties under United States tax law as well. Your company should never participate in a deal that involves prohibited payments—no matter how lucrative the promised contract seems. The penalties under United States law are just too severe. If any doubt arises about what is permitted, you must contact legal counsel.

International Boycott

Some countries, primarily Arab states, have tried to impose an international boycott of the state of Israel and have blacklisted companies that deal with Israel or Israeli companies.

It is a violation of United States law to participate or assist this international boycott. Your company is forbidden to sign any agreement or any statement certifying that you have not dealt with Israel or promising not to do so in the future. Nor can you furnish information about whether or not you company has dealings with Israel. If you asked to join in boycott activity, you may be required to report the request to the federal government. Violation of federal anti-boycott law is a serious matter that can result in substantial criminal penalties and income tax problems. If you are approached to participate in any boycott activity, you should seek legal counsel immediately.

CHAPTER 17

A Strategy for Intellectual Property and Contract Management

In every software company, there needs to be an ongoing process that keeps the company's legal affairs in order. It is not enough to implement the concepts discussed in this book on a sporadic basis. A software business needs to foster a culture in which intellectual property and contract management are attended to as a matter of course. And, no less than once a year, there should also be an audit to verify that legal affairs are under control.

For very important reasons, a software company needs to be able to verify its own legal health. Neglect of legal rights can weaken or cripple a software business, as I have explained in the chapters of this book. In addition, there are key moments in the life of a software business when it must be able to prove that it has control of its legal affairs. When a company borrows funds, obtains a substantial venture capital investment, sells stock to the public, or is acquired, it must be able to undergo "due diligence" scrutiny of its legal and financial affairs. If the party conducting the examination finds legal chaos, the deal may come to a dead stop or there may be a delay that can cause the deal to fall apart.

Of course there are legal matters that affect corporations that are beyond the scope of this book, such as federal, state, and local taxation, employee health and retirement benefits, corporate and securities law, liability insurance, and real estate issues, among others. These too need attention and the assistance of professional advisors. However, the focus here is on those legal issues that have particular application to software businesses—the issues that I have discussed in this book.

Keeping legal affairs in order is not cost-free. In a small company, it requires the owners to assume one more burden. In large companies, it means hiring staff to manage contracts and intellectual property matters. There are administrative costs for security measures and copyright filings; there are substantial legal costs for trademark and patent holdings. These burdens, however, are an essential part of running a software business, and the ultimate cost of failing to attend to legal affairs is much higher.

In the following pages, you will find lists of measures for intellectual property and contract management that are used by many software businesses. Of course, a list represents a distillation, and perhaps an oversimplification. The lists certainly must be read in light of the discussions of copyrights, trademarks, patents, and contract matters in the preceding chapters of this book. In the context of your business, particular items may require consulting with counsel.

There is no formula for managing legal matters that fits every business. You should adapt the listed items to your own company. Because every company is unique, there may be issues affecting your company not discussed or addressed here, and there are likely to be matters listed that do not apply to your company.

Intellectual Property Protection Procedures

Procedures for intellectual property protection should be a matter of routine. Your company should consider doing the following:

1. Implement a procedure to have the copyright on each version of the company's software products registered with the Copyright Office before the software is released.

2. Make sure that registration, use, and licensing of trademarks and service marks conforms to good legal practice.

3. Encourage employees to disclose patentable inventions. Consult counsel on the patentability and potential value of inventions.

4. Hold periodic meetings to educate officers and employees about the importance of trade secrets, and implement appropriate security measures for the company.

5. Create and maintain a program for security of the premises, including, alarms, after-hours access control, badges, and sign-in logs.

6. Verify use of appropriate copyright, trademark, and patent legends.

7. Give each officer and employee a copy of the company's policy on intellectual property protection.

Software Protection and Control

Because software and data are critical assets, your company should consider using the following measures to protect them:

1. Implement appropriate computer security systems, including password controls, that provide a high degree of assurance that only authorized users have access. Use security software that records each log-in, including the identity of the user and the time and duration of use. Monitor for unusual or inappropriate access. Change passwords periodically. Be sure that names of former employees are promptly removed from access lists.

2. Implement systems for tracking changes to source code for the company's software products and proprietary software tools, so that the company is in a position to prove what technology it had at various points in time. For the same reason, archive older versions of the software and documentation.

3. Perform regular backups of computer code and business data.

4. Have copies of proprietary source code and master disks in a secure location off-site, so that fire or other disaster will not destroy the software (and the company along with it).

5. Arrange for back-up computer facilities off-site to ensure the continuation of key business functions in case of an emergency.

6. Arrange for regular compliance with your escrow agreement updating obligations; verify compliance by your suppliers with any escrow obligations that were set up to protect your company.

7. Maintain lists of each piece of third-party software incorporated in the company's products, including memory management programs, printer drivers, etc. Verify that your company is licensed to use the third-party code and that

your company's field of use and geographic distribution is authorized by license.

8. Monitor competing products to see if your company's copyrights, trademarks, or patents are being infringed. Monitor the markets for counterfeit versions of your company's products.

9. Avoid "cloning" competitors' products in order to avoid copyright infringement concerns. Seek legal advice before any reverse engineering activity.

Contract Management

It is important for companies to manage contract documentation with customers. The company should take the following steps:

1. Maintain files containing every agreement, together with each amendment, schedule, and addendum. Contract files should be maintained for dealings with suppliers, dealers, independent programmers, and others with whom the company has a commercial relationship.

2. Maintain files of documentation relating to end-user agreements, such as shipping documentation, customer acceptance forms, reports of errors and bugs, records of service calls, installation of software patches, upgrades, and new software versions.

3. Use a database system to record installation dates, renewal and expiration dates, and other key milestones for each end-user agreement.

4. Establish controls on who is authorized to sign or negotiate changes in contracts.

5. Maintain export control documentation including export declarations, validated licenses, and correspondence with Commerce Department and State Department personnel.

Controlling Documentation

The solid foundation of managing legal affairs is to gather and store the relevant documentation as a matter of business routine. Where feasible, documents should be kept in looseleaf binders, so that they are easy to find and so that new materials can easily be added. Documents that should be kept include the following.

Intellectual Property Documents

1. Copyright registration certificates and copyright applications.
2. Trademark registration certificates and applications for trademark registration.
3. Invention disclosure forms, patents, and patent applications.
4. Correspondence with government agencies involved in intellectual property protection.
5. Summaries of technologies that the company considers to be trade secrets.
6. Agreements with other companies in which your company or the other has agreed to keep information confidential.
7. Agreements under which the company has acquired software technology or other intellectual property rights, including licenses, assignments, development agreements, publishing agreements, etc.
8. Agreements under which the company has granted software technology or intellectual property rights to others, including assignments, development and publishing agreements, etc.
9. Agreements relevant to security measures, including guard service contracts, contracts for purchase and service of alarm and entry control systems, contracts for procurement of encryption and password protection software, and any consultant reports on such matters.
10. All correspondence relating to intellectual property matters.

Litigation Records

1. All pleadings, correspondence, and other documents relating to any actual or threatened suit, claim, or arbitration concerning licensing or use of intellectual property or infringement of any intellectual property rights.
2. All pleadings, correspondence, and other documents relating to any actual or threatened suit, claim, or arbitration concerning alleged defects in the company's products.

Form Documents

1. Standard forms such as beta test agreements, employee confidentiality and non-competition agreements, confidential disclosure agreements, exit interview forms, end-user agreements, shrink-wrap licenses, bug reports and logs, and the like.

2. Standard sales, service, and other commercial contracts.

3. Samples of all disk labels and documentation with appropriate copyright, patent, and government contract legends.

4. Employee policy statements concerning intellectual property matters.

Marketing and Sales Material

1. Advertisements, sales literature, and other documents used to promote the company's products. These should be kept in order to monitor the company's use of its trademarks and its representations concerning its products.

Lists of Consultants and Professionals

1. A list of technical consultants and experts used by the company.

2. A list of professionals used by the company: lawyers, accountants, marketing consultants, advertising agencies, etc.

Employee Documentation

Managers in charge of hiring, or in the human resources department of large companies, must require and maintain appropriate employee documentation, including the following:

1. Employee confidentiality and non-competition agreements.

2. Confidentiality and non-competition agreements signed by consultants.

3. Records regarding employee access to laboratory notebooks and other trade secret information.

4. Completed exit interview forms for each departing employee.

Periodic Legal Audits

In addition to the ongoing process of protecting its intellectual property, a software company should conduct an audit of its intellectual property and contract management at least once a year. This kind of audit is needed in the same way that a person needs a regular physical examination by a doctor. The process is designed to make sure systems are functioning properly and to attempt to catch any problems before they become serious. The audit should cover both the implementation of the existing procedures and their effectiveness. An attorney can aid in the design of the process and in assessing its results. The involvement of the company's accountants may also be appropriate.

The audit should address all the subjects listed above. Key managers should take responsibility for verifying compliance with company procedures and for reporting all exceptions and problems. In addition, from time to time, counsel review form agreements and company policies from time to time to be sure that they reflect any changes in the law. Needless to say, problems found in policies or practices should be addressed and cured.

A Written Guide to Good Business Practice

Many high technology companies give every employee a written set of guidelines to good business behavior, often entitled "Ethical Guidelines" or "Guide to Business Practice." Many companies distribute the guidelines to every new employee. Some companies give every employee a new copy every year.

These guidelines cannot cover every topic and can only give general guidance on the subjects that they do cover. However they may serve to sensitize employees to potential problems and legal concerns.

I have included a sample form of guidelines as Form 17-1 (on diskette as ETH-ICS.W51). This form is based on one used at a sophisticated high technology company near Boston, which kindly gave its permission for this use.

CHAPTER 18

When You Need a Software Lawyer

Major software corporations have large legal staffs to draft new contracts, manage the protection of their intellectual property, and carry out other legal tasks. Most businesses and individuals, of course, do not have these resources and don't want to spend money on lawyers when they can avoid it. Unfortunately, there is a certain level of spending on legal affairs that is unavoidable for a software business.

In some cases, like litigation or applying for a software patent, it is obvious that you *must* hire an attorney. In these matters, the old adage is apt: "A person who represents himself has a fool for a lawyer." But there are other matters when an attorney is not really needed or can play a secondary role. Unfortunately, there are many times when a business fails to perceive that its needs counsel. This chapter gives you some guidelines in determining when you need a software lawyer.

How Lawyers Can Help Software Businesses

We live in an increasingly complex society. The number of laws and regulations that apply to businesses has increased many fold in the past few decades. There are matters affecting any business where good legal counsel is indispensable. We have looked at some in this book. Every software business should have a lawyer available who understands computers and software and can give advice on promoting the legal health of the business. At the very least, you need enough legal advice to tell you what legal risks your business is taking.

There are other legal areas, beyond the scope of this book, in which a software business is likely to need the services of good legal counsel (and/or an accountant or other professional advisor). These areas include:

- Financing (including private investments and the sale of securities to the public)

- Corporate law

- Taxation

- Real estate

- Employment matters

- Employee benefits.

In addition, any small or family-owned business should have the benefit of legal advice on estate planning.

Do You Need an Attorney for a Particular Job?

At times you may be unsure whether an attorney is needed for a particular transaction or task. Here are three questions that you should consider when you decide if you need a lawyer:

1. **How simple or complex is the job?** Some legal tasks can be very simple. For example, as is discussed in Appendix A, in most cases you can register a software copyright with the Copyright Office without an attorney's help. Included in this book and on diskette are two forms of software evaluation agreement (Forms 8-1 and 8-2). Also included is an employee confidentiality agreement (Form 4-3) that obligates employees to keep their employer's technology and proprietary techniques secret and to turn over any inventions to the company. And there are sample beta test agreements (Form 4-1 and 4-2). Many small businesses routinely use these simple forms without consulting legal counsel, while others consult counsel to review and approve the forms. Non-competition agreements (ones that attempt to keep your employees from working for

competitors after they leave your business), involve law that can be very tricky and require review by an attorney. Other tasks are even more complex. Contracts involving large sums of money, or a multifaceted or multiyear relationship, normally require the aid of a lawyer.

2. **How familiar are you with the legal task?** Sometimes you can become quite familiar with a comparatively complex legal task. For example, if you have negotiated five software publishing agreements with the aid of counsel, chances are you can do the sixth one yourself, using the prior deals as a template, and perhaps letting your lawyer give the deal one last look before it is agreed to and signed. The same is true of contracts to supply software or services to customers where the great majority of the provisions are "standard" and the variations are only in such non-technical matters as price, credit terms, and delivery dates. In these cases, common sense tells you that if your lawyer has reviewed and approved the form contract, further legal advice is usually unnecessary. One caution is that forms should be reviewed and updated from time to time, because the law changes.

3. **How important is the matter in your business?** The more important a legal matter is for your business, the more you need to seek an attorney's guidance. If you are negotiating a contract that governs an important part of your business, for example one that defines your relationship with an important supplier, publisher, distributor, or customer, you should surely have the draft contract reviewed by a lawyer before you agree orally or sign. Your intellectual property is important; from time to time you should ask an attorney to help design and carry out a legal audit to be sure that intellectual property is properly protected. This type of audit, discussed in Chapter 16, is like going to a doctor for a regular check-up.

Being Smart About Using an Attorney

When you do need a lawyer, you will get the most cost effective service when you have thought through the business issues thoroughly and are well organized. This book will help you do that.

In many contract negotiations you can bring the talks far along, and resolve most or all of the business issues without counsel, or with perhaps occasional consultations. If you do an outline or rough draft of a contract before you see your attorney, the attorneys' work will be much more focused and efficient and therefore less expensive.

Finding Legal Counsel

It is a good idea to have an attorney who works in the computer field available to advise your business. You can use an attorney as a consultant. Many attorneys who practice in the computer field will answer quick questions over the phone for a modest charge or for free.

You don't want just any business or corporate lawyer. Sometimes lawyers who don't understand the software field will take your money in good faith to review a contract, and then miss important issues. You need a lawyer who has experience with the law affecting software and who understands your technology.

If you are sued or bring a lawsuit, you also need an attorney with substantial litigation experience. Getting a trial lawyer who understands software is particularly important, because one key to software litigation is the counsel's ability to make complex ideas into simple concepts that judges and juries will be able to understand.

Getting legal help should not necessarily be "one-stop shopping." Depending on the needs of your software business, you may well need more than one lawyer or more than one law firm. The attorney that drafts your computer contracts probably is not the right one for the highly specialized field of patents—and vice-versa.

In areas where there are many technological business, such as the metropolitan areas in California and Texas, Boston, Seattle, and other high-technology centers throughout the United States, there are many qualified practitioners. In other areas where technology businesses are less common, you may have to ask lawyers and other business people to find the attorney you need.

Registering Your Software Copyright and Recording a License Agreement or a Transfer of Ownership Rights

Introduction

This Appendix covers two important copyright procedures that are discussed in Chapter 1.

The first is *registration*, the process by which a copyright gets on record at the Copyright Office. In Chapter 1, I reviewed the substantial advantages under the Copyright Act that come from copyright registration.

The second is *recordation* of an exclusive license agreement or an assignment. The recordation procedure applies when the copyright involved has previously been registered. As is discussed in Chapter 1, when some or all of the copyright exclusive rights are transferred, as they would be in a publishing agreement or in a variety of other types of deals, recording the license agreement or assignment protects the rights of the licensee or transferee.

There are three form letters included in this appendix. They can also be found on diskette in COPY-LTR.W51.

The Registration Process

The Three Elements of the Application

To register a software copyright you simply have to send the following to the Copyright Office.

- The application form
- The fee
- A deposit of copyrighted material

All three elements are discussed below. However, if you have any questions about copyright procedures, you can call the Copyright Office's Information Line at (202) 707-3000. If you prefer, you can write for information at:

Copyright Office
Library of Congress
Washington D.C. 20559

Who Can File an Application?

Under the Copyright Act, a copyright application can be filed by the owner of the copyright in a software program or the owner of "any exclusive right" in the work. Therefore, the author could register, as long as he or she has any exclusive rights and has not assigned them all. An exclusive licensee for worldwide rights, for example, or for a country, or for a particular application or field of use, could register. So could someone who bought all rights in a software program.

Of course, if a company licenses an unregistered program from the author, the license contract should specify who will be responsible for registering it. Registration need only be done once to make the copyright registered for all purposes.

One Application or Many?

As noted in Chapter 1, a program may have more than one copyrightable aspect; in addition to computer code, you may claim protection for screens and displays, sound, etc. And you can also copyright the documentation, which may be on disk or printed material. To cover all of these things, you need file only *one* application.

In the past people would file one application the program's code, another for program screens, and a third for the documentation. The Copyright Office, burdened each year with over 600,000 applications for all kinds of works, ended that practice in 1988. Now one form is all it takes to register software. Of course, each time you bring out a revision of your product that makes a significant change, you should register the new version by filing another copyright application as a matter of routine.

If your program consists of a number of discrete programs, as do, for example, some accounting packages, you have a choice of registering the package as a whole or the individual programs separately. If you are going to be marketing them separately, then use separate registration forms for each; otherwise use a single form.

The Registration Form

Getting the Right Application Form

In the great majority of cases, the correct form to use for a copyright registration of software is Form TX. Bound into this book is a tear-out copy of Form TX. The tear-out Form TX in the book is actually a bit longer than regulation size, for reasons known only to the authorities that run the publisher's production facility. If you use the form right out of the book, you must either trim it to 8.5" by 11" size or copy it onto an 8.5" by 11" piece of paper. Basic information and line-by-line instructions that the Copyright Office provides with Form TX are included at the end of this chapter.

Form TX is the form for literary works. Form TX is normally appropriate for software because the Copyright Office believes that since the computer program (or at least the source code) is text, "literary authorship will predominate in most works, including many in which there are screen graphics." However, if visual or graphic elements predominate (as it would, for example, in an arcade game), registration may be made on Form PA as an audiovisual work. You can order Form PA through the Forms Hotline (described below). Form PA is very similar to Form TX, although the numbering of spaces is different. The following guide to using Form TX will serve as well to guide you through Form PA. Current Copyright Office policy, at least at the time this was written, was to accept software registration filings on either form.

If you need copies of Form TX or any other forms, you can place an order on the Copyright Office Forms Hotline at (202) 707-9100. The hotline is a telephone answering machine that acts as a mailbox for form orders. You just call and, at the sound of the tone, record your name and address and identify the forms you need. For software registration, you should ask for Forms Package 113, which includes Form TX as well as additional information on software registration. A response to your order takes two or three weeks and there is no charge for the service. The Copyright Office will accept applications filed on photocopies of Form TX or any other official form—as long as the photocopying is done right. The key is to make the copy look just like the original on good quality paper. To copy Form TX the proper way, you need to make a two-sided copy. Copy the form so that the text on both sides of the page of paper is lined up head-to-head (so that the top of page 2 is right behind the top of page 1), just like the copy of Form TX in the book. If you foul up the copying, the Copyright Office may bounce back your application.

Some Notes on Filling Out Form TX

Before reading the rest of this discussion of copyright registration, please take a few minutes to read Form TX and to read the Form TX official instructions found at the end of this Appendix. For the most part the form is self-explanatory. But there are few sections or "spaces" in Form TX you need to know a bit more about.

Space 1: Your Software's Title

If you want a copyright, your program must have a title—even if the program is an otherwise nameless subroutine or if you haven't yet given it a commercial title. The Copyright Office uses the title for filing and classification. If you change the title later, there is a procedure, described below, to let the Copyright Office know.

Space 2: Who is "The Author"?

If the program is "work-for-hire," the *employer* is the author (see the discussion of "work-for-hire" in Chapter 1). For example, if employees of Digital Equipment Corporation wrote the program, then DEC is the author. If the program is not "work-for-hire," the persons who wrote the program are the authors. If there are more than three authors, you will need to list them separately, which means that you will need the official continuation sheet, Form TX/CON, which is available from the Forms Hotline. Informal attachments are not accepted.

Space 2 Continued: The "Nature of Authorship" Line   Space 2 also asks you for the "Nature of Authorship." This is the only really tricky line in the application.

There are "magic words" that the Copyright Office is looking for in the "Nature of Authorship" line.

There are two aspects of this line that can be troublesome. One is that if you get this line wrong, the Copyright Office will bounce your application back to you. The second is that, if you aren't careful, you can increase the amount of copyrighted material that you have to deposit without any apparent increase in your copyright protection.

Words That You *Should* Put in "Nature of Authorship"   The easiest course is simply to write in the blank for "Nature of Authorship" the following words:

Entire text of computer program.

If there is a user's manual included with your program, use the following:

Entire text of computer program with user's manual.

It is the position of the Copyright Office that these simple phrases register *every aspect* of the program that is within the scope of copyright protection.

Words That You *May* Put in "Nature of Authorship"   In the space for "Nature of Authorship," you have the option of mentioning "screen displays." If you do mention these two words, however, you will create more work for yourself. You will then be required to include pictures, or even videotapes, of those screen displays, along with computer code, in the deposit you make at the Copyright Office. The rules governing the deposit of these screen display materials are discussed below.

Why would someone make extra work for themselves by making an unnecessary claim of screen displays in Form TX? The reason is that some software owners (or perhaps their lawyers) don't want to run whatever risk there may be that the Copyright Office is wrong in its position that claiming the text of the program registers all aspects of it. Some argue that making the express claim puts would-be infringers on notice that the screen displays are claimed (but it is unlikely that infringers are really deterred by language in Copyright Office filings). Wishing to take no risks, these applicants always expressly claim protection for screen displays, and then supply the additional material required.

If this logic makes you feel that you want to make an express claim of screen displays in your application, the following terminology will work fine in the blank for "Nature of Authorship":

Entire text of computer program and screen displays

or

Entire text of computer program and screen displays with user documentation

Words That You Should *Not* Put in "Nature of Authorship"   In stating "Nature of Authorship" correctly, the operative principle is that Congress said you can copyright a computer *program*. Unfortunately, people often *say* that they are registering something else. In general the Copyright Office will *reject* applications with statements in this space that describe:

- An algorithm, method, or technique

- Program functions

- The medium on which the software is recorded

- Short ambiguous phases that don't sound like they describe a computer program

If you describe your material as something that sounds wrong, you will probably will get your application *rejected*. This will delay processing and require you to correct the error when you file for the second time. Therefore do *not* describe your program's features or functions, and do *not* use any of the following terms on the "Nature of Authorship" line:

Data format
File format
Menu
Structure, sequence, and organization
Look and feel
System design
EPROM chip
CD-ROM
Computer algorithm
Method for computer analysis

The problem with these terms is that, at least as far as the Copyright Office is concerned, none of them *sound* like something that Congress said you can copyright, and many of the terms are ambiguous at best. So stick to the "magic words."

Space 4: The "Copyright Claimant"

The "claimant" is either the author (which could be a corporation if the program is "work-for-hire") or someone else who owns *the entire rights to the program*. This could be a transferee of all rights in the program or the heir of the original owner. If you have an exclusive license, but not *all* rights, you are *not* the "claimant."

If the author and the claimant are not identical, then a very brief description of the transfer of rights is called for. For example, you could write:

Transfer of all rights by written contract
Purchase of all rights and title from author
Written assignment
All rights transferred by will

You should *not* attach the contract of transfer.

Space 6: "Derivative Works"

Use this space if the program has a substantial amount of material that was previously published, registered, or in the public domain. It would be used, for example, for the latest revision of your program. It is sufficient in Space 6a, "Pre-existing material," simply to write:

Previous version

For Space 6b, "Material Added to This Work," either of the following phrases will do:

Revised text of computer program
Revised and additional text of computer program

Do *not* refer to bug fixes or error corrections (which are not considered a sufficient change for a new filing), or to the new functions of the program (which the Copyright Office feels are not registerable elements).

Space 11: Your Certification

In Space 11, you state the interest that you have in the software that makes you eligible to file a registration. Check off Author, Other Copyright Claimant (i.e. transferee of *all* rights in the program), Owner of Exclusive Rights, or Agent of one of these. Then sign. Unless the application is signed, it will not be processed.

The Fee and Deposit Required with the Application

The Fee

Unless you seek expedited processing of your application (discussed later), the registration fee (as of this writing) is $20, payable by check or money order to *Register of Copyrights*. (Note that all fees referred to in this book are subject to change. It's a good idea to call the Copyright Information Line to verify the fee.)

The Required Deposit: Code From the Software Program

For software programs, other than those on CD-ROM, you must deposit a printout of the computer code to register your software. Most often parties deposit a printout of source code, but as described later, there is a procedure for submitting an object code printout.

The rules on making the required deposit are the following:

- For programs over 50 pages in length, submit the first and last 25 pages of the source code for the program, printed out on standard 8 1/2 by 11-inch paper.

- If the program is a revised version of copyrighted material and the first and last 25 pages do not both include revised portions, submit 50 contiguous pages of the source code from a portion of the program that does include revisions. (If there are revisions in the first and last 25 pages, send those).

- If your program is less than 50 pages in length, supply the source code for the entire program.
- If you register user documentation with the program, include one full copy.

Note to Macintosh mavins who are registering a HyperCard "stack": the Copyright Office considers the text of the script of the stack, written in HyperTalk, to be the "source code" that you should submit. The same would undoubtedly be true if you are submitting a script from an analogous Windows applications generator.

Protecting Your Trade Secrets

There is public access to material that is deposited in the Copyright Office under certain circumstances, and it is possible that your trade secrets will be revealed to competitors from the material on deposit. In a recent lawsuit, the court found that an employee of Atari Games Corporation, by misrepresenting the purpose of his visit, gained access to source code that Nintendo of America had deposited at the Copyright Office. Based on what it learned by this unauthorized inspection, Atari was able to create a "key" to open the ROM-based "lock" that controlled access to the Nintendo game system.

To provide a measure of protection for trade secrets while still securing copyright protection, the Copyright Office lets you limit the disclosure in your copyright deposit in the following ways:

For new computer programs:

- You may submit the first and last 25 pages of the source code for the program, with *up to 49 percent* of the code blacked out.
- You may submit the first and last 10 pages of the source code for the program, with no code blacked out.
- You may submit the first and last 25 pages of a printout of the *object code* for the program, together with any 10 pages of the *source code* with no code blacked out.
- For programs of less than 50 pages, you may submit the entire source code, with *up to 49 percent* of the code blacked out.

For revised computer programs:

- If the revisions are present in the first and the last 25 pages, any of the four options just mentioned.

- If the revisions are not in the first and the last 25 pages; 20 pages of source code containing the revisions with *no* portions blacked out, *or* any 50 pages containing the revisions with *up to 49 percent* blacked out.

Nothing in the rules requires that the most sensitive and innovative parts of the program be submitted. Programmers therefore should consider arranging the modules of the source code so that the first and last 25 pages contain rather routine code. In addition, it is permissible that the printout submitted be double-spaced.

If you take advantage of these options to protect trade secrets, you must include with your application a letter in the following form:

Object-Code-Only Filings and the "Rule of Doubt"

Sometimes you may wish to file *only* object code. This may be because of concern over trade secrets or because the source code, for some reason, is unavailable. You can make such a filing, by submitting a printout as follows:

- For programs 50 pages in length or over, the first and last 25 pages of the object code for the program.

- For programs less than 50 pages in length, the entire object code for the program.

If you make an object-code-only filing, the Copyright Office will register the copyright under its so-called "rule of doubt" because it cannot determine what the code is.

The effect of the "rule of doubt" is that in litigation you do *not* get the benefit of the two procedural presumptions that usually come with registration: (1) that until proven otherwise, your copyright is presumed valid; and (2) that until proven otherwise, all the statements in your copyright registration are taken as true. As we noted in Chapter 1, these presumptions can simplify proof somewhat at trial. However the matters that are the subject of this rule (such as the fact that the program is original and the identity of the author) are not difficult to prove in litigation. Therefore, it is really not a very serious detriment that the "rule of doubt" applies. Nonetheless, you should use this option only if you have a good reason for an object-code-only filing.

If you make such an object-code-only filing, you *must* send, with the application, a letter in the following form:

Form A-1: Sample Letter for Depositing Trade Secret Code

XYZ Software Corp.
123 Main Street
Anytown, California

[Date]

Register of Copyrights
Library of Congress
Washington, D.C. 20559

Dear Register:

Enclosed is a copyright application for [Title of Program] submitted by XYZ Corporation.

XYZ Corporation is submitting the deposit in the enclosed form in order to protect trade secrets that are contained in the computer code.

I certify that the statements in this letter are true.

Very truly yours,

[Name]
[Title]

Form A-2: Letter for Object-Code-Only Deposit

XYZ Software Corp.
123 Main Street
Anytown, California

[Date]

Register of Copyrights
Library of Congress
Washington, D.C. 20559

Dear Register:

Enclosed is a copyright application for [Title of Program] submitted by XYZ Corporation.

XYZ Corporation is submitting the deposit in the form of object code only.

[Title of Program] is an original work and the object code contains copyrightable authorship.

I certify that the statements in this letter are true.

Very truly yours,

[Name]
[Title]

Deposit of Other Items

Screen Displays

As noted, you needn't mention screen displays in your application. But if you do, you must make an additional deposit as follows:

- Visual representations of the screens in printouts, photos, or drawings no smaller than 3x3 inches and no larger than 9x12 inches. Be sure to include *all* screens used.
- If the work is "predominantly audiovisual," a VHS videocassette reproducing all the graphics.

Works on CD-ROM

For CD-ROM format works, deposit the entire CD-ROM package, including (1) any operating software, (2) the CD-ROM disk, (3) the manual, and (4) if the work also comes in printed form, a copy of the printed version.

Computer Databases

Special rules apply to computer databases. If you seek to register a database, you should contact the Information Line at (202) 707-3000 for details.

Submitting the Application

Sending It All In Together

It is important to mail the application, the deposit, and the fee in the same envelope. If you try sending them separately, you will likely get them back the same way—and have to start the application process all over again.

How Long Does Registration Take?

Normally registration takes about 16 weeks from the time that the application is received. When the process is completed, you receive a Certificate of Registration. If there are errors in the application, the process may take longer.

The effective date of registration is the date on which your properly prepared application is received, together with the appropriate fee and your deposit of program code. If you want assurance that your application was received, send it registered or certified mail, return receipt requested.

The Copyright Office Information Line will give you information about your pending application, but only after 16 weeks have passed from the time that your application was received.

Getting the Copyright Office to Process Your Application in a Hurry

As I explained in Chapter 1, under current law no lawsuit can be brought to enforce a copyright unless it is registered. (A bill to remove that requirement is pending before Congress, so this might change in the future.) If you need to get registration quickly because you have filed or are about to file litigation, you need to ask for special handing of your application. Special handling should get you your Certificate of Registration in about *ten working days*—rather than in four months. The cost for this is an *additional* $200, for a total fee of $220.

Presumably, by the time that you *need* expedited registration, you will already have litigation counsel. Counsel can handle the process of expedited registration as part of getting ready for the battle. However, if you wish, you can do it yourself.

If you want expedited treatment, you must *not* send the application to the address stated above for Form TX—because then your application will simply go on the pile for the normal, slow treatment. Instead, you *must* use the following address:

Library of Congress
Department 100
Washington DC 20540

Note that the address for special handling should *not* include a reference to the Copyright Office, because that may cause the mail to be misrouted and delayed.

In addition, you must request special handling. There is a form for this request, but it's not really necessary to use a form. It is good enough if you send your application with a letter requesting this relief. An example of such a letter is on the following page.

Form A-3: Letter Requesting Special Handling

> Jack Smith Software Corp.
> 34 44th Street
> Seattle, Washington
>
> [Date]
>
> Library of Congress
> Department 100
> Washington DC 20540
>
> RE: <u>Special Handling Application</u>
>
> Dear Register:
>
> On behalf of Jack Smith Software Corp., I enclose a copyright application, deposit and a fee of $220 and request <u>special handling</u>.
>
> The reason that special handling is needed is that copyright infringement litigation concerning the enclosed is imminent [has already commenced]. Jack Smith Software, Inc. is the plaintiff. The defendant is Jane Jones Data Corp. of Harvard, Massachusetts. The suit will be [has already been] brought in United States District Court for the Northern District of California in San Francisco.
>
> I certify that the statements in this letter are true and correct to the best of my knowledge and information.
>
> Very truly yours,
>
> Jack Smith
> President

Note that all of the information set forth in this sample is required for expedited handling. You must state:

- That litigation is imminent or has commenced

- The names of the plaintiff and defendant
- The court where the lawsuit is to be filed or has been filed
- A certification that your statements are true

If any of these elements is absent, the request for expedited treatment will be denied.

Corrections and Supplemental Information for Existing Registrations

To make corrections or supplement a registration, ask the Copyright Office Forms Hotline for Form CA. You can use this form only if:

- You made a mistake on your original registration: for example, the wrong publication date, the wrong author, or a misspelling.
- You want to change the title of the program.
- You want to register a change of address. Updating your address makes it easier for would-be licensees to find you through the Copyright Office. Note that failing to update your address will not invalidate your copyright registration.

Form CA is not for new versions of the software (which is done by a new Form TX filing) or for transfers of ownership (which are documented in the Copyright office by the recording process described below). Form CA is available by calling the Forms Hotline. When the form is filled out, mail it to:

Copyright Office
Library of Congress
Washington D.C. 20559

together with a fee of $20, payable by check or money order, payable to Register of Copyrights.

Recording Transfers of Ownership Rights

It is prudent for the licensee of any exclusive right (or the transferee of all rights) in a computer program to make a record of its ownership rights with the Copyright Office. (For convenience, I will use the term "transferee" to refer both to the exclusive licensee and the transferee of all rights.) As I explained in Chapter 1, the transferee should record the transfer within 30 days after the transfer or license grant (60 days if the transfer took place outside the United States). If transferees miss that window, their rights are subject to the conflicting rights of any assignee or exclusive licensee who files in good faith before they do.

It is easy for transferees to make a record of their interest in software by using the following procedure.

Procedure If the Copyright Is Not Yet Registered

If the program copyright is not yet registered, then, as is discussed previously in this appendix, the transferee itself is entitled to register the copyright. Simply follow the procedures discussed above.

Procedure If the Copyright Is Already Registered

If the copyright has already been registered, you must record the agreement, assignment, or other document with the Copyright Office. To record the transfer, send the copyright office:

- Two copies of the official Document Cover Sheet for recordation of documents
- The fee
- The original or a photocopy of the document to be recorded

Bound in this book is a tear-out copy of the Document Cover Sheet form produced by the Copyright Office. The tear-out Cover Sheet, like Form TX, comes from the printer slightly longer than regulation size. If you use the form right out of the book, you must either trim it to 8.5" by 11" size or copy it onto an 8.5" by 11" piece of paper. You can also get a copy of the Document Cover Sheet from the Copyright Office Forms Hotline.

You will find that the recordation information called for in the Document Cover Sheet is readily apparent. Note that in Space 2, you should check the box for "Transfer of Copyright" when you record a license to software.

Space 3 requires a listing of all registered copyrighted works transferred by document. With this form it is permitted to attach additional 8 1/2 by 11-inch sheets of paper if needed, to list all the transferred copyrighted works. While the Document Cover Sheet has a provision in Space 4 for recording incomplete documents, it is not advisable to do so. In fact, the recordation of an incomplete document may be invalid. Therefore, you should send complete documents for recording, including all attachments and schedules.

You may record an original of the document to be recorded, that is, the actual agreement or assignment with the original signature in ink. However, the Copyright Office prefers that you record a photocopy. Note, however, that if you are sending a copy, you must sign *both* the Affirmation and the Certification on the Document Cover Sheet. The Affirmation (which must be signed in any case) says that the statements in the Document Cover Sheet are true, and the Certification states that the photocopy accurately reflects the contents of the original.

The recording fee, payable by check or money order to the Register of Copyrights, is $20 for a document that assigns or transfers an interest in a single registered copyright. If the document assigns more than one copyright, there an additional $10 fee for each ten or less additional copyrights covered by the same assignment document. The amount of the fee enclosed should be stated on the Document Cover Sheet in Space 6. Fees are subject to change.

The mailing address for recordation is:

Documents Unit
Cataloging Division
Register of Copyrights
Library of Congress
Washington, D.C. 20559

In about four to six months after receipt, the Copyright Office will send back a Certificate of Recordation. The filing is a public document available to any member of the public on request.

As is noted above, if you need to record a transfer resulting from an inheritance, purchase in a bankruptcy, receivership, or divorce, similar procedures apply. However, to be sure the filing is correct in those situations, you should see a lawyer about the documentation that is required. A lawyer's advice is also needed for any transaction involving the pledge of a copyright as security for a debt or contractual obligation.

If you wish to sue on the basis of the assignment or license of a registered copyright, the assignment or license must be recorded before the suit is brought. If you are bringing such a lawsuit, your attorney can arrange expedited recordation under the special handling procedure described above.

A final note: any or all of the exclusive or non-exclusive rights of the copyright owner may be transferred. However, a transfer of exclusive rights will be valid *only* if the transfer is in writing and signed by the owner of the rights that are transferred (or the owner's authorized agent). The Copyright Office will not scrutinize filings to make sure that they are legally valid transfers; that is your responsibility. When in doubt, seek legal counsel.

Filling Out Application Form TX

These official instructions accompany Form TX, which is bound into the middle of this book. Read these instructions before completing this form.

When to Use This Form: Use Form TX for registration of published or unpublished non-dramatic literary works, excluding periodicals or serial issues. This class includes a wide variety of works: fiction, non-fiction, poetry, textbooks, reference works, directories, catalogs, advertising copy, compilations of information, and computer programs. For periodicals and serials, use Form SE.

Deposit to Accompany Application: An application for copyright registration must be accompanied by a deposit consisting of copies or phonorecords representing the entire work for which registration is to be made. The following are the general deposit requirements as set forth in the statute:

Unpublished Work: Deposit one complete copy (or phonorecord).

Published Work: Deposit two complete copies or one phonorecord of the best edition.

Work First Published Outside the United States: Deposit one complete copy (or phonorecord) of the first foreign edition.

Contribution to a Collective Work: Deposit one complete copy (or phonorecord) of the best edition of the collective work.

The Copyright Notice: For works first published on or after March 1, 1989, the law provides that a copyright notice in a specified form "may be placed on all publicly distributed copies from which the work can be visually perceived." Use of the copyright notice is the responsibility of the copyright owner and does not require advance permission from the Copyright Office. The required form of the notice for copies generally consist sof three elements: (1) the symbol "©," or the word "Copyright," or the abbreviation "Copr."; (2) the year of the first publication; and (3) the name of the owner of copyright. For example: "© 1989 Jane Cole." The notice is to be affixed to the copies "in such manner and location as to give reasonable notice of the claim of the copyright." Works first published prior to March 1, 1989, **must** carry the notice or risk loss of copyright protection.

For information about notice requirements for works published before March 1, 1989, or other copyright information, write: Information Section, LM-401, Copyright Office, Library of Congress, Washington, D.C. 20559.

LINE-BY-LINE INSTRUCTIONS

1 SPACE 1: Title

Title of This Work: Every work submitted for copyright registration must be given a title to identify that particular work. If the copies or phonorecords of the work bear a title (or an identifying phrase that could serve as a title), transcribe that wording *completely* and *exactly* on the application. Indexing of the registration and future identification of the work will depend on the information you give here.

Previous or Alternative Titles: Complete this space if there are any additional titles for the work under which someone searching for the registration might be likely to look, or under which a document pertaining to the work might be recorded.

Publication as a Contribution: If the work being registered is a contribution to a periodical, serial, or collection, give the title of the contribution in the "Title of this Work" space. Then, in the line headed "Publication as a Contribution," give information about the collective work in which the contribution appeared.

2 SPACE 2: Author(s)

General Instructions: After reading these instructions, decide who are the "authors" of this work for copyright purposes. Then, unless the work is a "collective work," give the requested information about every "author" who contributed any appreciable amount of copyrightable matter to this version of the work. If you need further space, request Continuation sheets. In the case of a collective work, such as an anthology, collection of essays, or encyclopedia, give information about the author of the collection work as a whole.

Name of Author: The fullest form of the author's name should be given. Unless the work was "made for hire," the individual who actually created the work is its "author." In the case of a work made for hire, the statute provides that "the employer or other person for whom the work was prepared is considered the author."

What is a "Work Made for Hire"? A "work made for hire" is defined as: (1) "a work prepared by an employee within the scope of his or her employment"; or (2) "a work specially ordered or commissioned for use as a contribution to a collective work, as a part of a motion picture or other audiovisual work, as a translation, as a supplementary work, as a compilation, as an instructional text, as a test, as answer material for a test, or as an atlas, if the parties expressly agree in a written instrument signed by them that the work shall be considered a work made for hire." If you have checked "Yes" to indicate that the work was "made for hire," you must give the full legal name of the employer (or other person for whom the work was prepared). You may also include the name of the employee along with the name of the employer (for example: "Elster Publishing CO., employer for hire of John Ferguson").

"Anonymous" or "Pseudonymous" Work: An author's contribution to a work is "anonymous" if that author is not identified on the copies or phonorecords of the work. An author's contribution to a work is "pseudonymous" if that author is identified on the copies or phonorecords under a fictitious name. If the work is "anonymous" you may: (1) leave the line blank; or (2) state "anonymous" on the line; or (3) reveal the author's identity. If the work is "pseudonymous" you may: (1) leave the line blank; or (2) give the pseudonym and identify it as such (for example: "Huntley Haverstock, pseudonym"); or (3) reveal the author's name, making clear which is the real name and which is the pseudonym (for example: "Judith Barton, whose pseudonym is Madeline Elster"). However, the citizenship or domicile of the author **must** be given in all cases.

Dates of Birth and Death: If the author is dead, the statute requires that the year of death be included in the application unless the work is anonymous or pseudonymous. The author's birth date is optional, but is useful as a form of identification. Leave this space blank if the author's contribution was a "work made for hire."

Author's Nationality or Domicile: Give the country of which the author is a citizen, or the country in which the author is domiciled. Nationality or domicile **must** be given in all cases.

Nature of Authorship: After the words "Nature of Authorship" give a brief general statement of the nature of this particular author's contribution to the work. Examples: "Entire text"; "Coauthor of entire text"; "Chapters 11-14"; "Editorial revisions"; "Compilation and English translation"; "New text."

3 SPACE 3: Creation and Publication

General Instructions: Do not confuse "creation" with "publication." Every application for copyright registration must state "the year in which creation of the work was completed."

Give the date and nation of first publication only if the work has been published.

Creation: Under the statute, a work is "created" when it is fixed in a copy or phonorecord for the first time. Where a work has been prepared over a period of time, the part of the work existing in fixed form on a particular date constitutes the created work on that date. The date you give here should be the year in which the author completed the particular version for which registration is now being sought, even if other versions exist or if further changes or additions are planned.

Publication: The statute defines "publication" as "the distribution of copies or phonorecords of a work to the public by sale or other transfer of ownership, or by rental, lease, or lending"; a work is also "published" if there has been an "offering to distribute copies or phonorecords to a group of persons for purposes of further distribution, public performance, or public display." Give the full date (month, day, year) when, and the country where, publication first occurred. If first publication took place simultaneously in the United States and other countries, it is sufficient to state "U.S.A."

4 SPACE 4: Claimant(s)

Name(s) and Address(es) of Copyright Claimant(s): Give the name(s) and address(es) of the copyright claimant(s) in this work even if the claimant is the same as the author. Copyright in a work belongs initially to the author of the work (including, in the case of a work made for hire, the employer or other person for whom the work was prepared). The copyright claimant is either the author of the work or a person or organization to whom the copyright initially belonging to the author has been transferred.

Transfer: The statute provides that, if the copyright claimant is not the author, the application for registration must contain "a brief statement of how the claimant obtained ownership of the copyright." If any copyright claimant named in space 4 is not an author named in space 2, give a brief statement explaining how the claimant(s) obtained ownership of the copyright. Examples: "By written contract"; "Transfer of all rights by author"; "Assignment"; "By will." Do not attach transfer documents or other attachments or riders.

5 SPACE 5: Previous Registration

General Instructions: The questions in space 5 are intended to find out whether an earlier registration has been made for this work and, if so, whether there is any basis for a new registration. As a general rule, only one basic copyright registration can be made for the same version of a particular work.

Same Version: If this version is substantially the same as the work covered by a previous registration, a second registration is not generally possible unless: (1) the work has been registered in unpublished form and a second registration is now being sought to cover this first published edition; or (2) someone other than the author is identified as copyright claimant in the earlier registration, and the author is now seeking registration in his or her own name. If either of these two exceptions apply, check the appropriate box and give the earlier registration number and date. Otherwise, do not submit Form TX; instead, write the Copyright Office for information about supplementary registration or recordation of transfers of copyright ownership.

Changed Version: If the work has been changed, and you are now seeking registration

to cover the additions or revisions, check the last box in space 5, give the earlier registration number and date, and complete both parts of space 6 in accordance with the instructions below.

Previous Registration Number and Date: If more than one previous registration has been made for the work, give the number and date of the latest registration.

6 SPACE 6: Derivative Work or Compilation

General Instructions: Complete space 6 if this work is a "changed version," "compilation," or "derivative work," and if it incorporates one or more earlier works that have already been published or registered for copyright, or that have fallen into the public domain. A "compilation" is defined as "a work formed by the collection and assembling of preexisting materials or of date that are selected, coordinated, or arranged in such a way that the resulting work as a whole constitutes an original work of authorship." A "derivative work" is "a work based on one or more preexisting works." Examples of derivative works include translations, fictionalizations, abridgments, condensations, or "any other form in which a work may be recast, transformed, or adapted." Derivative works also include works "consisting of editorial revisions, annotations, or other modifications" if these changes, as a whole, represent an original work of authorship.

Preexisting Material (space 6a): For derivative works, complete this space **and** space 6b. In space 6a identify the preexisting work that has been recast, transformed, or adapted. An example or preexisting material might be: "Russian version of Goncharov's 'Oblomov'." Do not complete space 6a for compilations.

Material Added to This Work (space 6b): Give a brief, general statement of the new material covered by the copyright claim for which registration is sought. **Derivative work** examples include: "Foreword, editing, critical annotations"; "Translation"; "Chapters 11-17." If the work is a **compilation**, describe both the compilation itself and the material that has been compiled. Example: "Compilation of certain 1917 Speeches by Woodrow Wilson," A work may be both a derivative work and compilation, in which case a sample statement might be: "Compilation and additional new material."

7 SPACE 7: Manufacturing Provisions

Due to expiration of the Manufacturing Clause of the copyright law on June 30, 1986, this space has been deleted

8 SPACE 8: Reproduction for Use of Blind or Physically Handicapped Individuals

General Instructions: One of the major programs of the Library of Congress is to provide Braille editions and special recordings of works for the exclusive use of the blind and physically handicapped. In an effort to simplify and speed up the copyright licensing procedures that are a necessary part of this program, section 710 of the copyright statute provides for the establishment of a voluntary licensing system to be tied in with copyright registration. Copyright Office regulations provide that you may grant a license for such reproduction and distribution solely for the use of persons who are certified by competent

authority as unable to read normal printed material as a result of physical limitations. The license is entirely voluntary, nonexclusive, and may be terminated upon 90 days notice.

How to Grant the License: If you wish to grant it, check one of the three boxes in space 8. Your check in one of these boxes, together with your signature in space 10, will mean that the Library of Congress can proceed to reproduce and distribute under the license without further paperwork. For further information, write for Circular R63.

9, 10, 11 SPACE 9, 10, 11: Fee, Correspondence, Certification, Return Address

Fee: Copyright fees are adjusted a 5-year intervals, based on increases or decreases in the Consumer Price Index. The next adjustment is due in 1995. Contract the Copyright Office in January 1995 for the new fee schedule.

Deposit Account: If you maintain a Deposit Account in the Copyright Office, identify it in space 9. Otherwise leave the space blank and send the fee of $20 with your application and deposit.

Correspondence (space 9): This space should contain the name, address, area code, and telephone number of the person to be consulted if correspondence about this application becomes necessary.

Certification (space 10): The application can not be accepted unless it bears the date and the **handwritten signature** of the author or other copyright claimant, or of the owner of exclusive

right(s), or of the duly authorized agent of
author, claimant, or owner of exclusive right(s).

Address for Return of Certificate (space 11):
The address box must be completed legibly
since the certificate will be returned in a window
envelope.

Glossary of Legal Terms

The following are legal terms commonly used in discussion of software law issues and in software agreements. Terms in italics are defined elsewhere in the glossary.

Acceptance: (1) Expressing agreement to the terms of an offer to enter into an agreement. The acceptance of the offer results in the formation of an agreement. (2) In the course of an agreement where one party is to deliver goods, the recipient's agreement to receive and keep the goods. Acceptance in this sense normally occurs when the recipient has had an opportunity to inspect the product and indicates acceptance. In some cases, failure to reject goods can constitute acceptance.

Agreement: A contract. An undertaking between or among two or more parties that is enforceable under contract law.

Alternative Dispute Resolution: Methods for business dispute resolution other than litigation, including *arbitration* and *mediation*.

Answer: In litigation, the document filed in court by which a defendant states formally its position on the matters alleged by the plaintiff and raises defenses.

Antitrust laws: State and federal laws designed to guard against anti-competitive practices and improper attainment or exploitation of economic power. Discussed in Chapter 10.

Arbitration: A process for binding non-judicial resolution of contract or other business disputes. Arbitration often takes place pursuant to an arbitration clause in a contract.

Assignment: The transfer of a legal right or interest from one person or company to another.

Berne Convention: One of several treaties that require signatory countries to provide copyright protection for works copyrighted in other countries. The United States and many other countries are signatories. See Chapter 16.

Beta Test Agreement: An agreement governing the trial use, or beta testing, of software. Discussed in Chapter 5.

Breach of Contract.   An act or omission by one party in the course of the performance of an agreement that is inconsistent with the terms of the agreement or which prevents the other party from receiving the benefit of the agreement.

Breach of Warranty: When products delivered under an agreement fail to conform to a *warranty*. The warranty may relate to product quality or non-infringement of the intellectual property rights of others.

Choice of Law: A field of law that governs what state's or country's law governs a document or a dispute. Often agreements have "choice of law clauses" that indicate which law will apply. Such clauses are often, but not always, enforced.

Clean Room: A method designed to avoid copyright infringement suits by duplicating the functions of a software (or firmware) program without copying its code or internal structure. The method requires use of technicians who are told what a program must do but have no exposure to the program itself, its code, or design. The method protects against copyright infringement claims only in rather limited circumstances. See discussion in Chapter 1.

Common Law: State and federal doctrines of law created by judges' decisions rather than by statutes passed by legislatures. Many claims, such as rights to sue for fraud, arise from common law decisions of the court system. In some states, some crimes are also defined by common law.

Complaint: The document, filed in court in litigation, that initiates the proceeding and states the nature of the claim asserted.

Confidentiality Agreement: An agreement between an employer and an employee that obliges the employee not to disclose confidential matters. Such agreements commonly also have additional provisions that assign all of the employee's inventions and discoveries to the employer. See Chapter 2. The term may also be used to describe any agreement that requires one or more parties to hold information in confidence.

Consequential Damages: Under the *Uniform Commercial Code* and other contract law, lost profit and lost opportunity damages that flow from a *breach of warranty* in the sale or licensing of goods.

Consideration: In contract law, what is paid for the performance of the other party.

Contract: An *agreement*. An undertaking of two (or more) parties that is enforceable under contract law.

Convention: A *treaty*.

Copyright: A right granted by the United States Copyright Act or by foreign copyright law. A copyright generally governs who can make or distribute copies of a software program (or other types of copyrighted works) or prepare works based on it. See Chapters 1 and 16.

Corporation: A business organization formed in accordance with state corporate law. In many cases, corporate status can limit liability of the principals of the business. See Chapter 13.

Counterclaim: In litigation, a claim that the defendant asserts in response against the plaintiff who brought a lawsuit.

Court Order: An order of a court of law that requires one or both of the parties to take a particular action or to refrain from a particular action.

Damages: The (dollar) amount of the plaintiff's recovery in litigation. Attorneys call the injury that the plaintiff suffers "damage" (singular) or "injury" and the amount of money that the judge or jury awards "damages" (plural).

Defendant: The party who is sued in litigation.

Derivative Work: In copyright law, a work based on another work. See Chapter 1.

Direct Damages: In contract law, the cost of replacement goods when the goods that the seller delivered did not conform to the agreement.

Distinctiveness: In trademark law, the quality of a trademark that makes it stand out from marks on similar products. Distinctiveness may come from the arbitrary sound and look of the mark, or from "secondary meaning"; that is, customer recognition of the mark as pertaining to a particular source of the goods.

Export Controls: The export licensing systems administered by the Department of Commerce and the Department of State designed to restrict foreign access to technology with military uses and to weapons by regulating exports of certain goods. See Chapter 16.

External Characteristics: In software copyright law, a shorthand expression for the way a program looks and acts on the screen; the visible and audible aspects of a computer program.

Fair Use: In copyright law, a doctrine that allows a party to make limited use of another's copyrighted work without permission under certain circumstances. An example of fair use would be an author's reproduction of a software product screen in a review of the product. In some limited circumstances, reverse engineering of a software program may be fair use. See Chapter 1.

Force Majeure: In contract law, an event, caused by a force that is not under the control of either party, such as fire or earthquake, that prevents one or both from performing a contract in a timely manner. An "act of God." Many agreements have a clause permitting delays in promised performance in case of force majeure.

Franchise Laws: Federal and state law designed to protect franchisees. Franchise laws may require certain disclosures to prospective dealers and may forbid dealer terminations in some cases. In some cases, software dealerships have been held to be covered by franchise laws. See Chapter 10.

Fraud: Under state law, obtaining something of value by means of a material misrepresentation of fact or by a half-truth. In most states, to prove fraud it is necessary to show that the misrepresentation was intentional or reckless. See Chapter 13.

Guaranty: An enforceable promise that goods or service will be a specified quality or grade or will have certain defined characteristics. A *warranty*. Also spelled "guarantee."

Hold Harmless: In contract law, a promise to pay any and all liability or costs that the party may incur for a specified cause. The phrase is commonly used when a software licensor indemnifies a licensee against any expense or loss due to a patent, copyright, or trademark infringement suit; in that situation the licensor agrees to "hold the licensee harmless" from such a suit.

Incidental Damages: In agreements relating to the sale of goods, damages which are "incidental" to inspecting defective goods and replacing them with goods that conform to the agreement. Examples are costs for an advisor to help select the replacement product, packing costs, freight, insurance for shipping for the new product, etc.

Indemnification: The payment of any and all liability or costs that another party may incur for a specified cause.

Infringement: In the law of copyrights, trademarks, and patents, the use of intellectual property rights that belong to another without permission.

Integration Clause: In contract law, a clause of an agreement stating that all earlier oral and written discussions or promises are superceded by the agreement. Also known as an "entire agreement" clause.

Intellectual Property: Intangible property rights consisting of copyrights, patents, trademarks, and trade secrets.

Lanham Act: A statue enacted by Congress that sets forth federal law on *trademarks* and *service marks*.

Letter of Intent: In contract negotiations, an informal summary, signed by the parties, summarizing some terms for a proposed contract.

License: In software law, the grant of the right, pursuant to an agreement, to use some or all of the intellectual property rights that relate to specified software. The grant of the right to use, copy, sell, or modify the software. Unlike an assignment, a license is revocable, when the license agreement expires or under other circumstances stated in the agreement.

Licensee: In software law, the party that receives a license.

Licensor: In software law, the party that grants a license.

Literal Elements: In software copyright law, the source code and object code of a software program.

Litigation: The process of resolving disputes through lawsuits and trials.

Look and Feel: An informal term for the way that a program acts and behaves. See *External Characteristics*.

Offer: In contract law, a proposal for an agreement. Offers can be made orally or in writing, although some oral agreements are unenforceable.

Magnuson-Moss Act: A federal statute governing the contents of warranties for consumer products. See Chapter 11.

Mediation: A voluntary process of dispute resolution in which a neutral third party makes a non-binding recommendation for solution of the dispute.

Misrepresentation: A misstatement of fact by which one obtains something of value. *Fraud*.

Negligence: Under state law, carelessness or failure to exercise ordinary care that results in personal injury or injury to property. Some states have held that advisors on computer-related matters may be held liable for negligent advice, a form of liability sometimes called "computer malpractice."

Nominal Damages: In contract and other fields of law, one dollar or some other nominal amount of monetary damages awarded in litigation when a party has violated an agreement or otherwise breached the law, but has caused no harm.

Non-Literal Elements: In copyright law, the elements of a computer program other than its literal code, such as how the program appears and operates.

Non-Competition Agreement: An employee's agreement to not participate in a business that competes with his or her former employer for a certain amount of time after leaving stated place of employment. See Chapter 3.

Non-Disclosure Agreement: A *Confidentiality Agreement.* '

Non-Solicitation Agreement: A form of *Non-Competition Agreement* in which an employee with customer contacts agrees not to solicit customers of the employer for a certain amount of time after leaving employment. See Chapter 3.

Paris Convention: A treaty that requires signatory states to provide patent and trademark rights to holders of such rights in other signatory states. See Chapter 17. The United States is a signatory to the Paris Convention as are many other countries.

Partnership: Under state law, an agreement of two or more persons to operate a business enterprise and share profits and losses. Partners may bear unlimited personal liability for claims and debts arising in a business. See Chapter 13.

Patent: An intellectual property right, granted by federal law, to prevent any manufacture, use, or sale of products incorporating a particular invention unless the patent holder has given permission. See Chapter 15.

Permanent Injunction: A court order, issued after a trial, that permanently forbids or requires a certain course of action by the losing party.

Plaintiff: The party that brings litigation against another by filing the claim in court.

Preliminary Injunction: A court order, issued during litigation (typically very early in a case) that forbids or requires a certain course of action during the pendency of the litigation.

Prior Art: In patent law, the existing state of knowledge at the time of a claimed invention as disclosed in publicly available information or as contained in prior inventions.

Products Liability: Liability, primarily under state law, for personal injury caused by a product. Normally, product liability is imposed if the product is hazardous, whether the manufacturer was negligent or not.

Punitive Damages: In some states, increased damages awarded in contract lawsuits and other cases in order to punish the wrongdoer for conduct that violates moral norms.

Rejection: In contract law, the buyer's refusal to accept goods under a contract, where the buyer claims the goods are defective or do not conform to the agreement.

Robinson-Patman Act: A federal antitrust statute that often forbids a company from giving one dealer better prices or terms than those made available to others, subject to certain exceptions. The intent of the law is to protect small businesses against the economic power of large dealerships or distribution operations. See Chapter 10.

Secondary Meaning: In trademark law, distinctiveness at a trademark that arises from the public's association of the mark with a particular kind of goods. See Chapter 14 and *Distinctiveness*.

Service Mark: A symbol or name by which the source of services is identified. See *trademark*.

Seizure Orders: Court orders issued under federal trademark laws to authorize law enforcement officers to seize counterfeit goods.

Shrink-Wrap License: An end-user license agreement for software sold in the mass-market. Typically, the shrink-wrap license is printed on an envelope containing software diskettes. The envelope contains a notice that states that by opening the sealed disk package the customer agrees to be bound by the terms of the printed agreement. The name "shrink-wrap license" comes from the clear plastic "shrink-wrap" that is used as a protective covering for retail software products. See Chapter 11.

Software Support Agreement: An agreement to maintain software for an end-user by fixing bugs and errors, and, in some cases to provide program enhancements. Also know as a "Maintenance Agreement" or a "Maintenance and Enhancement Agreement."

Specifications: In an agreement to supply or develop software, the portion of an agreement, normally included as a schedule, in which the functional and technical aspects of software are described. Also known as a Statement of Work.

Statute: A law passed by a legislature. Federal statutes are enacted by the United States Congress. State statutes are enacted by state legislatures. A statute may also be known as an "act" as, for example the Robinson-Patman Act.

Statute of Limitations: A state or federal statute limiting the number of years within which a suit or claim may be brought.

Statute of Frauds: A state or federal statute under which certain agreements are unenforceable unless they are in writing.

Statutory Damages: In copyright law, damages that may be assessed in a copyright infringement action without the requirement of proof of actual damages.

Strict Liability: Liability imposed by the law without regard to fault. *Product liability* imposed in the case of defective products is an example of strict liability.

Title: (1) Right of ownership of property, subject however, to licenses or other grants of rights to use the property. (2) The name given to a copyrighted work.

Tort: Under state law, rights to recover for certain wrongdoing by a defendant. Torts are a body of law largely created by judges rather than legislatures. Fraud and negligence are torts.

Trade Libel: Intentionally or recklessly false statements about another company or its goods or services that hurt its reputation and cause it injury in the market.

Trade Secret: Information used in a business that is held in confidence and gives the business an advantage over the company's competitors. Trade secrets arise under state law. See Chapter 2.

Trademark: A symbol or name by which the source of products is identified. See Chapter 14.

Treaty: An agreement between countries.

Unfair Business Practices: Under the law of some states, activities in competition that injure others and are unfair or deceptive. Some states allow the victim of unfair business practices to sue for redress. Also known as "unfair competition."

Uniform Commercial Code (UCC): A statute enacted, with occasional modifications, in every state and territory of the United States. Only a portion of the UCC is enacted in Louisiana. The UCC provisions most relevant to this book are those dealing with the sale of goods, which are often held to govern licensing of software.

Universal Copyright Convention: One of several treaties that require signatory states to provide copyright protection for works copyrighted in other states. The United States and many other countries are signatories. See Chapter 16.

Warranty: An enforceable promise that goods or service will be a specified quality or grade will not infringe the rights of others or will have certain defined characteristics. A *guaranty*.

Appendix of Forms

Introductory Note

The following forms consist of sample agreements and checklists for your guidance and for use in negotiations. (A copy of each form can also be found on the diskette included with this book.) Every business deal is unique, and your own business situation may well require different terms or involve conditions not addressed in these forms. Issues of your state law may affect the enforceability of some of these documents or alter their effect.

Even if you simply make selections from the following forms, you may end up with inconsistencies, gaps, or a provision that you may regret, or you may omit some important issue. Therefore you should consider using these sample agreements in negotiations or other business activities subject to review by counsel.

All of these documents are based on the assumption that all parties and all activities governed by the documents are within the United States.

The Format Used for the Sample Agreements

As you read through the sample agreements you will see that many aspects of the agreements have explanatory comments. These of course are not meant to be part of the text.

In many cases, the text presents options and choices. Text within sections presenting options is indicated by brackets [like this]. Terms to be filled in are indicated by italics within brackets. For example, in the Definitions section of an Agreement you may see:

"Effective Date" shall mean [*specify date*][the date upon which both parties have signed this Agreement].

This means that you should complete the sentence either by writing a specific date or by using the words "the date upon which both parties have signed this Agreement."

Sections that are *Optional Provisions* are so indicated. When the the reader has to make a choice among options, but where one of the options must be chosen, the alternatives are labeled *Option 1, Option 2,* etc. Each optional provision has a vertical black line at the left margin, so that it is always clear where the provision ends. (The forms on disk omit the vertical lines.)

All time limits or dollar amounts specified in the sample agreements are mere suggestions or illustrative examples and are subject to adjustment by the parties. Indeed all of the contents of the following forms may be altered as necessary to suit your needs.

The Forms

The following is a list of the forms found within this appendix and on the diskette. The forms are provided on the diskette in two formats: WordPerfect 5.1 and ASCII. The WordPerfect files have the ".W51" filename extension. The ASCII files have the same filename with the ".TXT" filename extension.

The WordPerfect files are formatted so that they can be printed with 10 character-per-inch (10 cpi) Courier (monospace) fonts printed on pages with a one inch margins all around, that is on the left and right and on the top and bottom. These settings should allow the forms to be printed out on laser, ink jet, dot matrix or daisy wheel printers. The paragraph numbering is done with the automatic function in WordPerfect. This means that if you delete or add provisions, the paragraph numbers will adjust accordingly. You must still be careful that all internal references are consistent. Depending on the editing that you do, some additional polishing may be required to put the forms into presentable shape. Of course if you want to use other fonts or formats, you can modify and edit the forms accordingly.

Depending on the word processor that you use, the ASCII files may also require formatting and polishing for proper appearance.

THE FORMS

Form Number	Description	Filename
1-1	Cease and Desist Letter	C&D-LTR.W51
2-1	Policy on Intellectual Property	POLICY.W51
2-2	Exit Interview Form	EXIT.W51
2-3	Employee Confidentiality Agreement	CONFID.W51
3-1	Employee Non-Competition Agreement	NON-COMP.W51
4-1	Letter of Intent	INTENT.W51
5-1	Basic Form Beta Test Agreement	BETA1.W51
5-2	Beta Test Agreement for Use with Beta Test Plan	BETA2.W51
6-1	Software Evaluation Agreement (Disclosing Party's Version)	EVAL-DIS.W51
6-2	Software Evaluation Agreement (Recipient's Version)	EVAL-REC.W51
7-1	Assignment of Rights in a Software Program	ASSIGN.W51
8-1	Software Development Agreement Checklist	DEV-CHK.W51
8-2	Annotated Software Development Agreement	DEV-AGR.W51
9-1	Software Publishing Agreement Checklist	PUB-CHK.W51
9-2	Annotated Software Publishing Agreement	PUB-AGR.W51
10-1	Dealer Agreement Checklist	DEAL-CHK.W51
10-2	Annotated Dealer Agreement	DEAL-AGR.W51
11-1	Shrink-Wrap License	SHRINK.W51
12-1	End-User Agreement Checklist	USER-CHK.W51
12-2	Annotated End-User Agreement	USER-AGR.W51
12-3	Source Code Escrow Agreement	ESCROW.W51

THE FORMS

Form Number	Description	Filename
15-1	Employee Brochure on Business Ethics	ETHICS.W51
A-1, A-2, A-3	Letter for Depositing Trade Secret Code; Letter for Object-Code-Only Deposit; Letter Requesting Special Handling	COPY-LTR.W51

Form 1-1: CEASE AND DESIST LETTER

Introductory Note

The following is a cease and desist letter (on diskette as C&D-LTR.W51) to send to a copyright infringer. The letter is very straightforward in order to make the message to the infringer quite clear. As I note in Chapter 1, the letter will have more clout if it is sent by an attorney.

XYZ Software Corp.
[*Address*]

[*Date*]

Via Registered Mail/Return Receipt Requested

ABC Software Corp.
[*Address*]

Dear Sir or Madam:

XYZ Corporation (XYZ) is the owner of the software game program [*title*], copyright registration no. _____.

It has come to our attention that ABC Software Corporation (ABC) is marketing [*title*], a computer program that is substantially similar to our program. Marketing of ABC's product is an infringement of XYZ's copyright.

XYZ hereby demands that ABC immediately cease and desist from marketing [*title*] or any similar infringing product. Copies of the program should be destroyed immediately. If copies of the infringing game are in the hands of distributors, they should also be immediately recalled and destroyed.

XYZ also demands an accounting for your sales of [*title*] and demands that you pay over the profits from that program to XYZ.

I would appreciate a positive response to this demand in ten days confirming your full compliance with these demands, otherwise XYZ will pursue appropriate legal remedies.

Sincerely,

[*Name, Title*]

Form 2-1: POLICY ON PROTECTION OF INTELLECTUAL PROPERTY

Introductory Note

Every company should have a written policy on protection of intellectual property. The form should be posted in the office and made part of the employee manual. Review of the procedures should be a part of new employee orientation.

The following is a sample (on diskette as POLICY.W51). It may not fit every software business. Where there are particular security systems in place that require explanation, they could be added to this document. This draft is written to be straightforward and easy for employees to understand.

This term refers to the employer as "the company," but it may be preferable to use the name of the employer instead throughout the form.

[NAME OF COMPANY] POLICY ON PROTECTION OF THE COMPANY'S INTELLECTUAL PROPERTY

To All Personnel:

An important foundation of our company's success is its ownership of intellectual property, which consists of trade secrets, copyrights on software and written materials, trademarks, patentable inventions, and patents.

Every employee should be aware of the policy on protection of intellectual property discussed in this memorandum and should act to promote this policy.

TRADE SECRETS

The company's trade secrets are all of the information used in our business that is held in confidence and gives our business an advantage over its competitors.

One type of trade secret in our business is technology. This includes, but is not limited to, all of our software object code that has not been publicly released, our source code, alpha and beta versions of our software products, the programming and design techniques that we use, and our methods of optimization of software.

Another type of trade secret is the company's business information. This includes, but is not limited to, our product plans, our product acquisitions strategies, our customers, our profits, our costs and revenue levels, and our customer and business files.

Careless disclosure may destroy or impair the company's trade secrets. Trade secret information should never be disclosed without express authorization from an authorized member of management. As a general rule, you should assume that any non-public information in the company is a trade secret.

All employees should cooperate with the following methods that the company uses to protect confidentiality:

Computer Password Protection

The password protection system helps preserve the confidentiality of data on the computer systems. The applicable controls on access are explained to every employee at employee orientation. To protect our computer systems against unauthorized access, never give another person your password. Changes in your password will be required periodically, and you may choose to change your own password at any time.

Entry Control and Badges

It is important for the company to track and control the persons who have access to the company premises. Always wear your identification badge when on company premises. Visitors, during or after hours, must sign in and out, and must wear "Visitor" badges. Visitors should always be escorted. Certain areas are marked "authorized personnel only" and only persons permitted access should enter such areas.

Control of Disclosure of Trade Secret
Information Outside the Company

From time to time technical data or business information is shared with the company's suppliers, consultants, or others. No such information can be disclosed to an outside party unless a written confidentiality agreement has been signed by the party, and unless the disclosure has been authorized by [*position of person who may authorize disclosure*].

Technical information may not be disclosed in any publication or seminar or otherwise made public without the written prior authorization of [*position of person who may authorize disclosure*].

Confidentiality Legends on
Documents and Other Data

Even where sharing of trade secret technical or business information is permitted, the information that is disclosed in writing must be marked with a clearly visible "legend" or notice to alert the recipient that such information is involved.

The confidentiality legend should be typed in all capital letters (in order to be more conspicuous) and read like this:

NOTICE: THIS [PROGRAM, DATABASE, DOCUMENT] CONSISTS OF TRADE SECRETS THAT IS THE PROPERTY OF [*NAME OF COMPANY*]. THE CONTENTS MAY NOT BE USED OR DISCLOSED WITHOUT EXPRESS WRITTEN PERMISSION OF THE OWNER.

These legends should be used regardless of the form in which information in maintained. For example, the legend should be placed conspicuously in or on:

Every source code and data base file (written several times into the source code, including at the beginning and the end).

Product plans, specifications, market research results, etc.

Every print-out or other hard copy of every type of trade secret technical information.

Confidentiality Agreements for Employees

All employees who have access to any form of trade secret information are required to sign a confidentiality agreement in order to be employed at the company. This agreement requires employees to refrain from using or disclosing such information while they remain employed. The same restrictions remain in effect after employees go on to their next job.

Ownership of Intellectual Property

In accordance with company policy, and under the terms of the confidentiality agreement, all copyrights, trade secrets, patentable inventions, and other valuable intellectual property developed by an employee during his or her employment belong solely to the company.

Novel technology may be patentable, and should promptly be brought to the attention of a supervisor.

All employees should cooperate with management, as requested, in securing copyright and patent protection for company software.

The only exception to the rule that intellectual property belong to the company is the following: A development belongs to an employee if: (1) the employee made the development entirely on his or her own without use of the company's facilities, knowledge, property, or resources, (2) the employee did the work entirely on his or her own time and (3) the subject matter does not relate to the company's business or research or to its planned business or research. Only if all three of these criteria are met does a development belong to the employee.

Exit Interviews

When employees leave the company, they are given an exit interview, and are provided with a written statement reminding them: (1) they remain obligated under their confidentiality agreement to keep company trade secrets and confidential information in strict confidence after leaving, and (2) they are obligated to return all materials belonging to the company.

**Questions Concerning
Confidentiality and Intellectual Property**

Any employee who has questions about the company's policy on confidentiality and intellectual property should contact: [*title of person in charge*].

Form 2-2: EXIT INTERVIEW FORM

Introductory Note

The following is a form (on diskette as EXIT.W51) to be used at an exit interview to remind the departing employee of his or her continuing obligations under a confidentiality agreement. The form may need modification to conform it to your business. For example, if the employee had signed a non-competition agreement (see Chapter 3), the form would be modified to mention the obligations that such an agreement imposes.

Many companies use an exit interview form such as this one that calls upon the departing employee to sign and acknowledge his or her obligations. Others companies have a version in which no signature is required. In either case, it is a good idea to make two copies, one for the employee and one for the employee's personnel file, in order to document that the employee was given the form. If the employee refuses to sign (it is not uncommon), the supervisor should note this fact on the form.

It is also good practice to give the employee a copy of his or her signed confidentiality agreement at the exit interview.

[NAME OF COMPANY]
EXIT INTERVIEW FORM

Name of Departing Employee:_____

Name of Employee or Officer:_____

Handling Exit Interview: _____

Date of Exit Interview:_____

To the Departing Employee:

[*Name of employer*] (the "Company") is providing this statement to you to remind you of your obligation to the Company under Company policies and under the Confidentiality Agreement that you signed.

You are obligated to keep strictly confidential all Confidential Information of the Company. You may not to use Confidential Information for any purpose or disclose Confidential Information to any person or entity. This obligation does not terminate, but remains in effect after your employment ends.

"Confidential Information" means any confidential or proprietary information of the Company including, but not limited to, any technical and scientific information, any information relating to software architecture, design or code, any research and development information, any plans or projections, any customer lists, advertiser lists, supplier lists, customer sales analyses, price lists and any other non-public information concerning the Company's business.

In addition, you are obligated to turn over to the Company all property of the Employer and all Confidential Information in any form. You many not keep any copies of such materials.

Employee Certification

To the Company:

I certify that I have complied with, and will continue to comply with the Confidentiality Agreement that I signed in connection with my employment by the Company, including, without limitation, my obligation with regard to Confidential Information.

_____

(Employee Signature)

Form 2-3: EMPLOYEE CONFIDENTIALITY AGREEMENT

Introductory Note

This is a sample employee confidentiality agreement (found on diskette as CONFID.W51). It provides not only that the employee observe obligations of confidentiality, but also that the employee turn over inventions and cooperate in protecting the employer's intellectual property.

It is best to have all personnel with access to confidential information sign a confidentiality agreement, including technical, sales, clerical and maintenance personnel. New employees should sign when hired. Current employees who have not yet entered into a confidentiality agreement should also be required to sign. Every consultant or temporary employee who may have access to confidential information should sign an agreement with substantially similar provisions.

This agreement is written in the first person singular, a format with two advantages. First, it makes it easier for the employee to understand. Second, the use of the first person avoids a choice of whether to make pronouns masculine or feminine. These agreements should be written in plain language, so that employees will understand what the agreement requires.

The employer and employee should execute two original copies: one for each party.

In using this form, you may wish to substitute the company name for "Employer" throughout.

[NAME OF EMPLOYER]
CONFIDENTIALITY AGREEMENT

This Agreement is made in consideration of my employment with [*Name of Employer*] ("Employer").

1. DUTIES. I accept new employment or continuing employment with Employer. I agree that I will devote my full business time, attention, and ability to the business affairs of Employer. I acknowledge that as an employee, I have a duty of loyalty to Employer.

2. COMPENSATION. I will be paid salary at the level specified by Employer from time to time and will receive benefits in accordance with Employer's plans and policies. Employer shall be entitled to withhold from amounts to be paid to me any federal, state or local withholding or other taxes, payroll deductions, or other charges which it is from time to time required to withhold. I acknowledge that benefit plans and policies are subject to change without prior notice.

3. TERM OF EMPLOYMENT. I understand and agree that Employer may terminate my employment without cause at any time upon two weeks written notice or, at Employer's option, by tendering two weeks severance pay. My employment may be immediately terminated for cause at any time. Cause includes, but is not limited to, substandard performance, failure to perform in accordance with company policies and rules, or any act of dishonesty. I can terminate my employment at any time subject to two weeks prior notice. I understand that certain terms of this Agreement remain in effect after termination of my employment, regardless of the reason for termination.

4. COMPANY CONFIDENTIALITY. I acknowledge that in the course of my employment, I will gain access to and may gain possession of Confidential Information (as defined below) of Employer. I agree to keep all Confidential Information strictly confidential and not to use Confidential Information for any purpose or disclose Confidential Information to any person or entity (a) during my employment, except as expressly authorized by and for the benefit of Employer and in the course of my duties as an employee or (b) at any time after my employment ends.

"Confidential Information" shall mean any confidential or proprietary information of Employer, including, but not limited to, any technical and scientific information, any information relating to software architecture, design or code, any research and development information, any plans or projections, any customer lists, advertiser lists, supplier lists, customer sales analyses, price lists and any other non-public information concerning Employer's business. Confidential Information shall not include: (a) information disclosed publicly in published materials or (b) information generally known to the public.

5. RETURN OF PROPERTY. At the time that my employment terminates, or at any other time that Employer so requests, I will turn over to Employer all property of Employer and all Confidential Information in any form. I will not keep any copies of such materials.

6. ABSENCE OF PRIOR AGREEMENTS. I represent as follows:

a. My entering into employment with Employer under this Agreement does not constitute a breach of any contract, agreement or understanding and I am free to execute this Agreement and to enter into the employ of Employer.

b. I am not bound by the terms of any agreement with any previous employer or other party (a) to refrain from using or disclosing any trade secret, confidential, or proprietary information of such previous employer or other party in the course of my employment with Employer or (b) to refrain from competing, directly or indirectly, with the business of such previous employer or any other party.

7. WORKS BELONG TO EMPLOYER. All Works (as defined below) shall be the sole property of Employer. Employer shall be the sole owner of all patents, copyrights, and other rights relating to Works. I acknowledge that all Works are work for hire that become property of Employer, and I assign to Employer any and all rights that I may have or acquire in all Works.

"Works" shall mean all items created or made, all discoveries, concepts, ideas and fixed expressions thereof, whether or not patentable or registrable under copyright or other statutes, including but not limited to software, source and object code, hardware, technology, products, machines, programs, processes, developments, formulae, methods, techniques, know-how, data and improvements, which: (1) I make or conceive or reduce to practice or learn alone or jointly with others who are retained, employed or acting on behalf of Employer; (2) occur during the period of, as a consequence of, or in connection with my employment by Employer; (3) result from tasks assigned to me by Employer; or (4) result from use of property, premises or facilities owned, leased or contracted for by Employer.

This paragraph shall not apply to any development which meets all of the following three conditions: (1) I do the work entirely by myself without use of Employer's facilities, property, or resources, (2) I do the work entirely on my own time, and (3) the development does not relate to Employer's business or research or to its planned business or research.

8. AGREEMENT TO DISCLOSE. I agree to disclose promptly to Employer or its authorized agent all information regarding Works as soon as is possible. I agree to maintain accurate and adequate records of all Works.

9. DUTY TO COOPERATE. At all times during and after my employment, I agree to perform all tasks and execute all papers necessary or appropriate to grant Employer the full benefits granted in this Agreement or to facilitate Employer's securing and enforcing all rights pertaining to this Agreement.

10. BINDING EFFECT. This Agreement shall inure to the benefit of and be binding upon Employer, its successors and assigns, and on me, my successors, assigns, heirs, executors, administrators and legal representatives.

11. NEED FOR THIS AGREEMENT. I agree that because of the nature of Employer's business, the restrictions contained in this Agreement are reasonable and necessary in order to protect the legitimate interests of Employer.

12. REMEDIES. I understand that if I violate any provision of this agreement relating to Confidential Information, to Works or to my duty to cooperate in matters relating to protection of intellectual property, Employer will suffer immediate and irreparable injury. If I violate any of such provisions, I agree that, in addition to any other remedies that may apply, my strict compliance with this Agreement should be ordered by a court of competent jurisdiction and Employer is therefore entitled to preliminary and final injunctive relief to enforce this Agreement.

13. SEVERABILITY. If any one or more of the provisions contained in this Agreement shall for any reason be held to be invalid, such invalidity will not affect any other provision of this Agreement.

14. APPLICABLE LAW. This Agreement is to be interpreted in accordance with the substantive law of [*specify state*].

15. ENTIRE AGREEMENT. This Agreement represents the entire agreement between Employer and me and supersedes all prior or contemporaneous oral or written agreements between us relating to this subject matter. This Agreement may not be amended or altered except by a writing signed by both parties.

16. I ACKNOWLEDGE THAT I HAVE READ THIS AGREEMENT CAREFULLY, AND THAT I FULLY UNDERSTAND AND AGREE TO ALL OF ITS TERMS.

_____

[*Signature of Employee*]

_____

[*Employee Name, print or type*]

Employee Address:

_____

_____

Employment Date:

_____

Date of this Agreement:

_____

Accepted by:
[*NAME OF CORPORATION*]

By: _____

[*Signature of Officer of Corporation*]

Form 3-1: EMPLOYEE NON-COMPETITION AGREEMENT

Introductory Note

This is a sample employee non-competition agreement. (It is on diskette as NON-COMP.W51.) If you have read the employee confidentiality agreement, Form 4-3, this sample will look very familiar; this agreement adds non-competition provisions to the earlier form.

As I discussed in Chapter 3, the law differs from state to state as to whether non-competition agreements are permitted. In addition, these agreements must be carefully tailored in duration and geographic scope, or they may be invalid. If you are an employer and intend to use this form, or one like it, it is imperative that you have your attorney review it first.

As you will see, there are several options in the text for clauses on non-competition and non-solicitation. More than one option may apply. The first optional clause, which is a rather broad restriction, forbids the employee from working for competitors in a defined territory. This clause might apply to either a technical or a sales employee. The second optional clause, normally used for a technical employee, forbids the employee from working for companies that use certain technologies, regardless of whether they are in direct competition, on the theory that they are at least competitors in developing (and possible licensing) the named technologies. A third optional clause is directed at employees with customer contact, such as sales personnel. Under this clause, the employee agrees not to solicit his current employer's customers, or accept business from them, for a specified period after his or her employment ends. In many contracts, the clause is narrowed (and therefore made easier to defend in court) by limiting it to those customers and prospects with whom the employee has had personal contact or by limiting its geographic scope. This non-solicitation clause is more narrow than a straight non-competition clause (such as the first optional clause), because it is used when the sales employee is permitted to go to a competitor as long as he or she refrains from soliciting the current employer's customers or prospects. A fourth optional clause is designed to prevent raiding of employees, and may be considered for all personnel.

Note that paragraph 14, which permits the employee to own publicly traded stock of a competitor would normally be limited to a very low percentage of the competitor's stock, such as one or two percent.

This agreement is written in the first person singular, a format with two advantages. First, it makes it easier for the employee to understand. Second, the use of the first person avoids a choice of whether to make pronouns masculine or feminine. These agreements should be written in plain language, so that employees will understand what the agreement requires.

[NAME OF EMPLOYER]
**EMPLOYEE CONFIDENTIALITY AND
NON-COMPETITION AGREEMENT**

This Agreement is made in consideration of my employment with *[Name of Employer]* ("Employer").

1. DUTIES. I accept new employment or continuing employment with Employer. I agree that I will devote my full business time, attention, and ability to the business affairs of Employer. I acknowledge that as an employee, I have a duty of loyalty to Employer.

2. COMPENSATION. I will be paid salary at the level specified by Employer from time to time and will receive benefits in accordance with Employer's plans and policies. Employer shall be entitled to withhold from amounts to be paid to me any federal, state or local withholding or other taxes, payroll deductions, or other charges which it is from time to time required to withhold. I acknowledge that benefit plans and policies are subject to change without prior notice.

3. TERM OF EMPLOYMENT. I understand and agree that Employer may terminate my employment without cause at any time upon two weeks written notice or, at Employer's option, by tendering two weeks severance pay. My employment may be immediately terminated for cause at any time. Cause includes, but is not limited to, substandard performance, failure to perform in accordance with company policies and rules, or any act of dishonesty. I can terminate my employment at any time subject to two weeks prior notice. I understand that certain terms of this Agreement remain in effect after termination of my employment, regardless of the reason for termination.

4. COMPANY CONFIDENTIALITY. I acknowledge that in the course of my employment, I will gain access to and may gain possession of Confidential Information (as defined below) of Employer. I agree to keep all Confidential Information strictly confidential and not to use Confidential Information for any purpose or disclose Confidential Information to any person or entity (a) during my employment, except as expressly authorized by and for the benefit of Employer and in the course of my duties as an employee or (b) at any time after my employment ends.

"Confidential Information" shall mean any confidential or proprietary information of Employer, including, but not limited to, any technical and scientific information, any information relating to software architecture, design or code, any research and development information, any plans or projections, any customer lists, advertiser lists, supplier lists, customer sales analyses, price lists and any other non-public information concerning Employer's business. Confidential Information shall not include: (a) information disclosed publicly in published materials or (b) information generally known in the industry.

5. RETURN OF PROPERTY. At the time that my employment terminates, or at any other time that Employer so requests, I will turn over to Employer all property of Employer and all Confidential Information in any form. I will not keep any copies of such materials.

6. ABSENCE OF PRIOR AGREEMENTS. I represent as follows:

a. My entering into employment with Employer under this Agreement does not constitute a breach of any contract, agreement or understanding, and I am free to execute this Agreement and to enter into the employ of Employer.

b. I am not bound by the terms of any agreement with any previous employer or other party (a) to refrain from using or disclosing any trade secret, confidential, or proprietary information of such previous employer or other party in the course of my employment with Employer or (b) to refrain from competing, directly or indirectly, with the business of such previous employer or any other party.

7. WORKS BELONG TO EMPLOYER. All Works (as defined below) shall be the sole property of Employer. Employer shall be the sole owner of all patents, copyrights and other rights relating to Works. I acknowledge that all Works are work for hire that become property of Employer, and I assign to Employer any and all rights that I may have or acquire in all Works.

"Works" shall mean all items created or made, discoveries, concepts, ideas and fixed expressions thereof, whether or not patentable or registrable under copyright or other statutes, including but not limited to software, source and object code, hardware, technology, products, machines, programs, process developments, formulae, methods, techniques, know-how, data and improvements, which: (1) I make or conceive or reduce to practice or learn alone or jointly with others who are retained, employed or acting on behalf of Employer; (2) occur during the period of, as a consequence of, or in connection with my employment by Employer; (3) result from tasks assigned to me by Employer; or (4) result from use of property, premises or facilities owned, leased or contracted for by Employer.

This paragraph shall not apply to any development which meets all of the following three conditions: (1) I do the work entirely by myself without use of Employer's facilities, property or resources, (2) I do the work entirely on my own time, and (3) the development does not relate to Employer's business or research or to its planned business or research.

8. AGREEMENT TO DISCLOSE. I agree to disclose promptly to Employer or its authorized agent all information regarding Works as soon as is possible. I agree to maintain accurate and adequate records of all Works.

9. DUTY TO COOPERATE. At all times during and after my employment, I agree to perform all tasks and execute all papers necessary or appropriate to grant Employer the full benefits granted in this Agreement or to facilitate Employer's securing and enforcing all rights pertaining to this Agreement.

> *[**Comment:** As is noted in the introductory note to this form, the employer should include one or more of the following provisions in its non-competition agreement.]*

[Optional Provision:]

10. NON-COMPETITION: EMPLOYER'S COMPETITORS. Except with the prior written consent of Employer, during my employment with Employer and for a period of ___ year(s) after that employment ends, I will not directly or indirectly run, operate, control, be employed by, hold an interest in or participate in the management, operation, ownership or control of any business if:

(a) such business is in competition with Employer; and

(b) if such business is conducted, or if its products are licensed, sold or used [within the following geographic area: *state geographic scope*] [within a _____ mile radius of the location where Employer conducts its business at the date of termination of my employment with Employer].

As used in this agreement, "business" includes any corporation, company, association, partnership, limited partnership, or other entity.

[Optional Provision:]

11. NON-COMPETITION: FIELD OF TECHNOLOGY. Except with the prior written consent of Employer, during my employment with Employer and for a period of ___ year(s) after that employment ends, I will not directly or indirectly run, operate, control, be employed by, hold an interest in or participate in the management, operation, ownership or control of any business if such business:

(a) is engaged in the research, development, manufacture, license, or sale of computer software [of the following types: *specify*] [using the following technologies: *specify*] and

(b) if such business is conducted, or if its products are licensed, sold or used [within the following geographic area: *state geographic scope*] [within a _____ mile radius of the location where Employer conducts its business at the date of termination of my employment with Employer].

[Optional Provision:]

12. NON-SOLICITATION OF CUSTOMERS AND PROSPECTS. Except with the prior written consent of Employer, during my employment with Employer and for a period of _____ year(s) after that employment ends, I will not directly or indirectly, either for myself or for any other business or person, solicit, call upon, attempt to solicit or attempt to call upon any of the customers or prospective customers of Employer [with whom I have had contact], and I will not accept any business from such customers or prospective customers of Employer for myself or for any employer during such period. [The restriction in this paragraph shall only apply [within the following geographic area: *state geographic scope*] [within a _____ mile radius of the location where Employer conducts its business at the date of termination of my employment with Employer].]

[Optional Provision:]

13. NON-SOLICITATION OF OTHER EMPLOYEES. Except with the prior written consent of Employer, during my employment with Employer and for a period of ___ year(s) after that employment ends, I will not solicit or have any discussion with any employee of Employer concerning employment for any business other than Employer, and I will not induce or attempt to influence any employee of Employer to terminate his or her employment with Employer.

14. OWNERSHIP OF PUBLICLY TRADE SHARES. Notwithstanding the above, I will not violate this Agreement solely by owning less than [*number*] percent of the publicly traded stock of a competing business.

15. ADJUSTMENT OF RESTRAINTS BY A COURT OF LAW. If the period of time or the geographic scope of any non-competition or non-solicitation restraint area specified in this Agreement is judged by a court to be unreasonable, I agree that the time and/or geographic scope for such restraint will be reduced so that the restraint can be enforced in such area and for such time as the court decides is reasonable.

16. EXTENSION OF RESTRAINTS DURING PERIODS OF VIOLATION. If I violate any non-competition or non-solicitation restraint specified in this Agreement, I agree that the period of the restraint shall not run during the period of the violation. I understand that the purpose of this paragraph is to give Employer the protection of the restraint for the full agreed-upon duration.

17. BINDING EFFECT. This Agreement shall inure to the benefit of and be binding upon Employer, its successors and assigns, and on me, my successors, assigns, heirs, executors, administrators and legal representatives.

18. NEED FOR THIS AGREEMENT. I agree that because of the nature of Employer's business, the restrictions contained in this Agreement are reasonable and necessary in order to protect the legitimate interests of Employer.

19. REMEDIES. I understand that if I violate any provision of this agreement relating to Confidential Information, Works, non-competition, non-solicitation, or my duty to cooperate in matters relating to protection of intellectual property, Employer will suffer immediate and irreparable injury. If I violate any of such provisions, I agree that, in addition to any other remedies that may apply, my strict compliance with this Agreement should be ordered by a court of competent jurisdiction, and Employer is therefore entitled to preliminary and final injunctive relief to enforce this Agreement.

20. SEVERABILITY. If any one or more of the provisions contained in this Agreement shall for any reason be held to be invalid, such invalidity will not affect any other provision of this Agreement.

21. APPLICABLE LAW. This Agreement is to be interpreted in accordance with the substantive law of [*specify state*].

22. ENTIRE AGREEMENT. This Agreement represents the entire agreement between Employer and me and supersedes all prior or contemporaneous oral or written agreements between us relating to this subject matter. This Agreement may not be amended or altered except by a writing signed by both parties.

23. I ACKNOWLEDGE THAT I HAVE READ THIS AGREEMENT CAREFULLY, AND THAT I FULLY UNDERSTAND AND AGREE TO ALL ITS TERMS.

_____

[*Signature of Employee*]

_____

[*Employee Name, print or type*]

Employee Address:

_____

_____

_____

Employment Date:

_____

Date of this Agreement:

_____

Accepted by:

[*NAME OF CORPORATION*]

By: _____

[*Signature of Officer of Corporation*]

Form 4-1: LETTER OF INTENT

Introductory Note

This is a sample letter of intent (on diskette as INTENT.W51). As is discussed in Chapter 4, this form is designed to summarize the current state of contract negotiations, and to make it clear that the parties are not bound until a formal contract is worked out and signed.

> ABC Software Corp.
> 80 86th Street
> Seattle, WA 98052

[*Date*]

Jerry Jones, President
XYZ Software Publishing, Inc.
77 Massachusetts Avenue
Cambridge, MA 02138

RE: Letter of Intent

Dear Jerry:

ABC Software Corp. and XYZ Software Publishing, Inc. have drafted the attached list of proposed terms for a software development agreement. We will seek to conclude a formal written contract in the next 90 days based on these terms.

However, it is agreed that we do not yet have a contract and that significant details need to be worked out. Neither party is now bound and neither will be bound in any way until the formal written contract is signed. Either party can call off these negotiations at any time without obligation or liability.

Please countersign below to indicate the agreement of your company to this letter.

> Sincerely,
>
>
> Jack Smith
> President

Agreed to:

_____

XYZ Software Publishing, Inc.
by Jerry Jones, President

Attachment: List of Proposed Terms

Form 5-1: BASIC FORM BETA TEST AGREEMENT

Introductory Note

The following is a sample basic form for a beta test agreement (on diskette as BETA1.W51). As noted in Chapter 5, this form is suitable for a software product that the end-user can install and use—the type typically sold at retail or through direct mail.

When using this form, you may wish to substitute the name of the company involved for "Supplier" and the product trademark for "Product."

Note that having a signature line for the company is optional. Of course, having the tester sign is essential.

[NAME OF CORPORATION]
BETA TEST AGREEMENT

INTRODUCTION

1. The undersigned company or individual ("Tester") and [*Name of Corporation*] ("Supplier") agree that Tester will participate in the [*Name of Product*] beta test under the terms of this Beta Test Agreement ("Agreement"). As used in this Agreement, the term "Product" refers to [*Name of Product*] software and its user manual and other documentation.

AGREEMENT OF TESTER TO TEST AND REPORT

2. Tester agrees to report to Supplier any flaws, errors, bugs or other problems with the Product. Such reports may be made by telephone (xxx-xxx-xxxx), fax (xxx-xxx-xxxx), by e-mail to [*e-mail address*] or by United States mail to [*address*]. The beta test will end six months from the date of this Agreement, or on the date of first commercial sale of the Product, whichever comes first. Tester understands that prompt and accurate reports are of great value to Supplier, and promises best efforts to provide such reports.

DISCOUNTED COPIES OF PRODUCT TO USERS

3. Supplier offers to all beta testers who complete and return a copy of this Agreement and report as provided by this Agreement, the released version of the Product (when available) [free of charge] [at a *number* percent discount from the initial list price] (plus shipping and any applicable taxes). Such copy will be provided subject to Supplier's standard License Agreement (copy available on request).

CONFIDENTIAL INFORMATION

4. Tester acknowledges that as a participant in the [*Name of Product*] beta test, Tester will be given confidential trade secret information. Specifically, Tester agrees that the characteristics, performance, and potential shipment date of the Product, the Product itself (including all software and any documentation) and this Agreement are all confidential information and constitute trade secrets of Supplier. (This information is referred to as "Confidential Information".) Tester acknowledges that the Agreement will induce Supplier to make such information available to Tester.

> *[Comment:* *In the following clause, the obligation of the tester to hold information in confidence ends just as soon as the software product becomes generally available. In some cases, the supplier may supply the tester with technical or product information that it wishes to keep confidential even after product introduction. If so, the following clause should be modified to impose a longer period of confidentiality. Of course, testers often talk to friends and the press about new products even after signing strict nondisclosure clauses, and usually the supplier can do little about it.]*

5. Tester acknowledges that disclosure of Confidential Information could cause serious harm to Supplier and, as an essential term and condition of participating in the test, agrees not to disclose Confidential Information to any person or organization until the earlier of (a) the date on which Supplier first makes this information publicly available, or (b) the date on which Supplier ships the Product to the general public, or (c) twelve months after the date of this Agreement ("Non-Disclosure Period"). During the Non-Disclosure Period, Tester agrees not to disseminate, publish, or otherwise communicate any review, account, description or other information concerning the Product, except directly to Supplier or with the express prior written consent of Supplier.

6. Tester agrees not to decompile or reverse engineer the Program at any time during or after the beta test.

7. If Tester is a company, Tester agrees to take all reasonable steps to see that its employees, officers, and agents guard against and prevent disclosure of Confidential Information and to act in accordance with the confidentiality provisions of this Agreement. Tester further agrees that information will be available to its employees and officers and agents strictly on a "need-to-know" basis.

8. Tester will promptly return the Product to Supplier postage prepaid, at the end of the period of the beta test or upon the request of Supplier, whichever is earlier.

OWNERSHIP OF THE PRODUCT

9. Tester acknowledges that the Product, its copyright, its trademark, and any other intellectual property rights in the Product is owned by Supplier. Tester acquires no ownership of the Product from this Agreement and no right to use the Product beyond the term of the beta test. Tester acquires no right to copy the Product, prepare derivative works or participate in development, manufacturing, marketing, and maintenance of the Product.

TESTER MAY NOT COPY THE PRODUCT; LIMITED LICENSE

10. Tester may not copy the Product, and may not provide any copy to any other person. Tester may not modify the Product in any way. Tester may install the Product on one hard disk for testing at Tester's sole risk, but must remove such copy from such disk at the end of the beta test or upon Supplier's request, which ever is sooner. Tester has a limited license to use the Product solely for the purpose of the beta test and solely during the period of the beta test.

RISKS FROM THE PRODUCT

11. Tester understands that the Product may have errors and may produce unexpected results. Tester agrees that any use of the beta version of the Product, whether as part of this beta test or otherwise, will be entirely at Tester's own risk. Tester agrees to backup data and take other appropriate measures to protect programs and data. Tester agrees not to allow any third party to use the Product on Tester's hardware or otherwise and to indemnify and hold Supplier harmless from any damages or claims arising from use by any third party.

> *[**Comment:** You will note in the provision that follows and in other forms in this Appendix, that many contracts contain disclaimers of warranties and limitation to liability typed in all capital letters. The wording used is keyed to specific statutory provisions of the Uniform Commercial Code (UCC) which governs sales in all states and territories of the United States, except Louisiana. There is discussion of the UCC provisions that relate to warranties, disclaimers and limitation of damages in Chapters 8, 11, and 12. As is noted in those chapters, under the UCC, certain warranty disclaimers are invalid unless "conspicuous," which usually means in clearly legible text in all capital letters as follows. It is customary to use the same conspicuous type style for any limitation to damage liability.]*

12. THE PRODUCT AND ANY SUPPORT FROM SUPPLIER ARE PROVIDED "AS IS" AND WITHOUT WARRANTY, EXPRESS OR IMPLIED. SUPPLIER SPECIFICALLY DISCLAIMS ANY IMPLIED WARRANTIES OF MERCHANTABILITY AND FITNESS FOR A PARTICULAR PURPOSE. IN NO EVENT WILL SUPPLIER BE LIABLE FOR ANY DAMAGES, INCLUDING BUT NOT LIMITED TO ANY LOST PROFITS, LOST SAVINGS OR ANY INCIDENTAL OR CONSEQUENTIAL DAMAGES, WHETHER RESULTING FROM

IMPAIRED OR LOST DATA, SOFTWARE OR COMPUTER FAILURE OR ANY OTHER CAUSE, EVEN IF SUPPLIER IS ADVISED OF THE POSSIBILITY OF SUCH DAMAGES, OR FOR ANY OTHER CLAIM BY TESTER OR FOR ANY THIRD PARTY CLAIM.

NO OBLIGATION ON BEHALF OF SUPPLIER
ON ACCOUNT OF INFORMATION PROVIDED BY TESTER

13. Supplier does not want to receive and Tester agrees not to disclose to Supplier any information that is confidential or proprietary to Tester or others.

14. Tester agrees that the contents of all oral and written reports to Supplier and any other materials, information, ideas, concepts, and know-how provided by Tester (including corrections to problems in the Product and documentation) become the property of Supplier and may be used by Supplier for all business purposes, without any accounting or any payment to Tester. Under no circumstances will Supplier become liable for any payment to Tester for any information that Tester provides, whether concerning the Product or otherwise, no matter how such information is used or exploited by Supplier or anyone else.

[Optional Provision:]

*[**Comment:** The following language permits the supplier to use the tester's name and the beta test results in publicity and advertising without compensation.]*

PUBLICITY

15. Tester grants Supplier the right, to be exercised in Supplier's sole discretion, to use the facts, contents and outcome of the beta test, tester's comments, and tester's individual name, the names of tester's employees and agents participating in the test, and tester's trade name and trademark in Supplier's promotions, press releases, public relations, advertisements, and other sales and marketing activities. Such right shall be unlimited in duration, and no compensation shall be required for Supplier's exercise of such right.

GENERAL PROVISIONS

16. This Agreement does not authorize Tester to use Supplier's names or trademarks or the fact of the beta test for any publicity or marketing or other activities.

17. Neither Tester nor Supplier has any obligation to purchase anything under this Agreement. No agency, partnership, joint venture, or other joint relationship is created by this Agreement. Supplier may enter into the same or similar Agreements with others.

18. This document is a complete statement of the contract between the parties, and any change or addition to this Agreement must be in a writing signed by Tester and Supplier.

19.   The substantive law of [*state*] shall govern this Agreement.

SO AGREED on the date set forth below between [*Name of Supplier*] and Tester:

TO TESTER:
PLEASE SIGN AND FILL
IN BLANKS AS INDICATED:

Tester Signature:

_____

_____

Tester (Type or Print Name
of Company or Individual)

_____

If Tester is a Company: Type or Print Name
and Title of Person Signing this Beta Test Agreement

_____

Street Address

_____

City   State   Zip

Date: _____

Form 5-2: FORM OF AGREEMENT FOR BETA TEST

(IN ACCORD WITH TESTING PLAN)

Introductory Note

The following form (found on diskette as BETA2.W51) is for a beta test where (1) the software is more sophisticated and requires installation, training, and support from the supplier and (2) the parties have agreed upon a beta test plan specifying how the supplier and end-user will cooperate during the test. I have not provided a sample beta test plan because the particular provisions required are highly dependant on the application and customer involved. As noted in Chapter 5, a beta test plan should include the following:

Required equipment and scale of the test. The number of computers or work stations to be involved and the hardware and software platforms to be used.

Test sites. The business locations where the software will be installed and used.

Installation details. The timing and sequencing of installation, and the work needed from both sides to prepare for and carry out installation.

Training and technical support. Provision for how and when training and technical support for users will be supplied, often including a "hot line" for quick trouble-shooting.

Contact persons. The personnel at the tester that will be in charge of coordinating the beta test and the contact persons for the publisher.

Bug reports. The method and format of reporting problems and bugs.

Meetings. The scheduling of regular meeting with the tester's staff to access problems and progress.

Final or periodic evaluation of the software. Evaluation procedures in which the software is compared to projected results and user satisfaction is rated.

You may wish to substitute the name of the company involved for "Supplier" and the product name for "Product." Note that this form is written so that the "tester" is a business, not an individual.

[*NAME OF SUPPLIER*]
BETA TEST AGREEMENT

INTRODUCTION

1. The undersigned company ("Tester") and [*Name of Supplier*] ("Supplier") agree that Tester will participate in the [*Name of Product*] beta test under the terms of this Beta Test Agreement ("Agreement"). As used in this Agreement, the term "Product" refers to the [*Name of Product*] software program and its user manual and other documentation.

AGREEMENT OF SUPPLIER AND TESTER
TO CARRY OUT PLANNED BETA TEST

2. Supplier and Tester agree to use the reasonable efforts to carry out the cooperative tasks and procedures set forth in the Beta Test Plan attached hereto as Exhibit A. The beta test commencing with software installation and concluding with the final reporting procedure shall go forward under the schedule and in accordance with the procedures set forth in the Beta Test Plan, unless the schedule or tasks are changed by mutual agreement in writing.

DISCOUNTED COPIES OF RELEASED PRODUCT

3. At the conclusion of the beta test, Tester shall have option, which it may exercise within 6 (six) months of the date hereof or sixty (60) days of the conclusion of the beta test (whichever is later) to purchase a copy of the Product as released for commercial sale in the version and configuration specified in Exhibit B at [*specify percentage*] discount from the then current list price (provided that Tester shall pay shipping and any applicable taxes). The Product delivered under the option shall be subject to the Supplier's standard User Agreement, a copy of which is attached as Exhibit C. Tester acknowledges that such option and the opportunity to use the Product are each sufficient consideration for the promises of Tester contained in this Agreement.

CONFIDENTIAL INFORMATION

4. Tester acknowledges that as a participant in the beta test, Tester will be given confidential trade secret information. Specifically, Tester agrees that the characteristics, performance, and potential shipment date of the Product, the Product itself (including all software and any documentation) and this Agreement are all confidential information and constitute trade secrets of Supplier. (This information is referred to as "Confidential Information".) Tester acknowledges that the Agreement will induce Supplier to make Confidential Information available to Tester.

5. Tester acknowledges that disclosure of this Confidential Information could cause serious harm to Supplier and, as an essential term and condition of participating in the test, agrees not to disclose Confidential Information to any person or organization until the earlier of (a) the date on which Supplier first makes this information publicly available, or (b) the date on which Supplier ships the Product to the general public, or (c) twelve months after the date of this Agreement.

6. Tester agrees not to decompile or reverse engineer the Product at any time during or after the beta test.

7. Tester agrees to take all reasonable steps to see that its employees, officers, and agents guard against and prevent disclosure of Confidential Information and to act in accordance with the confidentiality provisions of this Agreement. Tester further agrees that information will be available to its employees and officers and agents strictly on a "need-to-know" basis.

8. Tester will promptly return the Product to Supplier in accordance with the provision and procedure of the Beta Test Plan, Exhibit A hereto, or, in any case, within ten (10) days of the end of the beta test or upon Supplier's request.

OWNERSHIP OF THE PRODUCT

9. Tester acknowledges that the Product, its copyright, its trademark, and any other intellectual property rights in the Product is owned by Supplier. Tester acquires no ownership of the Product from this Agreement and no right to use the Product beyond the term of the beta test. Tester acquires no right to copy the Product, prepare derivative works, or participate in development, manufacturing, marketing, and maintenance of the Products.

TESTER MAY NOT COPY
THE PRODUCT; LIMITED LICENSE

10. Tester has a limited license to use the Product solely for the purpose of the Test and solely at the location specified in the Beta Test Plan attached as Exhibit A hereto. Tester may not copy the Product, and may not provide any copy to any other person. Each authorized user at the Tester's business location may install the Product on one hard disk for testing at Tester's sole risk, or in such other installation as is specified in Exhibit A hereto, but must remove all copies at the end of the test or upon Supplier's written request, which ever is sooner.

RISKS FROM THE PRODUCT

11. Tester understands that the Product may have errors and may produce unexpected results. Tester agrees that any use of the beta version of the Product, whether as part of this beta test or otherwise, will be entirely at Tester's own risk. Tester agrees not to allow any

third party to use the Product on Tester's hardware or otherwise and to indemnify and to hold Supplier harmless from any damages or claims arising from use by any third party. Tester agrees to backup data and take other appropriate measures to protect its programs and data.

> *[**Comment:** You will note in the provision that follows and in other forms in this Appendix, that many contracts contain disclaimers of warranties and limitation to liability typed in all capital letters. The wording used is keyed to specific statutory provisions of the Uniform Commercial Code (UCC) which governs sales in all states and territories of the United States except Louisiana. There is discussion of the UCC provisions that relate to warranties, disclaimers and limitation of damages in Chapters 8, 11, and 12. As is noted in those chapters, under the UCC, certain warranty disclaimers are invalid unless "conspicuous," which usually means in clearly legible text in all capital letters as follows. It is customary to use the same conspicuous type style for any limitation to damage liability.]*

12. THE PRODUCT AND ANY SUPPORT FROM SUPPLIER ARE PROVIDED "AS IS" WITHOUT WARRANTY, EXPRESS OR IMPLIED. SUPPLIER SPECIFICALLY DISCLAIMS ANY IMPLIED WARRANTIES OF MERCHANTABILITY AND FITNESS FOR A PARTICULAR PURPOSE. IN NO EVENT WILL SUPPLIER BE LIABLE FOR ANY DAMAGES, INCLUDING BUT NOT LIMITED TO ANY LOST PROFITS, LOST SAVINGS OR ANY INCIDENTAL OR CONSEQUENTIAL DAMAGES, WHETHER RESULTING FROM IMPAIRED OR LOST DATA, SOFTWARE OR COMPUTER FAILURE OR ANY OTHER CAUSE, EVEN IF SUPPLIER IS ADVISED OF THE POSSIBILITY OF SUCH DAMAGES, OR FOR ANY OTHER CLAIM BY TESTER OR FOR ANY THIRD PARTY CLAIM.

NO OBLIGATION ON BEHALF OF SUPPLIER ON
ACCOUNT OF INFORMATION PROVIDED BY TESTER

13. Supplier does not want to receive and Tester agrees not to disclose to Supplier any information that is confidential or proprietary to Tester or others.

14. Tester agrees that the contents of all oral and written reports to Supplier and any other materials, information, ideas, concepts, and know-how provided by Tester (including corrections to problems in the Product and documentation) become the property of Supplier and may be used by Supplier for all business purposes, without any accounting or any payment to Tester.

15. Under no circumstances will Supplier become liable for any payment to Tester for any information that Tester provides, whether concerning the Product or otherwise, no matter how such information is used or exploited by Supplier or anyone else.

[Optional Provision:]

PUBLICITY

16. Tester grants Supplier the right, to be exercised in Supplier's sole discretion, to use the facts, contents and outcome of the beta test, tester's comments, and the names of tester's employees and agents participating in the test, and tester's trade name and trademark in Supplier's promotions, press releases, public relations, advertisements, and other sales and marketing activities. Such right shall be unlimited in duration, and no compensation shall be required for Supplier's exercise of such right.

PERMISSION REQUIRED TO REVIEW AND REPORT

17. Tester agrees not to disseminate, publish, or otherwise communicate any review, account, description, or other information concerning the Product, except directly to Supplier or with the express prior written consent of Supplier.

GENERAL PROVISIONS

18. This Agreement does not authorize Tester to use Supplier's names or trademarks or the fact of the beta test for any publicity or marketing or other activities.

19. Neither Tester nor Supplier has any obligation to purchase anything under this Agreement. No agency, partnership, joint venture, or other joint relationship is created by this Agreement. Supplier may enter into the same, similar or different agreements with others.

20. This document is a complete statement of the contract between the parties, and any change or addition to this Agreement must be in writing and signed by Tester and Supplier.

21. The substantive law of [*state*] shall govern this Agreement.

SO AGREED on the date set forth below between [*Name of Supplier*] and Tester:

TO TESTER:
PLEASE SIGN AND
FILL IN BLANKS AS INDICATED:

        Tester Signature:

        _____

        Type or Print Name of Tester Company

        _____

        Type or Print Name and Title of Person
        Signing this Beta Test Agreement on behalf of Tester

        _____

        Street Address

        _____

        City   State   Zip

        Date: _____

        [*SUPPLIER*] Signature:

        _____

        Print Name and Title of Person
        Signing on Behalf of [*Supplier*]

        _____

        Date: _____

Form 6-1: SOFTWARE EVALUATION AGREEMENT

[Disclosing Party's Version]

Introductory Note

This is a sample software evaluation agreement, written from the disclosing party's perspective. (It is on diskette as EVAL-DIS.W51.) This is a form to be used by the disclosing party when it shares its confidential information in a negotiation.

This form defines confidential information broadly and requires the recipient to safeguard it and not exploit it in any way.

As is noted in Chapter 6, a company takes a substantial risk if it discloses trade secrets, software technology, source code, or other confidential information without this type of agreement in place.

EVALUATION AND CONFIDENTIALITY AGREEMENT

INTRODUCTION

This Evaluation and Confidentiality Agreement (the "Agreement") is entered into between _____ ("Disclosing Party") and _____ ("Recipient").

The parties contemplate Disclosing Party will disclose Confidential Information (as defined below) to Recipient, and they have entered into this Agreement to define the rights and duties of the parties concerning such disclosure.

1   Definition of Confidential Information

As used in this Agreement, "Confidential Information" shall mean:

    1.1   Disclosing Party's computer software program(s) [named] [codenamed] [*Name of Product*], including object code and/or source code, functionality, concept, processes, internal structure, design, external elements, user interface, technology, documentation, and information relating to markets, costs, prices and all other aspects of business operations concerning such product(s).

    1.2   Information disclosed by Disclosing Party to Recipient regarding [*Name of Process of Technology*] [*Other Subject Matter*];

    1.3   All other information that relates to Disclosing Party's products, designs, operations, plans, opportunities, finances, research, technology, developments, know-how, personnel, or any third party confidential information disclosed to Recipient; and

1.4   The terms and conditions of this Confidentiality Agreement, and the existence and content of the discussions between Recipient and Disclosing Party.

1.5   However, "Confidential Information" shall not include information (a) already lawfully known to Recipient, (b) disclosed in published materials, (c) generally known to the public or (d) lawfully obtained from any third party.

2   Nondisclosure and Nonuse of Confidential Information

2.1   Recipient acknowledges that Confidential Information is proprietary and trade secret information of the Disclosing Party.

2.2   Recipient shall not disclose Confidential Information to anyone other than its employees who legitimately need access to it. Recipient shall notify each of its employees who are given access to Confidential Information that they have an obligation not to disclose Confidential Information and shall take such steps as are reasonably necessary to insure compliance with this obligation.

2.3   Recipient shall not disclose Confidential Information to any consultant or independent contractor.

2.4   Recipient shall safeguard Confidential Information with reasonable security means at least equivalent to measures that it uses to safeguard its own proprietary information. Recipient shall store Confidential Information in a safe and secure location.

2.5   Recipient may not remove copyright, trademark, trade secret, confidentiality, and patent notices from Confidential Information.

2.6   Recipient agrees to receive and use Confidential Information solely for evaluation purposes related to its discussions with Disclosing Party. Recipient may not use Confidential Information for any other purpose, and in particular, may not use it for the purpose of developing software based on concepts, functions, or operations like those disclosed in Confidential Information.

2.7   Recipient may make copies of Confidential Information only as is necessary for its evaluation process. Recipient shall duplicate on any copy of Confidential Information all copyright, trademark, trade secret, confidentiality, and patent notices found on Confidential Information.

2.8   Recipient agrees not to use Confidential Information for its own or any third party's benefit at any time.

3   No Rights in Confidential Information

3.1   Nothing herein grants the Recipient any right in Confidential Information.

4   No Warranty

4.1   ALL CONFIDENTIAL INFORMATION IS PROVIDED "AS IS," WITHOUT ANY EXPRESS OR IMPLIED WARRANTY OF ANY KIND.

5   Return of Confidential Information

5.1   Within ten business days of receipt of Disclosing Party's written request or when negotiations between Disclosing Party and Recipient cease (whichever is earlier), Recipient shall return to Disclosing Party all documents containing Confidential Information. All copies of Confidential Information made by Recipient shall be turned over to Disclosing Party or destroyed. For purposes of this section, the term "documents" includes any medium, including paper, disks, tape, CD-ROM and any other means of recording information.

6   Equitable Relief

6.1   Recipient hereby acknowledges that unauthorized disclosure or use of Confidential Information will cause immediate and irreparable harm to Disclosing Party. Accordingly, Disclosing Party will have the right to seek and obtain preliminary and final injunctive relief to enforce this Agreement in case of any actual or threatened breach, in addition to other rights and remedies that may be available to Disclosing Party.

7   General Provisions

7.1   This Agreement constitutes the entire agreement of the parties concerning disclosure of Confidential Information and supersedes all prior or contemporaneous oral or written agreements concerning this subject.

7.2   This Agreement may not be assigned by the Recipient and its obligations under this agreement may not be delegated.

7.3   This Agreement is binding on the successors and assigns of the Recipient and inures to the benefit of the Disclosing Party's successors and assigns.

7.4   This Agreement may be amended only by a writing signed by both parties.

7.5   This Agreement will be governed by the substantive laws of the State of_____.

7.6   This Agreement is effective as of the date signed by the Recipient.

Agreed to by the parties:

_____

[*Name of Disclosing Party*]

By: _____

[*Signature*]

_____

[*Printed Name and Title*]

Date: _____

Recipient: _____

 [*Name of Company*]

By: _____

[*Signature*]

_____

[*Printed Name and Title*]

Date: _____

Form 6-2: SOFTWARE EVALUATION AGREEMENT

[Recipient's Version]

Introductory Note

This sample software evaluation agreement (on diskette as EVAL-REC.W51) is drafted for the recipient of software or information, who wants to evaluate the material without creating potential entanglements. In essence, this form promises very little except that the copyright and patent of the disclosed software will not be infringed (which is what the law requires anyway). The form expressly gives the recipient the right to develop products similar to those submitted for evaluation, and it gives no assurances of confidentiality.

The following sample, which is in the form of a simple letter agreement, is based on an actual software publisher's form. Perhaps the informality of the letter format is intended to make the form less unsettling to the disclosing party. Of course, more formal versions are used to accomplish the same purpose.

In Chapter 6 there is a discussion of the risks to the disclosing party when it discloses a product after signing such a form.

SOFTWARE EVALUATION AGREEMENT

Dear Developer:

Thank you for your interest in our company and for your offer to submit your program, material, and/or concept entitled _____ to our company for evaluation. This letter agreement will set forth the terms under which we will accept your material for evaluation.

1. We will use your material only for evaluation and will not make any copies of your material without your permission, nor will we distribute any copies of your material to any third parties.

2. We will return all copies of your material to you upon completion of our evaluation or on your earlier request.

3. We may, from time to time, receive submissions of material similar to yours, or we may be developing similar products. We cannot agree to treat as confidential your idea or any information which you may choose to disclose to us during the course of our evaluation whether or not marked as confidential or proprietary.

4. Our acceptance of your material for evaluation does not imply that we will market your material nor does it prevent us from marketing or developing other products which may be similar in idea or concept so long as we do not infringe your copyright or patent rights.

Please confirm your agreement to the terms set forth in this letter by signing in the space below and returning the signed copy of this letter to us. Please also supply the additional information requested below.

Sincerely,

_____

[*RECIPIENT COMPANY NAME*]

By: _____

Title: _____

ACCEPTED AND AGREED TO BY:

_____

[*Signature*]

If individual owner, print name:

_____

If corporate owner, print name of corporation, name of officer, and title:

_____

Address: _____

Date: _____

Form 7-1: ASSIGNMENT OF RIGHTS IN A SOFTWARE PROGRAM

Introductory Note

This form is for a simple assignment of rights to a software program. (It is on diskette as ASSIGN.W51.) As you will see, there are some choices and options presented. Pay attention in particular to the scope of rights transferred. As noted in Chapter 7, one can transfer all or only some of the rights to a software program.

This assignment is largely a one-way document; you can see that only the assignor (the seller of rights in the software) makes representations, promises, and warranties. The only performance by the assignee (the buyer of rights) is paying at the closing of the deal. Normally, the assignor should not sign and deliver the assignment form until the check is on the table. The assignee should not pay until all deliverable items are inspected and are found to be satisfactory.

Note that Form 7-1 does not require that all the physical objects (source code, object code, documentation, etc.) which the assignor delivers to the assignee be specified in detail; it makes such a list optional. Nonetheless, it is best to include a schedule that lists every item delivered and transferred; this practice can avoid disputes later on.

As noted in Chapter 7, this form is for a bare bones transaction. It is certainly not the right one for every transaction in which rights to software are transferred. If you have any doubts as to whether this is the appropriate way to accomplish your business goal, you should seek an attorney's advice.

This form contains the assignor's warranties and indemnification concerning the intellectual property rights that are being transferred. The risks involved in this type of provision are discussed in Chapter 8 and in the comments in this form.

As is noted in Chapter 1, after the assignment is done, the assignee should promptly register the copyright in the program with the Copyright Office, or if the copyright is already registered, it should promptly record the transfer of the copyright. Instructions for these procedures are found in Appendix A.

Although the following form speaks of transfer of "copyrights and other legal rights," some forms of intellectual property raise issues not addressed in Chapter 7 or this form. If any trade secret, patent right, patentable invention, or trademark is being transferred, it is advisable to seek an attorney's advice on how the transfer can best be accomplished.

ASSIGNMENT OF RIGHTS IN SOFTWARE PROGRAM
FROM [*NAME OF ASSIGNOR*] TO [*NAME OF ASSIGNEE*]

1   DEFINITIONS

1.1   "Assignor" shall mean [*Name of Corporation*] of [*City, State*].

1.2   "Assignee" shall mean [*Name of Corporation*] of [*City, State*].

1.3   "Program" shall mean the computer program entitled [*name of program*], including: its source code, documentation of the source code, object code, [user manual] [as are further specified in Schedule A attached hereto] and all copyrights and all other legal rights in all such items.

2   ASSIGNMENT

2.1   For $[*state amount*], receipt of which is acknowledged:

(a)   Assignor hereby grants, transfers, and assigns to Assignee [all right, title and interest in the Program, including all copyrights and all other legal interests and rights] [*specify other more limited transfer*] [except that Assignor retains rights to Commonly Used Code as stated below]; and

(b)   Assignor grants the warranties and indemnities set forth below.

2.2   This transfer and assignment is effective on the date indicated below.

3   WARRANTIES

[**Comment:** *A "warranty" is a guarantee that one party gives to another. Many assignment forms contain a broad warranty by the assignor that the code provided is original and does not infringe any intellectual property rights of third parties. This is an area where care is required. In reality, the assignor is usually in no position to give this sweeping intellectual property warranty. This is because it is difficult or impossible to know whether a program will infringe an issued or pending United States patent, much less a foreign patent. (See Chapters 8 and 15 for discussion of this difficulty with software patents.) For these reasons, assignors often resist giving a broad warranty of non-infringement. It is in the assignor's interest to give only a warranty that it knows of no infringement—as in Option 1. Option 2 is the broad warranty; under this option the assignor takes the risk that someday (even years later) the assignee will discover that the program infringes the rights of a third party. Then the assignor can be liable, for example, for all the assignee's lost profits due to loss of rights to the program or all the royalty payments required for a licence from the third party.*]

[Option 1: Warrants Only No Knowledge of Infringement]

3.1 Assignor warrants that, to its knowledge, it is the owner of all right, title, and interest in the rights in the Program that are the subject of this assignment, that it has granted no previous license inconsistent with the grant in this assignment, and that it knows of no other person or entity that has any license or ownership interest inconsistent with this assignment.

3.2 Assignor warrants that, to the best of its knowledge, the Program and all aspects of it are original, that it has no knowledge of any restraint or impediment to its absolute right to transfer and assign the rights in the Program that are the subject of this assignment, and that it knows of no rights existing under the laws of the United States or any state thereof that will be infringed by the commercial use and licensing of the assigned rights.

[Option 2: Broadly Warrants Non-Infringement]

3.3 Assignor warrants that it is the owner of all right, title, and interest in the rights in the Program that are the subject of this assignment, that it has granted no previous license inconsistent with the grant in this assignment, and that no other person or entity has any license or ownership interest inconsistent with this assignment.

3.4 Assignor warrants that the Program and all aspects of it are original, that Assignor has full and absolute right to transfer and assign the rights in the Program that are the subject of this assignment, and that the commercial use and licensing of the rights assigned will not infringe any rights existing under the laws of the United States or any state thereof of any other person or entity.

4 INDEMNIFICATION FOR CLAIMS ASSERTED BY OTHERS

[Comment: In the following section, the assignor indemnifies the assignee against infringement claims. Sometimes there is broad indemnification: the assignor must pay all costs and liability for any intellectual property lawsuit against the assignee (even if it turns out that the lawsuit is without merit). Sometimes there is a narrow indemnification: the assignor must pay only if it turns out that there was infringement and the assignor was aware of it. Obviously, the assignor will wish to give the narrow one, which is Option 1 below. The scope of indemnification is a matter for negotiation. The rather quaint terminology of "holding" the other party "harmless" is the same as a promise to pay any and all costs. The conditions of indemnification in clause 4.3 could apply to either a broad or narrow indemnification provision.]

[Option 1. Narrow Indemnification:]

4.1   If any third party brings any lawsuit or proceeding based upon a claim that the Program breaches the patent, copyright, or trade secret rights of such third party ("Claim") and if it is determined that such infringement has occurred and that the third party intellectual property rights involved were known to Assignor prior to the date of this assignment, then Assignor shall hold Assignee harmless against any loss, damage, expense, or cost, including reasonable attorneys' fees, arising from the Claim.

[Option 2. Broad Indemnification:]

4.2   Assignor agrees to indemnify and hold Assignee harmless against any loss, damage, expense, or cost, including reasonable attorneys' fees, arising out of any claim, demand, proceeding, or lawsuit by a third party based on any assertion that the Program breaches the patent, copyright, or trade secret rights of such third party ("Claim").

4.3   This indemnification obligation shall be effective only if: Assignee has given prompt notice of the Claim and permitted Assignor an opportunity to defend; Assignee has reasonably cooperated in the defense of the Claim; and infringement does not result from Assignee's modification of the Program. To reduce or mitigate damages, Assignor may at its own expense procure the right for Assignee to continue licensing and distributing the Program.

[Optional Provision:]

5   COMMONLY USED CODE AND TECHNIQUES

*[**Comment:** If the assignor is a software developer, it may request language to make it clear that it may continue to use the routine code and methods that are utilized in the program that is being transferred. The provision may be general, as in the example stated here, or may refer specifically to the techniques or body of routines which the developer will continue to have the right to use. Of course, what is "commonly used" may be a matter of debate, and therefore the use of general language can make the boundaries of what is permitted to the developer unclear.]*

5.1   Assignor and Assignee recognize that the Program contains computer code containing techniques, functions, routines, and subroutines that are commonly used in programming in the computer industry or are based on computer programming methods in common use. Assignor retains the right to use such code in any other software programs created for its own use or licensed to any third party.

6   **"AS IS" TRANSFER**

*[**Comment:** Simple assignments normally give no warranty about what the program will or will not do or that it is or is not error-free. The following language is included to make this clear.]*

6.1   The rights in the Program are transferred to Assignee "AS IS." EXCEPT AS OTH-ERWISE PROVIDED IN THIS ASSIGNMENT, ALL WARRANTIES, INCLUDING IMPLIED WARRANTIES OF FITNESS FOR A PARTICULAR PURPOSE, MER-CHANTABILITY, AND NON-INFRINGEMENT, ARE EXCLUDED.

[*NAME OF CORPORATION*] **(Assignor)**
By:

_____

[*Name of Officer*], [*Title*]

[*NAME OF CORPORATION*] **(Assignee)**
By:

_____

[*Name of Officer*], [*Title*]

Dated: _____

Form 8-1: SOFTWARE DEVELOPMENT AGREEMENT CHECKLIST

Introductory Note

This is a checklist (on diskette as DEV-CHK.W51) to use when negotiating a software development agreement. It is a general summary of important issues that arise in these agreements. There is no assurance that this form includes all issues that need to be addressed in your transactions.

The checklist is a tool to be used together with the information about these agreements in Chapter 8 and with the annotated software development agreement, Form 8-2 (on diskette as DEV-AGR.W51). These materials should help you set a strategy for your negotiations and develop negotiating tactics for key points.

As I noted in Chapter 8, a software development agreement is quite complex. Therefore these agreements should be negotiated subject to review by counsel.

1   Introduction or Preamble

This part of the agreement identifies the parties, states the general nature of the agreement, and recites a succinct statement of the work to be done.

2   Definitions

The definitions are shorthand terms that are used for convenience and help avoid ambiguities. Terms defined for this type of agreement commonly include "Developer," "Customer," "Program," "Confidential Information," and "Effective Date" (the date the agreement goes into effect).

3   Specifications

In the main text or in a schedule, the agreement should set out specifications for the software to be developed. Specification might include:

    3.1   Functional specifications: What functions must the program perform? How do the users interact with the program? How the program will look and sound? What data goes in and what comes out? What reports or data will the program create? How many users will the program support?

    3.2   Performance specifications: How fast will the program accomplished defined tasks? What throughput capacity the program will have?

    3.3   Required hardware and software compatibility.

    3.4   Data input and output formats.

    3.5   Applicable requests for proposals (RFPs) and the developer's response to the RFPs.

4   Deliverables and Scheduling

The agreement will often define "deliverables," the objects that developer must deliver under the agreement. Some common issues are:

    4.1   Are both source code and object code to be supplied, or only object code? If source code is to be supplied, there should be a requirement that it be adequately documented.

　　4.2　　What medium is the software to be delivered on? What format is to be used?

　　4.3　　Is the entire product to be delivered all at once or are various deliveries to be made over time?

　　4.4　　Is there to be early delivery of a prototype "alpha" version or a "beta" version for testing? Can prototypes be delivered without certain features? Must critical functions be developed first to demonstrate feasibility.

　　4.5　　Is user documentation a deliverable? Is only the text of the manual required or does the manual have to presented in a format suitable for production?

　　4.6　　Are there mechanisms for reasonable extensions in the delivery schedule?

5　Changes in Specifications

This provision sets up mechanisms to allow the parties to negotiate additions or changes to the job. Generally speaking, all changes in the program requirements, pricing, or in the schedule should be authorized in writing.

6　Resources

This section states what resources the customer will make available to the developer to permit it to do its work. The issues are:

　　6.1　　Is the customer supplying work space or computer hardware?

　　6.2　　Does the developer need access to the customer's computer system or network?

　　6.3　　Will the customer need technical information or data not included in the specifications?

　　6.4　　Does the developer require sample data from the customer's computer?

　　6.5　　Will the customer provide software tools, either its own or tools that it has licensed from third parties?

7　Confidentiality

This section governs confidentiality measures designed to protect trade secrets and confidential business information. The issues include:

　　7.2　　Are both parties under confidentiality obligations or is only one side obligated?

　　7.3　　What sort of measures to protect confidentiality are required?

　　7.4　　Must one or both parties require its employees to sign confidentiality agreements?

8　Subcontracting

These provisions deal with subcontractors who may be retained to work on the program. The issues are:

　　8.1　　Is use of subcontractors allowed?

　　8.2　　Must the developer take steps to cause its subcontractors to implement confidentiality safeguards?

　　8.3　　Must the developer require its subcontractors (or their employees) to sign confidentiality agreements?

　　8.4　　Must the developer require the subcontractors to agree that they will not supply software competitive with the program to the customer's competitors?

9   Restrictions on Developer's Competitive Activities

Is the developer restrained from licensing similar programs to software companies other than the customer, and if so, for how long?

10   Delivery and Acceptance

The section states the procedures under which the customer must accept or reject each deliverable. The issues are:

10.1   How is delivery made?

10.2   Is the acceptance criteria defined as the program's ability to perform in accordance with the specifications? Is it sufficient if the program "substantially" complies with the specifications.

10.3   Are the acceptance criteria defined to favor the customer, for example, as "customer's reasonable satisfaction"?

10.4   Are the acceptance criteria defined to favor the developer, for example, with reference to the customer's ability to run certain of developer's test data or to perform the functions in the user manual?

10.5   Does acceptance require a "live test" with the customer's actual data? Is a parallel test with the customer's old software required?

10.6   How much time, after each delivery, does the customer have to decide whether to accept the program or reject it? Under what procedure does the customer specify the reasons for rejection?

10.7   How much time does the developer have to cure defects?

10.8   What are the customer's rights if the developer fails to cure defects?

11   Payments

This section states the payment terms. The issues are:

11.1   What is to be the total amount paid?

11.2   What is the timing of payments? Is there a payment on signing? Are there progress payments? Is there a final payment?

11.3   What is the developer's remedy if the customer fails to make a required payment? Does the developer have an option to keep the program in lieu of damages for non-payment? Is the developer required to keep the program in lieu of damages for non-payment?

12   Copyright and Other Intellectual Property Ownership

This section governs the transfer of intellectual property to the customer, including copyrights, trade secrets, and patent rights. The issues are:

12.1   What intellectual property rights are conveyed? As in noted in Chapter 8, it is possible to grant the customer all or some part of the program rights, for example an exclusive license to certain fields of use, or even a non-exclusive license with a promise of royalties to the customer if additional copies are sold. The scope of the grant of rights to the customer is a matter for negotiation.

12.2   If patentable or trade secret technology is developed in the course of work under the agreement, does the customer own it exclusively?

12.3   When do the rights transfer to the customer? Together with each deliverable, or only after final payment to the developer?

12.4   Does the developer have the right to use routine portions of the code written for the program in applications that it develops in the future for other customers or for its own use?

13   Development Credit

Will the first user screen, the documentation, and/or the packaging give developer credit for writing the program?

14   Warranties; Disclaimers and Limitations

No one writes completely bug-free software. Even after thorough testing, bugs will appear. Therefore, the developer often gives a very limited warranty or "disclaims" or "excludes" all warranties on the program. Note that such a disclaimer must be stated conspicuously and in carefully crafted language (see Chapter 8 and Form 8-2) or the disclaimer may be ineffective.

An additional issue is the type of damages that may be sought if the developer fails to supply the program at all, or if the program is late. Will the agreement exclude consequential damages, that is, a claim for all the profits that the customer would have earned or the losses it would have avoided if the program had been supplied? The developer will normally insist that such damages be excluded.

15   Liability Cap

The parties can impose a limit on damages if things go wrong. The party who usually seeks this protection is the developer. The developer may fail ever to develop the program or may be held liable for some other reason, and therefore needs to limit its damage exposure.

As commonly worded, this type of clause places a limit on liability no matter what the cause, and therefore would normally limit any liability of the developer under the intellectual property warranty and indemnifications clauses discussed below.

16   Maintenance and Support

This section provides that the developer will have an ongoing obligation to fix bugs and errors. The issues here are:

16.1   How are bugs and errors reported?

16.2   How many months or years does the obligation to fix bugs last?

16.3   Is there a limit to the number of hours that the developer has to put into fixing bugs? After the time limit is reached, at what rate is the developer compensated for fixing bugs?

16.4   Is there a provision for the customer to extend the developer's obligation to fix bugs by paying a yearly software support fees?

16.5   What happens if the developer cannot or will not fix the bugs? Can the customer fix them and charge the developer?

17   Intellectual Property Warranties

This section states the developer's warranties about its legal right to supply the software to the customer. Breach of this type of warranty could lead to a suit by the customer for damages that result.

17.1   Does the developer warrant that the software does not infringe intellectual property rights of others (such as copyrights, trade secrets, or patents), or does developer warrant only that it knows of no infringement? From a developer's perspective, the latter is preferred.

18   Indemnification

This section deals with the developer's responsibility if intellectual property infringement claims based on the program are brought against the customer. Some other issues are:

18.1   What are the parties' obligations to report infringement claims to one another?

18.2   Who is responsible for legal fees and other costs of defense?

18.3   Who controls the defense or settlement of an infringement lawsuit? (The party that is responsible for paying a judgment or settlement will normally control.)

18.4   Is the developer required to pay for the defense, even if the infringement claim is without merit?

19   Remedies

This section can limit or expand litigation remedies for breach of contract. The section often specifies that injunctive relief should be available for breach of confidentiality or non-competition obligations.

20   Termination

This clause deals with terminating the agreement. The issues include:

20.1   Under what circumstances can one or another of the parties terminate the agreement? Is the triggering language a "material default of the other party"? Are additional defaults specified? Is there an opportunity to cure defaults before termination?

20.2   What obligations of the contract survive termination? Does the confidentiality clause? Does the exclusivity clause?

21   Arbitration

Are the parties required to submit any dispute to arbitration? Arbitration is generally faster and less expensive than litigation (but still quite expensive).

22   Legal Fees

Is the loser in arbitration, or litigation, required to pay the winner's legal fees? This can be a significant bargaining chip in many cases.

23   General Provisions

These provisions contain some fairly standard "legalese." Included are choice of state law, delays caused by "acts of God," responsibility for employment taxes, etc. See Form 8-2 for details.

Form 8-2: ANNOTATED SOFTWARE DEVELOPMENT AGREEMENT

Introductory Note

This is a sample software development agreement with annotations to aid you in negotiations. (A copy can also be found on diskette as DEV-AGR.W51.)

This draft includes many provisions that commonly occur in these agreements. It is based on a common format that requires delivery of the software program in stages under a milestone schedule. Your own negotiation may require a different payment arrangement or raise other concerns not addressed here.

In the following form, Schedule A (the specifications) is omitted because it is largely technical and depends so much on the type of software being developed. However, the parties should both remember that the specifications will be part of a legal document and therefore binding on both sides. The specifications should cover all functional and performance requirements with a high degree of specificity. A sample of the milestone schedule (Schedule B), is included, but the project stages and dates given are arbitrary. There could be an additional schedules. For example, a set of tests for determining acceptance could be specified in a schedule to the agreement.

In this form, the text of the agreement does not state whether source code and object code will be delivered, or only object code. Whether source code is required is stated in the specifications and in the definitions of "Deliverables" and "Final Deliverables" in the milestone schedule, which specifies the media and form of each delivery of software under the agreement. Software development agreements often require source code delivery.

This form contains straightforward provisions for software support and maintenance. The form gives several alternative provisions under which the customer may pay for having bugs fixed. More elaborate support arrangements, which include software upgrades and enhancements, are discussed in Chapter 12 in the context of end-user agreements.

This is a negotiation tool. Because a software development agreement is complicated, the final language needs to be reviewed by your attorney before you agree to it orally or in writing.

SOFTWARE DEVELOPMENT AGREEMENT
BETWEEN [*NAME OF CUSTOMER*]
AND [*NAME OF DEVELOPER*]

1   INTRODUCTION

*[**Comment:** The introduction should set forth succinctly the general nature and purpose of the agreement. This section of a contract is often written more formally, with the word "whereas" introducing each clause.]*

1.1   This is an agreement for [*Name of Developer*] to develop software for [*Name of Customer*] in accordance with an agreed-upon set of Specifications and Milestone Schedule.

2   DEFINITIONS

*[**Comment:** The definitions section should define key terms of the agreement to avoid ambiguity and to simplify drafting by providing shorthand names for persons and things. Additional definitions appear in Schedule B, the milestone schedule, and in the text. Depending on choices made in the remainder of the Agreement, you may need to add to these definitions or delete some of them. The definitions here are in alphabetical order.]*

As used in this Agreement, the following definitions shall apply:

2.1   "Agreement" shall mean this Agreement between Customer and Developer.

2.2   "Customer" shall mean [*Name of Corporation*] of [*City, State*].

2.3   "Commonly Used Code" shall include computer code, techniques, functions, routines, and subroutines that are common in the computer industry and computer programming methods in common use, whether or not created for use in the Program.

2.4   "Confidential Information" shall mean any information relating to or disclosed in the course of the Agreement, which is or should be reasonably understood to be confidential or proprietary to the disclosing party. "Confidential Information" shall not include information (a) already lawfully known to the receiving party, (b) disclosed in published materials, (c) generally known to the public or, (d) lawfully obtained from any third party.

2.5   "Deliverables" are the items that are specified in the Specifications and the Milestone Schedule as items to be delivered to Customer.

2.6   "Developer" shall mean [*Name of Corporation*] of [*City, State*].

2.7   "Effective Date" shall mean [*specify date*] [the date upon which both parties have signed this Agreement].

2.8   "Final Deliverables" are the items that are specified in the Milestone Schedule as the last and final delivery to Customer.

2.9   "Milestone Schedule" shall mean the schedule of time for delivery of the Deliverables, as set forth in Schedule B.

2.10   "Program" shall mean the computer program entitled [*name of program*] developed by Developer, which shall consist of all Deliverables [including the User Manual,], as stated in the Specifications (Schedule A), and the Milestone Schedule (Schedule B).

2.11   "Specifications" shall mean requirements for the Program's required operation, functions, capabilities and performance, and the documentation to be delivered therewith, as described in Schedule A attached hereto, or as revised by the parties under procedures set forth in this Agreement.

2.12   "User Manual" shall mean a complete description of all program functions and operations in readable English suitable for program users, including suitable examples, written in accordance with the requirements of the Specifications.

3   DEVELOPMENT OF SOFTWARE

[**Comment:** *In this section, the developer undertakes a duty to produce the program in accordance with the specifications.*]

3.1   On the Effective Date or within [*number*] of days thereafter, Developer shall begin work to program and develop the Program and shall apply such resources and efforts as shall be reasonably necessary to accomplish this task.

4   CHANGES IN SPECIFICATIONS AND MILESTONE SCHEDULE

[**Comment:** *A source of many disputes is changes to specifications that are not documented. Often customers will ask for additional features without expecting to pay more. Developers will do extra work as a result and expect extra pay. These conflicts can be avoided by documenting requests for extra work and the extra compensation involved. Similar problems can arise when delivery is late and arguments arise over whether this was agreed to. This draft requires the parties to negotiate changes in specifications and delivery schedules.*]

4.1   Either Customer or Developer may propose changes in the Specifications or to the Milestone Schedule. Customer and Developer must agree, in writing, to the changes prior to any such modifications, and to the effect, if any, on payments due under this Agreement.

4.2   Customer may not require work or features not set forth in the Specifications unless agreed to in writing. Developer will not be compensated, other than as stated in the Agreement, unless such additional payments are agreed to in advance in writing.

[Optional Provision:]

5　RESOURCES TO BE PROVIDED TO DEVELOPER

[Comment: Sometimes the developer needs technical or business information from the customer to do its work. Sometimes the developer needs access to the customer's computer system. The following clause is to deal with these and other such requirements.]

5.1　Customer shall supply to Developer all information and resources that Developer shall reasonably require to carry out the work required by this Agreement, including: [*include list*].

6　CONFIDENTIALITY

[Comment: The developer and customer share an interest in keeping the program and plans to market it confidential, as provided for in the following.]

6.1　Each party acknowledges that it will receive Confidential Information of the other party relating to technical, marketing, product, and/or business affairs. Each party agrees that all Confidential Information of the other party shall be held in strict confidence and shall not be disclosed or used without express written consent of the other party, except as may be required by law.

[Optional Provision:]

6.2　Developer is required to have all employees sign confidentiality agreements, in a form reasonably satisfactory to Customer, which include a promise to maintain confidentiality as required by this Agreement. Developer shall provide to Customer, upon request, a list of all employees who work on the Program and a copy of a current confidentiality agreement between each employee and Developer.

[Optional Provision:]

7　SUBCONTRACTORS

[Comment: The following language permits the developer to use subcontractors. It is possible, of course, to include language that forbids use of outside firms.]

7.1　Developer may retain third parties to work on the Program. All such third parties [and each of their employees who work on the Program] shall execute, before providing such services, an agreement, in a form reasonably satisfactory to Customer, which shall include a promise to maintain confidentiality as required by this Agreement and which includes an assignment to Developer of all rights in such work so that such rights may be licensed or transferred to Customer as required by this Agreement.

[Optional Provision:]

8   RESTRICTIONS ON DEVELOPER'S ACTIVITIES

8.1   From the Effective Date until the acceptance of the Final Deliverables, and for a period of [*number*] years thereafter or until [*date*], whichever is later, Developer shall not supply or agree to supply to any party other than Customer computer software with functionality similar to the Program or software that will or is likely to be competitive with the Program [including software on other software or hardware platforms] [excluding software on other software or hardware platforms]. [Unless otherwise provided, the provisions of this paragraph shall survive termination of this Agreement].

9   DELIVERY AND ACCEPTANCE OF DELIVERABLES

*[**Comment**: The following provision mandates delivery within dates specified in the milestone schedule. Optional language allows for some flexibility in the scheduling.*

There are many ways to write provisions under which the customer may accept or reject the program. The version that follows provides a time frame for customer's acceptance and allows a cure period if the program is rejected. As an option, this version also allows the customer to accept defective final deliverables of the program and to have the program fixed at the developer's expense.]

9.1   Developer shall deliver various Deliverables at the times and in the manner specified in the Milestone Schedule. [At its option, Developer can extend the due dates for any date of the Milestone Schedule by giving written notice to the Customer provided that the total of all such extensions shall not exceed [*specify number*] days.]

9.2   If Developer fails to make timely delivery of any Deliverable as specified in the Milestone Schedule, Customer may give Developer notice of the failure. After such notice, Developer shall have thirty (30) days to make the specified delivery. Failure to submit the Deliverables within such period shall be a material breach that shall entitle Customer to terminate this Agreement in accordance with the provisions on Termination.

9.3   Customer may inspect and test each of the Deliverables when received to determine if it [substantially] conforms to the requirements of the Specifications. [Testing shall be in accordance with the testing procedures specified in *Name of Testing Procedure Document or Schedule*].

9.4   [Any Deliverable not rejected in thirty (30) days shall be deemed accepted.] If any Deliverable is rejected, Customer shall give Developer notice of the rejection and the reasons for rejection. Developer shall then have thirty (30) days to cure deficiencies. After resubmission within such thirty (30) day period, Customer may again inspect the Deliverable to confirm that it [substantially] conforms to requirements of the Specifications. [If the resubmitted Deliverable is not rejected in the thirty (30) days after resubmission, the Deliverable shall be deemed accepted.] If the resubmitted Deliverable does not [substantially] conform to the requirements of this Agreement, the failure will be a material breach that shall entitle Customer to terminate this Agreement in accordance with the provisions on Termination. If the resubmitted Deliverable is rejected, Customer shall give notice to Developer stating the reasons for rejection.

9.5   Notice of failure to make timely delivery, rejection, or subsequent resubmission shall not affect the due date for subsequent Deliverables as required by this Agreement unless otherwise agreed in writing [or unless [*state other contingencies that will permit postponing due dates*]].

9.6   If the Final Deliverables in any material respect do not [substantially] conform to the Specifications, and such [substantial] non-conformity is not cured as provided in this Agreement, the failure will be a material breach that shall entitle Customer to terminate this Agreement in accordance with the provisions on Termination. [Alternatively, Customer, at its option, may accept the Final Deliverables as non-conforming. If it does so, it shall give prompt notice to Developer stating the known defects, and may withhold and deduct, from amounts otherwise due and payable to Developer upon acceptance of the Final Deliverables, the amount of reasonable out-of-pocket costs to correct, modify, and/or complete the Program in accordance with the Specifications. From time to time, and as soon as is practicable, Customer shall provide Developer with notice of all sums withheld and expended and shall turn over to Developer all funds withheld that are not so applied when such remedial work is completed.]

[9.7   Developer shall provide all necessary installation services and assistance that may be required for each Deliverable.]

[Optional Provision:]

[Comment: If a user manual or other documentation is to be written by the developer, these requirements should be included in the specifications and milestone schedule. Sometimes, the customer takes responsibility for the user manual or will hire another contractor to do this work. If this is the case, the following text may be appropriate.]

9.8 Developer shall provide to customer or to such other person as Customer shall designate, from time to time, as reasonably required before publication of the Program, all assistance and information reasonably necessary to ensure that a User Manual for the Program is complete and accurate. Developer shall review a draft of the User Manual upon request and promptly provide all corrections required to Customer.

10 PAYMENT

[Comment: The following text sets a time limit for payments and a remedy if prompt payment is not made.]

10.1 Customer shall pay Developer the amount due upon the execution of this Agreement as specified in the Milestone Schedule. Upon acceptance of each Deliverable, Customer shall pay Developer the amounts as specified in the Milestone Schedule. Payment shall be due within twenty (20) days of acceptance of each Deliverable. Payment by mail shall be deemed made when mailed. [Customer shall pay Developer interest on late payments at the rate of *specify number*.]

10.2 If any payment is not made as required, Developer may give notice of the failure to pay. The failure to pay, if not cured within thirty (30) days after notice, shall entitle Customer to terminate this Agreement in accordance with the provisions on Termination.

[Optional Provision:]

10.3 Should Developer fail to deliver acceptable Deliverables as required by this Agreement or should Developer deliver Final Deliverables that are properly and finally rejected by Publisher, Developer shall refund to Customer [all] [*specify percentage*] of amounts paid by Customer under this Agreement, and this Agreement shall terminate. SUCH REFUND SHALL BE CUSTOMER'S SOLE AND EXCLUSIVE REMEDY FOR FAILURE TO DELIVER THE PROGRAM IN ACCORDANCE WITH THIS AGREEMENT.

11   INTELLECTUAL PROPERTY

[Comment: The developer may seek a provision in the intellectual property section that lets it keep the program rights if customer fails to meet its payment obligations. The customer will want a provision that lets it get and keep the intellectual property rights for each deliverable as soon as it is delivered, in spite of any subsequent termination or dispute and no matter who may be at fault. Ownership of the intellectual property can be a very important leverage point in a dispute.

Option 1 provides that transfer occurs only after acceptance of the final deliverables and after payment. Option 2 in effect transfers the rights to the program to the customer from the acceptance of the first deliverable. Some agreements provide that the customer will receive rights in the program at the moment the agreement is signed.

Another matter addressed in the following section is what rights are transferred. As is noted in Chapter 8, it is possible to grant the customer all or some part of the program rights, for example an exclusive license to certain fields of use, or even a non-exclusive license with a promise of royalties to the customer if additional copies are sold. The scope of the grant of rights to the customer is a matter for negotiation.]

[Option 1. Transfer of Ownership Upon Final Payment:]

11.1   Upon Customer's acceptance of the Final Deliverables and the payment of all amounts due to Developer (net of such amounts as may have been properly withheld on account of Final Deliverables accepted as non-conforming, as stated above), Customer shall have and Developer shall be deemed to have irrevocably assigned to Customer [all right, title, and interest, throughout the world, in all copyrights, trade secrets, patentable materials, and all other proprietary rights in the Program and each Deliverable received and all the items and components thereof] [*specify other grant of rights*]. Until such payment is made, Developer shall retain ownership of all rights to the Program.

11.2   When transfer of the program to the Customer is effective, as specified above, the Developer shall execute such documents as Customer shall reasonably require to evidence and confirm the transfer of rights made under the Agreement.

11.3   Upon transfer of such rights, Customer may register the copyright to the Program [and any derivative work] in any and all countries and jurisdictions, place its copyright notice on the Program, and take such further steps as it deems fit to provide legal protection to intellectual property relating to the Program.

[Option 2. Transfer of Ownership Upon Delivery:]

11.4   Upon acceptance of each Deliverable hereunder, Developer irrevocably shall be deemed to assign to Customer [all right, title, and interest, throughout the world, in all copyrights, trade secrets, patentable materials, and all other proprietary rights in the Program and each Deliverable received and all the items and components thereof] [*specify other grant of rights*].

11.5   The Developer shall execute such documents as Customer shall reasonably require to evidence and confirm the transfer of rights made under the Agreement.

11.6   Upon transfer of such rights, Customer may register the copyright to the Program [and any derivative work] in any and all countries and jurisdictions, and take such further steps as it deems fit to provide legal protection to intellectual property relating to the Program.

[*Comment: Developers have an interest in remaining free to use code that is based on commonly known computer techniques in future programs, including such code that is developed in work on the program for the customer. If it is not careful, a developer may sign away the right to use code that does routine tasks like fetch information or display graphics. Therefore developers may request that a provision be added to allow continued use of commonly used code and methods. Of course, the customer should note that the general language of the definition of "Commonly Used Code" in the definitions section may make the boundaries of what the following clause permits somewhat unclear.*]

11.7   Notwithstanding any other provisions of this Agreement, Developer shall retain the right to utilize all Commonly Used Code in programs developed for others or for its own use.

[Optional Provision:]

12   DEVELOPMENT CREDIT

[*Comment: If the customer will be publishing or distributing the program, or letting others have access to it, developers often want credit for their creation of the program to appear on the work that they create. Credit for creation may enhance their reputation and lead to more work. The following is a provision to require that such credit be given.*]

12.1   Customer shall acknowledge Developer as the programmer in text displayed in the first screen of the Program and in the User Manual. Such development credit shall not give Developer any trademark, copyright, or other proprietary interest or rights in the Software. [Customer [shall] [need not] provide development credit in advertisements, including print and broadcast media, catalogs, and in direct mailings.]

13   [WARRANTY;] DISCLAIMER OF WARRANTIES

*[**Comment:** Most software development agreements have a provision for maintenance, that is, ongoing error correction. It is an unfortunate fact of life that no one writes completely bug-free software. Even after thorough testing, bugs may appear.*

Therefore developers resist giving a warranty that the code is bug-free or without errors. Rather developers prefer that the agreement state that no such warranty is given, but that bugs will be fixed when found. The customer may seek to impose an obligation to fix bugs for free for a substantial time. Developers will try to limit the work done for free and at some early point switch to paid bug-fixing.

The capitalized text of the following provisions is legally required to avoid giving an implied warranty that the code is defect-free. The odd-sounding language about warranties being "DISCLAIMED" is keyed to statutory provisions of the Uniform Commercial Code, which are discussed in Chapter 8. Sometimes a developer will give a warranty of a quite limited sort, in which it promises to make reasonable efforts to fix bugs during a specified time after acceptance, often 90 days or six months, and otherwise disclaims all warranties. Examples of both types of provisions are provided.]

[Option 1. Broad Disclaimer of Warranties:]

13.1   Developer and Customer agree that due to the nature of complex computer programs such as the Program, Developer cannot warrant that the Program will be completely free of all defects and errors. Accordingly, the Program is transferred and delivered to Customer "AS IS." EXCEPT AS PROVIDED BELOW IN THE PROVISION ENTITLED INTELLECTUAL PROPERTY WARRANTY, ALL WARRANTIES EXPRESS OR IMPLIED, INCLUDING IMPLIED WARRANTIES OF MERCHANTABILITY, FITNESS FOR A PARTICULAR PURPOSE AND NONINFRINGEMENT, ARE DISCLAIMED.

[Option 2. Warranty for Limited Duration, With Specified Remedy:]

13.2   Developer warrants that the program will perform in substantial conformity with the Specifications for a period of [*specify duration*] after acceptance of the Final Deliverables (the "Warranty Period"). However, Developer and Customer agree that due to the nature of complex computer programs such as the Program, Developer may not be able to find and remove all defects and errors. Accordingly, Customer's SOLE AND EXCLUSIVE REMEDY FOR ANY BREACH OF

THIS WARRANTY SHALL BE TO AVAIL ITSELF OF THE PROCEDURES SET FORTH IN THE SECTION OF THIS AGREEMENT ENTITLED "MAINTE-NANCE AND SUPPORT." EXCEPT AS EXPRESSLY STATED HEREIN, ALL WARRANTIES, INCLUDING WARRANTIES OF MERCHANTABILITY, FIT-NESS FOR A PARTICULAR PURPOSE, AND OF NON-INFRINGEMENT, ARE DISCLAIMED.

13.3   DEVELOPER WILL NOT BE LIABLE FOR INCIDENTAL OR CONSEQUEN-TIAL DAMAGES.

14   LIABILITY CAP

*[**Comment:** The parties can bargain about a limit to liability if things go wrong. The party who will usually seek this protection is the developer. You may wonder why this limit would be needed, if all warranties on the program are disclaimed. The answer is the developer may fail ever to develop the program. While the rules on damages are not always easy to apply, a developer who fails to deliver acceptable software could be liable for substantial sums. Or the program may be late and the delay may harm the customer. It is also possible that, for some unforseen reason, the warranty disclaimers may be ruled to be invalid. This clause serves as a "last resort" provision, if other clauses are held invalid, the developer tries to limit its exposure with this clause.*

Note that as worded, the following clause places a limit on liability for any and all reasons, and therefore would limit any product defect claim and would also limit any liability of the developer under the intellectual property warranty and indemnifications clauses found below.]

14.1   DEVELOPER'S LIABILITY TO THE CUSTOMER FOR ANY AND ALL CLAIMS IN ANY WAY RELATED TO THE PROGRAM OR THIS AGREEMENT SHALL NOT EXCEED *[SPECIFIC AMOUNT]* [THE TOTAL OF PAYMENTS MADE TO DEVELOPER].

15   MAINTENANCE AND SUPPORT

15.1   [During the Warranty Period,] [For a period of *[specify duration]* after Customer's acceptance of the Final Deliverables,] Developer shall use reasonable efforts to provide to Customer all corrections and/or modifications necessary to correct problems, logical errors, and bugs in the Program reported to Developer in writing. [The first *[specify number]* hours of the efforts of Developer's employees on such tasks shall be without charge. Thereafter Developer may bill for the time of its employees at [$*amount*] per hour. Such bills may be rendered to Customer at month end and are payable thirty (30) days after receipt.] Developer shall have no obligation to fix problems or errors resulting from Customer's modification of the Program.

15.2   If Developer fails to correct any problem, logical error, or bug reported during the Warranty Period within thirty (30) days of notice, Customer may contract for such work to be done by any third party that agrees in writing to hold in confidence the Confidential Information of Developer. The cost of such work, up to a maximum aggregate amount of [*$amount*], shall be reimbursed by Developer.

*[**Comment:** The following paragraph is a sample provision for on-going maintenance to be paid for yearly. Variations are obviously possible on the duration, the time when payment is due, the price, and the cap on price increases called for in this text.]*

15.3   After the expiration of the Maintenance Period, Developer shall provide Software Support for a period of one year, provided that Customer shall have paid, as payment therefor ("Support Fee"), a price equal to [fifteen (15)] [*other number*] percent of the total amount payable hereunder for development and delivery of the Program as specified on the Milestone Schedule as it may be modified by the parties. Developer grants Customer five (5) options to renew software support annually, exercisable by making payment in advance, in the amount of such Support Fee [as Developer shall specify from time to time] [, provided, however, that the yearly increase in the Support Fee shall at no time be more than [*specify number*] percent].

*[**Comment:** The following paragraph provides for on-going maintenance on a pay-as-you-go-model.]*

15.4   If, after expiration of the Warranty Period, Customer requests Developer to fix errors not reported to Developer in writing during the period of [*specify duration*] after acceptance of the Program, Developer shall make reasonable efforts to correct such errors, and shall be entitled to payment from Customer at Developer's then applicable rates and terms for such service and support, or at such other rates and upon such terms as the parties shall agree upon in writing.

16 INTELLECTUAL PROPERTY WARRANTY

[Comment: Many software development agreements contain an intellectual property warranty—a guarantee that the code provided is original and does not infringe the intellectual property rights of third parties. Breaching this warranty could require paying damages to the customer. This is an area where care is required. In reality, the developer is usually in no position to give a sweeping intellectual property warranty. It is difficult or impossible, for example, to know whether a program infringes a United States patent. (See Chapter 15 for a discussion of this problem with software patents.) For these reasons, developers may resist giving a broad warranty such as Option 3 below. Rather they should try to give only a warranty that they know of no infringement—as in Option 1. A warranty that copyrights are not infringed (Option 2) is somewhat safer, because there is normally no infringement unless another program has been copied to create the program. See discussion of software copyrights in Chapter 1.

The following text makes warranties only as to rights under United States law. Sophisticated developers will normally resist any warranty concerning foreign intellectual property laws, because it is more difficult to determine what foreign intellectual property rights the program might infringe. However when the customer plans to use the program in one or more foreign states, it way wish to negotiate a similar indemnification provision for the law of some or all foreign countries.]

[Option 1. Warrants No Knowledge of Infringement:]

16.1   Developer represents and warrants that it has no knowledge of any right, title, and interest in the Program other than its own, and that it has granted no license or ownership interest. Developer represents and warrants that it knows of no fact or circumstance indicating that commercial use and sale of the Program will infringe any rights existing under the laws of the United States or any state thereof of any other person or entity.

[Option 2. Warrants Non-Infringement of Copyright

and No Knowledge of Other Infringement:]

16.2   Developer represents and warrants that it owns the United States copyright for the Program and that it has no knowledge of any right, title, and interest in the Program other than its own, and that it has granted no license or ownership interest. Developer represents and warrants that it knows of no fact or circumstance indicating that commercial use and sale of the Program by Customer will infringe any rights existing under the laws of the United States or any state thereof of any other person or entity.

[Option 3: Broadly Warrants Non-Infringement:]

16.3   Developer represents and warrants that it is the owner of all right, title, and interest in the Program, and that no other person or entity has any license or ownership interest. Developer represents and warrants that the Program and all aspects of it are original, that Developer has full and absolute right to transfer the Program and that the commercial use or sale of the Program by Customer will not infringe any rights existing under the laws of the United States or any state thereof of any other person or entity whatsoever.

17   INDEMNIFICATION

*[**Comment:** In the following section, the developer indemnifies the customer against infringement claims. Sometimes there is broad indemnification: the developer must pay all costs and liability for any intellectual property suit against the customer (even if it turns out that the suit is without merit). Sometimes there is a narrow indemnification: the developer must pay only if it turns out that there was infringement and the developer was aware of it. Obviously, the customer, if it is sophisticated, will seek the broad one. The scope of indemnification is a matter for negotiation. The rather quaint terminology of "holding" the other party "harmless" is a promise to pay any and all costs.*

As is noted in Chapter 8, in some cases, agreements are negotiated in which the patent infringement indemnification is reversed, that is, the customer indemnifies the developer from patent infringement liability. These reverse provisions are sometimes negotiated where a large company is seeking to develop a new area of software technology, and has contracted with a small specialized developer.]

[Option 1. Broad Indemnification:]

17.1   Developer agrees to indemnify and hold Customer harmless against any loss, damage, expense, or cost, including reasonable attorneys' fees, arising out of any claim, demand, proceeding, or lawsuit by a third party based on any assertion that the Program breaches the patent, copyright, or trade secret rights of such third party ("Claim").

[Option 2. Narrow Indemnification:]

17.2   If any third party brings any lawsuit or proceeding based upon a claim that the Program breaches the patent, copyright, or trade secret rights of such third party ("Claim") and if it is determined that such infringement has occurred and that the third party intellectual property rights involved were known to the Developer prior to its delivery of the Final Deliverables, then Developer shall hold

Customer harmless against any loss, damage, expense, or cost, including reasonable attorneys' fees, arising from the Claim.

17.3   This indemnification obligation shall be effective only if: [Customer has made all payments required by this Agreement,] [Customer has given prompt notice of the Claim and permitted Developer an opportunity to defend,] [Customer has reasonably cooperated in the defense of the claim,] [the infringement does not result from Customer's modification of the Program.] [To reduce or mitigate damages, Developer may at its own expense procure the right for Customer to continue licensing and distributing the Program or replace it with a non-infringing product.]

18   TERM AND TERMINATION

[Comment: The term and termination clause of some form contracts grants the customer an absolute right to cancel at will on no notice, or on short notice. This would allow the customer to get out of further obligations if it decides that there no longer is any market for the product that is being developed. Ordinarily the developer will resist the inclusion of such an "escape" clause. The provisions which give a give a right to terminate in case of the bankruptcy of another party may be ineffective under United States bankruptcy law in some cases.]

18.1   The term of this Agreement shall commence on the Effective Date, and shall continue until all requirements of this Agreement are met, unless sooner terminated in accordance with the provisions set forth in this Agreement.

18.2   Either party may terminate this Agreement:

18.2.1   In accordance with provisions stated in this Agreement that provide for termination,

18.2.2   In the event that the other party ceases business operations or is in any bankruptcy or state insolvency or receivership proceeding not dismissed in thirty (30) days or assigns its assets for the benefit of creditors, or

18.2.3   In the event of any material breach by the other party which is not cured within thirty (30) days after notice.

[Optional Provision:]

18.3   Customer may terminate this Agreement at any time on thirty (30) days notice for any cause or no cause. In the event of such a termination, Customer shall pay the reasonable cost of Developer's services from the last delivery made under the Milestone Schedule to the date of receipt of notice of termination, not to exceed the amount specified in the Milestone Schedule for the next milestone.

19   EFFECT OF TERMINATION

19.1   Upon any termination of this Agreement by any party:

19.1.1   All provisions of the section of this agreement entitled Confidentiality shall remain in effect.

[Optional Provision:]

19.2   Upon termination of the Agreement by the Developer due to the material breach by the Customer:

19.2.1   Ownership of the copyright and all other rights in the Program pursuant to this Agreement shall revert to Developer.

19.2.2   Customer shall promptly execute and deliver to Developer all documents necessary to assign to Developer ownership of the copyright and all other rights in the Program.

19.2.3   Customer shall promptly return all objects and materials delivered by Developer.

[19.2.4   All provisions of the section entitled Restrictions on Developer's Activities shall be null and void.]

20   REMEDIES

20.1   Except as is otherwise provided in this Agreement, the parties shall have such remedies for breach or termination as are provided by applicable law.

20.2   The parties agree that in the case of the breach of any provision of the section of this agreement entitled Confidentiality [or Restrictions on Developer's Activities], the aggrieved party will suffer immediate and irreparable harm, and that immediate injunctive relief will therefore be appropriate.

[Optional Provision:]

21   ARBITRATION

*[**Comment:** Many of these agreements include arbitration clauses. These clauses require that disputes be settled by arbitration rather than litigation. The party with the stronger*

bargaining position will usually be able to pick the city where arbitration will take place. If there is no arbitration clause, disputes will normally be settled in court.

Sometimes one of the parties needs a type of relief that only comes from a court of law, such as an order that a party not disclose trade secrets or confidential information. This type of preliminary injunctive relief must be sought in a court of law. For this reason, the arbitration clauses often have an exception to allow a party to seek such injunctive relief.]

21.1   Any dispute relating to the terms, interpretation or performance of this Agreement (other than claims for preliminary injunctive relief or other pre-judgment remedies) shall be resolved at the request of either party through binding arbitration. Arbitration shall be conducted in *[specify city and state]* under the rules and procedures of the American Arbitration Association ("AAA"). The parties shall request that the AAA appoint a panel of three arbitrators and, if feasible, include one arbitrator of the three who shall possess knowledge of the computer software industry; however the arbitration shall proceed even if such a person is unavailable.

[Optional Provision:]

22   ATTORNEYS' FEES

22.1   In the event of any litigation or arbitration between the parties arising under this Agreement, the prevailing party shall be entitled to recover, in addition to any other relief awarded, its reasonable costs and expenses, including attorneys' fees, incurred in the proceeding.

23   GENERAL PROVISIONS

*[**Comment:** The following are some general provisions that are normally not controverted. Similar provisions are found in many commercial contracts.]*

23.1   **Relationship of Parties.** Developer shall be deemed to have the status of an independent contractor, and nothing in this Agreement shall be deemed to place the parties in the relationship of employer-employee, principal-agent, partners or joint venturers. Developer is responsible for all payments to its subcontractors [, and guarantees their observance of their confidentiality requirements referred to herein.]

23.2   **Payment of Taxes.** Developer shall be responsible for any withholding taxes, payroll taxes, disability insurance payments, unemployment taxes, and other taxes or charges incurred in the performance of the Agreement.

*[**Comment:** Most contracts have provisions to excuse delays for "force majeure" or "acts of God." Fires are obviously the commonest "act of God" that cause serious delays, but it's a good bet that many programmers in California will experience a serious earthquake. Some customers may want a shorter limit on extension of time than the six months provided for in this form.]*

23.3   **Force Majeure.** Neither party shall be deemed in default of this Agreement to the extent that performance of their obligations or attempts to cure any breach are delayed or prevented by reason of any act of God, fire, nature disaster, accident, act of government, shortages of materials or supplies, or any other cause beyond the control of such party ("Force Majeure") provided that such party gives the other party written notice thereof promptly and, in any event, within fifteen (15) days of discovery thereof and uses its best efforts to cure the delay. In the event of such a Force Majeure, the time for performance or cure shall be extended for a period equal to the duration of the Force Majeure but not in excess of six (6) months.

*[**Comment:** The following provisions relate to assignment of the agreement by the developer or the customer. There are a number of options presented in the following text. If there is an assignment, the developer may want the customer to remain responsible for payment if the assignee fails to pay. Owners of businesses may want the freedom to sell or assign all the assets of a business, including all its contracts. Normally the customer, who contracted for the skills of a particular developer, may resist granting the developer any right to assign the agreement.]*

23.4   **Assignments.** This Agreement may not be assigned by Customer in whole or in part without consent of Developer [which consent shall not be unreasonably withheld]. [Customer may assign this Agreement, without Developer's consent, to any third party which succeeds by operation of law to, purchases, or otherwise acquires substantially all of the assets of Customer and assumes Customer's obligations hereunder.] [Notwithstanding the above, Customer shall retain the obligation to pay if the assignee fails to pay as required by the payment obligations of this Agreement.] [Developer may not assign its obligations under this agreement without Customer's written consent, which Customer may withhold in its complete discretion.]

23.5   **Partial Invalidity.** Should any provision of this Agreement be held to be void, invalid, or inoperative, the remaining provisions of this Agreement shall not be affected and shall continue in effect as though such provisions were deleted.

23.6   **No Waiver.** The failure of either party to exercise any right or the waiver by either party of any breach, shall not prevent a subsequent exercise of such right or be deemed a waiver of any subsequent breach of the same or any other term of the Agreement.

23.7   **Notice.** Any notice required or permitted to be sent hereunder shall be in writing and shall be sent in a manner requiring a signed receipt, such as Federal Express, courier delivery, or if mailed, registered or certified mail, return receipt requested. Notice is effective upon receipt. Notice to Customer shall be addressed to [*specify name, title and address*] or such other person or address as Manufacturer may designate. Notice to Developer shall be addressed to [*specify name, title and address*] or such other person or address as Dealer may designate.

[***Comment:*** *The following "entire agreement clause" (also known as an "integration clause") is designed to eliminate any claim that oral promises not in the Agreement are effective. This clause, a standard feature of many types of agreement, will usually be enforced. If there are promises made or "side agreements" outside the text of the Agreement, it is important to get them into the text before the Agreement is signed.]*

23.8   **Entire Agreement.** This Agreement, including the Schedules thereto, states the entire agreement between the parties on this subject and supersedes all prior negotiations, understandings, and agreements between the parties concerning the subject matter. No amendment or modification of this Agreement shall be made except by a writing signed by both parties.

23.9   **Governing Law.** This Agreement shall be governed and interpreted in accordance with the substantive law of the State of _____.

23.10 **Venue and Jurisdiction of Legal Actions.** Any legal action brought concerning this Agreement or any dispute hereunder [, including but not limited to an action to enforce an arbitration award,] shall be brought only in the courts of the state of _____ [in the county of _____] or in the federal courts located in such state [and county], and both parties agree to submit to the jurisdiction of these courts.] or in the federal courts located in such state [and county].

IN WITNESS WHEREOF, [*Name of Customer*] and [*Name of Developer*] have executed this Agreement.

[*NAME OF Customer*]
By:

_____

[*Name of Officer*], [*Title*]

[*NAME OF DEVELOPER*]
By:

_____

[*Name of Officer*], [*Title*]

Schedule B
MILESTONE SCHEDULE

The following Schedule shall govern milestones and payments for the development of the Program.

1   DEFINITIONS

The following definitions and provisions apply to this Schedule:

1.1   "Working Model Code" shall mean Program code written by Developer that has Critical Features (as defined in the Specifications, Schedule A) implemented. This version of the Program demonstrates the technical feasibility of the project.

1.2   "Alpha Code" shall mean Program code written by Developer that includes all operations, functions, capabilities, and performance in the Specifications implemented, integrated and fully functional. It is code that is not necessarily "bug free" and may be in need of adjustment and tuning of functions, operations, and graphics.

1.3   "Beta Code" shall mean Program code written by Developer that includes all operations, functions, capabilities, and performance implemented, integrated and functional substantially in accordance with the Specifications. This version shall have all known bugs and errors corrected.

1.4 Working Model Code, and Alpha Code, Beta Code shall be supplied on two sets of 3 1/2" diskettes in MS-DOS high-density format, containing [respectively] the Program version's entire compiled object code [and the version's entire source code].

[Optional Provision:]

1.5 "Technical Documentation" shall mean commented source code and other documentation sufficient to permit the Program to be modified by a reasonably skilled technician with knowledge of the languages in which the Program is written but no prior knowledge of the Program.

*[**Comment:** The following text contains options as to how polished the final program code must be. Because the developer is unlikely to deliver code that is totally bug-free, the language may provide some leeway. Many Agreements have specific provisions for testing before final acceptance. A test plan could be set forth on an additional schedule.]*

1.6 "Final Deliverables" shall mean the version of the Program written by Developer that has passed through user tests and which [fully] [substantially] complies with the Specifications. [This version is the Beta Code version that has been corrected to address the bugs and other issues and problem that have been documented during testing.] Final Deliverables shall include:

  1.6.1 Two [sets of] 3 1/2" diskettes in MS-DOS high density format, each containing the Program's entire compiled object code;

  [1.6.2 Two [sets of] 3 1/2" diskettes in MS-DOS high density format, each containing the Program's entire source code and one printed copy of the computer source code.]

  [1.6.3 Two [sets of] 3 1/2" diskettes in MS-DOS high density format, each containing the complete User Manual for the Program in WordPerfect for DOS 5.1 format;]

  [1.6.4 Technical Documentation as follows: [*specify*].]

2 **DELIVERY AND PAYMENT SCHEDULE**

The delivery and payment schedule shall be as follows:

DUE DATE FOR DELIVERABLE (DAYS AFTER EFFECTIVE DATE OF AGREEMENT)	MILESTONE	ADVANCE PAYMENT AMOUNT
0 Days	Execution of Agreement by Both Parties	$10,000.00
50 Days	Working Model Code	10,000.00
110 Days	Alpha Code	10,000.00
140 Days	Beta Code	10,000.00
220 Days	Final Deliverables	20,000.00
	TOTAL	$60,000.00

Form 9-1: SOFTWARE PUBLISHING AGREEMENT CHECKLIST

Introductory Note

This checklist (on diskette as PUB-CHK.W51) contains topics and issues that often arise in negotiating software publishing agreements. You can use this checklist together with Chapter 9 and with the annotated software publishing agreement, Form 9-2 (PUBAGR.W51). These materials will help you develop your negotiating strategy. However, every publishing deal is unique, and there is no assurance that this checklist includes all issues that need to be addressed in your transactions. You may wish to modify this checklist to better suit the needs of your business.

As I noted in Chapter 9, a software publishing agreement is quite complex and its final language needs to be reviewed by your attorney. You should negotiate them subject to review by counsel.

The party supplying software is in the following discussion is called the "Developer." The term "Licensor" could also be used.

1   Introduction or Preamble

This section identifies the parties, states the general nature of the agreement, and contains a succinct statement of the work to be done.

2   Definitions

This section of the agreement defines terms. Its purpose is to create shorthand terms for convenience and to avoid ambiguities.

Definitions commonly found in software publishing agreements include: "Confidential Information," "Deliverables" (the items that are to be delivered under the agreement), "Developer," "Effective Date" (the date the agreement goes into effect), "Program," and "Publisher."

3   Specifications

In the main text, or more commonly in a schedule, the agreement should set out specifications for software to be developed or customized. Detailed specifications allow for realistic pricing and sensible expectations about what the program will do when completed. Of course if the program to be published already exists, a simple description will suffice. Specifications (also known as a Statement of Work) might include:

3.1   Functional specifications: What functions must the program perform, and how will the program interact with the user? How will the program look and sound? What reports or data will it create? How many users will the program support?

3.2   Performance specifications: How fast will the program accomplish defined tasks? What throughput capacity will the program have?

3.3   Data input and output formats.

3.4   Hardware and operating system compatibility.

3.5   Any applicable request for proposals (RFP) and the developer's response to the RFP.

4   Resources

If the software is to be written under the agreement, this section states what resources the publisher will make available to the developer to permit it to do its work. The issues are:

4.1   Is the publisher supplying work space and hardware for use in developing the software?

4.2   Does the developer need access to the publisher's computer system or network?

4.3   Will the publisher need technical information or data not included in the specifications?

4.4   Does the developer require sample data from the publisher's computer?

4.5   Will the customer provide or pay for software tools needed for the development work? Will the customer provide or pay for licenses for software to be imbedded in the program?

4.6   Are there other resources or assistance that the developer will need?

5   Confidentiality

This section governs confidentiality measures designed to protect trade secrets and confidential business information during the creation of the software and during the remainder of the relationship as well. The issues include:

5.1   Will there be confidential information passing from the publisher to the developer?

5.2   Will there be confidential information passing from the developer to the publisher?

5.3   Are both parties under confidentiality obligations or is only one side obligated?

5.4   What sort of measures to protect confidentiality are required?

5.5   Must one or both parties require its employees to sign confidentiality agreements?

6   Deliverables

The agreement needs to state the various objects that developer must deliver under the agreement. As is noted in Chapter 9, the agreement could refer to an existing program or to software to be created under the agreement. Common issues are:

6.1   Are both source code and object code to be supplied, or only object code? If source code is to be supplied, there should be a requirement that it be adequately documented.

6.2   Is the software product to be delivered all at once or are various deliveries to be made over time? Is there to be a prototype, an "alpha" version or a "beta" version? Are crucial functions to be delivered first to prove that they are feasible?

6.3   What medium is the software to be delivered on? What format is to be used?

6.4   Is user documentation a required deliverable under the agreement -- or is it the publisher's job to get the documentation done? Is only the text of the manual required or does the manual have to presented in a format suitable for printing?

7   Scheduling Deliveries of Software to the Customer

The agreement must specify when deliverables are to be supplied. These times are often stated in a milestone schedule.

7.1   Is the obligation to meet the schedule absolute?

7.2   How much flexibility, if any, is allowed in the schedule?

8   Changes in Specifications

Changes in the Specifications during programming are a potential source of friction. What is the mechanism to allow the parties to negotiate additions or changes in what is to be delivered? How are corresponding changes made in scheduling and advance payments? (Generally speaking, every change should be documented in a document that both parties sign.)

9   Delivery and Acceptance

The section states the procedures for the developer to deliver the program deliverables and for the publisher to accept or reject each deliverable. If a pre-existing program is to be delivered, a simplified acceptance procedure would be used. The issues are:

9.1   How is delivery made?

9.2   Is the acceptance criteria defined as the program's ability to perform in accordance with the specifications? Is it sufficient if the program "substantially" conforms to the specifications?

9.3   Is the acceptance criteria defined as ability to run certain test data? If so, what is the source of the test data?

9.4   Are the acceptance criteria defined to give the publisher discretion; for example, as "publisher's reasonable satisfaction?"

9.5   How much time after each delivery does the publisher have to make a rejection? Under what procedure does the publisher specify the reasons for rejection?

9.6   How much time does the developer have to cure specified defects?

9.7   When do program rights transfer to the publisher? With each deliverable, or only after final payment to the developer?

9.8   Under what circumstances can the publisher terminate the agreement if software is late or defective?

9.9   What are the publisher's rights if the publisher terminates the agreement because the developer has failed to deliver acceptable software? Does the developer have to return money already paid? Does the publisher own whatever software was developed to date even though the agreement was terminated? Can the publisher sue the developer for damages in excess of a refund of the amounts paid?

10   Subcontracting

If the program is to be written under the agreement, these provisions deal with subcontractors who may be retained to work on the program. The issues are:

10.1   Is use of subcontractors allowed?

10.2   Must the developer require subcontractors to implement confidentiality safeguards?

10.3 Must the developer require subcontractors (or their employees) to sign confidentiality agreements?

10.4 Must the developer require subcontractors to agree that they will not supply software competitive with the program to the publisher's competitors? For how long?

10.5 What provisions are there for verifying that required confidentiality measures have been taken?

11 Advance Payments

This section states the payment terms for royalty advances or other up-front payments to the developer. The issues are:

11.1 What is to be the total of the payments to the developer during the work to create the program?

11.2 What is the timing of payments? Is there a payment on signing? Are there progress payments? Is there a final payment? (Where multiple payments are contemplated, the payments are normally tied to a milestone schedule.)

11.3 Are the payments an advance on royalties, or are the up-front payments in addition to the royalties to be paid later on?

11.4 What is the developer's remedy if there is a payment default? Can the developer terminate the agreement, keep the copyright and sell the product to someone else? Does the publisher get a chance to cure the payment default?

12 Grant of License

This important section grants intellectual property rights, which include the rights to reproduce and license the program. It should be made quite clear exactly what rights are granted to the publisher. The issues are:

12.1 What is the territory granted? Are there areas excluded from the grant?

12.2 Is the licence limited to defined fields of use, markets, platforms, customer types, etc.?

12.3 Is the license that is granted exclusive or non-exclusive? (It could also be exclusive as to some rights and non-exclusive as to others.)

12.4   Does the publisher have the right to publish abroad by itself or through its sub-sidiaries? Does it have the right to sublicense others to publish the work in the United States or abroad?

12.5   If foreign publication rights are granted, does the publisher have a time limit for using such rights? If the publisher fails to use these rights, do they revert to the developer?

12.6   If foreign territories are included, is there a provision for the publisher to be responsible for compliance with all applicable United States export controls and restrictions?

12.7   Does the publisher get the right to create or arrange for the creation of derivative works, such as versions of the program for other platforms or other languages? If so, what rights to derivative works are granted? Does the publisher have a time limit for using such rights? If the publisher fails to use such rights, do the rights revert to the developer?

12.8   What types of intellectual property besides the copyright are granted to the publisher? For example, if it turns out that the developer has created a patentable invention, is that patentable technology exclusively licensed to the publisher? Are any trade secrets exclusively licensed?

12.9   Does the developer retain the rights to use the mundane routines or subroutines in the program's code in other programs that it writes for its other customers or uses internally?

12.10 Is there a grant to the publisher of rights to enhancements, improvements, or subsequent releases of the program?

12.11 Does the publisher have the right to modify the program or to require modification? Who pays for that work? Are the costs of modifications or improvements a deduction from the revenues on which royalties are based? Is there a cap on such deductions?

12.12 Are any trademark rights granted? Are provisions included that satisfy legal requirements for trademark licensing? (You should consult counsel about restrictions and requirements for trademark licensing and about trademark registration.)

13   Royalties

A publishing agreement must provide how royalties will be paid. Often royalties are based on net revenues from the program, which in turn is based on gross receipts produced by the program. It is also possible to have royalties based solely on the dollar volume of products shipped or to set a fixed royalty for each copy shipped. There are many other possible royalty arrangements. Some issues to consider are:

13.1   What is the basic royalty type? Is the royalty based on a percentage of "net revenues" from the program? On a percentage of "gross receipts?" Is there a minimum or a fixed royalty due for each copy of the program shipped?

13.2   What definition of "gross receipts" will apply? For example, is service or maintenance revenue part of gross receipts -- or is it limited to revenues from the licensing fees generated by the program? Normally the gross receipts figure is net of shipping costs and taxes.

13.3   What costs can be deducted from gross receipts to derive the "net revenues" figure on which royalties are based? Deductions may include return credits (which are rights granted to dealers to return a certain amount of software if it fails to sell), actual returns (due to defects or simply failure of the software to sell), and promotional and advertising credits (which are payments or credits given to dealers as sales incentives or to share advertising and promotion costs). Operating costs are normally not a deduction.

13.4   Is net revenues (or royalties) reduced by the publisher's out-of-pocket costs for replacement of product due to errors or bugs in the program, including cost of printing, diskette production, assembly labor, and shipping? Or does the publisher bear the risk of these costs? If they are deducted from royalties, is there a cap or limit on the percentage of royalties otherwise due that can be deducted in any period?

13.5   Is there a cap or limit on the percentage of gross receipts that can be deducted to arrive at net revenues?

13.6   What is the percentage royalty that applies? Does the percentage change based on the total number of copies sold?

13.7   What royalty applies if the program is sold "bundled" with other software or hardware products for a single price? How is the payment for the "bundle" allocated among the various products?

13.8   If sublicensing to other publishers, foreign or domestic, is permitted, does the developer get a higher percentage of revenue generated by such arrangements?

13.9   Are there minimum quarterly or yearly royalties due? What happens if net revenues are too low to justify minimum royalties? Can either party then terminate the agreement?

14   Timing of Royalty Payments

14.1   What period are royalties calculated for? Commonly they are calculated quarterly, but other arrangements are possible.

14.2   When is the calculation done?

14.3   When is payment due?

15   Recoupment of Advance Payments

Often software publishing agreements allow the publisher to recoup advance payments by reducing the amount of royalties otherwise due. The issues are:

15.1   Over what period of time and by what method are the advance payments recovered?

15.2   Are all of the advance payments recovered by the publisher or only part of them?

15.3   Is there a limit to the percentage of the royalties otherwise payable that may be deducted and applied to recoupment of advance payments during any given period?

16   Royalty-Free Copies

It is normal for the publisher to be able to supply demonstration copies of the program without paying royalties. The publisher may also want to use some copies of the program for its own internal use. The relevant questions are:

16.1   What controls will be required for the distribution of demonstration copies? What records of such distribution will be kept?

16.2   How will demonstration copies be labelled to preclude resale?

16.3   Is there a cap or maximum on the number of copies of the program that the publisher can use internally? After the cap is reached, how is the developer to be compensated for copies used internally by the publisher?

17   Accounting

The purpose of the accounting provisions is to require the publisher to keep adequate sales and royalty records and to allow the developer to check that royalties are being calculated and paid properly. The issues are:

17.1   What records of licensing revenues and royalties is the publisher required to keep?

17.2   How often does the publisher have to report revenue and royalty calculations to the developer? What is the form of the report?

17.3   Can the developer audit the publisher's records to be sure that royalties are properly calculated? On what notice?

17.4   What happens if there is a disagreement on royalty calculations? Is there an option to resolve such disagreements by arbitration? (See discussion of arbitration below.)

18   Marketing of the Program

An agreement may have very general or very specific provisions about the publisher's obligation to market the program. The questions to consider are:

18.1   Does the publisher have a marketing obligation stated in general terms, such as an obligation to use its "best efforts" or to use "reasonable efforts" to market the program?

18.2   Does the agreement impose affirmative obligations on the publisher to follow a particular marketing plan, or to spend a specified amount on marketing, or to devote specified staffing to a marketing effort?

18.3   Are there restrictions on how the publisher may market the program -- on selling methods or packaging?

18.4   Can the publisher cease or suspend publication if sales are poor?

19   Training and Technical Support

The publisher will often need to provide support for the program to customers, and will need to train personnel to provide that support. The agreement may require the developer to supply advice and information concerning the use and features of the program. The issues are:

19.1   What is the extent of the obligation of the developer to supply advice and information?

19.2   Will the developer be paid an hourly rate for such services?

19.3   Will the developer be paid its out-of-pocket expenses for providing such services?

20   Exclusivity

Exclusivity in a software publishing agreement can be a two-way street. The developer can agree not to supply competing products to others. The publisher can agree not to market products that compete with the program. The issues are:

20.1   What is the exclusivity obligation of the developer?

20.2   What is the exclusivity obligation of the publisher?

20.3   What is the duration of any exclusivity provision?

20.4   What is the definition of a "competing" product?

20.5   Can the developer supply to others a product similar to the program, but for a different platform?

20.6   Can the publisher market a product similar to the program for a different platform?

20.7   As noted above, there is an issue whether subcontractors who work on the program agree to the same restrictions.

21   Development Credit

Sometimes the developer will receive credit for writing the program in the text of the packaging or on the first user screen. If such a provision is included, the parties must agree where and how credit must be stated. For example, is development credit required in the user manual or in the publisher's advertisements and marketing materials?

22   Required End-User Warranty Disclaimer or License

Some software publishing agreements require that any packaging delivered to end-users contain a disclaimer of warranties and limits on liability and remedies. Some agreements for publishing products to be sold at retail require that the publisher use specified text in the shrink-wrap license included in the software package. Sometimes the form of a required end-user or shrink wrap license that is required is attached as a schedule to the software publishing agreement. (End-user agreements are covered in Chapter 12, and shrink-wrap licenses, and their limitations, are discussed in Chapter 11.)

23　Warranties; Disclaimers

No one writes completely "bug-free" software. Even after thorough testing, bugs will probably appear. Therefore developers give carefully narrowed warranties, if they give any at all, and "disclaim" most or all warranties on the program. Note that such a disclaimer must be stated conspicuously (in ALL CAPS). Getting the wording right is also important. See Form 9-2 for an example of disclaimer language.

An additional issue is the type of damages that the publisher may seek if the developer fails to supply an acceptable program. The agreement normally should exclude consequential damages, that is, money damages for all the profits that the publisher would have earned if an acceptable program had been supplied. The developer will also normally want the total amount of contract damages limited, as is discussed in the "liability cap" provision below.

24　Copyright Registration and Notices

The provisions require one party, usually the publisher, to register the copyright (unless it is already registered). Only an exclusive licensee can register a copyright.

The section also requires that copyright notices be used. If the program is licensed exclusively to the publisher, the publisher's name will normally go on the copyright notice. If the license is non-exclusive, normally the developer (or other holder of exclusive rights) will be referred to in the copyright notice.

If the program is already registered, the publisher should consider recording the license to the program with the Copyright Office. (Copyright procedures are discussed in Chapter 1 and in Appendix A.)

25　Maintenance and Support

This part of the agreement provides that the developer will have an ongoing obligation to fix bugs and errors found after the program is accepted. The issues here are:

25.1　How are bugs and errors reported?

25.2　How many months or years does the developer's obligation to fix bugs last?

25.3　Is there a limit to the number of hours that the developer has to put into fixing bugs? After the time limit is reached, is the developer compensated for fixing bugs? At what rate?

25.4 If bugs are not fixed in a given time, can the publisher have a third party fix the bugs? If the publisher pays, are the costs deducted from the net revenues on which royalties are based?

26 Intellectual Property Warranties

This section states the developer's warranties or guaranty about its legal right to supply the software and whether the software infringes the rights of anyone else. The developer can be liable to the publisher for the damage caused by any breach of this warranty. The issues are:

26.1 Does the developer warrant that the software does not infringe intellectual property rights of others (such as copyrights, trade secrets, or patents) -- or does developer warrant only that it knows of no infringement? From a developer's perspective, the latter is much better.

27 Indemnification

This section deals with the developer's responsibility if an intellectual property infringement claim is brought against the publisher. The scope of the indemnification clause is often related to the scope of the intellectual property warranty that we just discussed. If the developer has broadly warranted that there is no infringement, then the agreement will often place on the developer the entire cost of defending any infringement claim and the cost of paying any settlement or judgment. If the developer has warranted only that it knows of no infringement, then the agreement might provide that only if that warranty is false (if it did know of an infringement) would the developer be required to indemnify or defend the publisher or pay a settlement or a judgment. Other questions are:

27.1 What are the parties' obligations to report infringement claims to one another?

27.2 Who is responsible for legal fees and other costs of defense?

27.3 Who controls the defense or settlement of an infringement lawsuit?

27.4 Is the developer required to pay for the defense, even if the infringement claim is without merit?

27.5 May the publisher withhold royalties as security for the developer's obligations concerning infringement claims?

27.6 How long after termination of the agreement does the indemnification obligation last?

When, as is usually the case, the publisher has the deeper pocket, it will be the prime target in an infringement lawsuit. It usually makes sense, therefore, for the publisher to bear the "laboring oar" and to have control of the defense of an infringement claim.

28   Liability Cap

It is also common for an agreement specify a limit or cap for liability that the developer might have to the publisher under the agreement. The cap would come into play if the developer failed to deliver the promised software or if there are other breaches, including a breach of the warranties concerning non-infringement. (Some contracts provide that if the developer fails to develop an acceptable program, only part of the money paid in advance is returned, and that this is the publisher's sole remedy.)

28.1   Is there an overall damage cap? Is it a fixed dollar amount? Is set by a formula, for example, the total of advance payments and royalties paid to the developer under the agreement or a percentage of that amount?

28.2   Is there a separate cap on the amount of developer's obligation to indemnify the publisher if an infringement claim is brought against the publisher?

29   Infringement of Rights in the Program

The agreement should provide which party may act if a third party infringes the program copyright, for example, if a software "cloner" infringes the program's copyright by copying the program's external characteristics. Usually the publisher will have the choice of suing or not. In the case of a narrow license limited to a certain field of use or a non-exclusive license, the prerogative may belong to the developer. The questions are:

29.1   What are the obligations of each party to report an infringer to the other?

29.2   Which side has the right -- or the obligation -- to enforce the program copyright (or any patent rights) against the infringer?

29.3   If one side fails to pursue the infringer, may the other proceed?

29.4   How is any recovery treated for purposes of calculating royalties due to the developer?

30   Term and Termination

This section deals with amount of time the agreement is in effect and with ending it. The issues include:

30.1   When does the agreement commence?

30.2   How long does the agreement last? A defined number of years?

30.3   Does the publisher have an option to renew the agreement for additional terms?

30.4   As noted above, may one or another party terminate the agreement if royalties or revenue fall below a certain level? Can the publisher terminate at any time at its option?

30.5   Under what circumstances can one or another of the parties terminate the agreement due to the fault of the other party? Is the triggering language a "material default of the other party"? Are additional defaults specified? Is there notice and an opportunity to cure defaults before termination?

30.6   What happens to the license granted to the publisher upon termination. Normally it reverts to the developer. If the publisher is not going to be paying royalties any more, it usually has no need for rights to the program. Can the developer obtain the rights to any modifications to the program made by the publisher?

30.7   What obligations of the agreement survive termination (e.g., confidentiality, indemnification, exclusivity, etc.)? There is commonly a provision permitting licenses granted to end-users to remain in effect.

31   Source Code Escrow

Where only object code is delivered to the publisher, there might be a provision for the source code to be placed in escrow, and to be released if the developer fails to maintain the code. Software escrows are discussed in detail in Chapter 12.

32   Arbitration

If the parties want disputes to be subject to arbitration, they should add an arbitration clause. Arbitration is quite expensive but it is generally faster and less expensive than litigation. Some issues in drafting an arbitration provision might be:

32.1   Where does arbitration take place?

32.2   How many arbitrators sit and what rules apply?

32.3   Is familiarity with the computer industry a prerequisite for one or more panel members?

Note that injunctive relief, which is necessary to enforce confidentiality or exclusivity provisions, is not normally subject to arbitration. An exception to the arbitration clause often allows these claims to be pursued in court.

33   Remedies

This section can limit or expand litigation remedies for breach of agreement. The section often specifies that injunctive relief should be available for breach of confidentiality or exclusivity provisions. Some additional issues might be:

33.1   Is the publisher entitled to specified remedies if the program development runs late, for example a per diem reduction in the amount otherwise due?

33.2   If the publisher fails to pay the required advances, does the developer have an option to keep the program in lieu of damages for non-payment? Is the developer required to keep the program in lieu of damages for non-payment?

34   Legal Fees

Is the loser in arbitration, or litigation, required to pay the winner's legal fees? This can be a significant bargaining chip in many cases.

35   General Provisions

These provisions contain some fairly standard "legalese." Included are choice of state law, delays caused by "acts of God," responsibility for employment taxes, etc. See Form 9-2.

Form 9-2: ANNOTATED SOFTWARE PUBLISHING AGREEMENT

Introductory Note

This is a sample software publishing agreement with annotations to aid you in negotiations. (A copy can also be found on the diskette as PUB-CHK.W51.)

This draft includes many provisions that commonly occur in these agreements. There are many options presented in this form. As you will see, some of these options favor the developer and some favor the publisher. Your own negotiation may require different terms or choices or may raise concerns not addressed here. In negotiating these deals, you should read the text of each clause carefully and think through the way that each clause will affect your business. Your own perception of the technical and business risks will determine which clauses are most important to your business.

As noted in Chapter 9, there are two different settings in which parties negotiate publishing deals. The first is where the software is already written, perhaps needing minor modifications by the developer. In the second setting, the software that is being bargained for must be created under the terms of the agreement.

The following form is for the case where the software is to be written to specifications. If the software were already in existence, the form can be simplified to require a single delivery and acceptance and a single payment. The party termed the "Developer" can simply be an owner of the program, for example, a company that bought the rights to a program. In that case, the term "Licensor" can be substituted for "Developer."

In the following form, Schedule A (specifications) is omitted, because it is largely technical. However, both parties should remember that the specifications will be part of a legal document and therefore binding on both sides.

A sample milestone schedule (Schedule B) is included, but the project stages and dates given are arbitrary. There could, in appropriate cases, be additional schedules. For example, a set of tests for determining acceptance could be specified in a schedule to the agreement. There could also be a schedule containing warranty disclaimers required in sales documentation for end-users. A royalty scale, with differing percentage royalties based on different volumes of sales, could also be attached as a schedule. Marketing requirements for the publisher to carry out might also be in a schedule.

In this form, the text of the agreement does not specify whether both source code and object code will be delivered, or only object code. To find out whether source code is required, in this form one looks at the definition of "Deliverable" and "Final Deliverables" in the milestone schedule and specifications, which specify the form and media of each delivery of software under the agreement. Many software publishing agreements require source code delivery.

A software publishing agreement is a complex document. Negotiating one requires attention and patience. The final language needs to be reviewed by your attorney before you agree to it orally or in writing.

SOFTWARE PUBLISHING AGREEMENT
BETWEEN [*NAME OF PUBLISHER*] AND [*NAME OF DEVELOPER*]

1   INTRODUCTION

*[**Comment:** The introduction should set forth in plain and succinct language the general nature and purpose of the agreement. This section of a contract is often written more formally, with the word "whereas" introducing each clause.]*

1.1   This is an agreement between [*Name of Developer*] and [*Name of Publisher*]. Under this agreement, [*Name of Developer*] will [develop and] deliver certain software and under which [*Name of Publisher*] will publish such software under the terms and conditions stated below.

2   DEFINITIONS

*[**Comment:** The definitions section should define key terms of the agreement to avoid ambiguity and to simplify drafting by providing shorthand names for persons and things. Additional definitions appear in Schedule B, the milestone schedule, and in the text. Depending on choices made in the remainder of the agreement, you may need to add to these definitions or delete some of them. The definitions here are in alphabetical order.]*

As used in this Agreement, the following definitions shall apply:

2.1   "Advance Payment" shall mean each amount stated in the Delivery and Payment Schedule included in the Milestone Schedule, Schedule B.

2.2   "Agreement" shall mean this Agreement between Publisher and Developer.

2.3   "Commonly Used Code" shall include computer code, techniques, functions, routines, and subroutines that are common in the computer industry and computer programming methods in common use, whether or not created for use in the Program.

2.4   "Computer Trade" shall mean distributors, jobbers, direct mail sellers, resellers, wholesalers, and retailers that in the ordinary course derive revenue from the sale or licensing of computer hardware and software.

2.5   "Confidential Information" shall mean any information relating to or disclosed in the course of the Agreement, which is or should be reasonably understood to be confidential or proprietary to the disclosing party. "Confidential Information" shall not include information (a) already lawfully known to the receiving party, (b) disclosed in published materials, (c) generally known to the public, or (d) lawfully obtained from any third party.

2.6   "Deliverables" are the items that are identified in the Specification and the Milestone Schedule as items to be delivered to Publisher.

2.7   "Derivative Work" shall mean any work sufficiently based on the Program such that copying it without permission would infringe the copyright of the Program.

2.8   "Developer" shall mean [*Name of Corporation*] of [*City, State*].

2.9   "Documentation" shall mean the user manual and any other documentation that is supplied with or packaged with the Program when it is licensed to end-users, including but not limited to that delivered to Publisher under the terms of the Agreement.

2.10   "Effective Date" shall mean [*specify date*][the date upon which both parties have signed this Agreement].

2.11   "Final Deliverables" are the Program items that are specified in the Milestone Schedule as the final delivery to Publisher.

2.12   "Milestone Schedule" shall mean Schedule B to the Agreement.

2.13   "Program" shall mean the computer program entitled [*name of program*] developed by Developer, which shall consist of all Deliverables as stated in the Specifications (Schedule A), and the Milestone Schedule (Schedule B).

2.14   "Publisher" shall mean [*Name of Corporation*] of [*City, State*].

2.15   "Royalties" shall mean amounts calculated under the Royalty provisions of the Agreement.

2.16   "Quarter" shall mean each quarter [of Publisher's fiscal year] [of a calendar year].

2.17   "Specifications" shall mean requirements for the Program's required operation, functions, capabilities and performance and the Documentation to be delivered therewith, as described in Schedule A, or as revised by the parties under procedures set forth in this Agreement.

3 CHANGES IN SPECIFICATIONS AND MILESTONE SCHEDULE

*[**Comment:** A source of many disputes is changes to specifications. Often publishers may ask for additional or different features without expecting to pay more. Conflicts and misunderstandings can be avoided by documenting requests for extra work and extra compensation. Similar problems can arise when delivery is late and arguments arise over whether this was agreed to. This draft requires the parties to negotiate changes in specifications and delivery schedules.]*

3.1 Either Publisher or Developer may propose changes in the Specifications or to the Milestone Schedule. Publisher and Developer must agree, in writing, to the changes prior to any such modifications, and to the effect, if any, on payments due under this Agreement.

3.2 Publisher may not require work or features not set forth in the Specifications unless agreed to in writing. Developer will not be compensated, other than as stated in the Agreement, unless such additional payments are agreed to in advance in writing.

[Optional Provision:]

*[**Comment:** Sometimes the developer needs technical or business information from the publisher to do its work, for example, technical information about other products that the program must be compatible with. Sometimes the developer needs access to the publisher's software development tools. The following clause is to deal with these and other such requirements.]*

4 RESOURCES TO BE PROVIDED TO DEVELOPER

4.1 Publisher shall supply to Developer all specifications and other information or materials that Developer shall reasonably require to carry out the work required by this Agreement, including: *[include list]*.

5 CONFIDENTIALITY

5.1 Each party acknowledges that it will receive Confidential Information of the other party relating to its technical, marketing, product and/or business affairs. Each party agrees that all Confidential Information of the other party shall be held in strict confidence and shall not be disclosed or used without express written consent of the other party, except as may be required by law. Each party agrees to use reason measures and reasonable efforts to provide protection for Confidential Information.

6   DEVELOPMENT OF SOFTWARE

[Comment: In this section, the developer undertakes a contractual duty to produce the program.]

6.1   On the Effective Date or within *[number]* days thereafter, Developer shall begin work to program and develop the Program and shall apply such resources and efforts as shall be reasonably necessary to accomplish this task.

7   DELIVERY AND ACCEPTANCE OF DELIVERABLES

[Comment: There are many ways to write provisions for the acceptance of software. The version that follows is intended to be reasonably balanced. It provides a time frame for publisher's acceptance and allows a cure period if software is rejected. As an option, this version also allows the publisher to accept defective final deliverables for the program and to have them fixed at the developer's expense.]

7.1   Developer shall deliver various Deliverables at the times and in the manner specified in the Milestone Schedule. [At its option, Developer can extend the due dates for any date of the Milestone Schedule by giving written notice to the Publisher, provided that the total of all such extensions shall not exceed *[specify number]* days.]

7.2   If Developer fails to make timely delivery of any Deliverable as specified in the Milestone Schedule, Publisher may give Developer notice of the failure. After such notice, Developer shall have thirty (30) days to make the specified delivery. Failure to submit the Deliverables within such period shall be a material breach, which shall entitle Publisher, at its option, to terminate this Agreement in accordance with the provisions on Termination.

7.3   Publisher may inspect and test each of the Deliverables when received to determine if it [substantially] conforms to the requirements of the Specifications. [Testing shall be in accordance with the testing procedures specified in *[Name of Testing Procedure Document or Schedule]*].

7.4   [Any Deliverable not rejected in thirty (30) days shall be deemed accepted.] If any Deliverable is rejected, Publisher shall give Developer notice of the rejection and the reasons for rejection. Developer shall then have thirty (30) days to cure deficiencies. After resubmission within such thirty (30) day period, Publisher may again inspect the Deliverable to confirm that it [substantially] conforms to requirements of the Specifications. [If the resubmitted Deliverable is not rejected in the thirty (30) days after resubmission, the Deliverable shall be deemed accepted.] If the resubmitted Deliverable is rejected, Publisher shall state the reasons for rejection. If the resubmitted Deliverable does not [substantially] conform to the requirements of this Agreement, the failure will be a material breach that shall entitle Publisher to terminate this Agreement in accordance with the provisions on Termination.

7.5   Notice of failure to make timely delivery, rejection, or subsequent resubmission shall not affect the due date for subsequent Deliverables required under the Milestone Schedule unless otherwise agreed [or unless [*state other contingencies that will permit postponing due dates*]].

7.6   If the Final Deliverables in any material respect do not [substantially] conform to the Specifications, and such non-conformity is not cured as provided in this Agreement, the failure will be a material breach that shall entitle Publisher to terminate this Agreement in accordance with the provisions on Termination. [Alternatively, Publisher, at its option, may accept the Final Deliverables as non-conforming. If it does so, it shall give prompt notice to Developer stating the known defects, and may withhold and deduct, from amounts otherwise due and payable to Developer upon acceptance of the Final Deliverables, the amount of reasonable out-of-pocket costs to correct, modify, and/or complete the Program in accordance with the Specifications. From time to time, and as soon as is practicable, Publisher shall provide Developer with notice of all sums withheld and expended and shall turn over to Developer all funds withheld that are not so applied when such remedial work is completed.]

[Optional Provision:]

*[**Comment:** If the user manual or other documentation is to be written by the developer, these requirements should be included in the specifications and milestone schedule. Sometimes the publisher takes responsibility for the user manual or will hire another contractor to do this work. If this is the case, the following text would be appropriate.]*

7.7   Developer shall provide upon request, as reasonably required from time to time before publication of the Program, all assistance and information reasonably necessary to ensure that the Documentation for the Program is complete and accurate. Developer shall review a draft of the Documentation upon request and provide all required corrections to Publisher.

[Optional Provision:]

8   SUBCONTRACTORS

[Comment: The following language permits the developer to use subcontractors. It is possible, of course, to include language that forbids use of outside firms where security is particularly important.]

8.1   [Developer may retain third parties to work on the Program. All such third parties [and each of their employees who work on the Program] shall execute, before providing such services, an agreement, in a form reasonably satisfactory to Publisher, which shall include a promise to maintain confidentiality as required by this Agreement and which includes an assignment to Developer of all rights in such work so that such rights may be licensed or transferred to Publisher as required by this Agreement.] [Developer may not retain or permit third parties to work on the Program.]

9   ADVANCE PAYMENTS

9.1   Publisher shall pay Developer the Advance Payment amounts specified in the Milestone Schedule, within ten (10) days of acceptance of each Deliverable. Payment by mail shall be deemed made when mailed. Each Advance Payment will be treated as an advance on Royalties subject to recoupment by deductions from Royalties as provided below, provided however that each Advance Payment will otherwise be a non-refundable payment to Developer [except that should the Agreement be terminated due to Developer's failure to deliver acceptable Deliverables as required by this Agreement or due to Final Deliverables that are properly and finally rejected by Publisher, Developer shall return [all] *[specify percentage]* of the Advance Payments to Publisher]. [WHICH SHALL BE PUBLISHER'S SOLE REMEDY FOR ANY DAMAGE FLOWING THEREFROM.]

9.2   If any Advance Payment to Developer is not made on time and as required, Developer may give notice of the failure to make payment. Upon such notice, failure to make required payments shall automatically extend all remaining Milestone dates by the number of days from the date of notice until the required Advance Payment to Developer is made. If any such failure to pay is not cured within thirty (30) days after receipt of notice, Developer shall have the option to terminate this Agreement, effective upon Publisher's receipt of notice of termination from Developer. Notwithstanding such termination, in addition to any other remedy that Developer may have, Developer shall forthwith be paid all amounts due for milestones met under the Milestone Schedule that remain unpaid, plus the reasonable value of any additional work rendered in good faith and in accordance with the Agreement prior to termination. [In addition to other remedies, Publisher shall pay Developer interest on late payments at the rate of *[specify number]*.]

10   GRANT OF LICENSE

[Comment: This section governs the scope of the rights to the program that will be granted to the publisher. In reviewing the following section, please note the numerous choices that can be made in the scope of the license (and this is hardly a complete list).]

10.1   [Upon the Effective Date of this Agreement,] [Upon Publisher's acceptance of the final delivery under the Milestone Schedule,] Publisher shall have and Developer hereby grants to Publisher [an exclusive] [a non-exclusive] license to the Program as follows:

10.2   The license shall be effective solely for the territory defined as follows: [worldwide] *[list of countries, areas, or territories]* [with the following exceptions: *[list]*].

10.3   The license shall be subject to the following restrictions: *[list restrictions by field of use, market, platform, language, customer type, etc.]*

10.4   Subject to all limitations stated in the Agreement, Publisher may print, copy, distribute, display, demonstrate, market, and license the Program in object code form to end-users and to the Computer Trade [and to *[specify other permitted customers]*].

[Optional Provision:]

[Comment: This following optional sections deal with whether or not the publisher may authorize other companies to act as publisher. As is discussed in Chapter 9, if the publisher has the right to authorize others to publish the work in foreign states (or in the United States for that matter) and to take most of the revenue that results, the result may be unfair to the developer.]

10.5   Publisher shall not have the right to authorize any other company to act as publisher or manufacturer of the Program. Aside from vendors that replicate disks or print Documentation, packaging or other materials for the Program at Publisher's request without providing marketing or distribution services, Publisher may not authorize any third party to publish, copy, or replicate the Program. Except as otherwise provided for in this Agreement, no third party may receive the Program Source Code without the prior written permission of developer.

[Optional Provision:]

10.6   Publisher shall have the right to authorized any other company or companies to act as publisher or manufacturer of the Program outside the United States and its territories ("Foreign Sublicensing Right") [only as follows: *[specify territory, use restrictions, etc.]*]. Aside from vendors that replicate disks or print Documentation, packaging or other materials for the Program at Publisher's request without providing marketing or distribution services, Publisher may not authorize any third party to publish, copy, or replicate the Program within the United States and its territories without Developer's prior written permission [except as follows [*state exceptions*]]. If reasonable security measures are taken, Publisher may supply publishers or manufacturers of the Program outside the United States with Program Source Code without the prior permission of developer to the extent reasonably necessary to exercise such Foreign Sublicensing Right. [For any territory in which the Foreign Sublicensing Right is not used by Publisher in [*number*] months after the Effective Date, such right reverts to Developer.] Publisher shall be responsible for compliance with all laws affecting foreign commerce including all export licensing requirements and export controls.

10.7   [The license includes the right to create Derivative Works [only of the following types: [*list*]][subject to the following exceptions: [*list*], and to have the same rights in such Derivative Works as are granted in the Program.] [The license does not include any rights to Derivative Works.]

10.8   To the extent of the license grant stated above, the license to Publisher shall include Developer's copyrights, patents, patentable inventions, trade secrets, and all other proprietary rights in the Program under the terms and conditions stated in this Agreement.

10.9   All rights owned by Developer that are not granted by the Agreement are reserved to Developer.

10.10   Developer shall provide such written confirmations of this license grant as Publisher may reasonably require.

[Optional Provision:]

[**Comment:** *Developers have an interest in remaining free to use code that is based on commonly known computer techniques in future programs, including such code that is developed in work on the program for the publisher. If it is not careful, a developer might sign away the right to use code that does routine tasks like fetching information and displaying graphics. Therefore developers may request that a provision be added to allow continued use of commonly used code and methods. The publisher should note, however, that the general language of the definition of "Commonly Used Code" may make unclear the boundaries of what the developer may and may not do.]*

10.11   Publisher and Developer recognize that the Program will contain Commonly Used Code. Notwithstanding any other provisions of this Agreement, Developer shall retain the right to utilize Commonly Used Code in programs developed for others or for its own use.

[Optional Provision:]

[Comment: The publisher may want to insure that it has all rights to any program improvements that the developer may create. That is the purpose of the following clause, which does not require the developer to make improvements and does not commit the publisher to use improvements that are created. Any work to improve the program should be discussed by the parties before it is carried out. If there is to be a major upgrade of the program, there will need to be negotiations between the developer and the publisher to set the financial terms and work through the specifications in an amendment or new agreement.]

10.12   [For *period of time,*] [For the term of this Agreement,] Developer shall supply to Publisher free of charge, or upon such other terms as the parties may agree upon in writing, any Program enhancements, improvements, or subsequent releases that augment program functionality, utility or performance. Any such improvements that Developer supplies to Publisher shall be subject to the license provisions of this Agreement. [Each version of the Program delivered to Publisher shall include the source code with comments and with documentation sufficient for a reasonably skilled programmer to modify it.]

[Optional Provision:]

[Comment: If the publisher has an exclusive license and has received the program source code, it may want the right to modify the program. This right is provided in the following text. The text provides choices as to (1) who has control of whether modifications are made or not and (2) who ultimately pays for them.]

10.13   Publisher may modify the Program in order to improve its functionality or performance [without the permission of Developer] [with the permission of Developer which shall not be unreasonably withheld] [with the permission of Developer which Developer can withhold in its absolute discretion]. [Publisher shall bear all the costs of such modifications.] [Publisher shall have the right to charge [[*number*] percent of] the costs of such modifications [up to a limit of $[*amount*] per year] from Net Revenues From the Program (as defined below) used to calculate Royalties payable to Developer.] [Publisher shall first discuss such modification work with Developer. However, if the parties are unable to reach agreement promptly upon the terms under which the Developer shall make such modifications, Publisher may contract with other parties to do such modification work.] In contracting for such work, Publisher shall take reasonable steps to protect Confidential Information of the Developer.

[Optional Provision:]

[Comment: The following text is for the case where the program comes to the publisher with no trademark. If it is the intent of the parties to license a trademark, a simple statement granting a trademark license will not suffice. The trademark licensor has to maintain control of the use of its mark and risks invalidating its trademark rights if it does not. These are not simple matters. If you need provisions on trademark licensing as part of a publishing deal, they should be drafted by an attorney.]

10.14   Developer acknowledges that Publisher may select a trademark for the Program, and Developer shall gain no rights in the trademark.

11   ROYALTIES

[Comment: The following text presents a variety of choices for royalty types, and these are by no means all of the possible permutations. Where there is a sliding scale of royalty payments, for example, a scale varying with the amount of royalties received, the provision would normally be in a schedule to the agreement. It is also possible to provide different royalty formulas for different sales channels. For some products, revenues from software support and maintenance are important part of total revenue. For these products, the developer may wish to request that service revenue be included in the royalty calculation.]

11.1   Royalty payments shall be calculated for each Quarter as described below.

11.2   Royalty payments to Developer shall be due thirty (30) days after the end of each Quarter [provided that if accumulated and unpaid Royalties do not exceed $500.00, payments will be held until a Quarter when the balance exceeds $500.00 at which time the full balance will be paid].

[Option 1. Percentage Royalties Based On Net Revenues:]

11.3   Publisher shall pay Developer [a Royalty of [*number*] percent of Net Revenues from the Program] [a Royalty based on the various percentages of Net Revenues set forth on the Royalty Schedule attached as Schedule _].

11.4 "Net Revenues From the Program" shall mean Publisher's Gross Receipts less deductions for: (i) the amount of any credits or cash refunds for returns, and (ii) the amount of any credits, discounts, rebates, and promotional allowances [provided that all such deductions may not exceed [*number*] percent of Gross Receipts revenues for any Quarter].

11.5 "Gross Receipts" shall mean any and all revenues realized by Publisher (exclusive of sales, use, excise and other taxes and exclusive of all insurance and shipping costs) from all sales, licenses, or other transactions pursuant to which copies of the Program [or Derivative Works] are delivered or licensed to customers, distributors, dealers, or others [plus all revenues realized by Publisher for maintenance, training, or support for the Program paid by any person or entity].

[Option 2. Percentage Royalties Based On Gross Receipts:]

*[**Comment:** To use the following paragraph, you should also use the "Gross Receipts" definition from the preceding section.]*

11.6 Publisher shall pay Developer [a Royalty of [*number*] percent of Gross Receipts from the Program] [a Royalty based on the percentages of Gross Receipts from the Program set forth in the Royalty Schedule attached as Schedule __].

[Optional Provision. Minimum Per-Shipment Royalties:]

*[**Comment:** Whether royalties are based on net revenues or on gross receipts, developer's may seek a minimum royalty for each copy of the program shipped.]*

11.7 Notwithstanding the above, Publisher shall pay Developer, for each Quarter, a minimum royalty of no less than $[*number*] for each copy of the program shipped or licensed to a third party (promotional copies not included) during the Quarter.

[Optional Provision:]

*[**Comment:** Where royalties are based on net revenues or gross revenues, there is normally a clause to deal with "bundling" of the program with other software or with hardware for a single price.]*

11.8 If Publisher licenses or supplies the Program [or any Derivative Work] in a package or group with other products at a single price, the Net Revenues from such package or group shall be prorated according to the published list prices established by Publisher for the separate works contained in the package [provided however that, for the purpose of this allocation, the list price assigned to the Program shall be no less than $[*number*]].

[Optional Provision. Percentage

Royalties From Exercise of Foreign Sublicensing Right:]

[Comment: As noted in Chapter 11, if a foreign distributor will be publishing the program overseas as a sublicensee, the developer should get a substantially larger share of the revenue. This is because in the foreign market, the foreign party, not the publisher, is taking the risks and paying costs of publication. In this situation, where the publisher has very few costs after signing with the foreign party, the revenues used for the royalty calculation should be all or most of the revenues paid to the publisher by the foreign party.]

11.9   Publisher shall pay Developer a [royalty of [*number*] percent of Revenues From Foreign Sublicensing] [a Royalty on Revenues From Foreign Sublicensing based on the formula set forth in the Foreign Licensing Royalty Schedule attached as Schedule _]. "Revenues From Foreign Sublicensing" shall mean all Publisher's revenue derived in any way from exercise of its Foreign Sublicensing Right [except [*define any exceptions or deductions*]].

[Optional Provision. Minimum Quarterly Royalties:]

[Comment: Sometimes a publisher will guarantee a certain minimum quarterly or yearly royalty. Such provisions often have escape clauses, allowing the one or both parties to terminate the license agreement if the Program persistently fails to generate sufficient revenues to justify the minimum.]

11.10   Beginning with the first Quarter that begins no less than [*number*] months after the delivery and acceptance of the Final Deliverables, Publisher shall pay a total minimum Royalty for each Quarter of no less than $[*amount*]. [If such total minimum Royalty exceeds the Royalty calculated as stated above for more than [*number*] consecutive Quarters [not counting the first twelve months after the Effective Date], [Publisher] [either party] may terminate this Agreement.]

12   RECOUPMENT OF ADVANCE PAYMENTS

[Comment: This sample agreement is written so that the publisher may recoup the advance payments paid to the developer by deducting them from royalties later on. This is a common provision. The parties could, of course, negotiate a deal in which the advance payments are not deducted from royalties at all.]

12.1   Publisher shall recoup the Advance Payments made to Developer by deductions from Royalties [provided however that in any Quarter, the amount of Royalties as calculated under the provisions of the section entitled Royalties may not be reduced by such deduction by more than [*number*] percent].

13   DEDUCTION FOR COSTS FOR DEFECTIVE SOFTWARE

13.1   Publisher may deduct [from Net Revenues on which Royalties are calculated] [from Royalties] [all] [[*number*] percent] of Publisher's out-of-pocket costs for replacement of product due to errors or bugs in the Program, including cost of replacement printing, diskette production, shipping and assembly labor costs [provided, however, that in any Quarter such deduction from Royalties may not exceed [*number*] percent of Royalties otherwise payable]. No such deduction shall be made on account of errors or bugs created or introduced by modifications to the Program made by persons other than Developer.

14   DEVELOPER'S RIGHT TO TERMINATE BASED ON PERFORMANCE CRITERIA

[Comment: In the following section, the developer may terminate the agreement if net revenues or royalties are below a specified level.]

14.1   After the [second] [*specify other*] anniversary of the Effective date, Developer may at its option terminate this Agreement any time by notice during the [*number*] day period after receipt of the Royalty Report for the most recent Quarter, if the aggregate [Net Revenues][Royalties paid to Developer] on account of the Program during such Quarter plus the preceding three Quarters were less than $[*amount*].

15   ROYALTY-FREE COPIES

15.1   Notwithstanding the foregoing, no royalties shall be due for copies of the Program created and shipped by Publisher solely for demonstration purposes and clearly labelled: "Dealer Demonstration Copy; Not for Resale or Relicense." Publisher shall keep records of the number of such copies created and shall make such records available to Developer upon request.

15.2   Notwithstanding the foregoing, no Royalties shall be due for end-user copies of the Program created and shipped by Publisher for marketing and promotion purposes which have sufficient functions disabled or removed or are limited in the number of times they may be used, so as to render them substantially unusable for the functions for which the Program is normally intended.

15.3   No Royalties shall be due for the first [*number*] copies of the Program used by Publisher for its own internal purposes. Thereafter, Developer shall be paid the

Royalties for copies that Publisher uses internally at the rate that would have applied if the Programs were sold at [*number*] percent of retail list price. Publisher shall keep records of the number of copies put to use internally and shall make such records available to Developer upon request.

16   ACCOUNTING

[***Comment:*** *The purpose of the accounting provision is require the publisher to keep adequate sales and royalty records and to allow the developer to audit the publisher's records to verify that royalties are being calculated and paid properly.*]

16.1   Publisher shall maintain detailed records of receipts, revenues, and costs relating to the computation of the Royalty payments required by this Agreement.

16.2   Publisher shall deliver to Developer a report ("Royalty Report") within thirty (30) days after the close of each Quarter which shall provide all information reasonably required for computation of the Royalty payments required by this Agreement.

16.3   Developer may, upon reasonable notice, inspect the records of Publisher on which the Royalty Reports are based during Publisher's normal business hours. Developer may conduct such inspection itself or by its attorney, certified public accountant or agent [provided such person signs, at Publisher's request, a reasonable nondisclosure agreement].

17   MARKETING OF THE PROGRAM

[***Comment:*** *Depending on the bargaining power of the parties, the agreement may give the publisher absolute discretion in marketing, including the option (rarely taken) not to market at all. At the other extreme, the agreement may require that the publisher follow a definite marketing agenda. A common provision is an agreement of the publisher to use "best efforts."*]

[Option 1: No Minimum Marketing Requirement]

17.1   Publisher shall not be required to promote the product except as it deems appropriate; the level of effort and spending in promotion shall be in Publisher's sole discretion.

[Option 2: Specified Marketing Requirement]

17.2   Publisher shall be required to spend no less than $[*amount*] in computer magazines of national distribution in each of the first [*number*] years after publication, and shall be required during such period to hire a sales manager dedicated to the

Program for a yearly salary of no less than $[*amount*] per year. [Publisher shall also carry out the following marketing tasks: [*list other marketing requirements*]].

[Option 3: Best Efforts Marketing Requirement]

17.3 Publisher shall use its best efforts to promote the Program.

17.4 Publisher shall use its best efforts to commence distribution by no later than: [date] [[*number*] days after acceptance of the Final Deliverables].

17.5 Marketing of the Program shall be solely within the control of Publisher, including all decisions as to promotional means, and all matters of terms, conditions and prices [except [*list any exceptions or restrictions*]].

17.6 Publisher shall have the option to suspend or cease marketing the program if, in the judgment of the Publisher, results of marketing are insufficient to justify keeping the program on the market [except as follows: [*list any restrictions or exceptions*]]. Publisher shall promptly notify Developer of any decision to suspend or cease marketing of the Program.

18   TRAINING AND ADVICE

18.1 Developer agrees to provide such training, advice and information concerning the use and features of the Program as Publisher shall reasonably require. [Up to [*number*] hours of professional time shall be provided for this purpose without fee; thereafter the cost for professional services shall be $[*amount*] per day.] Publisher shall reimburse Developer for its reasonable travel and lodging costs incurred to provide such training, advice and information.

[Optional Provision:]
19   EXCLUSIVITY

19.1 From the Effective Date until termination of this Agreement, Developer shall not supply or agree to supply to any party other than Publisher computer software with functionality similar to the Program [including software on other software or hardware platforms] [excluding software on other software or hardware platforms] or software that will or is likely to be competitive with the Program. [Nothing in this clause shall affect Developer's rights to employ Commonly Used Code in products or work for competitors of Publisher.]

[Optional Provision:]

19.2 From the Effective Date until termination of this Agreement, Publisher agrees not to develop, acquire or market any product that will perform substantially the same functions as the Program or that would be directly competitive with the Program [and Publisher further agrees not to offer employment to any of Developer's employees without Developer's prior written consent].

[Optional Provision:]

20 DEVELOPMENT CREDIT

20.1   Publisher shall acknowledge Developer as the programmer in text displayed in the first screen of the Program and in the Documentation. Such development credit shall not give Developer any trademark, copyright or other proprietary interest or rights in the Software. [Publisher [shall] [need not] provide development credit in advertisements, including print and broadcast media, catalogs, and direct mail.]

[Optional Provision:]

21 REQUIRED END-USER LICENSE

[*Comment:* *Some software publishing agreements require that any sales to end-users or to dealers and distributors be under agreements or licenses that disclaim warranties and limit liability and remedies. Such limitation of liability clauses are discussed in Chapter 8.*]

21.1   [A license agreement shall be included in or on each box or container in which the Program is packaged for delivery to the end-user, and such license agreement shall contain [the following terms: *list*] [the terms set forth on Schedule __ to this Agreement].] [A license agreement substantially in the form set forth in Schedule __ to this Agreement shall be included in or on each box or container in which the Program is packaged for delivery to the end-user.]

22 WARRANTY DISCLAIMER; MAINTENANCE AND SUPPORT

[*Comment:* *Most software publishing agreements have a provision for maintenance, that is, ongoing error correction. No one writes completely "bug-free" software; even after testing and acceptance bugs and errors appear. Therefore, developers should not want to give a warranty that the code is bug-free or without errors. Often the agreement makes it clear that no such warranty is given. (Otherwise a broad warranty will normally be implied under state statutory law.) As is explained in Chapter 8, the upper case letters of the following provision are legally required for these types of disclaimers. The rather stilted language is necessary because it is keyed to statutory provisions.*]

22.1 Developer and Publisher agree that due to the nature of complex computer programs such as the Program, Developer cannot warrant that the Program will be entirely free of all bugs and logic errors. The Program is licensed "AS IS." EXCEPT AS PROVIDED BELOW IN THE PROVISION ENTITLED INTELLECTUAL PROPERTY WARRANTY, ALL WARRANTIES EXPRESS OR IMPLIED, INCLUDING IMPLIED WARRANTIES OF MERCHANTABILITY, FITNESS FOR A PARTICULAR PURPOSE AND NON-INFRINGEMENT, ARE DISCLAIMED.

22.2 [For the duration of this Agreement,] [For a period of [*number*] months after Publisher's acceptance of Final Deliverables under the Milestone Schedule,] Developer agrees to [make its best efforts to] deliver to Publisher all corrections and/or modifications necessary to correct bugs, errors and other program defects in the Program discovered by Publisher. Such corrections shall be delivered with reasonable promptness. [If such work exceeds __ hours, Publisher shall compensate Developer, in addition to Royalties otherwise due, at the rate of $ [*specify amount*] __ per hour.] [If Developer defaults in its obligations to provide such corrections, Publisher may do such work or have such work done at its own expense.] [If Developer defaults in its obligations to provide such corrections, Publisher may do such work or have such work done and deduct the cost thereof from Royalties otherwise due to Developer.]

22.3 EXCEPT AS OTHERWISE PROVIDED, THE REMEDY STATED IN THIS SECTION FOR ANY BUG, ERROR, OR OTHER PROGRAM DEFECT IS EXCLUSIVE.

[**Comment:** *The following provision will normally preclude the publisher from making any claim for lost profits, that is, the profits it would have made but for the developer's alleged failure to deliver adequate software. Again the language is dictated by statutory provisions.*]

22.4 DEVELOPER WILL NOT BE LIABLE FOR LOST PROFITS, LOST OPPORTUNITIES, OR INCIDENTAL OR CONSEQUENTIAL DAMAGES UNDER ANY CIRCUMSTANCES.

23 COPYRIGHT REGISTRATION AND NOTICES

[**Comment:** *The following provision relates to required copyright registration. Usually if the program is licensed exclusively to the publisher, the publisher will register the copyright (if it has not been previously registered). If the license is non-exclusive, normally the developer will handle registration.*]

23.1   When Publisher accepts the Final Deliverables, [Developer] [Publisher] shall promptly register the copyright and provide a copy of the Certificate of Registration to the other party. Both parties shall take reasonable steps to facilitate such registration.

*[**Comment:** The following provision relates to required copyright notices. Usually if the program is licensed exclusively to the publisher, the publisher's name will go on the copyright notice. If the license is non-exclusive, normally the developer (or other holder of the exclusive rights) will be referred to in the copyright notice. (See discussion of copyright notices in Chapter 1.) If patent rights or trademark rights are being licensed as well, you should see an attorney about the required provisions in notices that must appear on the products.]*

23.2   Publisher shall insure that each copy of the Program and any documentation contains a copyright notice indicating that the [Developer] [Publisher] holds the copyright for the Program and the Documentation. The copyright notice shall be placed on the Program and Documentation in all of the following places:

   23.2.1   Printed on each package, each license agreement and each diskette supplied to end-users;

   23.2.2   Displayed on the first screen seen by the end-user; and

   23.2.3   Printed on the first or second page of any Documentation.

24 INTELLECTUAL PROPERTY WARRANTIES

*[**Comment:** Some software publishing agreements contain a warranty that the code provided is original and does not infringe the intellectual property rights of third parties. Developers should seek to warrant only that they know of no infringement. Examples of both types of clauses are provided. In particular, the developer should seek to avoid a warranty that the product does not infringe patent rights, because it is virtually impossible to determine whether any patent or patent pending may be infringed. See discussion of patent issues in Chapter 15.*

The following text makes warranties only as to rights under United States law. Sophisticated developers will normally resist any warranty concerning foreign intellectual property laws, because it is hard to determine what foreign intellectual property rights the program might infringe. However, when the publisher plans to use the program in one or more foreign state, it may wish the indemnification provision to cover the law of some or all foreign countries.]

[Option 1: Warrants Only No Knowledge of Infringement]

24.1 Developer represents and warrants that, to the best of its knowledge: it is the owner of all right, title, and interest in the Program, it has granted no previous license inconsistent with the grant of rights contained in this Agreement, and it knows of no other person or entity that has any license or ownership interest in the Program.

24.2 Developer represents and warrants that, to the best of its knowledge: (a) all aspects of the Program are original, (b) there is no impediment to the grant of rights contained in this Agreement, and (c) no rights exist under the laws of the United States or any state thereof that the Program will infringe.

[Option 2: Broadly Warrants Non-Infringement]

24.3 Developer represents and warrants that it is the owner of all right, title, and interest in the Program, that it has granted no previous license inconsistent with the grant in this Agreement, and that no other person or entity has any license or ownership interest.

24.4 Developer represents and warrants that the Program and all aspects of it are original, that Developer has full and absolute right to make the grant of rights contained in this Agreement, and that no rights exist under the laws of the United States or any state thereof that the Program will infringe.

25 INDEMNIFICATION

*[**Comment:** In the following section, the developer indemnifies the publisher against infringement claims. Sometimes there is broad indemnification: the developer must pay all costs and liability for any intellectual property suit against the publisher (even if it turns out that the suit is without merit). Sometimes there is a narrow indemnification: the developer must pay only if it turns out that there was infringement and the developer was aware of it. Obviously, the publisher will want the broad indemnification and the developer will want the narrow one. Much less commonly, agreements are negotiated in which the patent infringement indemnification is reversed, that is, the publisher indemnifies the developer from patent infringement liability. These reverse provisions are sometimes negotiated where a large company is seeking to develop a new area of software technology, and has contracted with a small specialized developer. The issue of who indemnifies whom is for negotiation.]*

[Option 1. Narrow Indemnification:]

25.1   If any third party brings any lawsuit or proceeding based upon a claim that the Program breaches the patent, copyright, or trade secret rights of such third party ("Claim") and if it is determined that such infringement has occurred and that the third party intellectual property rights involved were known to the Developer prior to its delivery of the Final Deliverables, then Developer shall, for as long as copies of the Program sold by Publisher are in use, indemnify and hold Publisher harmless against any loss, damage, expense, or cost, including reasonable attorneys' fees, arising from the Claim.

[Option 2. Broad Indemnification:]

25.2   Developer agrees to indemnify and hold Publisher harmless against any loss, damage, expense, or cost, including reasonable attorneys' fees, arising out of any claim, demand, proceeding or lawsuit by a third party based on any assertion that the Program breaches the patent, copyright, or trade secret rights of such third party ("Claim").

25.3   The foregoing indemnification obligation shall be effective only if: [Publisher is not substantially in default of its Royalty obligations,] [Publisher has given prompt notice of the Claim and permitted Developer an opportunity to defend,] [Publisher has reasonably cooperated in the defense of the claim] [the infringement does not result from Publisher's modification of the Program.] [To reduce or mitigate damages, Developer may at its own expense procure the right for Publisher to continue licensing and distributing the Program or replace it with a non-infringing product.]

[Optional Provision:]

25.4   From the date of the notice from Publisher informing Developer of any Claim, Publisher shall have the right to withhold Royalty payments due Developer under the terms of this Agreement as security for Developer's obligation to indemnify Publisher.

26   LIABILITY CAP

*[**Comment:** The parties can bargain about a limit to liability if things go wrong. The party more exposed is the developer, who has promised to deliver valuable software and will harm the publisher if it fails to fulfill that promise. While the rules on damages are not always easy to apply, a developer who fails to deliver the software or delivers defective*

software could be liable for substantial sums, depending on circumstances and on which other provisions are included.

One common option, illustrated in the following text, is to place a cap on the developer's potential liability. Note that as worded, the following clause limits liability for any reason, and therefore would also limit any liability of the developer under the intellectual property warranty and indemnification clauses. It is common that a limitation of damages clause be stated in all capital letters.]

26.1   DEVELOPER'S LIABILITY TO PUBLISHER FOR ANY AND ALL OTHER MATTERS RELATED TO THE PROGRAM OR THIS AGREEMENT SHALL NOT EXCEED [*SPECIFIC AMOUNT*] [THE TOTAL OF PAYMENTS RECEIVED BY DEVELOPER].

27   INFRINGEMENT OF RIGHTS IN THE PROGRAM

*[**Comment:** The agreement will usually provide which party may act if a third party infringes the program copyright or wrongfully uses a licensed trade secret or patent. If the agreement grants the publisher a broad exclusive license, usually the publisher will have the choice of suing the third party. In the case of a narrow license or a non-exclusive license, the prerogative will normally belong to the developer. The following text reflects both options.]*

27.1   Each party shall notify the other of any infringements of the copyrights, patent, trademarks or trade secret rights of the Program. [Publisher] [Developer] shall have the option but not the obligation to seek redress for infringement at its own expense. If such party declines or fails to sue for infringement in a reasonable time, the other party may proceed.

27.2   Any recovery by Publisher from any proceeding or law suit or assertion of rights concerning the copyrights or other intellectual property rights in the Program shall go first to repay attorneys' fees and expenses, and any remainder shall be treated as Net Revenues for purposes of calculation of Royalties under the terms of this Agreement.

27.3   If Publisher has declined to pursue such claim or suit, and if the Developer enforces such rights, Developer shall retain any recovery from the claim or suit.

28   TERM

[Option 1. Specified Term:]

28.1   This Agreement shall commence on the Effective Date and [shall be in effect for a term of [*number*] years] [shall be in effect for the term of the copyright of the Program, unless sooner terminated in accordance with the provisions of this Agreement].

[Option 2. Automatic Renewal:]

28.2   This Agreement shall commence on the Effective Date and shall be in effect for a term of [number] years unless sooner terminated in accordance with the provisions of this Agreement. At the end of such term, and at the end of each successive term, this Agreement shall automatically be renewed for a term of an additional [*number*] years, unless terminated by either party by written notice given no less than sixty (60) days before the end of such period, or unless the Agreement is sooner terminated in accordance with the provisions of this Agreement.

29   TERMINATION

[Comment: Note that the part of the following provisions which allow a party to terminate in case of the bankruptcy of another party may be ineffective under United States bankruptcy law in some cases.]

29.1   Developer may terminate the Agreement:

29.1.1   Upon filing of any voluntary filing by the Publisher or upon any involuntary petition against the Publisher under the Bankruptcy Code that is not dismissed within thirty (30) days after filing, any receivership or any assignment of substantially all the assets of Publisher for the benefit of creditors.

29.1.2   Upon Publisher's ceasing to publish the Program or failing to make it available for licensing to the Computer Trade, end-users, or other permitted customers for more than thirty (30) days.

29.1.3   If any Royalty payment due Developer is not made on time and as required, and Publisher fails to cure such default within thirty (30) days after receipt of notice specifying the default.

29.1.4   If Publisher otherwise materially and substantially defaults on its obligations under this Agreement, and Publisher fails to cure such default within thirty (30) days after receipt of notice specifying the default in reasonable detail.

29.2   Publisher may terminate this agreement upon Developer's material and substantial breach of this Agreement, if such breach is not cured after thirty (30) days written notice specifying the breach in reasonable detail.

29.3   Notwithstanding termination of this Agreement:

29.3.1 The obligations of Developer under the section entitled Indemnification shall remain in effect.

29.3.2 The obligations of both parties under the section entitled Confidentiality shall remain in effect.

29.3.3 Publisher may market, license and distribute [up to [*number*]] copies of the Program manufactured as of the date of termination [including printed and produced but unassembled inventory].

29.3.4 Any unpaid Royalties and Royalties earned by post-termination sales or licensing of the Program, and those due or accrued as of the termination date, shall be paid promptly to Developer.

29.3.5 End-users that obtained the program pursuant to the terms of this Agreement may continue to use the Program indefinitely.

29.3.6 Each party shall return all papers and other media containing Confidential Information received from the other [including all source code].

29.3.7 Each party may pursue claims it has against the other for any breach of the terms of the Agreement.

29.4 Upon the termination of this Agreement, all rights in the Program granted to Publisher, including rights in all modifications created by Developer, shall revert to Developer (or such person or entity as Developer may designate in writing), and the license granted to Publisher in this Agreement shall terminate. [In addition, Developer's shall be entitled to obtain, at its option, a transfer of Publisher's rights to any other modifications to the Program in exchange for payment of Publisher's out-of-pocket cost for such modifications.] Publisher shall execute all instruments reasonably required to confirm such reversion of rights and termination of license [or to effect such transfer of rights to modifications].

[Optional Provision:]

30 SOURCE CODE ESCROW

[*Comment:* *As noted in Chapter 9, many publishing agreements provide for delivery of source code. Where source code is not delivered, the publisher may insist that the source code be put in an escrow, so that it can be reached if the developer becomes unwilling or unable to maintain it. Source code escrows are discussed in Chapter 12 and a sample source code escrow agreement (omitted here) can be found in this Appendix as Form 12-3 and on diskette as ESCROW.W51. The escrow agreement to be signed as part of a pub-*

lishing deal would normally be attached as a schedule to the agreement. The language noting that the escrow agreement is "supplemental" to this agreement is keyed to a provision of the Bankruptcy Code and is designed to help make the escrow agreement effective in case of a bankruptcy.]

30.1   Upon the delivery of the Final Deliverables, the parties shall enter into an Escrow Agreement, which is supplemental to this agreement, in the form attached as Schedule ___, and Developer shall make deposits of source code and documentation as required in the Escrow Agreement. The deposited materials shall be released to Developer or to Publisher as provided in the Escrow Agreement.

31   REMEDIES

31.1   Except as is otherwise provided in this Agreement, the parties shall have such remedies for breach or termination as are provided by applicable law.

31.2   The parties agree that in the case of the breach of any provision of the section of this agreement entitled Confidentiality [or Exclusivity] [or relating to the scope of permitted use of the Program], the aggrieved party will suffer immediate and irreparable harm, and that immediate injunctive relief will therefore be appropriate.

[Optional Provision:]

32   ARBITRATION

[Comment: As noted in Chapter 5, it is common to include arbitration clauses in these agreements. Arbitration is certainly not cheap, but it is quicker and less expensive than litigation in court. However, arbitrators cannot issue court orders such as injunctions requiring parties not to disclose trade secrets or confidential information. For this reason, arbitration clauses often carve out an exception which allows the parties to resort to a court of law to seek such relief.]

32.1   Any dispute relating to the interpretation or performance of this Agreement, other than claims for preliminary injunctive relief or other pre-judgment remedies, shall be resolved at the request of either party through binding arbitration. Arbitration shall be conducted in *[city, state]* under the rules and procedures of the American Arbitration Association ("AAA"). The parties shall request that the AAA appoint a panel of three arbitrators and, if feasible, include one arbitrator of the three sho shall possess knowledge of computer software and its distribution; however, the arbitration shall proceed even if such a person is unavailable.

33   ATTORNEYS' FEES

33.1   In the event of any litigation or arbitration between the parties arising under this Agreement, the prevailing party shall be entitled to recover, in addition to any other relief granted or awarded, its reasonable costs and expenses, including reasonable attorneys' fees incurred in the proceeding.

34   GENERAL PROVISIONS

*[**Comment:** The following are some general provisions that are fairly standard and normally not a subject of much serious negotiation or debate, with the possible exception of the clause on assignments. Similar provisions are found in many commercial contracts.]*

34.1   **Relationship of Parties.** Developer shall be deemed to have the status of an independent contractor, and nothing in this Agreement shall be deemed to place the parties in the relationship of employer-employee, principal-agent, partners or joint venturers. Developer is responsible for all payments to its subcontractors.

34.2   **Payment of Taxes.** Developer shall be responsible for any withholding taxes, payroll taxes, disability insurance payments, unemployment taxes and other taxes or charges incurred in the performance of the Agreement with respect to Developer's employees, servants, agents and subcontractors.

[Optional Provision]

*[**Comment:** Most contracts have provisions to excuse delays for "force majeure" or "acts of God." Some publishers may want a shorter limit on extension of time than the six months provided for in this form.]*

34.3   **Force Majeure.** Neither party shall be deemed in default of the Agreement to the extent that performance of their obligations or attempts to cure any breach are delayed or prevented by reason of any act of God, fire, natural disaster, accident, act of government, shortages of materials or supplies or any other cause beyond the control of such party ("Force Majeure") provided that such party gives the other party written notice thereof promptly and, in any event, within fifteen (15) days of discovery thereof and uses its best efforts to cure the delay. In the event of such a Force Majeure, the time for performance or cure shall be extended for a period equal to the duration of the Force Majeure but not in excess of six (6) months.

*[**Comment:** The following provisions on assignment are typical. Usually the developer will assent to an assignment, as long as the assignee of the agreement has the resources and the will to market, to promote the program, and to pay royalties. Owners of busi-*

nesses want the freedom to sell or assign all the assets of a business, including all its con-tracts; that is the purpose of the next optional clause, which gives the developer no ability to prevent an assignment in the case of a sale of substantially all the assets of the publish-er's business. The developer may want the publisher to remain responsible for payment if the assignee fails to pay; this is provided by an optional clause. Normally the publisher will have contracted for the skills of the developer and will resist granting the developer any right to assign its obligations under the agreement.]

34.4   **Assignments.** This Agreement may not be assigned by Publisher in whole or in part without consent of Developer [which the Developer may withhold in its absolute discretion] [which consent shall not be unreasonably withheld]. [Pub-lisher may assign this Agreement, without Developer's consent, to any third party which succeeds by operation of law to, purchases or otherwise acquires substantially all of the assets of Publisher and assumes Publisher's obligations.] [Notwithstanding any assignment, Publisher shall remain bound by the obliga-tions of this Agreement, and shall be obligated to fulfill all obligations if the assignee fails to perform as required by this Agreement.] Developer may not assign its obligations under this agreement without Publisher's written consent, which Publisher may withhold in its complete discretion.

34.5   **Partial Invalidity.** Should any provision of this Agreement be held to be void, invalid or inoperative, the remaining provisions of this Agreement shall not be affected and shall continue in effect as though such provisions were deleted.

34.6   **No Waiver.** The failure of either party to exercise any right or the waiver by either party of any breach, shall not prevent a subsequent exercise of such right or be deemed a waiver of any subsequent breach of the same or any other term of the Agreement.

34.7   **Notice.** Any notice required or permitted to be sent shall be in writing and shall be sent in a manner requiring a signed receipt, such as Federal Express, courier delivery, or if mailed, registered or certified mail, return receipt requested. Notice is effective upon receipt. Notice to Developer shall be addressed to [*specify name, title, and address*] or such other person or address as Developer may designate. Notice to Publisher shall be addressed to [*specify name, title, and address*] or such other person or address as Publisher may designate.

*[**Comment:** The following "entire agreement clause" (also known as an "integration clause") is designed to eliminate any claim that oral promises not in the agreement are effective. This clause, a standard feature of many types of agreements, will usually be*

enforced. If there are promises made or "side agreements" outside the text of the agreement, it is important to get them into the text.]

34.8   **Entire Agreement.** This Agreement, including the Schedules thereto, states the entire agreement between the parties on this subject and supersedes all prior negotiations, understandings and agreements between the parties concerning the subject matter. No amendment or modification of this Agreement shall be made except by a writing signed by both parties.

34.9   **Governing Law.** This Agreement shall be governed and interpreted in accordance with the substantive laws of the state of _____.

34.10   **Venue and Jurisdiction of Legal Actions.** Any legal action brought concerning this Agreement or any dispute arising from any act or omission arising from this Agreement [, including but not limited to an action to enforce an arbitration award,] shall be brought only in the courts of the state of _____ [in the county of _____] or in the federal courts located in such state [and county], and both parties agree to submit to the jurisdiction of these courts.

So agreed between the parties:

[*Name of Developer Corporation*]

BY _____

TITLE _____

DATE: _____

[*Name of Publisher Corporation*]

BY _____

TITLE _____

DATE: _____

Schedule B
MILESTONE AND PAYMENT SCHEDULE

[Comment: The following a merely an illustration. The actual deliverables and schedule would vary depending on the product, technology, functionality and specifications.]

1   DEFINITIONS

The following definitions and provisions apply to this Schedule:

1.1   "Working Model Code" shall mean Program code written by Developer that has Critical Features (as defined in the Specifications in Schedule A) implemented. This version of the program demonstrates the technical feasibility of the project.

1.2   "Alpha Code" shall mean Program code written by Developer that includes all operations, functions, capabilities, and performance in the Specifications implemented, integrated and fully functional. It is code that is not necessarily "bug free" and may be in need of adjustment and tuning of functions, operations, and graphics.

1.3   "Beta Code" shall mean Program code written by Developer that includes all operations, functions, capabilities, and performance implemented, integrated and functional substantially in accordance with the Specifications. This version shall have all known bugs and errors corrected.

1.4   Working Model Code, and Alpha Code, Beta Code shall be supplied on two sets of 3 1/2" diskettes in MS-DOS high-density format, containing [respectively] the Program version's entire compiled object code [and the version's entire source code].

[Optional Provision:]

1.5   "User Manual" shall mean a complete description of all program function and operations in simple English suitable for program users, including suitable examples, and written in accordance with Publisher's standard style for user manuals as described in the Specifications.

[Optional Provision:]

1.6   "Technical Documentation" shall mean commented source code and other documentation sufficient to permit the Program to be modified by a reasonably skilled technician with knowledge of the languages in which the Program is written but no prior knowledge of the Program.

*[**Comment:** The following text contains options as to how polished the final program code must be. Because the developer is unlikely to deliver code that is totally bug-free, the language may provide some leeway. Many agreements have specific provisions for testing before final acceptance. A test plan could be set forth on an additional schedule.]*

1.7   "Final Deliverables" shall mean the version of the Program written by Developer that has passed through user tests and which [fully] [substantially] complies with the Specifications. [This version is the Beta Code version that has been corrected to address the bugs and other issues and problem that have been documented during testing.] Final Deliverables shall include:

    1.7.1   Two [sets of] 3 1/2" diskettes in MS-DOS high density format, each containing the Program's entire compiled object code;

    [1.7.2   Two [sets of] 3 1/2" diskettes in MS-DOS high density format, each containing the Program's entire source code and one printed copy of the computer source code.]

    [1.7.3   Two [sets of] 3 1/2" diskettes in MS-DOS high density format, each containing the complete User's Manual for the Program in WordPerfect for DOS 5.1 format;]

    [1.7.4   Technical Documentation as follows: [*specify*].]

2   DELIVERY AND PAYMENT SCHEDULE

The delivery and payment schedule shall be as follows:

DUE DATE FOR DELIVERABLE (DAYS AFTER EFFECTIVE DATE OF AGREEMENT)	MILESTONE	ADVANCE PAYMENT AMOUNT
0 Days	Execution of Agreement by Both Parties	$10,000.00
50 Days	Working Model Code	10,000.00
110 Days	Alpha Code	10,000.00
140 Days	Beta Code	10,000.00
220 Days	Final Deliverables	20,000.00
	TOTAL	$60,000.00

Form 10-1: DEALER AGREEMENT CHECKLIST

Introductory Note

This is a software dealer agreement check list (on diskette as DEAL-CHK.W51). You may use it with Chapter 10 and the sample software dealer agreement, Form 102 (on diskette as DEAL-AGR.W51), to structure your negotiations. Of course, this checklist may not include all issues that need to be addressed in your transactions. You may wish to modify this checklist to better suit the needs of your business.

The order and numbering of this check list does not strictly correspond to the sections of Form 10-2, because this check list is somewhat broader in subject matter. However the order of discussion is quite similar.

1   Introduction (or Preamble)

This section of the agreement identifies the parties and states the general nature of the agreement.

2   Definitions

This section defines terms. Its purpose is to create shorthand terms for convenience and to avoid ambiguities. Terms commonly defined include: "Supplier", "Program", "Dealer", "Confidential Information", "Effective Date" (the date the agreement goes into effect).

3   Qualification of Dealer

This section contains the dealer's certification that it has sufficient technical and financial capabilities to qualify as a dealer of the supplier's software products. Often before an agreement is signed, the prospective dealer must disclose information on its financial resources and its technical experience and qualifications.

4   Grant of License

This portion of the agreement states the scope of the license that is granted to the dealer.

   4.1   What is the territory for which the license is granted?

   4.2   Is the license exclusive or non-exclusive? If it is exclusive, must the dealer meet specified sales levels to retain exclusivity?

   4.3   To whom may the dealer sell? Only to end-users? To other dealers?

4.4 Will the dealer be allowed to duplicate the software and documentation from master copies? Or will the dealers only sell copies created by the supplier? (Where the dealer is permitted to make copies, there needs to be reporting and audit mechanisms to be sure that the dealer pays for the copies that it makes.)

4.5 What products are included in the license grant? Is the grant only for listed products on an agreement schedule? Are a family of products included? Are future products included? Are rights to products only for a specified application or for a specified hardware or software platform included?

4.6 Will the supplier make custom modifications of the products as required by end-users? If so, there must be mechanisms for price estimates and for payment.

4.7 May the dealer sell only unmodified software, or may it make specified types of modifications, for example, to implement certain applications?

4.8 Does the supplier have the right to modify its products or change its product line, and to discontinue marketing some or all of its current products?

4.9 Does the supplier undertake that compatibility of data and file structure with existing software will be maintained in future versions?

4.10 Is the supplier barred from selling to end-users in the territory?

5 OEM Restrictions

5.1 Is the dealer only permitted to license the software to endusers as an OEM, that is, as part of a computer system that the dealer markets under its own trademark? If so, what are the minimum required components of the system? Must the system include both hardware and software? Must the system include the dealer's own proprietary software?

5.2 What monitoring and inspection is permitted to the supplier to insure that the dealer abides by the limitation to OEM marketing?

5.3 Can the dealer be terminated if it fails to limit its marketing of the software products to OEM transactions?

6 Trademark Issues

6.1 Does the agreement include a license for the dealer to use the supplier's trademarks?

6.2 Is the dealer permitted to identify itself as an "authorized dealer"?

6.3   What further use of the supplier's trademarks is permitted? How does the supplier control and monitor the dealer's use of its trademarks?

6.4   Does the supplier have the right to state rules for trademark use, including the use of the appropriate trademark symbol or legend?

7   Ordering, Delivery, and Payment

7.1   Does the dealer have an obligation to provide order forecasts for planning purposes?

7.2   What are the mechanics of ordering, acceptance of orders, and shipping of software products?

7.3   When is the dealer's payment for software due? In thirty days after shipment? In some other period?

7.4   What is the dealer's initial credit limit? Can the supplier adjust and alter the amount of credit allowed or change the terms of supply? Can the supplier cut off the dealer's credit altogether and require cash for any order?

7.5   If end-users return defective software products to the dealer, can the dealer get a refund in turn from the supplier? What is the process if the dealer discovers defective goods in its inventory? Can the dealer terminate the agreement if the supplier is unable to cure serious bugs and errors in the software?

7.6   What information concerning the dealer's customers goes to the supplier? Can the supplier use the information to sell non-competing products and services to the same customers?

8   Pricing

The dealer agreement must state how the dealer will be charged for becoming a dealer and for software products.

8.1   Is there an initial fee payable to the supplier on signing?

8.2   Are prices for the products specified in a schedule to the agreement?

8.3   Can the supplier change the prices charged to the dealer from time to time? Are the prices for products licensed to the dealer set at a percentage of "list price"?

8.4   Are there specified product quantity discounts for the dealer? If so, are discounts based on projected sales? If the dealer fails to order and pay for the projected volume of products, how is the discount amount reversed and paid over to the supplier?

8.5 Is there a "price protection" provision, a promise that the yearly increase in prices charged to dealers will be limited to a specified percentage?

8.6 Is there a provision for free demonstration copies?

9 Minimum Product Orders

9.1 Is the dealer required to order a minimum number or dollar amount of software products each quarter or each year? If so, how is the minimum requirement set?

9.2 Can the supplier adjust or increase the dealer's specified purchase quota?

9.3 Is the dealer required to achieve a minimum number of new customers or new installations each quarter or each year?

9.4 May the dealer be terminated if it fails to meet a specified yearly purchase quota or sales goal?

10 Other Dealer Marketing Obligations

10.1 Does the dealer undertake to use "best efforts" to make sales?

10.2 Does the dealer agree to maintain a specified level of inventory?

10.3 Must the dealer provide a specified number of sales and technical staff?

10.4 Must the dealer submit a marketing plan every year or on some other periodic basis?

11 Non-Competition

11.1 Is the dealer obligated not to carry competing products? Does this obligation extend beyond the termination of the agreement? For how long after termination? (These provisions are designed to prevent dealers from taking customers away from the supplier's product line after termination.)

11.2 Are there exceptions to the non-competition provision? For example, can the dealer market competing products if the dealer terminates the agreement because the supplier's products are defective or because product lines are discontinued?

12   Dividing the Support Obligation and the "Follow-on" Revenue

In many cases, the customer pays a yearly or other periodic fee in exchange for software support. The dealer and supplier must agree on who provides software support, and they must decide who receives what part of the substantial revenue stream generated by providing software support. There is also money to be made from licensing additional software to existing customers. The software dealer agreement sets out the framework for dividing "follow-on" responsibilities and revenue.

   12.1   Who does the customer pay for software support? The supplier? The dealer? Both?

   12.2   Does the end-user deal only with the dealer to obtain support or do support services come in part from the supplier and in part from the dealer?

   12.3   Assuming the dealer provides all software support, is there a yearly or monthly fee payable from the dealer to the supplier for every customer who receives software support?

   12.4   How do the dealer and the supplier coordinate the process of identifying errors, fixing bugs, and installing corrected software versions on the customers' computers? Is the supplier obligated to fix errors reported by the dealer (or to use "reasonable efforts" to fix them)?

   12.5   If the dealer licenses additional software to existing customers, is the discount from list price that the dealer gets less favorable than the discount that applies for licensing to new customers?

13   Supplier Marketing Support

   13.1   Is the supplier obligated to supply sales literature to the dealer?

   13.2   Is the supplier required to provide sales leads or other sales support?

   13.3   Is the supplier obligated to provide technical assistance to aid the dealer in responding to RFPs received from prospective customers?

14   Non-Infringement Warranties and Indemnification

This section deals with: (1) the supplier's warranty that it actually owns the software licensed to the dealer and (2) what happens if the dealer is sued by a third party on the claim that the product infringes the third party's trade secret, copyright, or patent. The issues include:

14.1 What warranty does the dealer give to the dealer that the supplier owns all necessary intellectual property rights in the program? What is the dealer's remedy if it turns out that the supplier does not have all required rights to the software?

14.2 If an infringement suit is brought against the dealer, is the supplier required to defend the claim? Does the supplier also agree to hold the dealer "harmless", that is, repay any amount that the dealer may have to pay account of the infringement claim?

14.3 Does the supplier have the right to control or settle the claim?

14.4 Does the supplier have the right to cure the problem by designing around it or providing non-infringing code, and does it then have the right to require the dealer, and the dealer's customers, to use substitute non-infringing code?

14.5 Does the supplier have the right to terminate distribution of a software product (and require the dealer to terminate its customers's right to use the software), if the supplier cannot find a cost-effective means to deal with the infringement claim?

15 Product Warranties and Remedies

A software dealer agreement will normally have a section in which the supplier disclaims product warranties and limits damage claims. The dealer likewise promises to include similar disclaimers and limitation in any contracts with its customers. There are a few variations to consider.

15.1 Does the agreement specify a form of end-user agreement that the dealer must use? May the supplier change the required end-user agreement form?

15.2 If the dealer gets sued by an end-user on account of allegedly defective software, does the supplier agree to defend the suit or bear the loss?

15.3 Is there a cap on the supplier's potential liability to the dealer under the agreement?

16 Confidentiality

16.1 Will the dealer be receiving confidential information of the supplier that it will be obligated to keep confidential?

16.2 Will the supplier be receiving confidential information of the dealer that it will be obligated to keep confidential?

17   Term and Termination

17.1   When does the agreement become effective? How long is the original term of the agreement? Is there an automatic renewal provision? Does either party or both parties have the option to terminate at any time or on specified notice?

17.2   Under what specified circumstances may the agreement relationship be terminated? Will the agreements provide that the agreement can be terminated upon a material breaches by the other party? On bankruptcy or insolvency? On failure to meet required sales levels (discussed above)? Will there be other specified events that allow termination? Are there opportunities to cure some defaults before the agreement can be terminated?

17.3   If the dealership is terminated, are the dealer's contracts with it existing customers to be assigned to the supplier or to a new dealer appointed by the supplier? Does the dealer have an obligation to turn over to the supplier records or information that relates to the customers?

17.4   If the agreement is terminated, what happens to the dealer's existing inventory of software products? May the dealer sell out its inventory? Will the supplier repurchase the inventory?

17.5   What obligations survive termination? Confidentiality? Non-Competition?

17.6   If the dealership is terminated, do the licenses held by end-users that are customers of the dealer remain in effect? (Normally they do.)

18   Remedies

This section can limit or expand litigation remedies for breach of agreement. Normally the agreement will provide for injunctive relief for breach of confidentiality and non-competition obligations.

19   Arbitration

This section governs whether the parties are required to submit any dispute to arbitration. Arbitration is quite expensive but it is faster and less expensive than litigation. Preliminary relief such as injunctions must be sought in court and are normally "carved out" from the issues to be submitted to arbitration. Some issues might be:

19.1   Where does arbitration take place?

19.2   What arbitration rules apply?

19.3   How many arbitrators sit, and how are they selected?

20   Legal Fees

Is the loser in arbitration or litigation required to pay the winner's legal fees?

21   General Provisions

These are some fairly standard clauses found in a variety of contracts. Included are: choice of state law, delays caused by "acts of God," responsibility for employment taxes, etc. See Form 12-2.

Form 10-2: ANNOTATED SOFTWARE DEALER AGREEMENT

Introductory Note

This is a sample software dealer agreement with annotations. (A copy can be found on the diskette as DEAL-AGR.W51.) This draft includes a number of provisions that commonly occur in these agreements. However, every deal is unique and no one form can include every possible variation.

For convenience, I have used the term "supplier" to refer to the party that contracts with and supplies the software dealer. In using this form, one could substitute other terms for "supplier," such as "publisher," "manufacturer," or "licensor."

As is noted in Chapter 10, the supplier and the dealer must share the revenue that comes from the dealer's customer, and must cooperate in providing software support to those customers. There are a number of ways that these issues of sharing benefits and burdens can be addressed. The following form contains one common solution: Only the dealer deals directly with the customer, and the dealer obtains fixes and technical support from the supplier. The dealer must pay license fees to get products. Before the dealer is permitted to supply software support to a customer (after the initial warranty period expires), the dealer must pay a yearly support fee to the supplier for that customer. In essence, the dealer pays each year for the right to sell support services to the customer. The dealer remains free to decide the license fees and fees for product support that it will charge to customers. Of course, there are many other possible arrangements, as is discussed in Chapter 10.

Suppliers often use counsel to create a "standard form" of software dealer agreement so that the terms of its relationship with its various dealers will be similar. In many cases, the attempt to impose uniform terms will limit the supplier's flexibility in negotiations.

A software dealer agreement is a document that both sides will need to live with for a number of years. While the following form and the other materials provided in this book can guide negotiations and help the parties create their initial draft, each side to such a bargain should agree to a deal and sign only with the benefit of advice of legal counsel.

The schedules to this dealer agreement are not included here because their details are highly dependant on the facts of particular deals, and their general content is self-explanatory.

As is noted in Chapter 10, many of the issues and terms in this sample dealer agreement may also arise in negotiations between a supplier and a sales representative or between a supplier and a distributor.

SOFTWARE DEALER AGREEMENT
BETWEEN [*NAME OF SUPPLIER*]
AND [*NAME OF DEALER*]

1   INTRODUCTION

[*Comment: The introduction should set forth in plain language the general nature and purpose of the agreement. This section of a contract is often written more formally, with the word "whereas" introducing each sentence.*]

1.1   This is an agreement for [*Name of Supplier*] to supply software products to [*Name of Dealer*] and to permit [*Name of Dealer*] to act as an authorized dealer and to license such software products to end-users.

2   DEFINITIONS

[*Comment: The definitions section should define key terms of the agreement to avoid ambiguity and simplify drafting by providing shorthand names for persons and things. Additional definitions may appear in schedules or in the text. The definitions here are in alphabetical order.*]

As used in this Agreement, the following definitions shall apply:

2.1   "Agreement" shall mean this Agreement between Supplier and Dealer.

2.2   "Confidential Information" shall mean any information relating to or disclosed in the course of the Agreement, which is or should be reasonably understood to be confidential or proprietary to the disclosing party. "Confidential Information" shall not include information (a) already lawfully known to the receiving party, (b) disclosed in published materials, (c) generally known to the public, or (d) lawfully obtained from any third party.

2.3   "Customer(s)" shall mean persons or entities that license Products from Dealer for their own business, commercial or personal use, but not for remarketing, time-sharing or service bureau use [, provided however that Customers may be only persons or businesses engaged in *specify field of use or particular industry*].

2.4   "Customer Agreement" shall mean a written license agreement between Dealer and a Customer relating to the Product(s).

2.5   "Dealer" shall mean [*Name of Corporation*] of [*City, State*].

2.6   "Dealer Discount Schedule" shall mean a list of applicable dealer discounts from the license fees stated on the Retail License Fee List. The Dealer Discount Schedule shall be subject to change without prior notice. The present Dealer Discount Schedule is attached to this Agreement as Schedule __.

2.7   "Delivery Date" for any Product shall mean the date that Dealer has shipped the Product to a Customer.

2.8   "Documentation" shall mean written or printed materials, and materials in non-software media, accompanying a Product.

2.9   "Effective Date" shall mean [*specify date*][the date upon which both parties have signed this Agreement].

2.10   "License Fee" shall be the amount payable from Dealer to Supplier for a license to Product(s) in accordance with the terms of this Agreement.

2.11   "Primary Support" shall mean the following services to be provided by Dealer to Customers:

2.11.1   Providing the Customer with a reasonable level of assistance in installing the Product(s).

2.11.2   Providing the Customer with a reasonable level of training.

2.11.3   Providing technical advice to the Customer on using the Product(s) by means of telephone support.

2.11.4   When a Customer reports a software error, accessing Supplier's error tracking system to determine whether the error matches an error previously reported and whether a software patch, a change to the current version of the Product, or other recommendation, has been identified as a response to the error.

2.11.5   Providing the Customer a reasonable level of assistance in installing any available software patch or version of the Product or in implementing any recommendation or solution to deal with software errors.

2.11.6   With regard to software errors not matching those in Supplier's error tracking system, acquiring and using tools required to acquire diagnostic reports, memory dumps, and other materials, and providing and employing such diagnostic services as may be required by the circumstances or requested by Supplier to aid in resolution of software errors.

2.11.7　Providing such other assistance to Supplier in dealing with Product errors as Supplier may request.

2.11.8　Providing Customer assistance in implementing fixes or recommendations as implemented by Secondary Support.

2.12　"Product" or "Products" shall consist of computer software products [identified as follows: [*list products to be licensed*]] [of the following type: [*specify field of use or product type*]] [on Supplier's Retail License Fee List, as it may be in effect from time to time] [including new versions, updates, patches and enhancements]. [Such Products shall consist of packages including software on diskette, tape, CD-ROM, or other computer media, Documentation, and such other materials for the user as Supplier may include.]

2.13　"Retail License Fee List" shall mean Supplier's list of available Products and retail license fees for such products. Such list is subject to change without prior notice. A copy of Supplier's current Retail License Fee List, relating to the Products, current as of the Effective Date, is attached as Schedule __.

2.14　"Secondary Support" shall mean the following services to be provided by Supplier to Dealer:

2.14.1　Using reasonable efforts to modify the Products to correct, fix, or circumvent errors, and modifying Documentation, as Supplier shall deem appropriate, to respond to reported errors.

2.14.2　Using reasonable efforts to assist Dealer in providing Primary Support.

2.14.3　In the discretion of Supplier, providing updates, enhancements, and new versions of the Products.

2.15　"Software Support Fee" shall be the amount payable from Dealer to Supplier on a periodic basis in exchange for the provision of Secondary Support from Supplier to Dealer and as a precondition for Dealer to supply Primary Support to a Customer for a Product.

2.16　"Supplier" shall mean [*Name of Corporation*] of [*City, State*].

2.17　"Supported Products" shall consist of Products for which Supplier is currently supplying software support and maintenance as listed from time to time in Supplier's Supported Products List. A copy of Supplier's Supported Products List is attached as Schedule __.

2.18　"Territory" shall mean [*define geographic scope of Dealer's territory*].

3   DEALER'S REPRESENTATIONS

3.1   Dealer represents that it has skill and expertise in computer and software licensing, installation, and marketing, and that it also has sufficient qualified staff and sufficient financial resources to carry out all of its obligations under this Agreement.

4   FINANCIAL QUALIFICATION OF DEALER

4.1   Dealer shall at all times maintain a good credit rating and sound financial condition. Dealer shall, upon request, promptly submit to Supplier financial statements and such other financial information as Supplier shall specify in order to verify Dealer's compliance with this provision. Failure to comply with this provision shall be a material breach of the Agreement which, in Supplier's discretion, shall be grounds for termination.

5   GRANT OF LICENSE

5.1   During the term of this Agreement, Supplier grants to Dealer [a non-exclusive] [exclusive] license solely to distribute and license the Products in unaltered form to Customers within the Territory.

5.2   Dealer may grant licenses to Customers only under a valid agreement containing substantially the same terms as those set forth in Supplier's form of Customer Agreement, as it may be in effect from time to time. Supplier's current form of Customer Agreement is attached as Schedule __. Supplier reserves the right to modify the Customer Agreement, or to specify that differing forms of Customer Agreement shall be used with some of the Products. Supplier reserves the right to specify that certain Products shall be supplied to Customer subject to restrictions to be stated in the Customer Agreement forms, on field of use, number of users or concurrent users, or subject to other restrictions or terms. However, Dealer shall have the right to set all prices charged to Customers.

5.3   Supplier grants to Dealer a nonexclusive right and license to use its trademarks for the purpose of marketing the Products only: (1) in signs and stationery of Dealer indicating its status as an authorized distributor, (2) in such marketing materials as Supplier may choose to supply to Dealer, and (3) in such advertising and other uses as Supplier may authorize in writing. Dealer may not use the trademarks in connection with any goods other than those of Supplier. Except as expressly authorized in writing by Supplier, no other uses of Supplier's trademarks are authorized. Supplier shall have the right, upon reasonable notice, to audit and inspect Dealer's use of its trademarks. Dealer shall provide to Supplier, upon request, such materials and information as Supplier may require to verify Dealer's compliance with this paragraph.

5.4 No ownership right is granted to any intellectual property relating to the Products. No right is granted for Dealer to replicate, produce, copy, or alter the Products. No right is granted for Dealer to use, distribute, rent, lease, lend, supply, or market the Products, except as expressly provided for in this Agreement. Dealer may not decompile, disassemble, or reverse engineer the Products.

[Optional Provision:]

6 DEALER'S OPTION ON NEW PRODUCTS

*[**Comment:** Sometimes the parties will agree that the dealer will have the option of carrying any new products that supplier may introduce. The following text contains such a provision.]*

6.1 If Supplier develops and markets new products [in the field of [*specify field*]], Supplier will give Dealer the option, exercisable within thirty (30) days after notice, to distribute such new products on the same terms and conditions as are applicable to Products.

[Optional Provisions:]

7 RESTRICTION TO OEM MARKETING

*[**Comment:** When the dealer is an OEM who will be marketing the software as part of a system sold under its own name, the agreement will restrict the dealer to OEM marketing. The following is a sample of the text to do so.]*

7.1 Dealer certifies and promises that it will license the Products only as part of a system (the "System") that shall include [computer hardware,] system software, and other applications software, and that such System will include services for installation and/or for training and technical support. The System with which the Products are distributed shall consist of at least the [hardware and] software items specified in Schedule __ to this Agreement. Licensing of the Products, other than as part of such a System, shall be a material breach of this Agreement. The failure of Dealer to abide by the restriction in this Section shall be grounds for Supplier, at its option, to terminate this Agreement.

7.2 Dealer represents that it has obtained all rights and licenses needed to market any and all [hardware and] software that may be supplied to Customers with the Products in the System.

[Optional Provision:]

8 **INITIAL FEE**

[*Comment:* It is common for a dealer agreement to require the dealer to pay a fee that is due on signing. The main purpose of the fee is to help defray legal and administrative costs of negotiation of the arrangement and help pay for initial support for the dealer. However, as noted in Chapter 12, these up-front payments may be construed as franchise fees in some states and thereby trigger franchise statute protection for dealers under state law. Controls imposed on dealers in the agreements may also be relevant to the application of franchise law. In some cases, one may avoid the applicable franchise statute if the agreement provides for a specified initial order of products, rather than a fee. You should contact legal counsel if you wish to determine how state franchise laws may affect your agreement.]

8.1 In consideration of the license granted by this Agreement, Dealer agrees to pay to Supplier an initial non-refundable fee of $[*amount*].

9 **PRODUCT ORDERS AND SUPPLY**

9.1 No less than thirty (30) days before the beginning of each calendar quarter, Dealer shall submit to Supplier in writing the volume of Products that Dealer expects to license to Customers in the upcoming quarter and for the next following quarter, specifying expected volume for each type and model of Product.

[Optional Provision:]

[*Comment:* The following clause requires the dealer to order and pay for a required quota of products. Such a quota could be set by formula, for example as a percentage of the previous years sales or as specified in dollars. Other requirements are possible, for example a minimum number of new customers.]

9.2 During the calendar year beginning on [*date*], and during each succeeding calendar year, Dealer shall order, accept, and pay the amount due for at least a certain specified amount of Products ("Required Yearly Quota of Products") as [specified in] [calculated in accordance with] Schedule ___ to this Agreement. Failure of Dealer to order, accept, and pay the amount due for the Required Yearly Quota of Products shall be grounds for Supplier, in its sole discretion, to terminate this Agreement, pursuant to the provisions on Termination. [The parties may increase or decrease the Required Yearly Quota of Products by written agreement at any time.]

9.3   Supplier shall use reasonable efforts to fulfil each of Dealer's orders within twenty (20) days of receipt. Supplier reserves the right to apportion Products in its sole discretion when demand exceeds available supply [, provided that Supplier may not terminate this Agreement due to the failure of Dealer to order, accept, and pay for the Required Yearly Quota of Products if such failure was due to lack of supply].

9.4   When Supplier delivers the Products to a common carrier, risk of loss and damage to the Products shall shift to Dealer.

9.5   Shipments will be deemed to comply with quantity and type ordered unless Dealer notifies Supplier of any errors in filing shipments within twenty (20) days of receipt.

10   DEALER'S PAYMENTS FOR PRODUCT LICENSES

*[**Comment:** The most common pricing mechanism is to give the dealer a discount from "list price," although other pricing mechanisms are possible. Often the discount increases with increased volume of purchases in accordance with a schedule. In some agreements the discount schedule is fixed for the duration of the agreement; in others, as in this sample agreement, the supplier has the right to change the discount schedule.]*

10.1   For all Products, Dealer shall pay the amount of Supplier's listed License Fee for the Products stated on Supplier's Retail License Fee List, as it may be published by Supplier from time to time, less the applicable Dealer Discount calculated in accordance with the then current Dealer Discount Schedule, which supplier may issue from time to time. Costs for shipment shall be borne by Dealer and included in the invoice price. Risk of loss shall be borne by Dealer upon shipment.

10.2   Payment shall be due thirty (30) days from the shipment date listed on the invoice, with the following exception: Supplier may set a limit on the amount of credit applicable to Dealer ("Credit Limit"), and for any order or part of an order that raises the amount due to Supplier to a level in excess of the Credit Limit, the Products shall be paid for in advance. The Credit Limit shall initially be the amount stated in Schedule __ to this Agreement. Supplier, in its discretion, may raise or lower Dealer's Credit Limit at any time or may require that all Products be paid for in cash.

10.3   Payments to Supplier not made when due shall bear interest, compounded monthly, at a rate of 1% per month or the highest rate then lawful, whichever is lower, from the date the payment was due until it is received by Supplier. Arrearage in excess of $[*amount*] that is not paid within ten (10) days of demand shall be grounds for termination of this Agreement at the option of Supplier.

11   SAMPLE COPIES

11.1   Supplier shall provide Dealer with [*number*] sample copies of each of the Products currently on Supplier's Retail License Fee List. From time to time, Supplier may provide additional sample copies of versions or Products. Dealer may not license, distribute, loan, or market any Product sent by Supplier that is marked "sample" or "not for relicensing." Such materials may be used solely for demonstration purposes.

12   OTHER OBLIGATIONS OF DEALER

12.1   Dealer shall use its best efforts to promote and market the Products. Dealer shall provide sufficient qualified staff to carry out its obligation to market. Dealer shall pursue any marketing leads received from Supplier.

12.2   Dealer shall require, prior to shipment of the Products to any Customer, that the Customer execute a Customer Agreement as provided for above.

[**Comment:** *The dealer's support obligations to customer, required by this agreement, must match the support obligation that the dealer will agree to provide under its own agreements with customers. The following provisions are based on the assumption that the customer will receive one year's maintenance included in the initial license fee that it pays to the dealer and then will have to pay a yearly fee for support. The initial period of support could be changed—or its duration could be made variable. The following provisions require that the dealer pay a software support fee to the supplier before each anniversary as a condition of the dealer providing continued support to the customer. Of course the dealer will seek a higher software support fee from the customer before making its own payment to the supplier. An alternative sometimes used is for the supplier to provide support to the customers and to have the customer pay support fees directly to the supplier.*]

12.3   For the period from the Delivery Date of each Product to a Customer to the first anniversary of the Delivery Date, Dealer shall provide Primary Support to such Customer for such Product.

12.4   If on or before each anniversary of the Delivery Date of the Product to a Customer, Dealer has paid to Supplier the Software Support Fee applicable to such Product with respect to such Customer, then Dealer shall continue to provide Primary Support to such Customer for such Product. If Dealer fails to make such Software Support Fee payment to Supplier, Dealer shall cease provision of Primary Support to such Customer for such Product. Dealer shall make each Software Support Fee payment to Supplier together with an identification in writing of the Product and Customer as to whom payment is made, in such form or format, and including such other information, as Supplier may require.

12.5 Applicable Software Support Fees shall be stated by Supplier in a list made available to Dealer ("Software Support Fees List"), which may change from time to time without prior notice. Supplier's current Software Support Fees List is attached as Schedule __ to this Agreement.

12.6 If Software Support has been terminated or has lapsed for a Product licensed to a Customer, Dealer may reinstate its right and obligation to provide such Customer with Primary Support if Dealer has paid to Supplier (1) the annual Software Support Fee in effect at the time, plus (2) a reinstatement fee equal to the greater of (a) the difference between the License Fee paid to Supplier for the Product to be supported and the applicable License Fee for the then-current version of such Product and (b) $[specify amount]. Upon reinstatement of Software Support, Dealer will be supplied with the current version of the Product, and Dealer shall arrange for the upgrade of the Product in the Customer's computer system to the current version.

12.7 Dealer assumes sole responsibility for the selection and recommendation of the Products to achieve the desired results and business purposes of Customers.

12.8 Dealer shall identify and promptly inform Supplier of any design or programming errors or omissions in the Products of which it becomes aware. Dealer may suggest features or improvements for the Products or ideas for additional products. Such information and suggestions and any product, modification or improvement that results from such information or suggestions shall be the sole property of Supplier.

12.9 No later than ten (10) days after the end of each month, Dealer shall deliver to Supplier, in the format set forth as Schedule __ to this Agreement, a written report of the following information:

12.9.1 A description of the amount and type of Products newly licensed to Customers during the month and the revenues derived from each such licensing transaction;

12.9.2 A statement of all revenues received from Customers on account of support;

12.9.3   A copy of each Customer Agreement signed during the past month;

12.9.4   An identification of each Customer who became entitled to Software Support and each Customer for whom Software Support lapsed or was terminated during the past month; and

12.9.5   Such additional information as Supplier may require.

12.10   Dealer shall use its best efforts to assist Supplier in the protection of its legal rights and to enforce the Customer Agreements, provided, however, that Dealer may not initiate litigation or arbitration concerning the Products against any third party, except a proceeding against a Customer to collect unpaid money due, without the prior written consent of Supplier. Dealer shall cooperate fully with Supplier in any action by Supplier in the event of an actual or threatened violation of Supplier's proprietary rights by any person or entity.

12.11   Dealer shall perform its duties in a manner that will preserve the reputation of Supplier and the Products.

12.12   Dealer shall perform its duties in compliance with all applicable laws and shall hold Supplier harmless from any claim, damage, liability, or expense, including attorneys fees, arising from any violation of law.

[Optional Provision:]

13   NON-COMPETITION

13.1   Dealer agrees that during the term of this Agreement [and for a term of [*number*] months after the termination of this Agreement], Dealer will not develop, market, or distribute any computer program or software product that is similar in function to or competes with the Products.

14   SUPPLIER'S OPTION TO MODIFY OR DISCONTINUE PRODUCTS

14.1   Supplier has the right, at any time, to make such modifications to the Products as it sees fit in the operation, performance, or functionality of the Products.

14.2   Supplier has the right, at any time, to discontinue distribution of any or all Products or versions of Products, to remove Supported Products or versions of Supported Products from Supplier's Supported Products List, or to discontinue support, maintenance, or the provision of new versions, updates, or corrections for any Product or for any version or for any hardware or software platform or operating system. [If such a termination of distribution of the Products or of support, maintenance, or the provision of new versions, updates, or corrections materially impairs the value of this Agreement to Dealer, Dealer shall have the option to terminate this Agreement; such option to terminate shall be exercisable within sixty (60) days of notice to Dealer of Supplier's decision to terminate such distribution, and such termination shall take effect sixty (60) days after Dealer's notice of termination is given. [If Dealer terminates the Agreement under this provision, Dealer shall be released and discharged from its obligations under the section entitled NonCompetition.]]

15   SUPPLIER SUPPORT OBLIGATION

15.1   Supplier will use its reasonable efforts to make the Products perform substantially in accordance with the product description set forth in the Documentation that accompanies the Product, as it may exist from time to time. However, Dealer acknowledges that inevitably some errors may exist in the Product, and the presence of such errors shall not be a breach of this provision. Supplier's sole obligation with regard to such errors shall be to provide Secondary Support as stated in this Agreement.

15.2   Supplier will make reasonable consulting services, technical advice, and training available to Dealer. Such services will be provided by phone or at Supplier's offices. Such services will be provided at such times as are mutually agreed upon the parties.

15.3   Supplier shall make reasonable efforts to aid dealers in advertising and promotion of Products.

*[**Comment:** The general model for software licensing to customers contemplated by this form of agreement (and the end-user agreement, Form 12-2) is that any problem in the products will be cured by a new version or by a software "patch" or "work-around." In theory, a refund is made only if the problem cannot be fixed in a reasonable amount of time. Of course other arrangements are possible. For example, for marketing reasons, the customer might be given a right to return the software after a trial if it is not satisfied. In any case, it may be hard to stop a customer from returning, and refusing to pay for, defective software. Where returns are made due to defects, the dealer understandably will want the supplier to grant a refund of the fee that the dealer paid for the product. The following text accomplishes this.]*

15.4   If, notwithstanding the language of the Customer Agreement, Products with material defects in logic, operation, materials, or workmanship are returned by Customers to Dealer within ninety (90) days of delivery to Customers, Dealer may return such Products to Supplier for a refund of the License Fee paid to Supplier, provided Dealer certifies in writing that it has refunded any license fee or other consideration paid by Customer for the Product, each such Customer has completed a signed statement of the reasons for the return, in the form attached as Schedule _ to this Agreement, and Dealer has forwarded the foregoing certification and signed Customer statement to Supplier.

[Optional Provision:]

[Comment: When software problems result in litigation, customers may sue the dealer or the supplier or both. Some dealer agreements have clauses that make the supplier responsible for defending the litigation. The following is language that accomplishes this.]

15.5   If Dealer has a Customer Agreement in force with a Customer that conforms to the requirements for such Customer Agreements stated in this Agreement, and if notwithstanding the language of such Agreement, the Customer seeks monetary damages from Dealer in arbitration or litigation on account of alleged defects in software logic or operation, Supplier agrees for as long as copies of the Products sold by Dealer are in use by Customers licensed by Dealer, to indemnify and hold Dealer harmless against any loss, damage, expense, or cost, including reasonable attorneys' fees, arising from such proceeding. The indemnification obligation in this section shall be effective only if: (1) Dealer is not in default of its obligations under its Agreement, (2) Dealer has given prompt notice of the claim and permitted Supplier to defend, and (3) Dealer has reasonably cooperated in the defense of the claim.

[Optional Provision:]

[Comment: Some dealer agreements have provisions that allow the dealer to terminate the agreement if there are persistent software errors that the supplier is unable to cure.]

15.6   If Supplier is unable to cure material defects or errors in logic in a Product six (6) months after Dealer gives notice of such defects or errors, and if Dealer reasonably believes that Supplier is therefore unable to fulfil its obligations to produce and deliver the Product, Dealer may, at its option, terminate this Agreement in accordance with the provisions on termination of this Agreement. [If Dealer terminates the Agreement under this provision, Dealer shall be released and discharged from its obligations under the section entitled NonCompetition.]

16   WARRANTY OF RIGHTS TO THE PRODUCTS; INDEMNIFICATION

16.1   Supplier warrants that the licensing of the Products to Customers for commercial use will not infringe or violate any copyright, patent, trade secret, trademark, or proprietary right existing under the laws of the United States or any state or territory thereof of any other person or entity.

16.2 Supplier agrees, for as long as copies of the Products sold by Dealer are in use by Customers licensed by Dealer, to indemnify and hold Dealer harmless against any loss, damage, expense, or cost, including reasonable attorneys' fees, arising out of any claim, demand, or suit asserting that the Product infringes or violates any copyright, patent, trade secret, trademark, or proprietary right existing under the laws of the United States or any state or territory thereof ("Claim").

16.3 The indemnification obligation in this section shall be effective only if: (1) Dealer is not substantially in default of its payment obligations, (2) Dealer has given prompt notice of the Claim and permitted Supplier to defend, and (3) Dealer has reasonably cooperated in the defense of the claim.

16.4 To reduce or mitigate damages, Supplier may at its own expense procure the right for Dealer to continue licensing and distributing the Product or replace it with a non-infringing product. If Supplier supplies a non-infringing update or version of the Product, Dealer shall promptly supply the same to its Customers and install the same at its Customer locations. If, in its judgment, Supplier deems that, due to the Claim or for any other reason, it is not in Supplier's interest to continue distributing the Products, Supplier, without breaching this Agreement, may terminate the distribution of any or all of the Products and may direct Dealer to exercise its right under Dealer's Customer Agreements to direct Customers to terminate use of the Products. [If such a termination of distribution of the Products materially impairs the value of this Agreement to the Dealer, Dealer shall have the option to terminate this Agreement; such option to terminate shall be exercisable only within sixty (60) days of notice to Dealer of the supplier's decision to terminate such distribution. Any such termination shall take effect sixty (60) days after notice of termination is given. [If Dealer terminates the Agreement under this provision, Dealer shall be released and discharged from its obligations under the section entitled NonCompetition.]]

16.5 Supplier shall have no obligation to Dealer to defend or satisfy any claims made against Dealer that arise from the use, marketing, licensing, or disposition of the Products by Dealer other than as permitted by this Agreement.

17   DISCLAIMER OF WARRANTY AND LIMITATION OF LIABILITY

17.1 THE REPRESENTATIONS AND WARRANTIES EXPRESSLY GRANTED IN THIS AGREEMENT ARE THE SOLE REPRESENTATIONS AND WARRANTIES, EXPRESS OR IMPLIED, MADE BY SUPPLIER. ANY AND ALL OTHER

REPRESENTATIONS AND WARRANTIES, EITHER EXPRESS OR IMPLIED, INCLUDING BUT NOT LIMITED TO IMPLIED WARRANTIES OF MERCHANTABILITY, FITNESS FOR A PARTICULAR PURPOSE, AND NON-INFRINGEMENT, ARE EXPRESSLY EXCLUDED AND DISCLAIMED.

17.2   THE REMEDIES SET FORTH IN THIS AGREEMENT SHALL BE DEALER'S SOLE REMEDIES FOR BREACH OF THIS AGREEMENT. SUPPLIER WILL NOT BE LIABLE FOR LOST PROFITS, LOST OPPORTUNITIES, OR INCIDENTAL OR CONSEQUENTIAL DAMAGES UNDER ANY CIRCUMSTANCES.

17.3   UNDER NO CIRCUMSTANCE MAY SUPPLIER'S LIABILITY TO DEALER, UNDER ANY AND ALL PROVISIONS OF THIS AGREEMENT, EXCEED THE SUM OF $[*specify amount*].

18   CONFIDENTIALITY

18.1   [Dealer acknowledges that it will receive Confidential Information from Supplier relating to technical, marketing, product, and business affairs of Supplier. Dealer agrees that all Confidential Information of Supplier shall be held in strict confidence and shall not be disclosed or used without express written consent of Supplier.] [Each party acknowledges that it will receive Confidential Information from the other party relating to technical, marketing, product, and business affairs. Each party agrees that all Confidential Information of the other party shall be held in strict confidence and shall not be disclosed or used without express written consent of the other party.]

19   TERM AND TERMINATION

[*Comment: Note that the part of the following provisions which allow a party to terminate in case of the bankruptcy of another party may be ineffective under United States bankruptcy law in some cases.*]

19.1   This Agreement shall take effect on the Effective Date. Unless sooner terminated in accordance with the provisions of this Agreement, the term of this Agreement shall be [*number*] years and shall be renewed successively for additional terms of [*number*] years, unless either party, in its sole discretion, gives notice of termination no less than ninety (90) days prior to the expiration of the then-current term.

19.2   In the event that Dealer fails to maintain a satisfactory credit rating or financial condition or if Supplier reasonably concludes that, for any reason, Dealer is or will become unable to discharge its obligations hereunder, Supplier may terminate this Agreement upon thirty (30) days notice.

19.3   In the event of a filing by or against either party of a petition for relief under the United States Bankruptcy Code or any similar petition under the insolvency laws of any jurisdiction not dismissed in thirty (30) days, or in the event that either party shall make an assignment for the benefit of creditors, permit any attachment on a substantial portion of its assets to remain undissolved for a period of thirty (30) days, or discontinue the business operations relevant to this Agreement, then the other party may immediately terminate this Agreement upon written notice.

19.4   In addition to provisions authorizing termination hereunder, either party shall have the right to terminate this Agreement because of a material breach of the Agreement by the other party that has not been cured thirty (30) days after the terminating party has notified the other party of the breach and advised the other party of its intention to terminate the Agreement if the breach remains uncured.

19.5   Upon termination of this Agreement, and except as otherwise provided in this Agreement:

19.5.1   The license granted to Dealer by this Agreement shall be terminated immediately; Dealer shall make no further use of all or any part of the Products or any Confidential Information received from Supplier, except that Supplier at its option shall either (1) permit Dealer to license some or all of its then existing inventory of Products to Customers or (2) direct Dealer to return to supplier or ship to such person or entity as Supplier may specify (at Dealer's cost and risk for shipping) some or all of such inventory for a refund of the amount paid for such inventory;

19.5.2   Dealer shall report to Supplier as to the then current status of its negotiations with all Customers and prospects and as to its obligations to Customers;

19.5.3   Dealer shall cease any public statement or representation that it is an authorized dealer or that it is in any way involved with Supplier, and shall immediately cease use of any trademark, service mark, or trade name of Supplier, except as may otherwise be authorized in writing by Supplier;

19.5.4   Any support fee or other service or support revenues relating to Products that are accrued or are received by Dealer after termination shall be turned over to, shall be the property of, and may be collected by Supplier or such person or entity as Supplier may designate;

19.5.5   Supplier shall be entitled to, but shall not be obligated to, deal with any Customers who have dealt with Dealer, and at Supplier's option, Dealer shall assign to Supplier or to such person or entity as Supplier may designate, those Customer Agreements and other contracts or agreements relating to the Products specified by Supplier; and

19.5.6   Dealer shall cooperate fully with Supplier and perform all acts appropriate to carry out the provisions of this Agreement relating to termination.

19.6   The provisions of this Agreement concerning Confidential Information, Indemnification, [and (except as otherwise provided) Non-Competition] shall survive the termination of this Agreement, and termination shall not relieve either party of the obligation to pay any amount due to the other.

19.7   It is understood and agreed that no termination of this Agreement, whatever the cause thereof, shall in any way terminate, restrict, limit, or affect in any way the right of any authorized Customer to utilize the Products in accordance with the terms of a Customer Agreement.

20   GENERAL PROVISIONS

20.1   **Relationship of Parties.** Dealer shall be deemed to have the status of an independent contractor, and nothing in this Agreement shall be deemed to place the parties in the relationship of employer-employee, principal-agent, partners, or joint venturers.

20.2   **Entire Agreement.** This Agreement, including the Schedules attached to this Agreement, states the entire agreement between the parties on this subject and supersedes all prior negotiations, understandings and agreements between the parties concerning the subject matter. No amendment or modification of this Agreement shall be made except by a writing signed by both parties.

20.3   **No Waiver.** The failure of either party to exercise any right or the waiver by either party of any breach, shall not prevent a subsequent exercise of such right or be deemed a waiver of any subsequent breach of the same of any other term of the Agreement.

20.4   **Notice.** Any notice required or permitted to be sent hereunder shall be in writing and shall be sent in a manner requiring a signed receipt, such as Federal Express, courier delivery, or if mailed, registered or certified mail, return receipt requested. Notice is effective upon receipt. Notice to Supplier shall be addressed to [*specify name, title, and address*] or such other person or address as Supplier may designate. Notice to Dealer shall be addressed to [*specify name, title, and address*] or such other person or address as Dealer may designate.

20.5 **Partial Invalidity.** Should any provision of this Agreement be held to be void, invalid, or inoperative, the remaining provisions of this Agreement shall not be affected and shall continue in effect as though such provisions were deleted.

20.6 **Force Majeure.** Neither party shall be deemed in default of this Agreement to the extent that performance of their obligations or attempts to cure any breach are delayed or prevented by reason of any act of God, fire, natural disaster, accident, act of government, shortages of materials or supplies, or any other cause beyond the control of such party ("Force Majeure") provided that such party gives the other party written notice thereof promptly and, in any event, within fifteen (15) days of discovery thereof and uses its best efforts to cure the delay. In the event of such Force Majeure, the time for performance or cure shall be extended for a period equal to the duration of the Force Majeure but not in excess of three (3) months.

20.7 **Assignment.** Supplier may assign this Agreement. This Agreement may not be assigned by Dealer, nor any duty hereunder delegated by Dealer, without the prior written consent of Supplier [, which consent shall not be unreasonably withheld] [, which consent may be withheld in Supplier's absolute discretion]. Subject to the foregoing, this Agreement shall be binding upon and inure to the benefit of the parties to this Agreement and their respective heirs, legal representatives, successors, and permitted assigns.

20.8 **Taxes.** Dealer shall pay, in addition to the other amounts payable under this Agreement, all local, state, and federal excise, sales, use, privilege, personal property, gross receipts, and similar taxes (excluding taxes imposed on or measured by Supplier's net income) levied or imposed by reason of the transactions under this Agreement. Dealer shall, upon demand, pay to Supplier an amount equal to any such tax(es) actually paid or required to be collected or paid by Supplier.

20.9 **Injunctive Relief.** The parties recognize that a remedy at law for a breach of the provisions of this Agreement relating to Confidential Information, use of Supplier's trademark, copyright, and other intellectual property rights, [and/or Non-Competition] will not be adequate for Supplier's protection, and accordingly Supplier shall have the right to obtain, in addition to any other relief and remedies available to it, injunctive relief to enforce the provisions of this Agreement.

[Optional Provision:]

20.10 **Arbitration.** Any dispute relating to the terms, interpretation or performance of this Agreement (other than claims for preliminary injunctive relief or other pre-judgment remedies) shall be resolved at the request of either party through binding arbitration. Arbitration shall be conducted in [*specify city and state*] under the rules and procedures of the American Arbitration Association ("AAA"). The parties shall request that the AAA appoint a panel of three arbitrators and, if feasible, include one arbitrator who shall possess knowledge of computer software and its distribution; however the arbitration shall proceed even if such a person is unavailable.

20.11 **Governing Law.** This Agreement shall be governed and interpreted in accordance with the substantive law of the State of _____.

20.12 **Exclusive Jurisdiction and Venue.** Any legal action brought concerning this Agreement or any dispute hereunder [, including but not limited to an action to enforce or challenge an arbitration award,] shall be brought only in the courts of the state of _____[in the county of ___] or in the federal courts located in such state [and county]. Both parties submit to venue and jurisdiction in these courts.

So agreed between the parties signing below.

[*NAME OF SUPPLIER*]

By: _____
[Signature]

Type Name:
Title:
Date:

[*NAME OF DEALER*]

By: _____
[Signature]

Type Name:
Title:
Date:

Form 11-1: SAMPLE SHRINK-WRAP LICENSE

Introductory Note

This is a sample shrink-wrap license for end-user sales of mass-market software. (A copy is found on diskette as SHRINK.W51.) This text is designed to be printed on the familiar sealed paper envelope that contains the software program diskettes. Normally the shrink-wrap license is printed in a font size that permits the entire text to be placed on the face of the envelope. As is discussed in Chapter 11, the enforceability of these documents is questionable, and their effect may be altered by state and federal law.

The following is a form suitable for a software product that is to be used by a single user on a single computer. Alternative language is provided that grants a license for installation on a network server. If the use of the program is to be restricted to a limited number of workstations or a specified number of concurrent users, the language would be modified accordingly.

Also included in the text is language designed to limit the rights of the United States government if it purchases the software. Again many attorneys have doubts that a shrink-wrap notice alone can limit the rights of the government. However, it best to include this language for whatever effect it may have. An overview of licensing software to the government is found in Chapter 12.

I have also provided additional text to place on the outside of the shrink-wrapped package. This additional text gives the retail buyer warning of some of the terms of the shrink-wrap license and a warning that the sale is subject to the enclosed license. Use of this text is recommended because it might give the licensor a better argument that the shrink-wrap license should be enforced.

SOFTWARE LICENSE AGREEMENT
OF [*NAME OF LICENSOR*]

[*NAME OF CORPORATION*] ("LICENSOR") IS WILLING TO LICENSE THE ENCLOSED SOFTWARE TO YOU ONLY IF YOU ACCEPT ALL OF THE TERMS IN THIS LICENSE AGREEMENT. PLEASE READ THE TERMS CAREFULLY BEFORE YOU OPEN THIS PACKAGE, BECAUSE BY OPENING THIS SEALED DISK PACKAGE YOU ARE AGREEING TO BE BOUND BY THE TERMS OF THIS AGREEMENT. IF YOU DO NOT AGREE TO THESE TERMS, LICENSOR WILL NOT LICENSE THIS SOFTWARE TO YOU, AND IN THAT CASE YOU SHOULD RETURN THIS PRODUCT PROMPTLY, INCLUDING THE PACKAGING, THIS UNOPENED DISK PACKAGE, AND ALL WRITTEN MATERIALS, TO THE PLACE OF PURCHASE PROMPTLY FOR A FULL REFUND.

Ownership of the Software

1. The enclosed Licensor software program ("Software") and the accompanying written materials are owned by Licensor [or its suppliers] and are protected by United States copyright laws, by laws of other nations, and by international treaties.

Grant Of License

2. Licensor grants to you the right to use one copy of the Software on a single computer. You may load one copy into permanent memory of one computer and may use that copy, or the enclosed diskettes, only on that same computer. [You may not install the software on a network.] [You may install the Software on a single network server.] [You may install the Software on a single network server, provided that you have a License for Network Station from Licensor for each station of the network at which the Software is used.]

3. This license is valid only for use within the United States of America and its territories.

Restrictions on Use and Transfer

4. If this Software package contains both 3.5" and 5.25" disks, then you may use only the size disks appropriate for your computer. You may not use the other size disks on another computer or loan, rent, transfer, or assign them to another user except as part of the permanent transfer of the Software and all written materials (as provided for below).

5. You may not copy the Software, except that (1) you may make one copy of the Software solely for backup or archival purposes, and (2) you may transfer the Software to a single hard disk provided you keep the original solely for backup or archival purposes. You may not copy the written materials.

6. You may permanently transfer the Software and accompanying written materials (including the most recent update and all prior versions) if you retain no copies and the transferee agrees to be bound by the terms of this Agreement. Such a transfer terminates your license. You may not rent or lease the Software or otherwise transfer or assign the right to use the Software, except as stated in this paragraph.

7. You may not reverse engineer, decompile, or disassemble the Software.

Limited Warranty

8. Licensor warrants that the Software will perform substantially in accordance with the accompanying written materials for a period of 90 days from the date of your receipt of the Software. Any implied warranties on the Software are limited to 90 days. Some states do not allow limitations on duration of an implied warranty, so the above limitation may not apply to you.

9. LICENSOR DISCLAIMS ALL OTHER WARRANTIES, EITHER EXPRESS OR IMPLIED, INCLUDING BUT NOT LIMITED TO IMPLIED WARRANTIES OF MERCHANTABILITY, FITNESS FOR A PARTICULAR PURPOSE, AND NON-INFRINGEMENT, WITH RESPECT TO THE SOFTWARE AND THE ACCOMPANYING WRITTEN MATERIALS. This limited warranty gives you specific legal rights. You may have others, which vary from state to state.

10. LICENSOR'S ENTIRE LIABILITY AND YOUR EXCLUSIVE REMEDY SHALL BE, AT LICENSOR'S CHOICE, EITHER (A) RETURN OF THE PRICE PAID OR (B) REPLACE-MENT OF THE SOFTWARE THAT DOES NOT MEET LICENSOR'S LIMITED WAR-RANTY AND WHICH IS RETURNED TO LICENSOR WITH A COPY OF YOUR RECEIPT. Any replacement Software will be warranted for the remainder of the original warranty period or 30 days, whichever is longer. These remedies are not available outside the United States of America.

11. This Limited Warranty is void if failure of the Software has resulted from modification, accident, abuse, or misapplication.

12. IN NO EVENT WILL LICENSOR BE LIABLE TO YOU FOR DAMAGES, INCLUDING ANY LOSS OF PROFITS, LOST SAVINGS, OR OTHER INCIDENTAL OR CONSEQUEN-TIAL DAMAGES ARISING OUT OF YOUR USE OR INABILITY TO USE THE SOFTWARE. Because some states do not allow the exclusion or limitation of liability for consequential or incidental damages, the above limitation may not apply to you.

13. This Agreement is governed by the laws of the State of _____.

14. If you have any questions concerning this Agreement or wish to contact Licensor for any reason, please write: [*Company name and address*] or call [*phone number*].

15. U.S. Government Restricted Rights. The Software and documentation are provided with Restricted Rights. Use, duplication, or disclosure by the Government is subject to restric-tions set forth in subparagraph (c)(1) of The Rights in Technical Data and Computer Soft-ware clause at DFARS 252.227-7013 or subparagraphs (c)(1)(ii) and (2) of Commercial Computer Software - Restricted Rights at 48 CFR 52.227-19, as applicable. Supplier is [*Com-pany name and address*].

[TEXT FOR OUTSIDE OF PACKAGE:]

Notice: [NAME OF COMPANY] IS WILLING TO LICENCE THE ENCLOSED SOFTWARE ONLY UPON THE TERMS OF THE LICENCE AGREEMENT THAT IS ENCLOSED. You can obtain a full copy of the license agreement by calling (xxx) xxx-xxxx. IF YOU DO NOT AGREE TO SUCH TERMS AFTER READING THE LICENSE, YOU MAY RETURN THIS

SOFTWARE FOR A FULL REFUND. EXCEPT FOR THE LIMITED WARRANTY EXPRESSLY STATED IN THE LICENSE AGREEMENT, [NAME OF COMPANY] DISCLAIMS ALL OTHER WARRANTIES, INCLUDING ANY IMPLIED WARRANTIES OF MERCHANTABILITY, FITNESS FOR A PARTICULAR PURPOSE, AND NON-INFRINGEMENT. IN NO EVENT WILL [NAME OF COMPANY] BE LIABLE FOR ANY DAMAGES, LOST PROFITS, LOST DATA OR INCIDENTAL OR CONSEQUENTIAL DAMAGES ARISING FROM USE OF OR ANY INABILITY TO USE THE SOFTWARE.

Form 12-1: END-USER AGREEMENT CHECKLIST

Introductory Note

This is an end-user agreement check list (found on diskette as USER-CHK.W51). You may use it with Chapter 12 and the annotated end-user agreement, Form 12-2, to structure your form agreements and your negotiations. If there is to be extensive software development work as part of you end-user agreement, you should also consult Forms 8-1 and 8-2, which deals with software development agreements, for guidance on additional issues that may arise.

This check list uses the term "vendor" to describe the party supplying the software. It is also common to use other terms, such as "supplier" or "licensor."

This check list is based on the assumption that there will be a single document that covers the initial licensing and subsequent software maintenance services. Some vendors divide these documents into two instruments: a license agreement and a separate software support agreement.

The topic numbering in this check list does not correspond to section numbers in the sample end-user agreement Form 12-2 (USER-AGR.W51), because the coverage of topics in this check list is somewhat broader. However many of the topics covered are the same.

Many vendors wish to create one or more "standard forms" of license agreements. Any vendor creating such a form should have it reviewed by counsel before using it. And any customer making a major expenditure on software (or hardware) should have the form of the agreement reviewed by an attorney and should negotiate modifications if appropriate.

1   Introduction (or Preamble)

This section identifies the parties and states the general nature of the agreement.

2   Definitions

This section defines terms. Its purpose is to create shorthand terms for convenience and to avoid ambiguities. Terms defined will vary with the contents of the agreement, but commonly include: "Vendor", "Program", "Customer", "Confidential Information", "Documentation", "Effective Date" (the date the agreement goes into effect), etc.

3   Grant of License

This portion of the agreement states the scope of the license that is granted to the customer. There are a number of aspects that must be considered. First, will the license be exclusive or non-exclusive? Usually the end-user will get only a non-exclusive license, although, as is discussed below, sometimes there is an exclusive license for custom modifications created at the customer's expense. Second, how will the agreement define and limit the scope of use permitted to the customer? Here are some of the choices.

3.1   Single user (i.e. a single individual).

3.2   Site license: What is the definition of the "site?" What happens if the site is expanded? What happens if other locations gain access to the software when LANs are linked together?

3.3   Corporation-wide license: What is the definition of the corporation? What happens if the corporation "grows" through merger or acquisition? Are "affiliates" and "subsidiaries" included, and if so, how are those terms defined?

3.4   Single server and a specified number of users: Is there a mechanism in the agreement to provide for monitoring of compliance with this limitation?

3.5   Single server and a specified number of workstations: Is there a mechanism in the agreement to provide for monitoring of compliance with this limitation?

3.6   Single server and a specified number of concurrent users: This limitation is normally enforced by a software-implemented monitoring mechanism included in the software product.

3.7   When the license is limited to a certain number of terminals, authorized users, or concurrent uses, on what terms can the customer increase the scope of the license? On what terms can the customer get additional user manuals, or, if needed, additional software diskettes? What is the cost of doing so?

4   Other Scope of Use Issues

For microcomputer software, the grant of the license may address other matters concerning scope of use including the following:

4.1   Employee home use of office software: If a vendor has granted a site license for a microcomputer program, is an employee of the customer allowed to install a copy of the program on a home computer? If the license has a specified per-workstation license fee, must the customer pay an additional fee for a copy of the software on the employee's computer at home?

4.2   Laptop and notebook computer use: May employees install copies of the program into portable computers to use on the job? Where there is a per-workstation license fee, will a portable computer and the desktop computer be counted as single installation if only one person has use of both machines?

5 Limitation To a Specified Hardware Or Software Platform

5.1 Does the agreement include a restriction as to general type of hardware and software that the software will be used on? Does the agreement specify the particular hardware on which the software must be used?

5.2 Does the vendor reserve the right to require that the customer upgrade the operating system software or its hardware as a condition for software support or the delivery of new versions of the software program? This provision may prove necessary when the installed user base as a whole moves to new software and hardware.

5.3 Does the customer have an option to change the assigned hardware or to downsize from a mainframe version of the program to a version that operates on networked microcomputers? What is the cost of exercising this option?

6 Options on Additional Software

6.1 Does the customer have the option to license additional software at stated price or at a stated discount from list price? Do the terms and conditions of the agreement cover all additional programs that may be licensed from the vendor? If additional software is licensed, are additional software support fees due? (See discussion of software support below.)

7 Ownership of Modifications

7.1 If substantial modifications to the software are to be made under the agreement, who will own them? (If the agreement does not grant the customer ownership of the modifications, then normally the vendor will own them.) Some end-user agreements provide that the vendor will own the modifications, but that the customer will be paid a royalty if the modifications are licensed to another customer. Some agreements provide that the customer owns the modifications.

8 The "Customer's Own Data" Restriction

8.1 Does the agreement restrict the scope of a software license to the "customer's own data" or the "customer's own use"? Does the agreement prohibit "service bureau" use of the vendor's software? (These limitations are very common.)

8.2 What is the customer's intended use of the software? Based on that use, is there ambiguity as to whether it is the "customer's own data" that is being processed?

9　Delivery and Installation

The end-user agreement must have provision concerning delivery and installation of the software.

9.1　When and how is delivery to be made? If the delivery time is missed, may the customer cancel the agreement?

9.2　Does the vendor supply installation or does the customer install the software? If vendor installation is required, is the price of installation included in the licensing fee or is it extra?

9.3　Is there a need to arrange conversion of data from the customer's existing format? Does the vendor supply data conversion or is it the customer's responsibility? If the vendor converts the data, what is the price for the data conversion service? Is the conversion of data guaranteed by the vendor?

10　Acceptance by the Customer

In many agreements, a portion of the license fee is due on "acceptance." There are several types of commonly used provisions for acceptance found in end-user agreements:

10.1　Are there vendor-specified acceptance criteria? Must the customer accept the software if it "substantially" performs the functions described in the user manual?

10.2　Are there customer specified criteria for acceptance based, for example, on the ability of the software to process certain test data and meet performance (throughput or response time) requirements? Is there a "parallel" test, in which the same data is run on the customer's old software and on the new software from the vendor? Is successful conversion of data part of the acceptance criteria?

10.3　Are there additional acceptance requirements included in the customer's original request for proposals (RFP) or in the vendor's response to the RFP? If so, have these documents been incorporated by reference into the agreement?

10.4　Is there a free trial? Does the customer have the right to test the software and then decide whether to accept or reject it? If so, how long is the test period? If the customer rejects the software, does the vendor keep a portion of the upfront fees or are all payments refunded?

11　The License Fee

In exchange for the license to the program, the customer pays a license fee.

11.1 How much is the license fee?

11.2 When is the license fee payable? Is it paid in part upon the signing of the agreement? Is part of the fee due on delivery and/or acceptance?

11.3 Does the customer get "price protection"; that is, does the customer get the benefit of any price reductions or special offers during a specified period after signing the agreement?

12 Protection of Intellectual Property

This section of the agreement includes provisions designed to protect the vendor's intellectual property rights. Usually there is an acknowledgement that the vendor (and/or its suppliers) maintains all ownership of intellectual property, and normally there are provisions prohibiting the customer from decompiling, reverse engineering, or modifying the software. Additional issues may be:

12.1 Does the agreement state that certain information which the vendor supplies to the customer is confidential? What information is so designated? Manuals and documentation? The program itself? What obligation are imposed on the customer to safeguard confidential information?

12.2 Where source code is delivered to the customer, what security and confidentiality protections are imposed? Restriction on access to source code to selected employees? Secure storage requirements? Other required security measures?

12.3 Does the agreement require that the customer take sufficient steps to prevent unauthorized coping of the software? Is the customer's obligation limited to taking "reasonable efforts" to prevent copying of the software? Is there a specified dollar limit to the customer's potential liability for copying and distribution of vendor's software by unauthorized users?

13 The Customer's Obligation to Protect Its Own System and Data

To limit potential vendor liability, many license agreements require customers to implement procedures to protect data against accidental loss or destruction.

13.1 Is the customer required to backup all data from hard disk to tape or other form of storage every business day?

13.2 Is the customer required to install anti-virus software?

14   Warranties, Disclaimers and Limitation of Damages

14.1   Is there a warranty given? For what period? Typical warranties are 90 days, six months or one year.

14.2   Is the warranty limited to "substantial compliance" with the user documentation?

14.3   Are the customer's consequential (lost profit and lost opportunity) damages disclaimed?

14.4   What are the provisions for remedies in case of breach of warranties? Is "reasonable efforts" at bug fixing the exclusive remedy?

14.5   Is there a "cap" on potential money damage claims under the agreement?

15   Intellectual Property Warranties and Indemnification

Some end-user agreements contain language indemnifying the customer if it turns out that the program infringes another party's rights under patent or copyright law and if a lawsuit against the customer results. Sometimes there is also a warranty of non-infringement (usually with very limited remedies for the customer for breach of that warranty). Here are some of the negotiable items:

15.1   If the end-user is sued for infringement by a third party, does the vendor have an obligation to defend the claim and pay any judgment or settlement? Who controls the defense of the litigation? What are the conditions to the vendor's obligation to defend and indemnify? Is there a cap or limit on the vendor's indemnification of the customer, and if so, how much is the cap?

15.2   If the vendor finds that there is an infringement problem, can the vendor cure it by "designing around" the problem or by procuring a license to the program?

15.3   If the vendor faces a claim of infringement, and cannot find a cost-effective cure, can the vendor "pull the plug" by terminating the customer's right to use the program in order to limit infringement damages? What are the customer's rights and remedy if the vendor "pulls the plug?"

16   Training Employees to Use the Program

When a customer licenses a new software package, it often needs training for its employees. The following are issues to consider:

16.1   What is the training curriculum?

16.2 What qualifications will the trainers have?

16.3 How many hours or days of training will be supplied?

16.4 How many of the customer's employees will be trained?

16.5 Will the customer or the vendor supply the location and the computers for the training sessions?

16.6 What data will be used in the training sessions? Will the customer supply the test data?

16.7 Will the training materials be supplied to the customer in advance of training sessions?

16.8 Is videotape instruction or tutorial software available?

16.9 What is the cost to the customer for training services and materials?

16.10 Is on-going training available? Is "advanced" training available? On what terms?

17   Period of Support Included in the License Fee

17.1 How long a period of software support is included in license fee? Ninety days? One Year? Some other period? (Usually this is the same as the warranty period.)

17.2 What are the provisions for the customer to renew or terminate software support? Does software support automatically renew each year? Can software support be cancelled, and if so, under what conditions?

17.3 If software support lapses or ends, under what conditions may the customer reinstate software support?

18   The Content of Software Support

Software support typically includes fixing software bugs by providing patches and maintenance releases for the software.

18.1 Does software support include provision for the vendor's technicians to log-in to the customer's computer system by modem and run diagnostic programs to find software problems and install "patches?"

18.2 Is on-site service required? If on-site service is called for, does the agreement set out a specified amount of time within which the vendor's personnel must arrive at the customer's location when a problem occurs? Does the customer have to pay travel and other out-of-pocket costs for on-site service?

18.3   Does the agreement provide that the vendor can comply with its software support obligations by providing a method to use the software without encountering the bug, a so-called "work around" -- rather than fixing the error in the software?

18.4   Is there a time limit in which serious bugs must be fixed? Can the customer cancel the agreement if the time limit is exceeded?

18.5   Does the vendor have an "escape clause" provision in the agreement that allows the vendor to exit from the agreement if the vendor is unable to fix the software? Can the vendor discontinue support, refund some or all of the license fee or support fee, terminate the license, and cease further obligation to the customer?

19   New Versions of the Software

19.1   What is the procedure for the customer to get new and improved versions of the program? Does the software support fee include a right for the customer to get new versions of the software that may become available from time to time? If new versions are not included in the support fee, are they available at a stated discount from list price?

19.2   Is the customer's use of the most recent (or one of the two most recent versions) of the software a condition of the vendor's obligation to provide support? What provision is made for the vendor to discontinue support of old versions?

20   The Software Support Fee

20.1   How much must the customer pay for software support?

20.2   When is software support fee payable? Yearly? Monthly?

20.3   Are there several software support plans available, each with its own fee structure?

21   Technical Support

21.1   Does the vendor provide technical advice by phone on use of the program? Is the amount of technical advice limited to a specified number of hours?

21.2   Does the customer have the option of obtaining technical advice on a pay as you go basis, for example as a "900" telephone number at a $2.00 or $3.00 per minute charge?

22 Restrictions on Relocation

22.1 Can the vendor terminate some of its software support obligations, for example, obligations to provide on-site service, if the customer moves to a new site more than a specified distance from the vendor's service location?

23 Term and Termination

23.1 Does the payment of the license fee grant the customer a perpetual license or is it limited to some term of years?

23.2 May either party terminate their obligations based on material breach by the other?

23.3 What are the obligations of the customer that are triggered by termination? Usually the customer must erase the software from the hard disk, tape or other storage media, destroy any archival copies, and return the original diskettes or other media and documentation to the vendor.

23.4 What obligations survive termination? Usually the obligation to safeguard the vendor's confidential information will survive termination.

24 Audit

24.1 What rights does the vendor have to audit the customer's premises to verify compliance with the agreement?

25 Escrow Agreement

Where software has an essential role in a customer's business, a source code escrow agreement may be required to insure the customer's ability to maintain the code. Some issues to consider are the following:

25.1 Who pays for the software escrow fees? Normally the customer pays, but there are exceptions.

25.2 What are the release conditions, that is, the conditions under which the escrowed source code is released to the customer? Do the release conditions include the vendor's cession of business operations, its bankruptcy, its failure to fix errors within a specified time, its loss of key technical employees?

25.3 What is the release mechanism? If the customer and the vendor disagree on whether a release condition exists, will the escrow agent continue to hold the source code until a court of law orders that the source code be released to the customer? Or will the source code be released to the customer unless a court order prevents the release?

25.4   What provisions exist for verification that the source code is complete and properly documented -- and that it in fact compiles into the most recent version of the program?

26   A Transferable or Non-Transferrable License

26.1   Is the customer's license transferable to another corporation? May the customer transfer the license to another corporation under specified circumstances, such as the sale of the business operation that is using the software?

26.2   May the vendor assign or delegate its obligation to provide software support?

27   Public Reference

Is the vendor authorized to mention publicly that the customer licenses software from the vendor? Can this fact be used in advertisements, press releases, etc.?

28   Software Time Bombs and Locking Devices

28.1   Does the software contain a "bomb" or "lock?" As is discussed in Chapter 12, if it does, the device must be expressly authorized in the agreement.

28.2   If such a device is mentioned in the agreement, under what condition may the "bomb" or "lock" be triggered? If the customer fails to pay a bill? If the customer transfers ownership of the program in violation of its provisions? If the customer uses the program substantially in excess of the agreed-upon scope of use?

29   Resolution of Disputes

29.1   If there is a dispute between the customer and the vendor, is it subject to litigation or to arbitration? Can the vendor resort to a court of law for a preliminary injunction to enforce confidentiality or field of use restrictions of the agreement?

29.2   If the customer fails to pay charges due and owing, can the vendor recover, in addition to the amount due, its attorneys fees and other costs of collection?

30   General Provisions

Most end-user agreements have general provisions of the types that we have seen earlier in this book, examples of which will be found in Form 12-2.

31   Schedules

A variety of schedules may be appropriate depending on the terms of the agreement. Schedules to the agreement might include:

31.1   A schedule identifying the software to be licensed and stating the applicable license fees.

31.2   A schedule specifying the customer, site, and/or hardware for which the software is licensed.

31.3   A schedule stating the limit on the number of authorized users or concurrent users.

31.4   A schedule stating acceptance criteria.

31.5   A schedule of currently supported versions of the software products.

31.6   A schedule stating training services provided.

31.7   A schedule stating the software support provided and the currently applicable fee.

31.8   A schedule setting forth the escrow agreement that will be executed in connection with the agreement.

Form 12-2: ANNOTATED SOFTWARE END-USER LICENSE AGREEMENT

Introductory Note

This is a sample software end-user license agreement with annotations to aid you in negotiations. (A copy can also be found on the diskette as USER-AGR.W51.)

The business using the end-user agreement may be a dealer or reseller (including a VAR or OEM), a distributor, a software developer, or a software manufacturer. I have used the term "Vendor" to describe the party supplying the software. It is also common to use other terms, such as "Supplier" or "Licensor," or you could simply use your company name.

Many vendors wish to create one or more "standard forms" of license agreement that can be used for end-user licensing transactions. This sample text is designed as a form that could be used with a variety of different products—and for this reason the software products licensed, the cost, the nature ,and price of software support and maintenance, and other information may be attached as schedules. It is also possible to create an end-user agreement that covers all products that are being licensed or may be licensed in the future. This form covers that option as well. Note, however, that some of the options in the following text are best suited to licensing a single software product or system.

There are many ways that these agreement may be written. The are variations depending on the price level of the software products involved, the degree of customization required, the sophistication of the negotiators, the level of support required after installation, the method of pricing software support and a variety of other factors. Some of the variations are covered in the following form, but it is not possible to cover them all. The following form is a general guide—but it may not be the right form for your product or your deal.

Schedules that are self-explanatory are omitted. I have included a sample schedule that sets forth provisions for software support to be provided on a yearly (or other periodic) basis. Again this is just one of many possible variations. A vendor could prepare several such schedules to offer varying levels of software support at different prices.

Any vendor creating an end-user agreement form should have it reviewed by counsel before using it. And any customer making a major purchase of software (or hardware for that matter) should have the form of the agreement reviewed by an attorney and should seek to negotiate modifications if appropriate.

SOFTWARE LICENSING AGREEMENT

1   INTRODUCTION

*[**Comment:** The introduction should set forth in plain English the general nature and purpose of the agreement. This section of a contract is often written more formally, with*

the word "Whereas" introducing each clause. This paragraph could be drafted with a blank for the name of the customer, to be typed in when the form is used.]

1.1   This is an Agreement between [*Name of Vendor*] and its customer [*Name of Customer*] under which [*Name of Vendor*] is licensing software on a non-exclusive basis for the customer's own use under the terms and conditions stated below.

2   DEFINITIONS

*[**Comment:** The Definitions section should define key terms of the Agreement to avoid ambiguity and simplify drafting by providing shorthand names for persons and things. Additional definitions may appear in schedules to the agreement or in the text. It is important to review the definitions carefully, because the interpretation of many terms of the agreement can be affected by how key terms are defined.]*

As used in this Agreement, the following definitions shall apply:

2.1   "Agreement" shall mean this Agreement between Vendor and Customer.

2.2   "Confidential Information" shall mean any information relating to or disclosed in the course of the Agreement, which is or should be reasonably understood to be confidential or proprietary to the disclosing party. "Confidential Information" shall not include information (a) already lawfully known to the receiving party, (b) disclosed in published materials, (c) generally known to the public or (d) lawfully obtained from any third party.

2.3   "Customer" [shall mean [*Name of Corporation*] of [*Address*]] [shall mean the party so designated on the first page of this agreement].

2.4   "Delivery Date" shall mean the date that Vendor ships the Program to Customer.

2.5   "Documentation" shall mean the user manual(s) and any other materials supplied by Vendor for use with the Program or with any Release.

2.6   "Effective Date" shall mean [*specify date*] [the date upon which both parties have signed this Agreement] [the date upon which both Customer and a duly authorized officer of Vendor at Vendor's headquarters has approved and signed the Agreement].

*[**Comment:** The following definitions give the user the choice of creating an agreement covering any program licensed from the vendor (in the present or future) or covering specified programs only. An optional provision below, on "Scope of the Agreement," can be used to make it explicit that broad coverage of all programs is intended.]*

2.7   "License Fee" [shall mean the fee for any Program licensed to Customer as set forth on Vendor's then current License Fee Schedule] [shall mean the fee for licensing the Program or Programs specified in the Program Description and Price Schedule attached as Schedule _ to the Agreement.]

[2.8   "License Fee Schedule" shall mean Vendor's listing of Programs and Licence Fee as it may be in effect from time to time. Vendor reserves the right to change the License Fee Schedule without notice.]

2.9   "Program" shall mean the machine-readable object code of [any of Vendor's software products which Customer is currently licensing from Vendor or licenses now or in the future from Vendor] [the computer software program or programs described in the Program Description and Price Schedule attached as Schedule _ to the Agreement] [and such additional Releases of such programs as shall be supplied by Vendor to Customer from time to time] together with its Documentation.

2.10   The term "Release" shall mean any version of a Program or any materials which are supplied by Vendor at or after the delivery of a Program, including any software provided for the purpose of improving the functions or performance of the Program, changing the intellectual property contained in the Program, expanding the capability or ease of operation of the Program, or for the purpose of fixing errors in program logic, together with Documentation.

2.11   The term "Software Support" shall mean support and maintenance services for Programs provided for in this Agreement.

2.12   The term "Software Support Fee" shall mean that applicable annual fee due for Software Support in accordance with Vendor's Software Support Schedule.

2.13   The term "Software Support Schedule" shall mean Vendor's written statement of Software Support offered and the fees due for such Software Support as it may be in effect from time to time. Vendor reserves the right to change the Software Support Schedule without notice.

2.14   The term "Supported Products List" shall mean a list of Program versions, together with associated computer hardware and operating system software platforms, for which Vendor provides Software Support. Vendor reserves the right to change the Supported Products List without notice.

2.15   "Vendor" shall mean [*Name of Corporation*] of [*Address*].

3   **GRANT OF LICENSE**

[Comment: The license granted can be limited in a number of ways. For example, there may be a limit on the number of authorized users. The agreement may restrict the number of concurrent users. The vendor may grant a site license, that is, a license for use at a particular location. The license may be limited to use with a certain specified hardware type. In licensing software for use on mainframe or minicomputer systems, it is common to limit the use of the program to specified hardware. In the following text, several choices are presented from which the negotiator can mix and match.]

3.1   Vendor hereby grants to Customer, and Customer hereby accepts, a permanent non-exclusive license to use the Program subject to the terms and provisions of this Agreement.

[Optional Provision:]

3.2   The license granted by this Agreement authorizes use of the Program by no more than *[specify number]* [users] [concurrent users], who shall be employees of Customer ("Authorized Users").

[Optional Provision:]

3.3   The license granted by this Agreement authorizes use of the Program only at the location listed in Schedule __to this Agreement ("Authorized Location") by employees of Customer ("Authorized Users").

[Optional Provision:]

3.4   The license granted by this Agreement authorizes use of the Program only on the computer hardware listed in Schedule _ to this Agreement.

[Optional Provision:]

3.5   One copy of the Program must be licensed for each computer or work station on which the Program is installed.

[Optional Provision:]

3.6   The Program [may not be installed on a network] [may be installed on a single network] [however access may be permitted only as follows: *state restrictions as to sites where use is allowed, authorized users, etc.*].

[Optional Provision:]

3.7   Customer shall maintain adequate records of usage of the Program by Authorized Users to assure compliance with the limitations of this license. Such records shall be available to Vendor for inspection upon reasonable request.

[Optional Provision:]

3.8   Where a Program is properly licensed for a particular workstation, Authorized Users of the Program at such workstation may install a copy of the Program on a single home and/or a single portable computer without the Customer paying an additional licence fee, if (a) such use constitutes no more than twenty (20) percent of such Authorized User's usage of the Program and (b) the Authorized User has only one copy of the Program in use at any time. Customer shall take all necessary steps to assure compliance with the limitations of this provision.

[Optional Provision:]

4   SCOPE OF THE AGREEMENT

4.1   This Agreement shall apply to each Program or Release of a Program that Customer is currently licensing from Vendor or shall licence in the future.

5   RESTRICTION AGAINST THIRD PARTY USE

*[**Comment:** Many end-user agreements forbid use of the program by third parties or for third parties' data. The purpose of these restrictions is to prevent customers from using a program to operate as a "service bureau," that is a business that receives data belonging to others and processes it. The customer would normally have to pay substantially higher fees for a service bureau license. The following provisions put this restriction into effect.]*

5.1   The Program may not be used by any person or entity that is not [an Authorized User] [an employee of Customer].

5.2   The Program may be used for Customer's internal business use and only to process information or data of Customer. Customer may not process information or data belonging to other parties.

6   COPIES OF THE PROGRAM

6.1   Vendor shall furnish to Customer [one copy] [*specify number* copies] of the Program.

6.2   Customer shall have the right to make one copy of the machine-readable object code for the Program solely for archive purposes. On such archival copy, Customer shall mark copyright, trademark, patent, and/or trade secret notices identical to those on the copy of the Program provided to Customer. Customer may not otherwise make copies of the Program.

[Optional Provision:]

6.3   Vendor shall furnish to Customer [*specify number*] copies of the Documentation. Upon request, at Vendor's option, additional copies of the Documentation may be supplied to Customer at Vendor's then current price. Customer may not, without the prior written consent of Vendor, copy or otherwise reproduce any Documentation.

[Optional Provision:]

6.4   Customer shall be entitled to make [*number*] additional copies of the Program [and Documentation] to the extent necessary for use of the Program [by Authorized Users] [at the Authorized Location] [on the Authorized Hardware]. Customer shall reproduce and include copyright or trade secret notices on any copies in the same text as stated in the copies provided to Customer.

7   INSTALLATION

[**Comment:** *The following are some common provisions on installation.*]

[Option 1:]

7.1   Vendor shall load the Program on Customer's computer hardware and conduct Vendor's standard test procedures on the installed Program. Vendor shall be relieved of its obligation to perform the installation, and the Program shall be deemed accepted, if Customer's computer hardware or operating system software, in whole or in part, is defective or is not otherwise in good operating condition. Customer shall provide Vendor with access to the computer hardware and electrical power, work space and such other items as may be required to complete the installation.

[Option 2:]

7.2   Installation of the Program on a computer shall be Customer's responsibility. Customer shall follow the installation procedures contained in the Documentation.

8   DATA CONVERSION

[Comment: Where data must be converted from another file format, the vendor may provide the conversion service, or the customer may arrange for a third party to do the conversion. Both options are provided for below. Note that customers may wish to make data conversion part of the acceptance procedures.]

8.1   [The conversion of Customer's data files from Customer current system shall be carried out by Vendor [for a price of [*specify rate*]] [at a charge determined by Vendor's current fee schedule for such work] payable [upon completion of the conversion] [thirty (30) days after invoice]. Customer shall provide all information reasonably required for conversion. Vendor shall use reasonable efforts in converting the data; however, all converted data files shall be supplied "AS IS" AND VENDOR DISCLAIMS ALL WARRANTIES, EITHER EXPRESS OR IMPLIED, INCLUDING BUT NOT LIMITED TO IMPLIED WARRANTIES OF MERCHANTABILITY AND FITNESS FOR A PARTICULAR PURPOSE WITH REGARD TO CONVERTED DATA FILES. It shall be Customer's obligation to test the converted date files to verify the accuracy of the conversion of data.] [The conversion of Customer's data files from Customer current system shall be the Customer's responsibility. At Customer's request, Vendor shall provide technical information about the file structures used by the Program to the Customer or to a file conversion vendor selected by Customer.]

9   ACCEPTANCE

[Comment: If the program is a relatively simple product to use and install, payment may simply be due upon delivery or within a specified total number of days of delivery, or even in advance. However, it is common with more sophisticated software products to have acceptance procedures. In some cases, the customer specifies a test procedure using its actual data in a live test. The following presents some of the common alternatives for acceptance provisions.]

9.1   The Program will be deemed accepted [when the Program has been delivered] [when the Program has been installed] [when the Program has been installed and passes Vendor's standard test procedures] [when the Program has been installed and performs substantially as described in the Documentation] [when the Program has been installed and performs to Customer's reasonable satisfaction] [when the Program has been installed and performs the test procedures specified in Schedule _ to this Agreement].

10   PAYMENT OF PROGRAM LICENSE FEE

*[**Comment:** Payment terms vary. Often a down payment is made, with the balance due on delivery and installation. Sometimes an additional payment is due upon acceptance. In some agreements, the customer may use the program on a trial basis and return it if not satisfied.*

10.1   In consideration of the license granted under this Agreement, Customer shall pay to Vendor the License Fee to be paid as follows:

10.1.1   Upon execution of this Agreement, [*number*] percent of the License Fee shall be paid.

10.1.2   Upon [the Delivery Date] [delivery and installation of the Program] [Customer's acceptance of the Program], the remaining [*number*] percent of the License Fee shall be paid.

[Optional Provision:]

11   OPTION TO RETURN PROGRAM

11.1   For a period of [thirty (30)] [sixty (60)] [*specify duration*] days ("Return Option Period") after [delivery] [installation] of a Program under this Agreement, customer shall have the option to return the Program for a refund of all amounts paid [except for: [*specify dollar amount*] which shall be retained by Vendor]. Customer may exercise this option only by giving notice of its exercise of this option and by returning the Program to Vendor within the Return Option Period. IF CUSTOMER EXERCISES THIS OPTION, SUCH REFUND SHALL BE CUSTOMER'S SOLE AND EXCLUSIVE REMEDY FOR ANY CLAIMS ARISING FROM OR RELATING TO THE PROGRAM.

12   ACKNOWLEDGMENT OF VENDOR'S OWNERSHIP RIGHTS

10.1   Customer acknowledges that it obtains no ownership rights in the Program under the terms of this Agreement. All rights in the Program including but not limited to Confidential Information, trade secrets, trademarks, service marks, patents, and copyrights are, shall be and will remain the property of Vendor [or any third party from whom vendor has licensed software or technology]. All copies of the Program delivered to Customer [or made by Customer] remain the property of Vendor.

13   CONFIDENTIAL INFORMATION

[Comment: The following is a typical provision on confidential information. If the agreement were one that granted rights to source code, more elaborate security provisions would be required, such as obligations to keep source code under lock and key, provisions for employees with source code access to sign confidentiality undertakings, provisions for the vendor to audit security measures, etc. Where only object code is licensed, which is most often the case, such provisions are not typically used.]

13.1   Customer acknowledges that the Program and the Documentation contain proprietary and Confidential Information of Vendor. Customer agrees to keep the Program and Documentation in confidence and to take all reasonable precautions to ensure that no unauthorized persons have access to the Program and Documentation and that no unauthorized copies are made [provided however, that any liability of Customer on account of unauthorized copies shall be limited to $[amount].] Breach of this provision shall be grounds for immediate termination of this Agreement without further obligation to Customer, at Vendor's option.

13.2   Customer may not alter any proprietary markings on the Program, including copyright, trademark, trade secret, and patent legends.

13.3   Customer may not decompile, disassemble, or reverse engineer the Program.

14   CUSTOMER'S OBLIGATION FOR DATA PROTECTION

14.1   Customer is required to perform daily backups of the data on the computer system used by the Program so that the likelihood of data loss is minimized. Customer shall be solely responsible for backup software and hardware. Customer shall provide the safe storage of all backup tapes and/or disks. Customer shall be responsible for keeping its computer system free of computer viruses.

15   WARRANTY

15.1   Vendor warrants that the Program will perform substantially in accordance with accompanying Documentation for a period of [90 days] [six months] [one year] from the date of Customer's [receipt of the Program] [acceptance of the Program] ("Warranty Period") [and for any period in which Software Support is paid for and in effect under the terms of this Agreement].

[Comment: Sometimes "flow down provisions" in dealership agreements (see Chapter 10) require that clauses be inserted in end-user agreement that protect not only the ven-

dor but also the supplier who licensed the product to the vendor. The following includes optional text to protect third parties that licensed technology to the vendor.]

15.2 VENDOR [AND ANY THIRD PARTY FROM WHOM VENDOR HAS LICENSED SOFTWARE OR TECHNOLOGY] DISCLAIM[S] ALL OTHER WARRANTIES, EITHER EXPRESS OR IMPLIED, INCLUDING BUT NOT LIMITED TO IMPLIED WARRANTIES OF MERCHANTABILITY, FITNESS FOR A PARTICULAR PURPOSE AND NON-INFRINGEMENT, WITH RESPECT TO THE PROGRAM AND THE ACCOMPANYING WRITTEN MATERIALS.

15.3 VENDOR [AND ANY THIRD PARTY FROM WHOM VENDOR HAS LICENSED SOFTWARE OR TECHNOLOGY] WILL NOT BE LIABLE FOR LOST PROFITS, LOST OPPORTUNITIES, OR INCIDENTAL OR CONSEQUENTIAL DAMAGES UNDER ANY CIRCUMSTANCES.

15.4 EXCLUSIVE REMEDY: CUSTOMER'S EXCLUSIVE REMEDY AGAINST ANY PARTY FOR BREACH OF THIS AGREEMENT SHALL BE, AT VENDOR'S CHOICE, (A) CORRECTION OF ANY ERROR OR DEFECT IN THE PROGRAM AS TO WHICH CUSTOMER HAS GIVEN NOTICE (B) REPLACEMENT OF THE PROGRAM INVOLVED.

15.5 If any problem, operational failure or error of the Program has resulted from any alteration of the Program, accident, abuse, or misapplication, then this warranty shall be null and void, at Vendor's option.

16 OVERALL LIMITATION OF DAMAGES

*[**Comment:** Even though the agreement has a broad disclaimer of warranties, there is always a risk that the disclaimer will be found ineffective or inapplicable and that damages will be imposed. Damages also might flow from the intellectual property indemnification set forth below. Therefore in addition to warranty disclaimers, the vendor should include a reasonable "cap" on damages.]*

16.1 IN NO CASE SHALL THE AGGREGATE AMOUNT OF DAMAGES PAYABLE TO CUSTOMER FROM ANY AND ALL PARTIES FOR ANY CLAIM ARISING FROM THE PROGRAM OR THIS AGREEMENT (INCLUDING, WITHOUT LIMITATION, ITS WARRANTY AND INDEMNIFICATION PROVISIONS) EXCEED THE AMOUNTS PAID BY CUSTOMER TO VENDOR UNDER THIS AGREEMENT.

17   INDEMNIFICATION

17.1   Vendor agrees to indemnify and hold Customer harmless against any loss, damage, expense, or cost, including reasonable attorneys' fees, arising out of any claim, demand, or suit asserting that the Program infringes or violates any copyright, patent, trade secret, trademark, or proprietary right existing under the laws of the United States or any state or territory thereof ("Claim"), subject to the overall limitation of damages hereunder.

17.2   The indemnification obligation in this section shall be effective only if (1) at the time of the alleged infringement, Customer was using a currently supported version of the Program listed in Vendor's then current Supported Products List, (2) Customer gave prompt notice of the Claim and permitted Vendor to defend, and (3) Customer has reasonably cooperated in the defense of the claim. Vendor shall have no obligation to Customer to defend or satisfy any claims made against Customer that arise from the use, sale, licensing or other disposition of the Program by Customer other than as permitted by this Agreement or from the Customer's modification of the Program.

17.3   To reduce or mitigate damages, Vendor may at its own expense procure the right for Customer to continue licensing and distributing the Program or replace it with a non-infringing product. If Vendor supplies a non-infringing Release of the Program, Customer shall promptly [install it] [permit its installation] on its computer system, and terminate use of prior Releases of the Program. If Customer is not entitled to such non-infringing Release under the terms of the Vendor's Software Support arrangement with Customer, Customer shall pay any applicable fee for upgrading to the non-infringing Release, as stated in Vendor's then current fee schedule, within thirty (30) days of delivery of such Release. If, in its judgment or for any other reason, Vendor deems that, due to the Claim or for any other reason, it is not in Vendor's practical interest to continue distributing a Program, Vendor may require customer, upon thirty (30) days written notice, to terminate use of a Program. Thirty days after notice to terminate use of a Program, this Agreement shall terminate as to the Program involved, Customer shall receive a refund of a percentage of the current year's Software Support Fee for the Program corresponding to the remaining portion of the year, and in addition, if such termination takes place during the first year after the Delivery Date, a refund of a percentage of the License Fee for such Program corresponding to the remaining portion of the first year. THE FOREGOING IS CUSTOMER'S EXCLUSIVE REMEDY AGAINST ANY AND ALL PARTIES FOR ANY CLAIM ARISING

FROM OR RELATING TO LOSS OF USE OF THE PROGRAM OR TO ANY OTHER DAMAGE ARISING AS A RESULT OF THIS PROVISION.

18   TRAINING

*[**Comment:** The parties will often wish to have an agreed-upon training program. The issues that should be covered are discussed in Chapter 12 and in the end-user agreement checklist, Form 12-1 (USER-CHK.W51).]*

18.1   Upon delivery and installation, Vendor will provide Customer with Training Services as specified on Schedule _ upon the payment terms stated therein. Thereafter training services will be provided on the terms and at prices stated in Vendor's then current schedule of fees for training services.

19 SOFTWARE SUPPORT

19.1   Software Support for the Program [shall consist of the services listed on Vendor's then current Software Support Schedule, which may change from time to time.] [shall consist of the services set forth on Schedule _ hereto].

19.2   During the Warranty Period specified above, Customer shall be entitled to software support without additional charge. "Expiration Date" shall mean the date of the expiration of the Warranty Period and each subsequent anniversary of such date. Before each Expiration Date, Customer shall be billed for the then applicable annual Software Support Fee. If Customer has paid the applicable Software Support Fee on or before the Expiration Date, Customer shall be entitled to receive an additional year of Software Support. Vendor shall have no obligation to provide Software Support after the Expiration Date if the applicable Annual Software Support Fee is unpaid.

19.3   The Software Support Fee shall be sent to Vendor at the address set forth above, or such other address as Vendor may designate. Information as to the amount of the currently applicable Software Support Fee for the Program is available from the Vendor on request.

19.4   Vendor's current policy is to support the most recently released version of the software and the next prior version, and to cease maintenance of earlier versions. However, Vendor reserves the right to change this policy in its discretion and reserves the right to discontinue support of Programs or versions of Programs for hardware and/or operating systems that are used by numbers of customers that Vendor deems inadequate to justify the cost of support.

19.5   Customer agrees that in order to receive Software Support for a Program, Customer must use a currently supported version of the Program, as listed in Vendor's Supported Products List, which is available from Vendor. Customer acknowledges and agrees that it may be necessary to update its computer hardware and/or operating system to achieve compatibility with the currently supported version. Customer acknowledges and agrees that if it has allowed its subscription to Software Support to lapse, and if its version of the Program is not currently supported, it may have to obtain a current version to obtain Software Support, as is discussed below.

19.6   If Customer is not using a currently supported version of the a Program as listed in Vendor's Supported Products List, Vendor may suspend provision of Software Support for the Program until Customer cures this condition without refunding the Software Support Fee.

19.7   Customer may terminate Software Support by written notice to Vendor prior to any Anniversary of the Delivery Date. However, Vendor shall not be required to refund any Software Support Fee.

19.8   If Software Support has been terminated or has lapsed, Customer may reinstate its subscription to Software Support upon payment of (1) the annual Software Support Fee in effect at the time, plus (2) a reinstatement fee equal to the greater of (a) the difference between the License Fee paid hereunder and the applicable license fee for the then current version of the Program and (b) $[*specify amount*]. Upon reinstatement of Software Support, Customer will be upgraded to the current version of the Program.

[19.9   Any installation required for an upgrade to a currently supported version of a Program under any paragraph of this Agreement, when performed by Vendor, will be charged to Customer at Vendor's then current hourly rates plus reimbursement for any out-of-pocket costs or expenses incurred by Vendor. Such installation charges shall be in addition to other fees or charges that may be due.]

[Optional Provision:]

20   RESTRICTIONS ON TRANSFER TO A NEW LOCATION

[*Comment: Where the end-user has a site license, it is common for the agreement to require the vendor's permission before moving the program to a new location. Such provisions are often used if a move to a distant location would make it more expensive or difficult to provide onsite service or to monitor the Customer's compliance with the restrictions in the agreement. Some agreements permit moves within a stated geographic area. Many agreements allow off-site use in the case of an emergency. The following are samples of the provisions that might be used.]*

20.1   Customer may not transfer the storage or operation of a Program to a location other than the Authorized Location, except that Customer may move a Program to new site within [*number*] miles by road of [the nearest designated service center] [the offices of Vendor] as of the date the Program is moved or to a location approved in writing by Vendor before the move ("Permitted New Location").

20.2   If the storage and operation of a Program is moved to a location other than a Permitted New Location, Vendor may suspend Software Support. However, Vendor shall not be required to refund any Software Support Fee.

20.3   If Customer is temporarily unable to use a Program at the Authorized Location because of conditions beyond Customer's control, Customer may use the Program at another location [and on different hardware] on a temporary basis [except as follows: [*specify limits to permissible move*]]. Such use, if not otherwise authorized by this Agreement, shall be permitted only as long as is necessary in response to such conditions. Customer shall provide Vendor notice within five (5) days if this provision is invoked, and shall also give notice within five (5) days when the Program is returned to the Authorized Location.

20.4   In case of any move of the Program permitted under this Agreement, shipment of the Program to the new site shall be at Customer's sole expense, risk, and control, and Customer shall be solely responsible for the protection of the Program during transport. Installation of the Program required by a move or the preparation of the Program for moving, when performed by Vendor, will be charged to Customer at Vendor's then current hourly rates plus reimbursement for any out-of-pocket costs or expenses.

21   TERM AND TERMINATION

*[**Comment:** Note that the part of the following provisions which allow a party to terminate the agreement in case of the bankruptcy of another party may be ineffective under United States bankruptcy law in some cases.]*

21.1   The term of this Agreement shall commence upon the Effective Date and shall continue in effect until terminated as provided for herein. [This document shall not become effective unless a duly authorized officer of Vendor at Vendor's headquarters has approved and signed the Agreement.]

21.2   It is agreed that either party may terminate this Agreement immediately upon written notice to the other party in the event that such other party (a) becomes insolvent or makes an assignment for the benefit of creditors; (b) files or has filed against it any petition under any Title of the United States Code or under any applicable bankruptcy, insolvency, reorganization or similar debtor relief law which is not discharged within thirty (30) days of said filing, or (c) requests or suffers the appointment of a trustee or receiver, or the entry of an attachment or execution as to a substantial part of its business or assets.

21.3   Vendor may terminate this Agreement in the event Customer (a) fails to make when due any Licence Fee payment or other payment required under this Agreement; (b) commits a material breach of any of its obligations concerning scope of use or the protection of the Program, Documentation, intellectual property of Vendor, and Confidential Information; or (c) materially breaches any of its other obligations under any provision of this Agreement, which breach is not remedied within thirty (30) days after notice thereof by Vendor to Customer. [In its discretion, upon the occurrence of any the of foregoing conditions, Vendor may terminate the Agreement as to any or all Programs covered by this Agreement.]

22   RIGHTS UPON TERMINATION

22.1   Upon termination of this Agreement, Customer's licence to use the Program shall terminate, and Customer shall immediately turn over to Vendor all copies of the Program and Documentation, and any other Confidential Information relating to the Program and Documentation and shall remove and erase completely any copies of the Program installed or recorded on any hard disk or other storage medium. Customer shall promptly certify to Vendor in writing that it has complied with this requirement.

22.2   Upon termination of this Agreement, Customer shall pay to Vendor all fees due through the effective date of such termination. Unless otherwise specified herein or otherwise agreed in writing, all fees collected or accrued prior to the date of termination shall be retained by Vendor without any pro rata refund to Customer.

22.3   The termination of this Agreement shall not extinguish any rights or obligations of the parties relating to protection of Confidential Information.

23   AUDIT

23.1   During the term of this Agreement [and for a term of [one year] [*specified period*] after termination], upon reasonable notice, Vendor may enter the premises of

Customer and perform reasonable audit and inspection procedures to confirm that Customer is in compliance with the terms and conditions of the Agreement, including, but not limited to, provisions relating to scope of use of the Program, protection of Confidential Information, and termination. Customer shall cooperate in any such inquiry.

[Optional Provision:]

24   ESCROW AGREEMENT

[Comment: As is discussed in Chapter 12, a source code escrow agreement is used when the software is crucial for the customer. The customer may need access to the source code in order to maintain the program if the vendor is unable or unwilling to do so. Commonly the escrow agent for software is a specialized company known as an escrow house. Each of the various escrow houses has its own form escrow agreement, which it will supply on request. A sample escrow agreement is included in this book as Form 12-3 and on diskettes as ESCROW.W51.]

24.1   Simultaneously with the execution of this Agreement, the parties shall execute and enter into the Source Code Escrow Agreement, a copy of which is attached as Schedule _ hereto. The Source Code Escrow Agreement shall be deemed supplementary to this agreement for purposes of the Bankruptcy Code.

25   ASSIGNMENT

[Comment: The following provisions on assignment present some, but by no means all, of the possible choices. Option 1 is pro-vendor; it forbids the customer from assigning its license to the program, but permits the vendor freedom to assign its contractual obligations. Option 2 is more evenhanded; it blocks both parties from making an assignment without the consent of the other party. Option 3 adds a provision that permits assignments as part of the sale of a business. Customers may insist on the right to transfer their rights under the agreement if the assets of their business are sold. Also included is an optional provision, often used, that states that even if the Customer assigns the agreement, the Customer remains legally responsible along with the assignee. Some customers are anxious about a clause permitting the vendor to assign the agreement, because they bargained for the software-related skills of the vendor and have no assurance that an assignee will actually be able to perform the agreement.]

[Option 1:]

25.1   Customer may not sell, pledge, assign, sublicense, or otherwise transfer or share its rights or delegate its obligations under this Agreement without the prior written consent of Vendor, which Vendor may withhold in its sole discretion. Any attempted sale, pledge, assignment, sublicense or other transfer in violation hereof shall be void and of no force or effect. Vendor may assign its rights and delegate its duties hereunder at any time without the consent of Customer.

[Option 2:]

25.2   Either party may assign some or all of its rights and/or obligations under this Agreement only with the express prior written consent of the other party, and that consent may be granted or withheld in the other party's sole discretion. Any purported assignment, except as provided for in this paragraph, shall be null and void and a material breach of this Agreement.

[Option 3:]

25.3   Either party may assign all of its rights granted in the Agreement as part of the sale or transfer to an acquiring entity of substantially all the assets of that party's business operations in which the Program is employed. Otherwise, either party may assign some or all of its rights and/or obligations under this Agreement only with the express prior written consent of the other party, and that consent may be granted or withheld in the other party's sole discretion. Any purported assignment, except as provided for in this paragraph, shall be null and void and a material breach of this Agreement.

[Optional Provision:]

25.4   The Customer's assignment of this Agreement shall not discharge Customer from its obligations, but shall make Customer's assignee an additional obligor under this Agreement. Any assignment by Customer will be invalid unless the assignee agrees in a writing delivered to Vendor to be bound by and perform all obligations and terms of this Agreement.

26   GENERAL PROVISIONS

26.1   **Applicable Law.** This Agreement shall be construed pursuant to substantive law of the State of _____.

26.2   **Shipping Costs and Risk of Loss.** All costs relating to the shipment of the Program and the Documentation, including freight and insurance costs, shall be borne by Customer. Upon delivery and installation of the Program and the Documentation, Customer shall assume all risk of loss and damage to the Program and the Documentation, and shall at its sole cost and expense replace any lost or damaged portion thereof.

26.3   **Taxes.** Customer shall pay, in addition to the other amounts payable under this Agreement, all local, state and federal excise, sales, use, personal property, gross receipts and similar taxes (excluding taxes imposed on or measured by Vendor's net income) levied or imposed by reason of the transactions under this Agreement. Customer shall, upon demand, pay to Vendor an amount equal to any such tax(es) actually paid or required to be collected or paid by Vendor.

26.4   **Required Consents.** Customer warrants that it has obtained lawful permission to use all hardware and software required in order for the Program to be used on Customer's computer system.

26.5   **Public Reference.** Customer consents to the public use of its name as a customer of Vendor.

[Optional Provision:]

26.6   **Software Lock.** Customer consents to acts by Vendor to disable the Program (including the triggering of software features that prevent operation of the Program) in the event that Customer fails to pay the License Fee for the Program or uses or transfers the Program in breach of this Agreement.

[Optional Provision:]

26.7   **Required Acceptance by Officer of Vendor.** This Agreement is not binding upon Vendor until executed by an authorized representative of Vendor at Vendor's headquarters office.

26.8   **Modification.** This Agreement may not be modified or amended except by a writing which is signed by authorized representatives of each of the parties. [No purported modification or amendment shall be binding until approved in writing by an authorized representative of Vendor at Vendor's headquarters office.]

26.9   **No Waiver.** The failure of either party to exercise any right or the waiver by either party of any breach, shall not prevent a subsequent exercise of such right or be deemed a waiver of any subsequent breach of the same of any other term of the Agreement.

26.10   **Notice.** Any notice required or permitted to be sent hereunder shall be in writing and shall be sent in a manner requiring a signed receipt, such as Federal Express, courier delivery, or if mailed, registered or certified mail, return receipt requested. Notice is effective upon receipt.

26.11 **Force Majeure.** Neither party shall be deemed in default of this Agreement to the extent that performance of their obligations or attempts to cure any breach are delayed or prevented by reason of any act of God, fire, natural disaster, accident, act of government, shortages of materials or supplies or any other cause beyond the control of such party ("Force Majeure") provided that such party gives the other party written notice thereof promptly and, in any event, within fifteen (15) days of discovery thereof and uses its best efforts to cure the delay. In the event of such Force Majeure, the time for performance or cure shall be extended for a period equal to the duration of the Force Majeure but not in excess of three (3) months.

26.12 **Entire Agreement.** This Agreement constitutes the sole and entire agreement of the parties with respect to the subject matter hereof and supersedes any prior oral or written promises or agreements. There are no promises, covenants or undertakings other than those expressly set forth in this Agreement.

26.13 **Equitable Remedies.** The parties recognize that money damages is not be an adequate remedy for any breach or threatened breach of any obligation hereunder by Customer involving intellectual property, Confidential Information or use of the Program beyond the scope of the license granted by this Agreement. The parties therefore agree that in addition to any other remedies available hereunder, by law or otherwise, Vendor [and any third party from whom vendor has licensed software or technology] shall be entitled to an injunction against any such continued breach by Customer of such obligations.

[Optional Provision:]

26.14 **Arbitration.** Any dispute relating to the terms, interpretation or performance of this Agreement (other than claims for preliminary injunctive relief or other prejudgment remedies) shall be resolved at the request of either party through binding arbitration. Arbitration shall be conducted in [*specify city and state*] under the rules and procedures of the American Arbitration Association ("AAA"). The parties shall request that the AAA appoint a panel of three arbitrators and, if feasible, include one arbitrator who shall possess knowledge of computer software and its distribution; however the arbitration shall proceed even if such a person is unavailable.

26.15 **Late Fees, Costs and Attorneys Fees.** A late payment charge of 1.5% per month, compounded monthly, shall apply to any payment due from Customer that is in arrears for a period exceeding thirty (30) days. [In any legal action or arbitration proceeding brought by Vendor on account of Customer's breach, Customer shall be liable for all of Vendors' cost of litigation or arbitration, including reasonable attorneys' fees.] [In any legal action or arbitration proceeding brought on account of a breach, the prevailing party shall recover from the other party all costs of litigation or arbitration, including reasonable attorneys' fees.]

26.16 **Exclusive Jurisdiction and Venue.** Any cause or action arising out of or related to this Agreement [, including an action to confirm or challenge an arbitration award,] may only be brought in the courts of applicable jurisdiction in [*state*] at [*location*], and the parties hereby submit to the jurisdiction and venue of such courts.

So agreed between the parties signing below.

[*Name of Vendor*]

BY: _____

PRINT NAME: _____

TITLE: _____

Date: _____

[*Name of Customer*]

BY: _____

PRINT NAME _____

TITLE: _____

Date: _____

Schedule _
SOFTWARE SUPPORT

*[**Comment:** Support can vary greatly. It may consist of simply providing software updates. It may include on-site visits to diagnose and fix problems. It may include diagnostic services to monitor load on the system. The following provisions include several of these options, but there are many other variations possible. Under the following provisions, payment of the software support entitles the customer to all new and improved versions of the program. An alternative would be to provide that an additional license fee must be paid for major upgrades of a program.]*

1   **SERVICES PROVIDED.** Software Support shall consist of the following services:

1.1   Vendor shall assist customer in diagnosing errors and malfunctions which occur when the Program is used by Customer. Vendor is not responsible for errors or malfunctions caused by any hardware or any third party operating system.

1.2   Vendor shall provide support services to Customer to attempt to correct diagnosed errors and malfunctions. Vendor shall attempt to provide Releases that implement corrections and shall attempt to assist Customer in using the Program in a way that can avoid diagnosed errors, malfunctions and defects.

1.3   Vendor shall provide support services to Customer to attempt to keep the Program compatible with the then current version of the operating system of the computer hardware.

1.4   Vendor may provide Customer with new Releases for the Program licensed to Customer. Releases may include new features and functions added to the Program and/or may provide corrections to errors or malfunctions. The timing and content of Releases will be at the sole discretion of Vendor.

1.5   Vendor will effect delivery of each Release to Customer. All deliveries and shipments of Releases will be at Vendor's expense. [The Customer will install each Release.] [Vendor will install each Release as its sole expense. Vendor shall be relieved of its obligation to perform the installation, and the Program shall be deemed accepted, if Customer's computer hardware or operating system software, in whole or in part, is defective or is not otherwise in good operating condition. Customer shall provide Vendor with access to the computer hardware and electrical power, work space and such other items as may be required to complete the installation.]

1.6   Vendor will perform remote diagnostics monthly or, on such other schedule as Vendor deems appropriate based on reported errors. Vendor shall use its best efforts to respond to Customer's notification of material errors on the same day as notification is given to Vendor or on the following day.

1.7   All Software Support shall be performed during the Service Hours unless other arrangements are mutually agreed to by the parties in writing. "Service Hours" shall mean the hours of on-call service coverage under this Agreement which are [from __ a.m. to __ p.m. seven (7) days per week] [*specify times*].

1.8   Vendor will provide reasonable technical support by telephone concerning use of the Programs and diagnosis of problems or errors.

1.9   Vendor shall provide Customer with telephone number(s) and/or other contact information in order to allow Customer to accomplish the required notification and request information.

1.10   Software Support does not entitle Customer to Software Modules available from Vendor which are designed to increase the number of terminals, to add additional applications or to cover business functions that are not included in the Program currently licensed to Customer. Such Software Modules may be licensed from Vendor. If such additional Software Modules are licensed by Customer, Releases relating to them will be available as part of Software Support under this Agreement [without additional fee] [upon current payment of the then current Software Support Fees for such Modules].

2   CONDITIONS OF SOFTWARE SUPPORT.   The following terms and conditions shall apply at all times while Software Support are in effect:

2.1   Customer shall provide Vendor with access at the site to its computer hardware, system software, the Program and customer data files with sufficient work space required to perform the Software Support services. Customer shall also provide sufficient electrical current, telephone and power outlets for Vendor's use in performing Software Support.

2.2   Customer shall supply Vendor with access to the computer hardware, system software, the Program and customer data files through the use of telephone line(s) and modem(s). The computer system must be equipped by Customer with hardware and communications software approved by Vendor capable of originating telephone calls to and receiving calls from Vendor. Specification for suitable communications hardware and software are available from Vendor on request.

2.3   Customer shall designate an individual who shall be the System Manager. The System Manager must have a working knowledge of the Program and the system hardware and will be responsible for the computer system backups, user access, and for recording and reporting errors and malfunctions.

Form 12-3: SOURCE CODE ESCROW AGREEMENT

Introductory Note

This is a sample Source Code Escrow Agreement (on diskette as ESCROW.W51) to aid you in nego-tiation of a escrow arrangement.

As is discussed in Chapter 12, usually the escrow agent for a source code escrow is a specialized com-pany known as an "escrow house." These companies are chosen to hold source code in escrow because they can provide reasonably secure, climate-controlled storage and because they have the expertise to conduct verification when needed. It is possible to have other types of escrow agents, such as banks, attorneys, or other third parties. Any escrow agent will charge a fee.

Escrow houses each have their own preferred form of escrow agreement, but all are generally similar to the following text. Some terms are subject to negotiation, particularly: the conditions under which the source code is released to the customer and the process by which the source code is released. You may also find that the escrow fees are negotiable.

The following form of agreement provides that if the customer and the vendor disagree on whether a release condition exists, the escrow agent will continue to hold the source code until an arbitration panel orders it released to the customer. Some Escrow Agreements provide the opposite: that the code will be released immediately and may be used by the customer until the arbitrators order that it go back into escrow. The parties need not choose to have an arbitration provision; it is also common to provide that a dispute over releasing code from escrow will be settled by a court of law.

I have used the term "vendor" to describe the party supplying the software. It is also common to use other terms, such as "supplier" or "licensor."

The text of this agreement is generally self-explanatory, but two legal matters may need clarification. This form of agreement contains some technical language intended to make it effective even if the ven-dor goes into bankruptcy proceedings. It is often possible to get escrowed source code free from a bankruptcy situation, but not always. It will probably be necessary to seek the aid of counsel when you seek to enforce escrow rights against a vendor operating under bankruptcy court supervision. Any software escrow agreement will be related to an underlying agreement; for technical reasons relating to bankruptcy law, the escrow agreement should recite that it is "supplementary" to the underlying agreement.

The following agreement is written so that each new version of the source code is added to the pre-viously deposited material. It is also possible to provide that new versions are substituted for old ones and that only source code for the most recent version of the software product remains in escrow.

A further explanatory note: Section 9 of this form allows the escrow agent the option to file an inter-pleader lawsuit if it is at a loss as to its proper action in a dispute over possession of the source code. Interpleader is a legal way of placing an object or money before a court of law and asking the court to decide who is entitled to get it.

SOURCE CODE ESCROW AGREEMENT

1   Introduction

1.1   This is a Source Code Escrow Agreement under which [*Name of Vendor*] ("Vendor") will deposit source code to be held in escrow by [*Name of Escrow Agent*] ("Escrow Agent") and under which the source code will be released to [*Name of Customer*] ("Customer") only upon the occurrence of certain conditions specified herein.

1.2   Vendor and Customer agree that this Agreement is supplementary to [*Name of Underlying Agreement*] entered into on [*date*] ("License Agreement") in accordance with §365(n) of Title 11, United States Code (the "Bankruptcy Code").

2   Deposit in Escrow

2.1   Within ten (10) days after execution of this Agreement, Vendor shall deliver to Escrow Agent in a sealed package the completely documented current version of the Source Code for the Programs, in machine readable form, as described more fully in Exhibit A and collectively referred to hereinafter as the "Source Material." Vendor shall identify each item in the package and certify the completeness and accuracy of the description of the Source Material in a cover letter sent to Escrow Agent, with a copy to Customer. Within five (5) days after receipt of the Source Material, Escrow Agent shall notify Customer of receipt.

2.2   Vendor shall deliver each revision of the Source Material to Escrow Agent within thirty (30) days of the date when the corresponding revision of the object code for any of the Programs become publicly available. Delivery to the Escrow Agent shall be made together a description of the contents of the deposit and with Vendor's certification of the completeness and accuracy of description of each deposit. At such time as any revisions to the Source Material are deposited, Escrow Agent shall give written notice of such deposits to Customer, including a photocopy of Vendor's description of the deposit and Vendor's certification of the completeness and accuracy of the description of the deposit. As used herein, the term "Source Material" shall include all versions deposited.

2.3   Escrow Agent shall hold the Source Material in a climate-controlled facility and shall release the same only upon the terms and conditions provided in this Agreement.

3   Release from Escrow

3.1   <u>Delivery by Escrow Agent to Customer</u>. The Source Material shall be released and delivered to Customer only in the event that:

(a)   Vendor directs Escrow Agent in writing to make delivery to Customer at a specific address, and the notification is accompanied by a certified or cashier's check payable to Escrow Agent in an amount equal to one hundred dollars ($100.00) plus any amounts outstanding and due to Escrow Agent under this Agreement; or

(b)   Escrow Agent has received from Customer:
   (i)   Written notification that Vendor has failed in material respects to support the Programs as required by the License Agreement or has otherwise materially defaulted under the License Agreement ("Vendor Default");
   (ii)   Evidence satisfactory to Escrow Agent that Customer has previously notified Vendor of such Vendor Default in writing;
   (iii) A written demand that the Source Material be released and delivered to Customer;
   (iv)   A written undertaking from Customer that the copy of the Source Material being released to Customer will be used only as permitted under the terms of the License Agreement;
   (v)   Specific instructions from Customer on where and how to make delivery; and
   (vi)   A certified or cashier's check payable to Escrow Agent in an amount equal to five hundred dollars ($500.00) plus any amounts outstanding and due to Escrow Agent under this Agreement.

3.2   In the event that the provisions of paragraph 3.1(b) are met, Escrow Agent shall, within five (5) days of receipt of all of the items specified in paragraph 3.1(b), send to Vendor notice that Customer has demanded release of the Source Material and shall include a photocopy the items specified in paragraph 3.1(b). Vendor shall have thirty (30) days from the date such items are mailed or sent by Escrow Agent to make written notice of any objection to the release of the Source Material. Vendor shall send a copy of any such objection to Customer.

3.3   In the event that Vendor sends such notice of objection to Escrow Agent within the thirty (30) day period, the matter shall be submitted to, and settled by arbitration. Three (3) arbitrators shall be chosen by the American Arbitration Association office located in the city of *[specify city and state]* in accordance with the rules of the American Arbitration Association. The arbitrators shall apply *[specify state]* law. The parties shall request that, if feasible, the AAA appoint one arbitrator to the panel of three arbitrators who shall possess knowledge of the computer software industry; however the arbitration shall proceed even if such a person is unavailable. The decision of the arbitrators shall be binding and conclusive on all parties involved. Judgment on the arbitrator's decision may be entered in any forum, federal or state, having jurisdiction. All costs of the arbitration, including reasonable attorneys' fees and costs incurred by the prevailing party and Escrow Agent shall be paid by the non-prevailing party.

3.4   If, within thirty (30) days after mailing or sending the items specified in paragraph 3.1(b) to Vendor, Escrow Agent has not received written notice of objection to the release of the Source Material, then Escrow Agent shall release the Source Material to Customer in accordance with the delivery instructions referred to in paragraph 3.1(b)(v).

3.5   <u>Delivery By Escrow Agent to Vendor</u>. Escrow Agent shall release and deliver the Source Material to Vendor upon the occurrence of any of the following conditions:

    (a)   <u>Mutual Termination</u>. The presentation to Escrow Agent of a written notice of termination:

        (i)   Executed by authorized representatives of Vendor and Customer, stating that this Escrow Agreement has been terminated by the agreement of Vendor and Customer, and

        (ii)   Directing Escrow Agent to release and deliver the Source Material to Vendor by a specified method of delivery to a specified address within ten (10) days of receipt by the Escrow Agent; or

    (b)   <u>Non-Payment</u>. Escrow Agent shall give notice to both Customer and Vendor of the non-payment of any fee due and payable hereunder. Both Customer and Vendor shall have the right to pay the unpaid fee within thirty (30) days from the date of mailing or sending the notice from Escrow Agent. Upon timely payment of the unpaid fee by either Customer or Vendor, this Agreement shall continue in force and effect.

4   Ownership of Source Material

4.1   Absent release and delivery of the Source Material to Customer, ownership of the source code itself and any accompanying documentation (together with all copyrights and proprietary rights therein) shall remain with Vendor.

4.2   Upon release and delivery of the Source Material to Customer, Customer shall have the right to possession of the Source Material, and Customer shall be licensed to use, maintain, modify and update the Source Material as are reasonably required to receive all benefits that are due to Customer under the terms of the License Agreement. Any source code or object code resulting from Customer's modification, modification, or updating of the Source Material shall be Customer's property. However, nothing herein shall discharge Customer from the obligations of the License Agreement, which shall remain in full force and effect.

5   Fees and Term

5.1   Escrow Agent shall be entitled to the fees described in Exhibit B, which shall be paid by Customer.

5.2   Escrow Agent shall issue an invoice for its initial fee to Customer which shall be due at the time of the execution of this Agreement, and shall issue additional invoices to Customer from time to time as additional fees become due. Payment is due within twenty (20) days of invoice date.

5.3   The initial term of this Agreement shall be one (1) year commencing the date all parties have signed.

5.4   The term of this Agreement shall be automatically renewed for successive one (1) year terms unless otherwise terminated. The fees set forth on Exhibit A may be increased, by Escrow Agent in its sole discretion, by a maximum of ten (10) percent per year for any term after the initial term.

5.5   This Agreement shall terminate upon the delivery of the Source Material to any party, provide however that all fees due to Escrow Agent shall remain due and owning notwithstanding the termination of this Agreement. No fee shall become refundable or be discharged on account of such termination.

6   Bankruptcy

6.1   Vendor acknowledges that if Vendor or its trustee in bankruptcy rejects the License Agreement or this Agreement under the provisions of the Bankruptcy Code, Customer may elect to retain its rights under the License Agreement and this Agreement as provided in Section 365(n) of the Bankruptcy Code. Vendor or such trustee in bankruptcy shall not interfere with the rights of Customer as provided in the License Agreement and this Agreement, including the right to obtain the Source Material from Escrow Agent.

7   Liability

7.1   Except for actual fraud, gross negligence, or intentional misconduct, Escrow Agent shall not be liable to Vendor, Customer or to any other party for any act, or failure to act. Any liability of Escrow Agent under this Agreement, regardless of cause, shall be limited to the actual cost of new blank magnetic media or blank documentation of the same type and quality of any lost or destroyed source code copy. Escrow Agent will not be liable for special, indirect, incidental, or consequential damages.

8   Indemnity

8.1   Vendor and Customer shall indemnify and hold harmless Escrow Agent and each of its directors, officers, and stockholders from any and all claims, damages, suits, liabilities, obligations, costs, fees, and any other expenses whatsoever, including legal fees, that may be incurred by Escrow Agent or any of its directors, officers, or stockholders relating to the duties or performance of Escrow Agent under this Agreement, except as otherwise provided in paragraph 7.1.

9   Disputes

9.1   In the event of any dispute between Vendor and Customer or any other party claiming rights under this Agreement, Escrow Agent may submit the matter to any court of competent jurisdiction in an interpleader or similar action. However, Escrow Agent shall not be obligated to bring such a proceeding. Vendor and Customer shall indemnify and hold harmless Escrow Agent harmless from all costs and fees incurred in such a proceeding, including legal fees.

9.2   If Escrow Agent shall be uncertain as to its duties or rights hereunder, Escrow Agent may, without incurring any liability, refrain from taking any action until it receives direction in writing in the form of the order, decree, or judgment of a court of competent jurisdiction; but Escrow Agent shall be under no duty to institute or defend any such proceeding.

10   Verification

10.1   Upon receipt of a written request from Customer and payment by the Customer of the applicable fee, Escrow Agent shall compile and inspect the Source Material to verify its contents, completeness, accuracy, and functionality, and shall send its written Technical Verification Report to Customer. Upon request from Vendor, Escrow Agent will send Vendor a copy of its written Technical Verification Report.

10.2   Vendor shall cooperate with Escrow Agent by making available promptly facilities, computer systems, object code, technical and support personnel, and all other materials and assistance as Escrow Agent may reasonably request for the purpose of verification. Upon request by Customer, Vendor shall permit one employee of Customer to be present at Vendor's facility during verification of Source Material.

11   Source Material

11.1 . Except as otherwise provided in this Agreement, Escrow Agent shall have no responsibility with respect to the accuracy or completeness of the Source Material or any revisions thereto.

12   Notices

12.1 All notices required or permitted by this Agreement shall be in writing and sent by registered or certified mail, return receipt requested, or by any form of express delivery that generates a receipt. The following addresses shall be used for notice:

(a)   If to Vendor:

(b)   If to Customer:

(c)   If to Escrow Agent:

13   Governing Law

13.1   This Agreement shall be governed by the laws of *[specify state]*.

So agreed among the parties to this Agreement:

[Name of Escrow Agent]   Witness:

By _____   _____

Print Name:

Title: _____

Date: _____

Tel. No.: _____

[Name of Vendor]   Witness:

By: _____   _____

Print Name:

_____

Title: _____

Date: _____

Tel. No.: _____

[Name of Customer]   Witness:
By: _____   _____

Print Name:

Title: _____

Date: _____

Tel. No.: _____

EXHIBIT A

Vendor Name: _____

Customer Name: _____

Product Name: _____

Version No.: _____

Date of Deposit: _____

Description of Materials Deposited:

_____

_____

_____

Form 15-1: COMPANY STATEMENT OF GOOD BUSINESS PRACTICE

Introductory Note

The following is a form (on diskette as ETHICS.W51) designed to give all employees guidance in ethical and legal norms for their employment at a software company. Many large- and medium-size high technology companies provide such statements to every new employee. Some companies provide each employee with a copy once a year. Often the form is signed by the company president, chairman, or CEO.

The following form discusses, in simplified terms, many matters of good business practice, including many of the topics that we have addressed in this book. Such a reminder, while by no means an insurance policy, can help employees avoid acts detrimental to the company. Every business is different, and this form will likely need to be customized to fit your business.

The following form is based on one used by a public company (with the kind permission of its general counsel) and has comments concerning trading of the employer's stock that may not be needed for privately held companies. This form refers to the employer as the "Company," but it would probably be better to use the name of the company involved.

[*Name of Company*]
Guide to Good Practice
For Our Software Business

To All Employees:

　　Good ethics are good business. Trust and respect is the foundation of our relationship with everyone that encounters our Company, including our employees, customers, shareholders, suppliers, competitors, neighbors, friends, and the general public.

　　Public interest in business ethics has increased in recent years. So has the burden of laws affecting the ethical conduct of our business. These guidelines are provided because the complexity of modern business makes it more difficult to determine what the law permits or what is right and what is wrong.

　　This brochure is designed to acquaint you with some of the laws that affect business ethics, and to lay out ethical principles. It certainly does not cover all the issues, but it touches on many important ones.

General Policies and Procedures

　　The Company's policies and procedures, some written and others unwritten, have been established over the years. You should do your best to learn and follow the policies that affect your job.

If you are asked by anyone to depart from an established policy or practice, you have both the right and the responsibility to clarify any ethical questions that may arise. You should take the matter up with your supervisor and pursue it until you satisfy yourself that you understand clearly the Company policy which applies to your issue.

In the event you cannot resolve any question about ethical conduct with your supervisor, you should contact [*specify contact person*], who will assist you in resolving the matter.

Fairness Toward Your Fellow Employees

The Company believes in mutual trust and respect among all employees. We value the virtues of skill, hard work, honesty, and fairness. It is our policy to make decisions on hiring and advancement without regard to sex, age, handicap, disability, religious creed, racial background, or national origin.

Statements in Sales, Advertising, and Publicity

The Company's promotional materials and advertising must provide fair characterizations of the Company's products. There must be no misleading statements about competitors' products. Comparisons with competitive products must always be fairly based on the facts. This rule of practice applies equally to our employees' discussions with customers.

Open and Fair Competition

It is the policy of the Company to comply fully with the laws of the United States, including export controls and antitrust laws, and the laws of all states. It is also our policy to comply with the laws of the other countries where the Company does business, unless doing so would violate United States law.

Under the antitrust laws of the United States, many states, and many other countries, it is illegal to collaborate with competitors for the purposes of fixing or maintaining prices. Our employees should not discuss prices with competitors under any circumstances, except in legitimate sales or purchase transactions with the competitor.

Estimates Must Be Reasonable

Many of us are responsible for providing prices, and cost and expense estimates to government procurement personnel, taxing authorities, and audit agencies, and to customers and suppliers. Estimates also are used in the Company's operations. Any employee providing such a number must have a reasonable basis for every estimate. A "reasonable basis" means that there are known facts or a sensible, realistic, and honest basis underlying every significant assumption. Price estimates should provide a fair profit, taking into account relevant factors such as risk, technical innovation, and product demand.

Policy on Gifts and Entertainment

No employee may solicit a gift from any company or persons that we do business with. Even unsolicited gifts may often be improper. Any gift is inappropriate if the value of the gift gives the appearance that it is intended to influence our business decisions. Decline any inappropriate gift politely but firmly.

The same criteria applies to gifts that our employees might present to a customer. Never give a gift of such value that it appears calculated to influence a business decision.

In general, never give or accept a gift if public disclosure of the gift would be embarrassing to either to the Company or any donor or recipient.

It is also the Company's policy that moderation prevail in entertaining on the Company's behalf or in accepting entertainment accepted from others. Extravagance or excess is not good business.

Proper Government Relations

The Company's products are frequently purchased by agencies of state and national government. Our policy is to seek our fair share of this business solely on the basis of superior price, performance, reliability, delivery, or customer service versus our competitors.

The Company's policy, and the law, prohibits the use, directly or indirectly, of any corporate funds for any contribution to any political party, committee, candidate, or official.

So that we can act in accordance with the federal and state law and the United States Foreign Corrupt Practices Act, no employee may ever give a gift (directly or through any intermediary) to any official of any domestic or foreign government or political organization. The only exception is business meals or infrequent and inexpensive entertainment which accords with the Company's general policy on gifts and entertainment.

Inside Information and the Stock Market

Occasionally we have information about the Company that is not known to the investing public, for example, sales levels, prospects for profitability, acquisition of new products, technological achievements, financial reverses, etc. If this inside information is "material," that is, if it is likely to affect investors' decisions regarding the trading of the Company's stock when the information becomes public, our general policy is to disclose this information as promptly as possible to the public. Sometimes, however, it will not be possible for the Company to disclose material information to the public until certain events have passed or complete information is available.

Until disclosure to the public takes place, employees with knowledge of the material inside information, and their immediate families, have very important responsibilities under United States securities law:

1. They cannot buy or sell the Company's stock until the material information has been released to the public; and

2. They cannot disclose the information to others who might use it in buying or selling the Company stock until the information has been released to the investing public.

Violation of these rules may be a criminal offense. Officers and Members of the Board of Directors of the Company may have additional restrictions on their ability to purchase and sell the Company's stock.

Avoiding Conflict of Interests

Employees should avoid outside activity that may raise an actual or potential conflict with job responsibilities in the Company. Even the appearance of a conflict should be avoided.

The potential for problems exist, for example, if the employee, or a close friend or relative, has an interest in a competitor or in a company from which the Company purchases goods or services. Any such situation must be immediately disclosed to your supervisor.

Protecting the Company's Proprietary Information

The Company's trade secrets, proprietary information, and other internal information are valuable assets. Protection of this information plays a vital role in the Company's ability to compete.

A trade secret is information, knowledge, or know-how which gives the owner some advantage over competitors who do not possess the "secret." A trade secret must be secret, that is, not generally or publicly known, but it need not be patentable to qualify as a trade secret. Under the laws of most states and most countries, a trade secret is treated as property.

The Company's trade secrets is not just its technical know-how. Trade secret information includes the Company's strategic, business, marketing, financial, and new product plans, its sales, profits, and any unpublished financial or pricing information, its methods and systems, employee lists, customer and vendor lists, and information regarding customer requirements, preferences, business habits, and plans. This list, while not complete, suggests the wide scope and variety of the Company's proprietary information which must be protected.

Employee obligations to protect trade secret and confidential information of the Company are:

1. Not to disclose this information to persons outside of the Company, in conversations with visitors, suppliers, family, or anyone else;

2. Not to use this information for your own benefit or for the profit or benefit of persons outside of the Company;

3. To disclose this information to other Company employees only on a "need to know" basis and then only to employees who have been informed that the information is the Company's proprietary information; and

4. To place appropriate trade secret legends on all documents and in all software files that contain confidential information.

Special procedures apply for sharing confidential information with suppliers and customers, which you may discuss with your supervisor.

A person leaving the employ of the Company has an obligation to protect the Company's trade secrets and proprietary information until the information becomes publicly available or until the Company no longer considers it trade secret or proprietary.

Departing employees should note that correspondence, printed matter, software files and programs, documents, or records of any kind are all property of the Company and must remain at the Company. Of course, skills and general knowledge acquired or improved on the job are personal assets of the employee.

Respecting Trade Secrets and Property Rights of Other Firms

It is the Company's policy to respect trade secrets of others. This applies especially to knowledge you may have of trade secrets of a former employer. You should give no person at the Company any information which you have reason to believe is a trade secret of a former employer. If you have signed a confidentiality or non-competition agreement with any other company that might affect you work for the Company, you should inform your supervisor.

Receive Information from Outside of the Company Only on a NonConfidential Basis

It is the Company's policy to refuse to receive or consider any trade secret information, that is, non-disclosed ideas, inventions, patent applications, etc. submitted from companies or person outside of the Company without the prior written approval of a departmental supervisor or *[specify person in charge]*.

Fair Software Licensing Practices

It is the Company's policy that software licensed by the Company should not be duplicated or used in any manner inconsistent with the Company's rights and the vendor's rights as spelled out in licensing agreements. When we license to others any software products that contain computer code supplied by other companies, we must be sure that we have a valid license that authorizes our use and distribution of the code.

Respecting the Company's Property

Company equipment, tools, materials, and supplies with which we accomplish our tasks have been purchased for a specific purpose. Unauthorized removal or misapplication of these items places an unnecessary financial burden on the Company to the disadvantage of all of us and may be a violation of criminal law.

You Set the Standards

You are urged to keep this brochure for reference during your work at the Company. Should you have any question which cannot be answered by reference to this brochure, you are encouraged to speak with your supervisor or *[specify contact person]*.

Forms A-1, A-2, A-3: LETTERS FOR USE WITH COPYRIGHT REGISTRATION

Introductory Note

The following sample letters are discussed in Appendix A. To use them, substitute appropriate names for the fictitious ones used in these forms. (These forms are on diskette as COPY-LTR.W51.)

Form A-1 is for use in copyright registration when you are depositing with the Copyright Office source code that has portions blocked out to protect trade secrets. Form A-2 is used when depositing object code, rather than source code in connection with copyright registration. Form A-3 is used to obtain "special handling," that is, expedited processing of a copyright registration application when there is pending or imminent litigation.

Form A-1: Sample Letter for Depositing Trade Secret Code

XYZ Software Corp.
123 Main Street
Anytown, California

[*Date*]

Register of Copyrights
Library of Congress
Washington, D.C. 20559

Dear Register:

Enclosed is a copyright application for [*Title of Program*] submitted by XYZ Corporation.

XYZ Corporation is submitting the deposit in the enclosed form in order to protect trade secrets that are contained in the computer code.

I certify that the statements in this letter are true.

Sincerely,

[*Name*]
[*Title*]

Form A-2: Letter for Object-Code-Only Deposit

XYZ Software Corp.
123 Main Street
Anytown, California

[*Date*]

Register of Copyrights
Library of Congress
Washington, D.C. 20559

Dear Register:

Enclosed is a copyright application for [*Title of Program*] submitted by XYZ Corporation. XYZ Corporation is submitting the deposit in the form of object code only.

[*Title of Program*] is an original work and the object code contains copyrightable authorship.

I certify that the statements in this letter are true.

Sincerely,

[*Name*]
[*Title*]

Form A-3: Letter Requesting Special Handling

Jack Smith Software Corp.
8086 Main Street
Seattle, Washington

[*Date*]

Library of Congress
Department 100
Washington DC 20540

RE: Special Handling Application

Dear Register:

On behalf of Jack Smith Software Corp., I enclose a copyright application, deposit and a fee of $220, and request special handling.

The reason that special handling is needed is that copyright infringement litigation concerning the enclosed is imminent [*has already commenced*]. Jack Smith Software, Inc. is the plaintiff. The defendant is Jane Jones Data Corp. of Harvard, Massachusetts. The suit will be [*has already been*] brought in United States District Court for the Northern District of California in San Francisco.

I certify that the statement in this letter are true and correct to the best of my knowledge and information.

Sincerely,

Jack Smith
President

Software Business and Intellectual Property Resources

This is a list of selected software-related resources for your convenience. While I believe all listed private companies and organizations are quite reputable, I can offer no guarantees as to the service they will provide or the cost of the service. I am grateful for the assistance and cooperation I received from all of the listed government agencies.

Trademark Materials

Trademark Search Services

The following companies provide trademark search services. They will each provide brochures on request that describe their methods and their fee structure. These services will not interpret the results of their search; only an attorney is legally qualified to do that.

Thompson & Thompson
500 Victory Road
Quincy, MA 02171
Phone: (617) 479-1600 or (800) 421-7881
Fax: (617) 786-8273

The Rugge Group
2670 Mountain Gateway
Oakland, CA 94611
Phone: (510) 530-3635
Fax: (510) 530-3325

Trademark Research Corporation
300 Park Avenue
New York, NY 10010
Phone: (212) 228-4084 or (800) TRC-MARK
Fax: (212) 228-5090

On-Line Trademark Search

The following are on-line services for trademark searches. As noted in Chapter 14, Dialog Information Services includes marks found in the state and federal registration system in its TRADEMARKSCAN database and many other marks in other databases. Compu-Mark includes only marks in the federal and state registration systems. Both services are rather costly. You can call the phones numbers listed below to arrange for an subscription to these services. TRADEMARKSCAN is also available through CompuServe. (Type "GO TRADERC".)

Dialog Information Services
3460 Hillview Avenue
Palo Alto, CA 93404
Phone: (800) 334-2564 or (415) 858-2700

Compu-Mark
500 Victory Road
Quincy, MA 02171
Phone: (800) 421-7881

Books that Contain Listings of Trademarks, Products, and Corporate Names

The following are works, updated from time to time, that list software businesses and trademarks and United States trademarks in general. None of them give a complete listing of all relevant trademarks. However, they do cover a very large number of marks in use. These books can be found in major metropolitan libraries.

Datapro Directory of Software (Delran NJ: Datapro Information Services Group)

Brands and Their Companies (Detroit MI: Gale Research, Inc.)

Trademark Register of the United States (Washington DC: Trademark Register)

Compu-Mark Directory of U.S. Trademarks (North Quincy MA: Compu-Mark U.S.)

Computer Industry Information

Computer and Software Trade and Industry Organizations

American Electronics Association

1225 Eye Street NW, Suite 950	*and*	5201 Great America Parkway
Washington, DC 20005		P.O. Box 54990
Phone: (202) 682-9110		Santa Clara, CA 95056-0990
Fax: (202) 682-9111		Phone: (408) 987-4200
		Fax: (408) 970-8565

American Electronics Association (office for Japan)
Yonbancho 11-4
Chiyoda-Ku, Tokyo
JAPAN 102
Phone: 011 81-3-3237-7195
Fax: 011 82-3-3237-1237

American Electronics Association (office for the European Community)
Place St. Lambert 14
B-1200 Brussels, BELGIUM
Phone: 011 32-2-773-4911

Software Publishers Association (SPA)
1101 Connecticut Avenue NW
Washington, DC 20036
Phone: (202) 452-1600

Software Dealers Information and Directory

National Association of Computer Dealers (NACD)
13103 FM 1960 West No. 206
Houston, TX 77065
Phone: (800) 223-5264 or (713) 894-1983

The NACD sells the *National Directory*, a listing of computer dealers.

United States Government Agencies

Copyright Office

Copyright Office
Library of Congress
Washington, DC 20559
Information Line: (202) 707-3000
Forms Hotline: (202) 707-9100

Patent and Trademark Office

Patent and Trademark Office (PTO)
U.S. Department of Commerce
Washington, DC 20321
Information Line: (703) 557-INFO (557-4636)

Export Controls

Bureau of Export Administration (BXA)
Exporter Counseling Division
U.S. Department of Commerce
14th and Constitution Avenue NW
Washington, DC 20230
Information Line: (202) 482-4811

Office of Defense Trade Controls (DTC)
PM/DTC Room 200, SA-6
Bureau of Politico-Military Affairs
U.S. Department of State
1701 N. Fort Myer Drive
Arlington, VA 22209-3113
Phone: (703) 875-6644 (General Information)
(703) 875-5664 (Assistant to the Director)
(703) 875-7050 (Office of the Director)

Anti-Boycott Compliance

Bureau of Export Administration
Office of Export Licensing
Bureau of Anti-boycott Compliance
Department of Commerce
14th and Constitution Avenue, N.W.
Washington, DC 20230
Phone: (202) 482-2381

Software Escrow Houses

The following companies serve as escrow agents. Contact them for fee schedules
and escrow agreement forms.

Data Securities International, Inc.

49 Stevenson Street	*and*	101 Cambridge Street
Suite 550		Suite 210
San Francisco, CA 94105		Burlington, MA 01803
Phone: (415) 541-9013		Phone (617) 273-5432

Fort Knox Safe Deposit, Inc.
235 DeKalb Industrial Way
Decatur, GA 30030-2203
Phone: (404) 292-0700 or (800) 875-5669
Fax: (404) 292-0421

Zurich Depository Corporation
1165 Northern Boulevard
Manhasset, New York 11030
Phone: (516) 365-4756
Fax: (516) 627-4394

Source Books on Software Law

If you are interested in a more technical discussion of points of software law written for attorneys, consult the following texts. These books are available in major libraries, in university or court law libraries, or though bookstores.

Brown, Peter, and Richard Raysman, *Computer Law: Drafting and Negotiating Forms and Agreements*, New York: Law Journal Seminars Press, 1984. *(loose leaf)*

Kutten, L., *Computer Software* , New York: Clark Boardman Co., 1987. *(loose leaf)*

Scott, Michael D., *Scott on Computer Law,* 2nd edition. Englewood Cliffs: Prentice-Hall Law and Business, 1991.

INDEX

© (copyright) symbol, 23, 26, 268
® (trademark) symbol, 236, 237, 241

A

Acceptance
    definition of, 317
    and end-user agreements, 193-95
    optional (free trial), 194
    and parallel tests, 194
    and performance criteria, 194
    and software development agreements,
        114-15, 116
    and specified corrections, 194
Accolade case, 18-19
Affidavits
    definition of, 40
    "of Use," 240
Agreements
    definition of, 317. *See also* Beta test
        agreements; Confidentiality
        agreements; Dealer agreements,
        software; Development agreements,
        software; End-user agreements,
        software; Evaluation agreements,
        software; Non-competition
        agreements; Non-solicitation
        agreements; Publishing agreements,
        software; "Standard" agreements;
        Work-for-hire agreements
AIDS test, 211
American Arbitration Association, 87
American Chamber of Commerce, 272
American Electronics Association, 272
Amiga, 111

Antitrust law
    and dealer termination, 163
    description of, 317
    and distributor and dealer prices, 163
    and license terms, 162
    and price discrimination, 153
    and price fixing, 162
    and restrictions on pricing to dealers,
        163
Appeals
    description of, 42
    and trade secrets, 65-66
Apple Computer, 146
    and copyright litigation, 41
    and software patents, 249, 258
    suit against Microsoft, 41
Arab states
    and international boycotts, 278
Arbitration, 86-87
    definition of, 318
    and end-user agreements, 204-5
    and international distribution, 275
    and software publishing agreements,
        139
ASSIGN.W51 file (form of assignment of
    rights in a software program), 106
Assignments, software, 103-6
    assignment of rights in a software
        program (form), 367
    definition of, 103, 312
    form of, 106
    that make "business sense," 104-5
    and transferring rights in a computer
        program, 103-4
Atari Games Co., 258, 259, 299

Fraud, 217-18
> definition of, 321
> statute of, 325

FTC (Federal Trade Commission), 159, 160, 161, 175, 177

G

Game programs
> and copyrights, 9, 1-12, 18-19, 37-38
> and royalty calculation, 134
> and software development agreements, 111
> and software patents, 258-59.

"Genericide," 226-27, 245-46

Genesis game console, 18-19

GEnie, 146

Geographic scope
> and non-competition agreements, 72-73
> and software publishers, 129

Germany, 269, 270

GSA (General Services Administration), 205, 207

Guidelines (for employees)
> good business practice, drafting and use of, 285

H

Hays, David, 173, 174

Heckel, Paul, 258

Hiring
> and non-competition agreements, 69, 77
> and trade secrets, 46, 54, 58, 59, 64. *See also* Departing employees; Employee(s)

Hitachi, 249

Home offices
> trade secret data kept in, 54-55
> use of office software in, and end-user agreements, 190

Hypercard (Claris), 258

I

IBM (International Business Machines), 248, 249

Illinois law, and franchises, 159, 160
> and shrink-wrap license provisions, 179

Import/export, 276-277

Incorporation, 319
> and defense against personal liability, 218-19
> and trademarks, 223

Indemnification
> definition of, 321
> and end-user agreements, 200
> and software dealer agreements, 158
> and software development agreements, 119, 120-21

Independent contractors, 21, 108

India
> and software piracy, 275

Infringement
> basic definition of, 321
> intentional, 255, 256-57

Ingram Micro Inc., 143

Installation
> and end-user agreements, 193

Insurance
> liability, 210, 212, 217

Intel, 228, 242

Intellectual property
> and audits, 285
> and copyrights, 16-17, 120, 280-82, 283
> definition of, 321
> and end-user agreements, 195, 200
> and international distribution, 265, 268-72
> management, and protection procedures, 279-85
> and policy on protection of intellectual property form, 332
> and software dealer agreements, 157

Attention 3 1/2" Disk Drive Users:

The disk for *The Software Developer's and Marketer's Legal Companion* is available in 3 1/2" format. Please return the order form below with a check for $10.00 payable to Addison-Wesley to:

Addison-Wesley Publishing Company
Order Department
1 Jacob Way
Reading, MA 01867-9984

- -

Please send me the 3 1/2" disk (ISBN 0-201-62736-1) to accompany *The Software Developer's and Marketer's Legal Companion* by Gene K. Landy. I am enclosing a check for $10.00.

Name:

Address:

City: State: Zip: